COLLISION AND COLLUSION

The Strange Case of Western Aid to Eastern Europe

Janine R. Wedel

ST. MARTIN'S GRIFFIN ✸ NEW YORK

Cartoons by Chris Suddick © 1998

ISBN 978-0-312-23828-5

Library of Congress Cataloging-in-Publication Data

Wedel, Janine R., 1957-
   Collision and collusion : the strange case of western aid to
Eastern Europe / Janine R. Wedel
     p. cm.
   Includes bibliographical references (p.) and index.
   ISBN 0-312-21215-1 cl. ISBN 0-312-23828-1 pbk.
    1. Economic assistance—Europe, Eastern—Evaluation. 2. Economic
assistance—Former Soviet republics—Evaluation. 3. Europe,
Eastern—Economic conditions—1989- 4. Former Soviet republics—
Economic conditions. 5. Economic assistance—Evaluation.
I. Title.
HC244.W364 1998
338.91'0947—dc21   98-38646
                                               CIP

Design by Acme Art, Inc.
First paperback edition: January 2000

Transferred to Digital Printing in 2015

To my parents

CONTENTS

Acknowledgements v

Acronyms. vii

Maps ix

A Note about Terms xiii

A Note about Interviews xiii

Introduction: Some Enchanted Era 1

Chapter I   East Meets West:
             A New Order for the Second World 15

Chapter II   Consultants for Capitalism 45

Chapter III A Few Favored Cliques. 85

Chapter IV   A Few Good Reformers:
             The Chubais Clan, Harvard, and "Economic" Aid 123

Chapter V   A Few Good Financiers:
             Wall Street Bankers and *Biznesmeni*. 175

Chapter VI   Insights from the Second World 195

Appendix 1: Tables 209

Appendix 2: Methodology. 219

Appendix 3: Interviews 225

Appendix 4: Economic Aid to Russia 239
             Players
             Institutions, Organizations, Commissions
             GAO Chart: Organizational Profile of the Harvard Institute
             for International Development

Notes 245

Selected Bibliography 295

Index 311

ACKNOWLEDGEMENTS

I have been following the aid story in Central and Eastern Europe since 1989. I am grateful to the Council for the International Exchange of Scholars for the two terms in Poland as a Fulbright scholar during 1989-90 and 1991-92 that piqued my interest in the topic. My subsequent, more systematic, study would not have been possible without research and writing support provided by the National Science Foundation, the John D. and Catherine T. MacArthur Foundation, the Woodrow Wilson International Center for Scholars, the Friedrich Ebert Stiftung, and the Kosciuszko Foundation. I am greatly indebted to these institutions. The project has been intense and ambitious in its breadth, scope, information-gathering, and fieldwork. Crucial to the conduct of this nearly ten-year project was the help of so many people who granted interviews, located materials, and checked facts, not all of whom wished to be named here.

A number of people and institutions provided administrative and logistical help in my places of fieldwork: In Poland, Pani Antonina Dachów, Michał and Irena Federowiczowie, Aśka Mikoszewska, and Jacek Poznański and the Council of Ministers; in Bratislava, Ellie Sutter; in Russia, Debbie Seward, Svetlana Glinkina, Boris Greenberg, Masha Zolotukhin, and Vadim Ivanov and the Institute for the Economy in Transition; in Ukraine, Grigory Gubsky, Marta Kolomayets, and Ian Brzezinski; in Berlin, Yvonne Barber; in Bonn, Beth Pond; and in Belgium, Deanne Lehman and Benno Barnard.

Invaluable support in the United States was provided by Catherine Allen and the Department of Anthropology, Joseph Tropea and the Department of Sociology, and James Millar and the Institute for European, Russian, and Eurasian Studies, all of The George Washington University. I also very much appreciate the support of Carolyn Ban, dean of the Graduate School of Public and International Affairs at the University of Pittsburgh, my new academic home, and other colleagues at the school.

I am especially grateful to Vivian Keller for her skilled organizational help at crucial points of manuscript preparation. I also would like to acknowledge Lynne Taylor, Karen Coats, and Paul Smolarcik for editorial help, and my mother and father, Dolores and Arnold Wedel, for indexing the book. I wish to thank Chris Caltabiano, Katrina Greene, Anthony Gualtieri, Haley Hendrickson, Christina Herzler, Erind Pajo, Martina Pechova, and Doug Pyle for research assistance.

I was fortunate to have the help of talented readers. I am especially indebted to Jeff Dumas, Chris Hann, Bill Harwood, Antoni Kamiński, Phil Parnell, and Adam Pomorski. Igor Barsegian, Michael Bernstam, Steve Collier, Stephen F. Cohen, Gerald Creed, Steve Ebbin, Dan Guttman, Michael Illner, Kristine Kassekert, David Kideckel, Dave Lempert, Dave Mathiasen, Erind Pajo, Elena Petkova, Karla Scappini, Brian Wickland, Anne Williamson, and Lou Zanardi also provided valuable guidance on issues in the manuscript.

I am grateful to Chris Suddick for her creative cartoons and willingness to work with me on the project. And I wish to thank Karen Wolny, my editor, and Diana Finch, my agent, for their support.

Throughout the project, many people assisted in selfless and gracious ways. I am indebted to Igor Barsegian, Nancy Dunne, Renata Frenzen, Charles McMillion, Ron Potter, Karla Scappini, and, as always, especially to Jeff Dumas and Adam and Basia Pomorscy for their generous help and abiding interest.

Although many people helped with the project, any shortcomings in the final product are my responsibility alone.

ACRONYMS

ACAP	American Committee for Aid to Poland, Washington, D.C.
AID	Agency for International Development (also known as USAID)
CCET	Centre for Co-operation with Economies in Transition, OECD, Paris
CIPE	Center for International Private Enterprise, Washington, D.C.
CSO	Clearing and settlement organization
EBRD	European Bank for Reconstruction and Development, London
EC	European Commission, Brussels
ECU	European Currency Unit
EU	European Union
EURO	European Monetary Unit
FIP	Forum for Nongovernmental Initiatives, Poland
FTUI	Free Trade Union Institute, AFL-CIO
G-24	Group of Twenty-Four (Canada, United States, Japan, Australia, New Zealand, Austria, Belgium, Denmark, Finland, France, Germany, Greece, Iceland, Ireland, Italy, Luxembourg, Netherlands, Norway, Portugal, Spain, Sweden, Switzerland, Turkey, United Kingdom)
G-7	Group of Seven (Canada, France, Japan, United Kingdom, Germany, Italy, United States)
GAO	General Accounting Office (U.S. government body)
GKI	*Goskomimushchestvo* or State Property Committee (Russian government body responsible for privatization)
GKOs	Russian short-term treasury bills
HIID	Harvard Institute for International Development, Harvard University
HMC	Harvard Management Company, Harvard University
IBRD	International Bank for Reconstruction and Development (also known as World Bank)
IDA	International Development Agency, Poland
ILBE	Institute for Law-Based Economy (USAID-funded organization in Russia)

IMF	International Monetary Fund
IQC	Indefinite Quantity Contract (contracting mechanism under USAID)
ITCA	International Team for Company Assistance (American consulting firm)
JRL	Johnson's Russia List (Internet mailing list, *davidjohnson@erols.com*)
KPN	*Konfederacja Polski Niepodległej,* or Confederacy of Independent Poland (Polish political group)
LPC	Local Privatization Centers (USAID-funded organizations in Russia)
NACC	North Atlantic Cooperation Council
NATO	North Atlantic Treaty Organization
NDI	National Democratic Institute for International Affairs, United States
NED	National Endowment for Democracy, United States
NGO	Nongovernmental organization
NIK	Najwyższa Izba Kontroli (Supreme Control Board), Poland
NIS	Newly Independent States (successor countries of the Soviet Union)
NRI	National Republican Institute for International Affairs, United States
NSC	National Security Council (U.S. government body)
ODA	Overseas Development Administration (UK government body)
ODA	Official Development Assistance (development category)
OECD	Organization for Economic Cooperation and Development (based in Paris)
PFP	Partnership for Peace (program for military cooperation with Central and Eastern Europe)
PHARE	Poland and Hungary Aid in Restructuring the Economy (EU program)
PMU	Program Management Unit
ROAD	*Ruch Obywatelski Akcja Demokratyczna* or Citizens' Movement for Democratic Action (former Polish political party)
RPC	Russia Privatization Center (USAID-funded organization in Russia)
SEC	Securities and Exchange Commission (U.S. government body)
SEED	Support for East European Democracy Act
TACIS	Technical Assistance for the Commonwealth of Independent States (EU program)
UNDP	United Nations Development Program
USAID	United States Agency for International Development (also known as AID)

CENTRAL AND EASTERN EUROPE

NEWLY INDEPENDENT STATES OF THE FORMER USSR

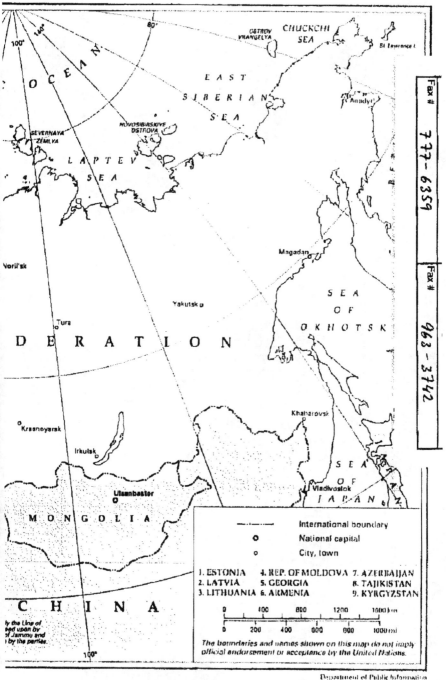

	International boundary
o	National capital
o	City, town

1. ESTONIA   4. REP. OF MOLDOVA 7. AZERBAIJAN
2. LATVIA   5. GEORGIA   8. TAJIKISTAN
3. LITHUANIA 6. ARMENIA   9. KYRGYZSTAN

0   400   800   1200   1600 km
0   200 400 600 800 1000 mi

The boundaries and names shown on this map do not imply
official endorsement or acceptance by the United Nations.

A NOTE ABOUT TERMS

"Central Europe" here refers to the Visegrád countries of Poland, Hungary, and former Czechoslovakia, on which this study concentrates. "Central and Eastern Europe" includes the Visegrád countries of Central Europe and two largely European countries of the former Soviet Union— Russia and Ukraine.

I use the terms "communism" and "socialism" (as well as "communist" and "socialist") interchangeably to denote the system that prevailed in the Eastern Bloc countries and the Soviet Union. I find both these terms somewhat inadequate: while "communism" in its pure form was never achieved, "socialism" would also seem to apply to some vastly different northern European nations.

"Second World" here refers both to the nations of the former Eastern Bloc and the former Soviet Union.

A NOTE ABOUT INTERVIEWS

I personally carried out hundreds of interviews for this book. Unless otherwise specified, I conducted all interviews cited in the text and in endnotes. (See Appendix 3: Interviews.)

Janine R. Wedel

Some Enchanted Era

ON AN EVENING IN FEBRUARY 1991, at the conclusion of an official banquet held in an opulent room of the U.S. Department of Treasury building, a chamber orchestra played Rodgers and Hammerstein's "Some Enchanted Evening."

For many of those in attendance—elegantly dressed men who had earlier participated in a conference titled "Economies in Transition: Management Training and Market Economies Education in Central and Eastern Europe," cosponsored by the White House and the Treasury Department—it may well have seemed an enchanted evening. One year earlier, after the fall of the communist East Bloc, the United States had authorized nearly $1 billion in aid to the region to "promote the private sector, democratic pluralism, and economic and political stability." With that aid effort heating up, the conference brought leaders from the region together with officials from the U.S. Agency for International Development (USAID), which led the aid effort, along with other U.S. agencies and representatives of the private sector to discuss and coordinate aid programs.

At the conference, high officials offered more optimism than substance or experience. One of these officials assured the visiting Central and Eastern Europeans: "America will not fail you. It will stick with you in this decisive moment." The West had an important role to play by assisting in the transition to democracy, he said, and would not squander the opportunity.

The "need for transition" to democracy and a market economy and the need for training, upon which everyone agreed, seemed to be repeated a hundred times. Speakers echoed the truisms they and the "experts" had uttered with missionary zeal at dozens of similar conferences. The need for change away from centrally planned economies had spawned a number of metaphorical clichés of "transition." An Eastern European minister parroted this trendy mantra: "It's easy to make an aquarium into fish soup. But can the fish soup be turned back into an aquarium?" Going from communism to capitalism would be no less dramatic and difficult. "Strong medicine" would be required to "jump to a market economy."

The Central and Eastern Europeans, who had been brought over specially for the conference, listened politely. Behaving (and being treated) more like bystanders than participants, they did nothing to undermine its upbeat tone, all the while underscoring the difficulty of transition in that charming, understated style in which the savvy elites of poor countries often present themselves.

Away from the music, I spoke with a Polish official who was to coordinate foreign assistance to his country. He was too gracious and well bred to be overtly critical of the conference. After a long conversation, however, he meekly suggested that some "training of the donors" might be helpful. He said he was struck by how Americans seemed driven to do good and thought they could just draft a statement and assume that good would follow. "But that isn't enough," he said. "They need to have some idea about what they're trying to accomplish."

Indeed, in the aid story, ideas about what could or should be accomplished have not always been wise or wisely set in motion. Problems that would emerge later in the field as aid arrived in Central and Eastern Europe and the nations of the former Soviet Union could be seen to take root in that banquet room on that "enchanted evening." The conference was symbolic of a genuine desire to do good and at the same time exposed a wide gap between the two sides—a gap in perspectives, goals, and experience. In the years ahead, that gap would grow wider before it narrowed and would create a situation in which many were far from enchanted with aid efforts.

THE DISCONNECT

At the start of the aid story, there was a gigantic disconnect between East and West—a disconnect forged by the Cold War and exacerbated by the barriers of language, culture, distance, information, and semiclosed borders. Before the revolutions of 1989, only a handful of scholars, journalists, diplomats, and descendants of emigrants from nations in the region had ventured behind the Iron Curtain. By the end of the decade, the volume of foreign traffic flowing through Central and Eastern Europe was enormous. Yet the disconnect lived on, even as circumstances changed after the collapse of the Berlin Wall.

I was in a unique position to observe the disconnect: When the Berlin Wall fell in 1989, I had already spent six years in Poland as an anthropologist, Fulbright scholar, and freelance journalist. I had a wealth of friends and acquaintances, many of whom were to become leaders in politics, business, and public life. Before the collapse of communism opened up so many new avenues to the West, the region's 40-plus years as a semiclosed world had shaped the many expectations natives had of foreigners and their ways of relating to them. I had observed how Poles welcomed foreign guests and showered them with hospitality and graciousness. Westerners were the bearers of gifts and opportunities. But at the same time, many Poles regarded Westerners as childlike because they were naive about the hard realities of the Eastern world as well as the political skills it took simply to survive under communism. I had recorded what I came to call the Poles' *ritual of listening to foreigners,* in which the naive but self-assured Westerner would encounter the shrewd Pole, who deftly charmed his guest while revealing nothing of what he truly thought. The same Pole would laugh at the Westerner's gullibility behind his back, as one might poke fun at a child. Many Poles had mastered the sophisticated art of impressing Westerners while maneuvering to get what they wanted.

The opportunities for Poles and their Central and Eastern European neighbors to use this skill expanded enormously after 1989. With America "winning" the Cold War and sensing history in the making, all sorts of Westerners came to tout the virtues of capitalism and democracy and to help transform the liberated satellites from centrally planned to market economies.

Under communism, Central and Eastern Europe had been a wilderness of too many regulations that many citizens did not obey and rigid ideologies that most did not believe in. The need for new rules brought with it questions about what those rules should be and who should formulate them. Over this landscape poured a flood of fixers and nostrum peddlers, real experts, and self-assertive frauds. Rising up to meet them was an array of bewildered new officials, privatization pirates, and entrepreneurs. The tradition of the fix and the deal took on a new vitality in this uncharted world—a world that was not quite communist, not quite capitalist, not quite anything else.

The peoples of Central and Eastern Europe, having finally attained their long-awaited independence, hoped that the "transition" would be simple, straightforward, and painless. They expected that the new leaders could transform their devastated economies overnight, with a little monetary help from their friends in the West. But before the amateur politicians found time to visit a tailor, they were beset by the blandishments of million-dollar lawyers and economists offering their services, some claiming to have brought Latin American republics out of economic disarray overnight. Grzegorz Kołodko, director of Poland's Institute of Finance, observed in 1990: "The traffic is . . . only from West to East. Economists from the West come to the East. Now people are getting interested in Czechoslovakia. Just watch. Prague—beautiful city, good beer. It will be a crowded place. Budapest—a very beautiful city. I don't know how it will be with Bucharest," he said wryly.[1]

As "transition to democracy" came into vogue, carpetbaggers and consultants, foundations and freelancers rushed to explore, and sometimes to exploit, the new frontier. A Washington, D.C., attorney observed that "every attorney in Washington did a week or two stint in Eastern Europe to train the poor natives in constitutional law." Historic castles once used as Communist Party resorts were converted to conference and training centers in business and capital markets. Visitors peddled authoritative expertise on functions—ranging from banking to environmental cleanup—that the newly arrived Central and Eastern European officials and entrepreneurs had yet to define, let alone learn how to evaluate. Perceiving the influx of visitors as the world coming to their aid, the virgin leaders made themselves accessible. At least at first.

This frontier attracted, indeed seemed set up to encourage, a jet set of "operators" on both sides. In the West, instant experts on the region and "transition" sprang up. Western historians and political scientists found themselves less needed; financiers, economists, bankers, and accountants were in demand. In the East, former communist leaders became arbiters of reform and mavens of business. Those actually needed were fixers, people who could arrange things—who could "play on any team," as one friend put it. On both sides, those who could play on any team seemed to be the

most sought after; operator-speculators were the disproportionate beneficiaries of the frontier's fortunes and opportunities.

During this influx into Central and Eastern Europe from 1989 to 1991,
I was based mostly in Poland and found myself witness to many encounters
between visiting foundation, government, and business representatives on
one hand and Poles I had known for years on the other. My writings on the
region had brought me to the attention of some of these representatives. As
most major American foundations (along with minor ones) moved into
Central and Eastern Europe in 1989 and 1990 looking for projects to
support, I received calls from emissaries scouting for the most useful
projects and contacts.

I was invited to attend many meetings between Eastern pacesetters
and visiting Western envoys. At first glance, such encounters had a novel,
surreal quality to them. In December 1989, on a trip to Poland, an
impeccably dressed Elizabeth Dole, then U.S. secretary of labor, visited
her down-to-earth, sometimes brash Polish counterpart, Jacek Kuron—a
prisoner under the communists, who typically sported a work shirt, jeans,
and Earth Shoes along with his earthy smile. The meeting was filled with
good intentions and good feelings, optimism, and hope for the future. If the
Berlin Wall, which had kept East and West artificially divided all those
years, could fall, any other problems could not be so difficult to solve. In
the euphoria of the moment, West and East appeared to come together.

I watched. Beneath the sheer intrigue of these encounters and my
sense of privilege in participating in this theater of the absurd, there
appeared to be a serious schism. Despite good intentions, I could see
danger signs. Such delegations, although welcomed, proved problematic to
the new leaders. The large Dole mission arrived while the Polish government was hammering out the stabilization plan to be implemented January
1, 1990. In the midst of intense negotiations to thrash out the critical
changes that were to come only weeks later, the country's highest officials
spent four days in fraternal meetings with the Dole delegation, explaining
the fundamentals of Poland. Stefan Kawalec, general director of the
Ministry of Finance, confided to me, "It was a very nice visit, but we have
had too many such nice visits already."

Whatever the expectations, Kawalec's understated tone, like the
contrast between Kuron's work shirt and Dole's dress-for-success ward-
robe, foreshadowed a lack of understanding and difference in styles that
would deepen the disjuncture. It was the disjuncture between what donors

and recipients defined as "help"; the discrepancy between how aid was perceived by its recipients and the "success stories" conveyed in donors' reports; the difference between the glossy brochures of aid agencies and the realities on the ground; and the disconnect between the resounding words echoed at international conferences and the actions actually taken.

AID IN THREE PHASES

In short, it was about politics and, crucially, the relationships between donors and recipients—not only at the higher echelons, but at all levels of contact. Transplanting know-how and ideas from one setting into another is an inherently troublesome process. Yet depending on how donors design and deliver assistance, and the relationships they develop with recipients, aid can either help to bridge the gap or serve to widen it. In the case of Central and Eastern Europe and later the former Soviet Union, this was precisely what was so often overlooked. Donors and the aid community talked about categories of aid to be proffered: privatization, private-sector, democracy, or humanitarian assistance. But rarely was careful consideration given to the donors' and recipients' agents, the relationships formed between them, and the effects of those relationships on aid outcomes. In the study of aid and development, little attention has been paid to how aid actually happens. Yet *how* aid happens—through whom and to whom, under what circumstances, and with which goals— determines not only the nature of what recipients actually get and how they respond to it, but its ultimate success or failure.

This book shows how relationships, both between Easterners and Westerners and among fellow Easterners, shaped the outcomes of nearly all of the strategies that the major donors employed in aid to Central Europe, Russia, and Ukraine: technical assistance through person-to-person contacts, grants to political-economic groups and nongovernmental organizations (NGOs) in the recipient nations, and loans to small businesses. Although these strategies differed significantly, in all of them it was crucially important exactly who participated and how these participants connected to their counterparts and compatriots—whether it was a Western consultant who made tens of thousands on projects of dubious merit or a well-meaning but unversed aid officer in Washington authorizing funds for projects unneeded and unwanted in the target country. Too often, relationships between donor and recipient representatives failed to facilitate, and even frustrated, partnerships. And too often, poorly conceived and structured projects, or lack of cultural understanding, led to impasse or even disaster.

It was not only the rapacity of Western agents or the errors of planning and implementation that led to problems in the aid effort. Further complicating the relationships between donors and recipients were the legacies of decades of communist rule. The pervasive distrust of foreigners and officialdom, the powers of the old elites, and the persistence of established relationships and mentalities could not be eliminated as easily as the ubiquitous statues of Lenin. Consequently, the legacies of the Cold War and communism played a large part in the story of aid to Central and Eastern Europe, Russia, and Ukraine. Donors could either help to dismantle communist-style relationships and mentalities or inadvertently support them. In some instances, unwitting donors sustained and even reinforced those legacies through their sheer misunderstanding of them. The Eastern champions of democracy who used aid for their own personal and political purposes, or the government-funded loan officers who preferred to feather their own nests rather than to help fledgling businesses, were among the many who, through their manipulation of aid and aid officials, kept those legacies alive. They, and the tradition they represent, cannot help but be an important focus of this book.

The progression of the aid effort to Central and Eastern Europe, and later to the former Soviet Union, can be traced in terms of three major phases. The initial euphoria on the part of donors and recipients alike was the first phase, which I call "Triumphalism." This phase was almost inevitably followed by a period of frustration and resentment in both East and West—a phase I call "Disillusionment." Eventually, in some cases and especially in Central Europe (Poland, Hungary, and the former Czechoslovakia), the donors and recipients adjusted to each other—a phase I term "Adjustment." They began to examine the relationships between them and how those could best be managed for successful aid outcomes, or at least to suit their own purposes. In other cases, notably that of Russia, there has been little successful adjustment, only scandal and ever-increasing tension. This book follows the tortuous path of aid efforts first in Central Europe, and, when the aid effort moved east, in Russia and Ukraine, in terms of those three phases.

CHEMICAL REACTIONS

"West" and "East" represent different types of social, economic, and political systems and distinct Cold War reference points. What happens when these two types of systems intersect through their representatives over the issue of aid? How do actors, operating in terms of different constraints, interests, procedures, and circumstances of power, interact and respond when brought together under the mantra of assistance?[2] (Although "West" and "East" are problematic categories given the vast variations within each, they organize the aid story in that the "West" gives aid and the "East" receives it.)

Foreign aid delivery often is thought of as a "transmission belt"—a conveyor transmitting advice from one side to another. But, in the cases I have studied, aid appears more like a series of chemical reactions that begin with the donor's policies, but are transformed by the agendas, interests, and interactions of the donor and recipient representatives at each stage of implementation and interface. Each side influences the other, and the result is often qualitatively different from the plan envisioned. This view of aid processes differs from approaches suggesting that "aid delivery" is like transferring knowledge from one society to another. In such approaches, which call to mind the metaphor of physics, one system is transferred to another, as in electrical induction.

By contrast, this study charts how the representatives of each system respond to the differences of the other—and the changes this produces. Because interactions between donors and recipients occur on (and between) several levels and over time, this book is an *ethnography across levels and processes.*[3] With aid issues as the common thread, I follow the interactions between actors who are shaping political and economic dimensions of relations between nations and "global" processes and those who are shaped by them.[4] The interactions I track are not only between actors on the ground (donor and recipient representatives), but also between the larger systems they represent.

I set out to understand aid *processes* rather than to cover the majority of aid projects (which would be impossible). To this end, I attempt to sample processes that appear to account for aid outcomes and report my analyses of some representative projects. The interactions associated with each phase of the East-West encounter occasion "chemical reactions" that can lead to the next phase. The three phases of aid—

Triumphalism, Disillusionment, Adjustment—signify palpable bench-marks along the way.

To tell the story, I outline the donors' major approaches in terms of the relationships engendered in the interface between donors and recipients. Because each approach nicely corresponds to a topical area (privatization, democratization, economic reform, or business development), chapters 2 through 5 present case studies, each of which links an approach with one such topical area. Chapter 2 examines the role of technical assistance, a chief strategy of the donors, in fostering a leading donor priority—the privatization of Central European state-owned enterprises. Another significant scheme has been giving grants to chosen recipient groups to further the building of democracy and civil society (chapter 3) and as political aid to a specific group under the guise of economic aid (chapter 4). Finally, providing monies for local business development has often coincided with loans to businesspeople in the recipient countries (chapter 5).

The study builds on the many works in development anthropology that have highlighted how cultural, social, and political conditions of recipient societies influence the success (or lack thereof) of aid programs. I concentrate especially on the ways in which donors organize aid efforts and the effects these have on relationships among people and institutions and, ultimately, aid results.[5] I found that while *relationships* of aid are little studied, they have crucial consequences for development outcomes.

A critical, yet often overlooked, component of the puzzle is recipients' responses to aid and how these shape the implementation of aid policies. Although recipients often are viewed as passive and voiceless, their responses, agendas, and interests influence aid administration, implementation, and outcomes.[6] Recipients can, actively or passively, frustrate, encourage, subvert, facilitate, or otherwise alter aid programs as they are conceived by the donors.

Here knowledge about the organization of Central and Eastern European social relations informs the study of aid processes. Anthropologists have shown how informal economic and social relationships under socialism transformed formal economic and bureaucratic procedures.[7] Many of these informal relationships, noted for their resilience, not only survived "transition," but shaped how recipients used aid and also how they interacted with donor representatives.

In some cases, donors were attracted to this environment of working through personal networks and enlisting the support of close-knit circles of people who had long worked together. The Central and Eastern European aid milieu of personal ties often contrasted starkly with the formalism and bureaucratic procedures of Western donors. Plugging into such a ready-made operation facilitated a donor's job in that contacts were easily accessible. Two effects of this approach, however, were that it tended to discourage the development of new contacts (as witnessed in chapters 3 and 4) and could enmesh donor agents in "corrupt" practices on the host side (as illustrated in chapter 4).

The case studies in chapters 2 through 5 that make up the heart of this work point to a trade-off between aid administration that goes "by the book" and ensures accountability (but fails to encourage relations among recipients and donors and impedes recipient input) and aid administration that gives a free hand to selected donor and recipient representatives (but at the expense of accountability).

The aid story is not a static one. I chart a process of change through the 1990s, from the phase of Triumphalism through Disillusionment, and finally, in some cases, Adjustment, in which donors and recipients swayed each other. Donor standards sometimes influenced those of recipients in positive and welcome ways. In some postsocialist contexts, for example, I observed a trend toward incorporating impersonal "professional" standards and a growing movement away from practices in which economic and bureaucratic transactions were shaped by personal relations. In these contexts, young people who came into their own during the 1990s often appreciated and appeared to adhere to different standards from some of their elders. This contrasts with some earlier anthropological work by myself and others showing the pivotal role of informal relationships in economic and political life.

In addition to a focus on relationships, this work notes the language of aid generated by donors and sometimes emulated by recipients. I have learned a lot from the works of anthropologists who have dissected the discourses of development and analyzed the history, evolution, and power relations of "development" and development institutions.[8] Several insightful anthropologists have shown that, although aid agencies tend to promise neutral technical solutions, they nonetheless reflect political ideologies that have important unanticipated consequences for the recipients.[9] As we shall see in chapters 2 and 4, certain privatization and economic reform strategies, which appear to have been driven by ideological orientations, had powerful consequences.

This study differs from nearly all other works in development anthropology in its focus on the "Second World," the nations of the former Eastern Bloc and the former Soviet Union. Nearly all studies in development anthropology concentrate on the "Third World"; critiques of development have thus grown out of fieldwork there. The ideas of the "Third World" and "development" both evolved in the context of postcolonialism and the Cold War; the idea of the "Third World" is closely intertwined with development models and institutions (as elaborated in chapter 1). The world after the Central and Eastern European revolutions of 1989 presented a dilemma for a development community now trying to operate in the "Second World": While problems such as overpopulation and illiteracy figure prominently in development models, the industrialized and highly literate countries of the "Second World" presented a new development domain. And so, by its concentration on the "Second World," this study further complicates the very idea of "development" and casts another pall over its post-Cold War future. With this study, I hope to encourage new domains of exploration in the anthropology of development as well as in the anthropology of policy.

IN THE FIELD

I began systematic study of this topic in 1991 in the Central European "Visegrád" countries of Poland, Hungary, and Czechoslovakia (named after their joint 1991 declaration signed in Visegrád, Hungary, to pursue common goals vis-à-vis the West), with interviews and participant observation. The West focused its aid efforts on these nations, which were seen as "models"—the most likely to succeed of the transitional countries. Because Poland is the most populous nation in the region and was the first to overthrow communism and to undertake radical economic reforms, Poland received nearly half the aid to the former Eastern Bloc. Thus, Poland is an essential part of the aid account, and the story, as told here, contains many illustrations from that country. (There are many parallels between the aid story in the more "advanced" Visegrád nations and the other nations of the Eastern Bloc. I focus on the Visegrád nations, where most of my fieldwork has been concentrated.) Later, when the aid frontier moved east, I began to examine assistance to Russia, generally the major donor priority in the former Soviet Union. When donors began to see Ukraine as important, I then followed some aid projects in that nation. (Despite some similarities, the political and strategic importance to the West of Russia and Ukraine renders their aid legacies significantly different from those of many other ex-Soviet states.)

I focus on "grant" aid—the technical assistance, training, and donations that do not have to be repaid by the recipients. Of the $80 billion in aid committed by the industrialized countries to Central and Eastern Europe from 1990 to 1996, some 40 percent consisted of grant aid (See appendix 1: Table 1). This study does not encompass such aid instruments as export credits or macrostabilization assistance, or loans provided by international financial institutions, except in cases in which the latter combine with grant aid projects otherwise under study. I set out to analyze some representative projects. I have included examples from the major (and some minor) donors and all recipient countries here covered (Poland, Hungary, the Czech Republic, Slovakia, Russia, and Ukraine). Although I did not attempt to study donors or recipients equally, the disproportionate attention I give to projects in Poland and Russia largely reflects donor priorities. And, because I set out to study the inter-reactions of the donors and recipients involved, there may be more cases in the book detailing problematic projects than "successful" ones. I describe positive cases in which donors influenced recipients' adaptation of "professional" practices, but my focus on social processes is constant. (See appendix 2 for a discussion of methods.)

Conducting an ethnography across levels and processes has meant going back and forth between donor and recipient representatives and bodies and doing so frequently. During the course of my research, which has spanned more than a decade, I have spoken at length with aid principals in all the countries here named. This included on-the-ground fieldwork (in 1989-90, 1991-92, 1994, 1995, 1998, and 1999) in Central Europe, Russia, and Ukraine. An equally important part of my research has been extensive, in-depth interviews with representatives of the major Western donors: the United States, the European Union, Germany, and the United Kingdom.

Although I interviewed many prominent figures, the most valuable information was gleaned from repeated conversations over many years with many aid officials at all working levels (see appendix 3, Interviews).

I also was privy to numerous meetings between donors and recipients at many levels. An international working conference I co-organized to bring donors and recipients together in an informal mode at the Woodrow Wilson International Center for Scholars in Washington, D.C. in April 1995 helped to frame many issues here discussed. The conference was titled "Western Aid to Central and Eastern Europe: What We Are Doing Right, What We Are Doing Wrong, How We Can Do It Better." It is my hope that this book will help to advance the spirit and desire for understanding in which that conference was conceived—the spirit in which the East and West began the "transition to democracy."

CHAPTER ONE

East Meets West:
A New Order for the Second World

> The radiance of Western justice and success is the power that
> caused the east European nations and the Soviet Union to
> abandon what they were and attempt to become what we, the
> democracies, have made of ourselves. . . . It is a moment to
> seize.
>
> —*Foreign Affairs*[1]

IN THE FALL OF 1989, a mood of triumph swept West and East alike. The long-suffering peoples of Eastern Europe (Poland, Hungary, Czechoslovakia, Bulgaria, Yugoslavia, and even more isolated Romania and Albania) had risen up. Remarkably and unexpectedly, the Soviet Union, the nation Ronald Reagan had christened the "Evil Empire" and the West's nemesis of the postwar era, was crumbling. Having won a victory that was not only political, but also moral and ideological, the West now had an unparalleled, historic opportunity to spread the fruits of freedom and free markets, to unite Europe, and to break down isolation between the two worlds. There was, it seemed, a meeting of the minds at last: The West had supported the spirit of resistance embodied in the movements led by Polish Solidarity leader Lech Wałęsa and Czech playwright Václav Havel, and in the aftermath of their success, the peoples of

Eastern Europe embraced the democratic ideals and financial support offered by the West.

The prevailing idea, in both East and West, was that Eastern Europe should look to the West not only for financial help and political models, but also for economic strategies and cultural identity. "Democracy," "freedom," "markets," and "civil society" became the bywords of 1989 and the early 1990s. Talk of a "return to Europe" filled cafes in Warsaw, Budapest, and Prague. Discarding the Soviet-tainted "Eastern" association, and believing they had been unwillingly pulled away from Europe by the politics of the Cold War, Poles, Hungarians, and Czechoslovakians asserted that they belonged to *Central* Europe. The end of communism reinvigorated enduring discussions of a "return to Europe."[2] The image was of a "lost-child-returning-home," as Czech sociologist Michal Illner has characterized it.[3]

Given the abandonment of communism, Western capitalism and democracy were seen as the only reasonable choices: virtually no alternatives to the Western capitalist models of reform espoused by the international financial institutions were seriously entertained on either side.[4] Part of the reason for this single-mindedness was that the peoples of the newly dubbed Central Europe were looking for simple answers. With little warning of impending difficulties from within or from the West, they hoped that their transition to democracy and free markets would be easy. And as Central Europe espoused Western models, so Western and Central European nations alike expected the West to open its doors and accept new responsibilities, to come in with accolades, affirmation, and aid.

The Marshall Plan became the reference point for the aid the West would provide to the "other Europe." Leaders, policymakers, and pundits in both East and West compared post-1989 aid to Central and Eastern Europe, and later, after the dissolution of the Soviet Union in December 1991, to Russia, with the post–World War II effort to rebuild Europe. Alexander King, who participated in the Marshall Plan as director of the European Productivity Agency of the Organization of European Economic Cooperation from 1957 to 1960, asserted that "A new Marshall Plan in Eastern Europe could be very successful in giving those countries the infrastructure and attitude in labor and management that will enable them to compete."[5] Offered as an economic life raft by the United States to the ravaged states of all of Europe after World War II, the Marshall

Plan, after Soviet dictator Joseph Stalin refused its aid, had helped to reconstruct only Western Europe.[6] Now, a post–Cold War "Marshall Plan" would accomplish similar objectives in the East. Both plans celebrated, and even symbolically consummated, America's winning of a war—first in a literal sense, and 50 years later in a symbolic sense. Both "Marshall Plans" were to assist "First World" Europeans—first to remake Western Europe, and 50 years later to bless Central Europeans in their "return to Europe." Furthermore, Central Europeans could now accept the Western generosity that Stalin had prevented them from accepting in 1947.[7] The words "Marshall Plan" became almost a metaphor for America's role as a white knight. They carried a powerful sentimental appeal that called to mind one of America's most celebrated moments of global leadership and enlightened self-interest. A "new Marshall Plan" implied that Americans were still capable of grand and unselfish acts—and Central Europeans did not hesitate to make that flattering connection. Solidarity leader Lech Wałęsa, speaking to a joint session of the U.S. Congress on November 15, 1989, proclaimed:

> It is worth recalling this great American plan which helped Western Europe to protect its freedom and peaceful order. . . . And now it is the moment when Eastern Europe awaits an investment of this kind—an investment in freedom, democracy and peace, an investment adequate to the greatness of the American nation.[8]

Throughout the West, donor nations, agencies, and individuals expressed their commitment to helping Central Europe. The European Union (EU) established Poland-Hungary Aid for Restructuring the Economy (PHARE), the largest aid program to the region. PHARE focused on Poland and Hungary, the first nations to dismiss their communist leaders in fall 1989. Other nations of the Soviet Bloc, whose governments subsequently collapsed that same fall, later joined the list of recipients.[9] The Group of Seven (G-7) countries (Canada, France, Japan, United Kingdom, Germany, Italy, and the United States) convened meetings to organize multilateral activities. The Group of Twenty-Four (G-24),[10] a larger body that included the nations of the G-7 and most of Western Europe, was established in 1989 to coordinate assistance to Central and Eastern Europe. The G-24 was chaired by the Commission of the European Communities in Brussels, which was given an unprecedented role in coordinating international assistance.[11]

In the United States, legislation was enacted on the very heels of communism's collapse. In the last days of November 1989, the U.S. Congress rushed through the so-called SEED (Support for East European Democracy) legislative package.[12] Championing the two nations that had led the revolutions, SEED authorized nearly $1 billion "to promote political democracy and economic pluralism in Poland and Hungary by assisting those nations during a critical period of transition."[13] Other nations of the region were added later. In addition, President George Bush established "Enterprise Funds" to promote the development of the private sector and other initiatives that would make American know-how available to the region.

Western development agencies were similarly galvanized into action. They reoriented resources and diverted personnel from the "Third World" nations of Africa, Asia, and Latin America to the "Second World" of Central and Eastern Europe, and later the former Soviet Union. In the aid community, the Second World became where the action was. By the end of 1992, the twilight of the aid push to the former Communist Bloc, the G-24 countries had committed $48.5 billion in aid (including export credits, loans, and rescheduled debt), of which $18.1 billion was grants, to help the nations of the region (see Appendix 1: Tables 1-4).[14] Meanwhile, following the collapse of the Soviet Union at the end of 1991, aid was gearing up farther east. By the close of 1992, the G-7 countries had committed $81 billion,[15] of which $16.8 billion was grant aid, to the former Soviet Union (see Appendix 1: Tables 5-8).[16] The now independent states of Russia and Ukraine were to receive the lion's share of Western aid to the ex-superpower. These sums appeared to be in the grand tradition of the Marshall Plan—more than enough to extend a firm lifeline to the beleaguered inhabitants of the former Eastern Bloc.[17]

COUSINS IN THE EAST

Apart from providing the West with an opportunity for major philanthropy, the collapse of communism offered it an historic opportunity to reconnect with the East. For the West, it was understandable, natural, and practical to help "our cousins." The region's "transition" was likened to the recovery of an ill patient with whom "we" had close cultural and historical bonds and from whom "we" had been separated only by an accident of history. The nations of Central Europe had been torn from Europe and forced into the Soviet orbit by the politics of the Cold War, not free will. There was to be "integration" and "partnership" between East and West, concepts much more easily accepted with regard to Poland, Hungary, and Czechoslovakia than, say, Africa. Psychology played a role: social critic Pascal Bruckner has observed that "Our estimation of a nation is tied in with our capacity to identify with it, to project ourselves in it."[18] Indeed, the West's capacity to identify with the peoples of the East lent a familial feel to the aid effort. Central Europeans were European. And the timing was fortuitous: the Communist Bloc collapsed at a moment when the idea of European unity (and a push for expansion of the European Community) was gaining great momentum in the West.

Not all of the newly independent countries of the Second World were considered candidates for joining Europe. The idea of European nations as aid recipients had upset the worldview of the development community. It could not readily classify the region as either "underdeveloped" or "developed"—the traditional development scheme, which, in application, is self-legitimating.[19] To resolve this ambiguity, the more "developed" countries of Poland, Hungary, and what was then Czechoslovakia were categorized almost as Western European countries that needed simply to catch up.[20] On the other hand, the "underdeveloped" countries of the Balkans and southeastern Europe were hardly candidates for "partnership" or "integration." They had fewer historical and cultural ties to the West, generally had less "developed" national economies, and were less industrialized.

The "model" countries of Poland, Hungary, and Czechoslovakia, which were to be the first of the former Bloc countries to "return to Europe," became the primary targets of most initial Western assistance. These countries, with Western Christian traditions, could claim deep historical and cultural ties to the West and identified with the West. During the martial-law crackdown of the early 1980s, Polish psychologist Zbigniew Nęcki noted that "we compare ourselves to Western countries, the most developed ones such as the United States, Japan, France, Sweden, and the Federal Republic of Germany."[21] Bulgaria and Romania, on the other hand, although also newly freed from the Soviet orbit, had an Eastern Orthodox tradition, and were inclined to look East.

Further, the considerable intellectual freedom and permission to travel that Poles and Hungarians had enjoyed since 1956 gave them closer contact with the West than Bulgarians and Romanians, whose travel and intellectual freedom had been severely restricted.

One of the West's key criteria for prospective partners was the extent to which a particular country figured in the West's security, political, and economic considerations. With the Soviet Union still in existence, and taking care not to annoy their giant eastern neighbor, the nations of Central Europe banded together to join the West. Polish president Lech Wałęsa, Czechoslovak president Václav Havel, and Hungarian prime minister Jozsef Antall met in an ancient castle on the banks of the Danube River to sign the "Visegrád declaration" of February 1991, which called for the three nations to coordinate their international strategies, especially in the context of entry to the EU and the North Atlantic Treaty Organization (NATO). It was hoped that Western aid would help to bring these nations "up to the level of" their Western neighbors and thus help them prepare for entry.

Moving eastward from the Visegrád countries, there were many fewer potential Europeans, according to the donors. As nations and regions of the former Soviet Union came to the attention of the donors, decisions about their status had to be made. Here donors made a distinction similar to the one they had made in the Eastern Bloc between the "more developed" and the "underdeveloped" countries. In some schemes, the nations with nuclear weapons—Russia, Ukraine, Kazakhstan, and Belarus—were dubbed the more "developed" ones. Almost invariably, the "underdeveloped" countries were the ethnically troubled Central Asian republics of Uzbekistan, Kyrgyzstan, Turkmenistan, and Tajikistan and the southern Caucasus republics of Armenia, Azerbaijan, and Georgia. The Organization for Economic Cooperation and Development (OECD), for example, classified these nations under its traditional category of Official Development Assistance (ODA).[22]

Russia, with its mixed European-Asian background, was not quite "our cousin" or a candidate for joining Europe. But as a fallen foe it had to be pampered so as not to be provoked into reasserting its rivalry. Later, Ukraine, also geopolitically important, began to enjoy more Western political and press attention. As donors looked for an alternative to aiding Russia, Ukraine became the target of considerable assistance.

At first glance, the reasons for assisting the Second World appeared to be much the same as those for aiding the Third World: to hold communism at bay, to ensure economic and political stability, and to create markets for the West. But aid to the Second World was about more than just keeping those nations out of the clutches of communism. It was about exorcising the legacies of communism itself—a quest that implicitly required more dramatic and wide-ranging change than heretofore had been expected of the Third World. The Second World had been "misdeveloped," not "underdeveloped" as the Third World, pundits said. Aid to India, as an example, tended to be couched mainly in terms of economic growth, not institutional and social change. But exorcising the legacies of communism in the Second World often required changing the very nature of recipient institutions, including those of banking, industry, international trade, social security, and health care.

According to the economic analysts and pundits of the time, change was supposed to be not only comprehensive, but accomplished quickly. Although a persevering debate about "shock therapy" versus "gradualist" approaches to reform raged in academic circles, the international institutions advocated and the leading donors supported, at least initially, the former approach.[23] And so the Western missionaries of change came armed with slogans that emphasized both the difficulty and the necessity of radical and rapid change. Harvard economist Jeffrey Sachs (of whom we will see more in chapters 2 and 4) had three favorites:

1. You can't cross a chasm in two jumps [you have to cross it in one].[24]
2. The dentist is cruel to pull slowly and faintly on a diseased tooth over a period of days. To shrink from what needs to be done merely prolongs the pain and agony.[25]
3. Suppose the British were to decide to switch from driving on the left side of the road to the right side? Would you recommend that they do so gradually, starting with trucks one year and cars a year later?[26]

The thinking of the day was that "we" had a once-in-a-lifetime "window of opportunity" to effect change. Many attuned to politics suggested that opposition to reform would more likely arise if reforms were made in a leisurely fashion. Many economists held that every change in the system would affect every other part of the system and lead to still more adjustments, so that all of the changes should be made at once. For these reasons, most agreed that it was imperative to demonstrate support for economic reform through aid that would deliver quick and tangible results.

American and European donors generally operated according to different projections of how long "the transition" would take. U.S. aid planners appeared to place more faith in change. They designed the aid effort on the assumption that "transition" would take just five years and that assistance would thus be required for a five-year period only. The American strategy was to "get in and get out," which recalled wartime strategy in the quick and certain impact it anticipated.[27] After five years, the recipient nations would "graduate," implying that, if they completed the American-designed course, the United States would certify them as having attained the benchmark of no longer needing aid. By contrast, Europeans, with generally deeper cultural ties and wider contact with the nations contiguous to the east, conceived of a commitment of a decade or more.

Whatever the time frame, the questions of how much aid the West would provide and the speed of transition became intertwined. The principle was, as anthropologist Gerald Creed put it, "the quicker you change the more we'll give; the more you give the quicker we can change."[28] If the West declined to send aid or sent insufficient aid, argued aid proponents, the nations of the Second World might fall into a chaotic abyss, suffer economic collapse and political turmoil, and even revert back to communism.

Thus, in the early days of independence, Central and Eastern Europe and the West were agreed: the West would help the East, and the East would show its gratitude through loyalty and quick reform.

THE WEST AS SAINT AND SAVIOR

For the peoples of Central Europe, Western assistance was never in doubt. They were predisposed to believe that the West cared and would fulfill its promises. Ironically, life under communism was largely responsible for this belief: two generations of isolation and communist experience had made the West a potent symbol of both good and evil and a curious "mixture of imitation and infatuation, jealousy and principled rejection," as anthropologist Chris Hann has described it.[29] The West as both saint and demon were powerful themes of life in the East, themes that did not evaporate with the collapse of communism. These themes set the stage for two distinctive phases in East-West relations in the Cold War's aftermath.

The East's idea of the West as saint (and the West's idea of the East as oppressed) provided the underpinnings for a period of intense euphoria, or Triumphalism, that occurred after the collapse of communism. It was a honeymoon between East and West in the spirit of a break from the past and a new start. This phase was relatively short, lasting roughly from 1989 to mid-1991 in the Visegrád countries. The late Rita Klimova, who served as the first Czechoslovak ambassador to the United States after the fall of communism, said that her compatriots then "imagined the United States to be a kind of rich Soviet Union." Her implication was that Central European recipients anticipated some continued economic dependency, with the West taking the place formerly held by the Soviet Union, but that the rewards for them would be greater than during the period of Soviet hegemony.[30] Some observers have compared these anticipations to Cargo Cults.[31] Indeed, the model of dependency on Big Brother, combined with ideas of Western prosperity, had formed the basis for aid expectations that would be difficult, if not impossible, to meet even under the best of circumstances.

Isolation, relative unavailability of consumer goods, and generally lower standards of living under communism had contributed to idealized views of the West. Particularly for Easterners who had not traveled there, people in the West seemed to live "the good life," or at least a less trying one. The West was a source of precious goods, money, and opportunities. In Poland, for example, where the peasantry had undergone nearly a half century of urbanization and many had traveled to America to work, America was perceived as a land of milk and honey. The waves of immigration to the New World (more than nine million Americans claimed Polish origins)[32] had mostly come from the peasantry and had sustained contact between Poland and the United States. During times of perceived national dispossession and hardship, such as the martial law imposed in Poland in the early 1980s, millions of households received relief parcels both from private relatives abroad and from religious and charitable organizations. Images of the prosperous West were refined to commercial icons: imported Swiss chocolates, French perfume, German wine, Viennese coffee, Bic razor blades, Johnny Walker whiskey, and Marlboro cigarettes could be purchased only in Pewex stores, retail outlets operated by the Polish government where Poles could buy imported goods for hard currency. Associations with the West, including Western products or relatives living abroad, were status symbols. Many Poles gained status in the eyes of their peers because they had worked or studied in the West or made friends with Westerners.

Furthermore, many Central Europeans had experienced the West as the standard-bearer of freedom and democracy, despite the official propaganda that promoted the West as demon in the game of East-West rivalry. As anthropologist David A. Kideckel has noted:

> Generations of communist state leaders used images of the West as *bête noire,* manifestly for consolidation and maintenance of their own power in society. For example, the chronic economic difficulties and shortages in the socialist states were regularly blamed on the machinations of the imperialist powers, Wall Street bankers, and financial lackeys like the International Monetary Fund.[33]

This negative image of the West was promulgated through the state-controlled media. However, these media were often not taken at face value: Many Central and Eastern Europeans found the official form of the news aired on television and printed in newspapers in conflict with the facts of daily life. They therefore distrusted official renditions, and, as Václav Havel put it, learned to "live in the lie."[34] This undercurrent of disbelief actually endowed the media with a powerful effect; often, people reactively assumed that the truth was the opposite of whatever the media claimed. In the early 1980s, one Polish physicist who was a visiting scholar in the United States was surprised to learn that racial segregation was a fact of life in South Africa. She had assumed that the Polish media had invented apartheid.[35] As Gerald Creed has observed, only after communist criticism of the West ceased to be part of official rhetoric did Central and Eastern Europeans entertain the idea that such criticism could be valid.[36]

Against the backdrop of East-West rivalry, Western actions during the Cold War encouraged black-and-white views of the West as right and the East as wrong. The West warmly welcomed defectors from Central and Eastern European countries. Radio Free Europe and Voice of America broadcasts presented benevolent images of America and the West. Politicians and diplomats expressed sympathy for the "casualties" of communism. And Western supporters funded resistance movements such as Poland's Solidarity movement both before and after it was outlawed by the communist government in the early 1980s. Support from outside helped to sustain the Opposition, as one prominent activist pointed out:

> The Opposition's main source of financial support was the West. Donations came from inspired individuals, from subscriptions, trade unions, social and political organizations, as well as from corporations, Polish emigré organizations, and government bodies such as substantial grants [about $1 million] from the U.S. Congress.[37]

Such Western acts of compassion during the Cold War enhanced the view of the West as saint and played no small role in Central and Eastern Europeans' expectations of Western help after the Cold War. Many in the East believed that the West would readily come to the assistance of the oppressed peoples of the East.

As the Berlin Wall fell, these idealized views crystallized to form an even more potent image. In the months after the revolutions of 1989, the West was much more than a saint. It became a savior. The triumphalism of the subsequent end of the Cold War left little room for voices to temper idealized views of the West or quell expectations of its role in Central and Eastern Europe's transformation. Misleading information circulating in the press in 1990-91 fueled expectations. For instance, Polish news reports that the West was sending billions of dollars in aid neglected to explain that this aid included export credits and loans that would have to be repaid. And the flood of visitors from the West conveying their interest in the region and their willingness to help contributed to a whirlwind of goodwill and anticipation—one that encouraged the East's predisposition to the idea that the West cared, would be involved, and would make good on its promises.

BUILDING THE AID MACHINE

As it ground into gear, the Western aid effort seemed to be all that the East could hope for. Western packages combined multinational aid (mostly loans from the international financial institutions, notably the

International Monetary Fund [IMF] and the World Bank) and bilateral assistance (often supplied by an array of "private" providers, such as consulting firms and nongovernmental organizations [NGOs]. The idea that the aid effort to Central and Eastern Europe, and later Russia and Ukraine, was unique—and not akin to Third World aid efforts— prompted Western donors to reorganize their aid efforts and management institutions to suit the gravity and import of their task. All manner of Western governmental agencies scrambled to take part in the action: in the United States alone, some 35 federal agencies, including the Departments of Energy and Labor and the Environmental Protection Agency as well as the United States Agency for International Development (USAID), got involved in the aid effort.[38]

Aid operations to the Second World differed from those to other regions in the role played by foreign policy officials and agencies, the higher visibility in the press, the interest taken by legislative bodies, and the considerable political sensitivity surrounding them. USAID official Steve Dean characterized the sentiment at the time: "I don't think the agency [USAID] has done anything like this [before]. Communism doesn't fall every ten years. I don't think you could compare it with anything else [in Latin America, Africa, et cetera]—not with the scope in this region."[39]

With large sums appropriated and pressure built up to disburse them and to show results, donors cranked up their aid machines quickly. Aid programs in the areas that donors established as priorities—generally economic reforms such as the privatization of state-owned industries or private-sector development, as well as areas given less attention such as public administration, health, or local governance—were to be coordinated at meetings attended by representatives of the G-24. The very founding of the G-24 especially to coordinate the Central and Eastern European effort illustrated the import initially placed on that effort.[40]

The high profile of the undertaking led the United States to appoint a special Department of State "coordinator" who was primarily responsible for policy formation and coordination, while USAID created the Bureau for Europe and the New Independent States to manage its programs. The Assistance Coordination Group, chaired by the State Department, managed assistance to Central and Eastern Europe, while the Office of the Coordinator for U.S. Assistance to the New Independent States (appointed under the Freedom Support Act of 1992) handled assistance to the former Soviet Union provided by a number of agencies.

In the United Kingdom, aid to the region was supervised primarily by the Foreign and Commonwealth Office, responsible for foreign affairs, rather than by the Overseas Development Administration (ODA). In Germany, the Ministry for the Economy (Bundesministerium für Wirtschaft) handled aid to the former Communist Bloc, not the traditional Third World aid arm, the Ministry for Economic Cooperation (Ministerium für Wirtschaftliche Zusammenarbeit).

Most aid work, whether funded by the United States, the EU, the United Kingdom, or Germany, was contracted to consulting firms and other providers. On their own, donor agencies generally lacked the resources to carry out aid agendas. Civil servants administered aid projects: they issued calls for proposals and evaluated them, organized competitive bidding, and managed task orders and projects. Any firm could compete, and the donors ostensibly followed fair and transparent selection procedures. In practice, however, those consultants and NGOs that had won previous contracts and/or put considerable effort into learning a contracting system and developing contacts were those most likely to be successful in contract competitions. In the United States, a cadre of "Beltway Bandits," Washington-based firms or firms with Washington offices, were experienced at winning USAID contracts. Successful competitors, especially at the beginning of the aid effort, tended to have worked in Latin America, Asia, or Africa. Later on, those who had worked in Central Europe were advantaged in winning contracts farther east. In 1992, Andrew Rasbash, economic adviser to PHARE in Poland, observed that "everyone wants to be involved in Poland. . . . If they get their foot in the door here, then they can go to Ukraine."[41]

Heading the award lists tended to be accounting firms, notably the "Big Six"—Deloitte & Touche, Coopers & Lybrand, KPMG Peat Marwick, Arthur Andersen, Ernst and Young, and Price Waterhouse. The Big Six, with track records in the Third World, appear to have been designated by the major donors as the most suitable agents of Central and Eastern European "transition." These firms received contracts from USAID, the EU, the British Know How Fund, the World Bank, and the European Bank for Reconstruction and Development (EBRD). They cornered a large portion of USAID contracts to Central and Eastern Europe and the former Soviet Union.[42]

With many jumbo "umbrella" and "omnibus" contracts, the Big Six had more substantial and all-encompassing portfolios in Central and

Eastern Europe than in the Third World, at least partly because the scope of work in the former was conceived of as much broader than in the latter. Donors retained the Big Six for a variety of tasks, from auditing, privatizing, and setting up stock exchanges, to writing tax and environmental legislation, to activities that could hardly have been further afield of these tasks, such as assessing the changing position of women under "transition."

The pressure to spend money quickly appeared to have played a role in the choice of contractors. An aid program's "success" was often evaluated simply in terms of having spent money. As one U.S. congressional staff member put it, "AID is supposed to move the money. That's what managers in Washington look at, that's what Congress looks at."[43] Ambassador Richard L. Morningstar, U.S. assistance coordinator to the former Soviet Union, has recounted that

> the pressure to get money out the door . . . that's why we favored large contractors, which met with some success. Programs in that part of the world are not a lot different from R&D [research and development] in a business because no one has done it before. Time was not given by virtue of political necessity, and so the program got skewed toward big contractors and large technical assistance programs. . . . At a time when there's pressure to get money out quickly and there's a lot of money, it's a lot less risky than giving contracts to small contractors.[44]

The climate of urgency led donors to attempt to build some flexibility into the aid machine by changing or circumventing standard foreign aid procedures. For example, competition could be waived by USAID's assistant administrator under "notwithstanding authority," an exception introduced especially for use in Central and Eastern Europe at the inception of the aid effort.[45] Notwithstanding authority was invoked in contracts granted for USAID's linchpin privatization program in Central Europe, as well as in its privatization and economic restructuring package for the former Soviet Union.[46] Moreover, some USAID awards were approved for "foreign policy"—that is, national security reasons— a justification that career procurement officer Stanley R. Nevin said, to his knowledge, had not before been used in USAID.[47]

Aid donors generally established funding ceilings, under which contracting decisions could be made without competition. EU rules

stated that all projects above 50,000 ECU (European Currency Unit)—
the common currency used in Europe—had to be competed in all 15
member states. Likewise, competition for British Know How Fund
awards above 50,000 pounds was obligatory.[48]

Thus, within a matter of months after the revolutions of 1989, donors
had at their fingertips new agencies, procedures, and mechanisms to
facilitate aid efforts in the Second World.

A MARSHALL PLAN OF ADVICE

With the superstructure of the aid machine in place, it might have seemed
to innocent observers in both East and West that implementation was the
only obstacle to relief for millions of Central and Eastern Europeans. But
even as the aid effort was in its nascent design stages, portents of trouble
were beginning to appear.

One such portent was the initial hint of suspicion on the part of Central
and Eastern Europeans that aid from the West was seriously mismatched to
their needs. Despite talk of a new "Marshall Plan" for reviving the
economies of the former Communist Bloc, few Western policymakers had
advocated a serious commitment on the order of tens of billions of dollars
in capital assistance. In the United States, for example, this magnitude of
capital investment never hit the budget agenda, although some politicians
and pundits called for such an investment. "We didn't do a Marshall Plan,"
a catch phrase of later years, was an acknowledgement that a comprehensive aid package for Central and Eastern Europe (implying strategic
planning, commitment of high-level officials, and, above all, massive
capital assistance) was not made available. As early as May 1990, the
United States had ruled out a modern-day Marshall Plan for reviving the
economies of the former Communist bloc.[49]

Still, there remained a huge disconnect between Western plans and
what Central and Eastern Europeans believed was possible. Minister
Witold Trzeciakowski, Poland's aid coordinator from 1989 to 1990, has
stated that when he called, in 1989, for a $10 billion "Marshall Plan" for
the former Eastern Bloc, he envisioned not only aid in large amounts, but
also an aid package largely of grants, as in the Marshall Plan, not primarily
of technical assistance and loans.[50] Although the Marshall Plan had
consisted of nearly 90 percent grant aid—largely capital assistance to

rebuild war-damaged infrastructures and industries—as of the beginning of 1992, Western aid to the former Eastern Bloc offered little more than 10 percent in grants.[51] Most aid to the region was in the form of export credits, loans, and debt relief. Technical assistance through advisers who provided expertise and training made up the bulk of grant aid. American technical experts had played key roles in the Marshall Plan, but as part of targeted, strategic assistance that accompanied massive capital investment.[52] It was not until 1993, Trzeciakowski says, that it finally became clear to him that a new Marshall Plan would not be forthcoming.[53]

Because few people in the region, including officials, had anticipated that the assistance would take the form it did, an even wider gulf was created between Marshall Plan rhetoric and the aid that was sent. Discussions about aid occurred in a highly charged political climate, in which the main actors were only beginning to confront the enormous task of converting social aspirations into reality. Even the highly educated and well-traveled elite generally had little knowledge of Western assistance goals, institutions, and results in the Third World.

The recognition on the part of Western officials of the limits of assistance (a "Marshall Plan of advice" or a "Mini Marshall Plan"), as Western aid officials sometimes referred to it among themselves, did not seem to affect the expectations of billions of dollars in aid in the East. As Poland's chief coordinator of foreign assistance, Jacek Saryusz-Wolski, explained in 1991, at the height of the country's frustration with aid efforts: "When people in Poland hear that billions of dollars come to Eastern Europe, they expect that Poland gets one-half or one-third of that money. . . . Very often people ask us what happened to it."[54] In 1992, Polish president Lech Wałęsa articulated the growing resentment when he spoke at the European Parliamentary Forum in Strasbourg, charging that "it is you, the West, who have made good business on the Polish revolution. . . . The West was supposed to help us in arranging the economy on new principles, but in fact it largely confined its efforts to draining our domestic markets."[55] Similarly, Hungary's chief aid coordinator, Béla Kádár commented that "the public learns from official statements that the Western world has transferred resources on the order of $40 billion to $70 billion so far to promote transition in the post-communist countries. One has to ask, where have all these billions gone?"[56]

Where indeed? There was a considerable gap between donors' allocations and actual disbursements in the region. In 1992, only an estimated 11 percent of the committed monies had actually been disbursed.[57] Not only was there a wide gap between the loose rhetoric about a Marshall Plan and the donors' actual promises, but another chasm yawned between the donors' promises and their deliveries.

Assistance to Central and Eastern Europe bore little resemblance to postwar aid in still other ways: The Marshall Plan, which entailed strategic and targeted assistance and the commitment of high-level officials, was directed by the United States, the world's only economic superpower at the time. The aid effort to the Second World, on the other hand, involved many donor nations that dispensed limited funds among many recipient targets and projects. The nature of the aid efforts coming from Western Europe and the United States were necessarily distinct, reflecting differences in politics and cultures, ties to recipient nations, and strategic agendas. Each donor nation dispersed resources among myriad constituent groups, each of which laid claim to a piece of the pie.

With regard to U.S. assistance alone, the State Department was given only a nominal "oversight and coordination" role. The SEED legislation of 1989, which made possible U.S. aid to Central Europe, established some 25 priority areas and called upon the expertise of up to 35 federal agencies, all with their own agendas. Similarly, the Freedom Support Act of 1989, which authorized U.S. assistance to the former Soviet Union, engaged 19 agencies.[58] The legislation did not consider how the expertise of all these agencies was to be coordinated, and there were few guidelines for managing the process. The structure of U.S. coordination to the former Soviet Union was so convoluted that Congress asked the General Accounting Office (GAO), the body charged by Congress with investigating how appropriated monies are spent, to investigate. GAO's subsequent report was titled "Former Soviet Union: U.S. Bilateral Program Lacks Effective Coordination."[59]

Also less than optimal was the lack of coordination among the various donors, which carried out both diverse and often overlapping aid programs. As Ambassador Robert L. Hutchings, Special Adviser for East European Assistance, Department of State, acknowledged in congressional testimony, "There is too much duplication and competition among donors, and too little coordination of activities so that we can make the best and most effective use of our collective resources."[60] Bilateral donors tended to operate in isolation from one another and often, in priority areas, to compete for projects.[61] The very structure of bilateral aid lacked incentives to encourage sharing pertinent information or working together in the interest of the recipient nation. An evaluation of a British Know How Fund employment project in Hungary described a duplication of effort that was far from unique:

> The project was successful in its immediate objectives. However, unknown to the British, at the same time, the Hungarians were receiving Canadian assistance with World Bank funding to establish a wider network of Job Clubs. . . . With the benefit of hindsight this may not have been the best use of scarce resources from both donor and recipient.[62]

But some donor officials argued that time and money were often wasted by requiring recipient governments to correspond with a wide variety of agencies, each with its own procedures, criteria, and information flows. Reducing project duplication, for example, would have required each specific donor to review other donors' projects before issuing a call to potential contractors for proposals. With individual strategic goals, capabilities, and time frames, it often was not in the self-interest of bilateral donors to coordinate assistance.

Nevertheless, "aid coordination" was a popular topic of discussion among donors, and many meetings, including those of the G-24—charged with the daunting task of coordinating all the programs—were devoted to this purpose. Meetings among G-24 officials at high political levels bore few concrete results in coordinating specific projects, because the officials present often were not at the working level and not well enough versed in actual conditions and projects. As Alan Mayhew, the former head of the EU's PHARE program, summed it up, "The G-24 coordination process never coordinated."[63] Through invocations that would continue for the duration of the aid effort, officials called for "better coordination" and critics decried the "lack of coordination." The Institute for East West Studies, which conducted several studies of aid to the region, concluded that "emphasis should not be on increasing financial commitments but rather on improving disbursement procedures of the donors and the absorptive capacity of recipients."[64]

To rectify problems of coordination (or at least to appear to be doing so), donors widely discussed and even set up some databases and "clearinghouses." One clearinghouse that received a lot of attention was set up by the OECD. The *OECD Register,* an online database of technical assistance to Central and Eastern Europe, was located at OECD head-quarters in Paris. Established for use by donors and recipients in planning and coordinating aid projects, the information contained in the *Register* ostensibly provided "an overview of assistance being given in relation to needs and priority areas, with a view to identifying duplication, overlap, mismatches and gaps."[65] But no database or technology, no matter how sophisticated, could overcome the fundamental reality that programs were set up to serve the strategic and cultural agendas of individual donors. Technical mechanisms could not provide incentives to solve problems that were fundamentally political.

However, there were cases in which multiple donors funded "demonstration" projects, often high-profile ones, as we will see in chapters 2 through 4. Some donor officials suggested that coordination among donors could occur when they worked together, even sharing costs, on specific large and complex projects.[66] But only in cases in which multiple donors saw *individual* benefits in coordinating projects did aid coordination occur.

Just as important as impediments to coordination, neither the organization of the aid effort itself, nor the pressure to spend quickly, were generally conducive to innovating, incorporating recipient input, or dealing effectively with the societies of the region. Despite new mechanisms, institutions, and programs created amid the excitement of the aid effort to the Second World, the nuts and bolts employed in much of the effort were similar to those employed in the Third World. This was partly due to long-established regulations and procedures, designed to minimize misuse of funds, that could not be bypassed or could be skirted only through the special authorities or high-level political interventions described earlier. As the EU's Mayhew reported, to reduce corruption, the PHARE program was "set up in the African style . . . where you have a delegation in country that has to carry out all sorts of checks, so it becomes bureaucratically very heavy."[67]

Further, although donors perceived the Second World as unique, they had little real understanding of its historical, economic, political, and sociological experiences, and little organizational capacity to deliver new programs. Following 40 years of Cold War foreign aid, during which capitalist and communist countries aided the Third World in an attempt to buy loyalties, the aid programs most available were those that had been implemented in the Third World. Almost by default, donors set many of them into motion. Many were ill-matched to recipient needs and stifled innovation.

For example, USAID, with its panoply of preexisting, standardized rules and congressionally mandated regulations, generally discouraged risk taking and allowed little flexibility.[68] There was pressure to put a well-crafted square peg into the latest round hole, in the manner of "We have this program in Honduras. We can implement it in Hungary." Civil servants who had handled Cold War aid were given Second World assignments, in which, they strongly suspected, their careers would benefit more by fulfilling bureaucratic mandates and maximizing spending than by developing programs tailored to recipient needs. Almost any bureaucrat, no matter how removed from the setting or lacking in host-country expertise, could perform adequately simply by adhering to the guidelines.

Standard contracting procedures also worked against aid flexibility. Under a long-developing body of regulations,[69] contracting procedures could be numbingly complex and time consuming. Administered from Brussels, PHARE was constrained by regulations designed to ensure fairness that often worked against effectiveness. The mandated "geographical balance" among its 15 member states sometimes meant not hiring the consultants with the most expertise. This point was not lost on the recipients. As a Polish newspaper reported in 1994: "In the post-war years everyone knew what the Marshall Plan was. Today in Central and Eastern Europe it is common knowledge that there are strings attached to the money coming from Brussels."[70]

And so the donors' bureaucracies, largely designed for operations elsewhere, rattled and clanked into Central Europe, and later into Russia and Ukraine. There they encountered, and colluded and collided with societies that functioned in some fundamentally different ways from their own. A high-level donor official characterized the challenge as such: "The bureaucracy puts all sorts of obstacles in the way to prevent you from reaching your political objectives and then criticizes you for failing to meet them."[71]

DILEMMAS OF AID RELATIONSHIPS

One of the most critical aspects of aid-program structure was the extent to which it incorporated recipient input (and from whom it drew this input). The EU tended to treat the nations of Central Europe more as potential partners than did the United States. This difference in attitude was evident in the way control was exercised and recipient input structured. U.S. assistance maximized Washington's control over aid to Central Europe, with planning and management authority in the United States, rather than with U.S. personnel overseas. Important decisions (as well as many less important ones) were made at home, rather than in the field. At first, USAID field representatives had no signature authority to disburse funds and served only as advisers to the U.S. ambassador in the recipient country and reporters to Washington. Because USAID staff in the region generally had little authority (a clause in some consultants' contracts stipulated that any agreements made with USAID representatives overseas were not legally binding), decision making was often delayed.

And information did not always flow well from Washington. USAID officials in the field sometimes learned about contracts signed in Washington only when contractors arrived on assignment. As USAID's Budapest representative remarked in 1991, "I get surprised every day [when] people on contract for USAID call and I don't know anything about it."[72] Following congressional direction that authority be delegated to the field ("in order to avoid planning and contracting in Washington for specific activities without the concurrence of the people in the field who have more intimate knowledge of the particular country"), Washington-based management changed somewhat in early 1993,[73] although field representatives still lacked the authority of their Third World counterparts.

Throughout the aid effort, Central European recipients pointed out that they had little or no input into aid decisions, and often were not consulted in advance or even informed of decisions.[74] Officials in Warsaw, Budapest, and Prague complained that their concerns were ignored despite the presence of American-government aid bureaus in these cities and numerous fact-finding missions from the West.[75] Polish officials responsible for aid coordination were unable to obtain reliable information about how much U.S. money was being spent on particular projects, although the local USAID office was just several blocks away. In 1992, the GAO looked into U.S. aid to Poland and Hungary, the major recipients of U.S. aid to the region at the time. GAO reported that, in Hungary, many assistance transactions, including those of the United

States, occurred without the knowledge of the Hungarian government's assistance coordination unit.[76]

As late as 1994, speaking before a Polish parliamentary commission, Minister Jacek Saryusz-Wolski, aid coordinator of Poland, reported:

> The principle of distribution of [American aid money] is such that we, as an agency, are simply informed about what they are doing with that money. At the most, we can protest, or object to a particular type of activity that we don't like. But the Americans do what they like, and we must accept that, at the most voicing our veto.[77]

In contrast to U.S. aid, EU assistance to Central and Eastern Europe was structured to compel input from recipients, as well as from in-country representatives. Many of the EU's PHARE programs were administered through Program Management Units (PMUs), which were set up either inside the government ministries or in parallel with them.[78] Although EU representatives typically were assigned as advisers to PMUs, the PMUs were staffed and directed by recipients, who naturally had access to local contacts. EU representatives sometimes worked alongside their local counterparts, shared office complexes for several years, and developed collegial relationships. Some high-level EU representatives were keenly aware that their host officials were to be treated as equals. One such official remarked that "One day he [the host official] may well be *my* boss [in the EU structure]."

Responding at least in part to recipients' requests and political considerations, the EU began to supply more capital assistance to finance trans-European network projects, in the form of railway lines, roads, and border infrastructure, following a Copenhagen summit in June 1993.[79] As one EU official explained, "Investment finance is more visible to the public. That's one of the reasons we're going into it. . . . [Investment] can be seen and touched."[80] In the mid-1990s, as U.S. assistance to Central Europe was winding down, the EU's PHARE program continued to evolve. PHARE began to fund projects to support pending EU members in the EU's "pre-accession strategy." PHARE became a major component of this strategy, "designed to help them [selected Central and Eastern European countries] align their political, economic and legal systems with those of the European Union."[81] In June 1998, the European Union adopted guidelines reorienting the PHARE program from a "demand-driven" program to one addressing the priorities of the "Accession Partnerships."[82] The new PHARE guidelines emphasized institution-building and investment support.[83]

However, the EU was much less partnership-oriented in its TACIS (technical assistance for the Commonwealth of Independent States, or CIS) program. Because Russia, unlike some Central European nations, was not a pending EU member, the EU was not driven by the necessity to harmonize laws with Russia. Although PHARE was composed both of technical assistance and investment, TACIS was confined almost entirely to technical assistance, as the acronym indicates.[84] Further, TACIS, which was centered in Brussels, entailed much less delegation to its in-country representatives than did PHARE. (TACIS had a coordinating unit in all NIS countries, but with delegations only in Russia, Ukraine, Georgia, and Kazakhstan.)[85] Although there was to be increasing decentralization away from Brussels, Michael B. Humphreys, counselor for the European Commission Delegation in Ukraine, explained that the TACIS countries should first prove themselves: Brussels, he said, has "less confidence in the ability of [TACIS] countries" [to manage their own programs] than it did in the PHARE countries.[86]

The EU and most other donors operated in standard (Third World) fashion in that they structured aid through government-to-government relations. By contrast, the target of U.S. assistance was almost exclusively the "private" sector. This allowed the United States to develop some "innovative ways of delivering assistance," as Ambassador Robert L. Hutchings of the Department of State rightly stated in congressional testimony.[87] One notable example of this innovation was the Enterprise Funds designed to support private business, discussed in chapter 5.

However, such a radical avoidance of government also resulted in problems. Supporting "private" actors was a way of bypassing recipient governments that were seen as suspect and full of holdover communist bureaucrats. Government-to-government links were intentionally weak. A 1992 letter from the Department of State to the GAO stated: "We have also designed our programs to deliver assistance primarily to the private sector rather than to the government. Indeed, we have intentionally avoided government-to-government aid agreements, which contrasts with the EC PHARE program approach." As the GAO concluded, the fundamental drawback of this approach was that the U.S. assistance program "lacked coordination in working with the host governments."[88] The weakness of government-to-government links sometimes resulted in a lack of mechanisms to establish aid priorities and instruments. This made it difficult for aid coordinators in the recipient countries to anticipate and coordinate projects.[89] Thus, in the case of U.S. assistance to Central Europe, neither government was systematically involved, communication channels were often unclear, and consultation on the recipient side was weak. As we will see especially in chapter 2, this meant that U.S. economic aid to Central Europe was not set up for optimal access to recipient governments or local contacts.

By contrast, as detailed in chapter 4, there also were cases in which aid contractors, with carte blanche from the donor, colluded with selected recipient elites, bypassed aid regulations, and were subject to little or no donor oversight. For example, U.S. aid to Russia delegated its economic aid portfolio to a private entity—the Harvard Institute for International Development (HIID)—which worked exclusively with a specific circle of "reformers" in (and out of) government and excluded other reformer groups in (and out of) government. As we shall observe, both extremes— of avoiding government contacts, as in the U.S. economic aid strategy to Central Europe, and of working with only one group in the government, as in the U.S. aid economic strategy to Russia—had problematic outcomes. Whatever the results, the tension between policies that regarded Central and Eastern Europeans as potential First World partners (and usually allowed for more recipient input and flexibility in programming) and the practice of aid as usual (bureaucratic procedure and precedent) became a significant feature of aid efforts.

Thus, despite talk of resurrecting a First World model through a "Marshall Plan," donors, in a hurry and with restricted and scattered resources, largely implemented a Third World model. Neither model was informed by sociological, political, or economic insights from the Second World or took into account the historical legacies of nearly a half century or more of communism from Berlin to Vladivostok.[90] But these legacies would be a key ingredient shaping perceptions and relations between East and West and, ultimately, aid outcomes.

PRIDE OF THE SECOND WORLD

Although in theory, donors recognized the distinctiveness of Central and Eastern Europe, the point of reference for many aid providers was their

Third World experience. This was an insult to people who were proud of their achievements and of their historical and cultural ties to the West. Despite Soviet domination, the nations of the Second World had made significant progress in the decades following World War II. They had rebuilt war-torn infrastructures, industrialized their economies, and educated their populations. Hungary and Romania, for example, routinely scored in the top three in the International Mathematical Olympiad, an annual international secondary-school competition.[91] As Walter Mientka, Secretary of the Olympiad Advisory Board, explained, "The former socialist countries always did quite well. . . . The key is the nature of their education."[92] Literacy levels and educational standards generally far surpassed prewar levels.

Many Central and Eastern Europeans considered themselves exemplars of European culture and civilization and saw communism as a forcibly imposed alien system. They were insulted to see their nations likened to Third World ones and not to be consulted about the course of development.

This sentiment contributed significantly to difficulties of the United States in working out bilateral assistance agreements with many countries in the region.[93] When the United States presented boilerplate aid agreements typically made for the Third World to the Visegrád countries (Poland, Hungary, the Czech Republic, and the Slovak Republic) and expected them to sign on the dotted line, all four evinced reluctance to comply. Their officials explained that the hesitation was due in large part to being treated like Third World peoples. Of particular concern to recipient officials were the U.S. requests for diplomatic immunity and privileges for all technical assistance workers—that is, for aid-paid consultants who did not have diplomatic standing (and thus did not already have such privileges). The draft agreements also included requests for aid workers to be exempted from income taxes and duties on alcohol and tobacco, a request that also was viewed as unnecessary "high living," and was poorly received.

The Visegrád countries responded by delaying the completion of bilateral negotiations for several years and refusing U.S. requests for American diplomatic immunity. Their officials indicated that no other donor countries had made such requests, and that, although such arrangements might be acceptable in Third World settings, they were not in Central Europe. As one official remarked, "We have flatly refused [the request for diplomatic immunity]. It is the product in our eyes of some bureaucrats who have difficulty distinguishing the Czech Republic from Shangri-La."[94] Although an August 1992 cable from the U.S. Department of State addressed to the ambassadors of all Central and Eastern European posts urged them to conclude bilateral agreements as quickly as possible,[95] two years later (in July 1994) protracted negotiations were still under way in the Visegrád countries. Poland never signed the agreement, although in time the Polish government granted consultants privileges through other means.[96]

Although few Western officials expressed frustration with their Central and Eastern European counterparts in public, they sometimes denigrated them in private: "They just can't handle it," "They are so disorganized," or "They have no sense of democracy." Underlying these views was the common Western perception that the new Eastern leaders were either unreformed communists or former dissidents. Neither had any experience with democracy, and all were terribly disorganized. Western aid representatives who treated them as "communist" products replicated the very ethnocentrism that Central Europeans had hated in the Soviets.

While affronted pride was widespread in the region, the Czech government was more emphatic than its Central European neighbors in responding to what the West offered. It spurned much of the aid. If the Third World was defined as a region in which governments received development assistance,[97] and if accepting aid signaled that "we're not yet part of the West" and meant remaining in a supplicant position, then the Czech government's stance was a way of defining the nation as already part of the West, refusing risk of any affronts to national pride. By refusing to play by the West's rules, Czech officials differentiated themselves both from their neighbors and from Third World associations. In a speech at the World Bank in 1993, Prime Minister Václav Klaus (previously minister of finance) explained that "after three years of relatively successful fundamental systemic transformation of the Czech economy and society, my experience tells me that the role of external factors in this process is relatively small and that the reform begins and ends at home."[98] Zdeněk Drábek, former aid coordinator of Czechoslovakia, further elaborated: "Many Czechs now proudly believe that Westerners have little to teach us, to show us, to advise. . . . The attitude has been essentially that we don't need the money."[99] By, in a sense, beating the West at its own game, the Czech Republic may have helped make itself "deserving" in the competition for the bigger Western favors of membership in the EU and NATO.

Western donors had tended to assume that the East would take whatever was offered. After all, the aid was a gift. Why were they complaining? What the donors had failed to see was that to many Central and Eastern Europeans, a gift was something designed to serve the needs of the recipients. The two sides had differing expectations for what the "gift" would consist of and just what constituted "help." In the East, "help" from the Soviet Union had usually been regarded as no help at all. Help from the West, on the other hand, in some Eastern countries had come to mean either tangible goods like relief packages or, in the context of an active, organized underground resistance, sizable sums of hard currency to fund opposition activities. The realization that Western "help" now often meant advice, not cash, hit hard.

The issue was a critical one. Anthropologist Marianne Gronemeyer argues that the success of many aid efforts depends on whether aid is interpreted as "help" by the recipients: "However obviously fraudulent use of the word 'help' to describe development aid may be, the word continues to be taken as the gospel truth, not least by those upon whom the fraud is committed."[100]

Just as "help" wasn't really help in the new parlance that invaded Central and Eastern Europe, "partnership" wasn't really partnership. Lurking beneath the donors' rhetoric of partnership were telltale patronizing idioms, such as that of the development practitioner as physician. The physician-patient analogy implied that the doctor knew best, that the ailing patient would take gratefully to the treatment—no matter how painful—and that the patient was generic (the results would be uniform and predictable from recipient to recipient). János Kornai, an economist and expert on centrally planned economies, wrote in an article on medical metaphors in economics that while much of economic theory "tries to outline the *ideal* economic system or its individual parts," a reasonable physician does not ask whether the anatomical structure and physiological functioning of the healthy human organism is ideal, or whether, for example, an optimal human organism should have two hearts.[101]

In time, the paper-thin deceptiveness of the slogans of transition became apparent. Although metaphors of turning fish soup back into an aquarium, having a tooth pulled, or crossing a chasm were colorful ways of explaining a position, they represented a bumper-sticker mode of thinking. After all, what made "transition" away from a centrally planned economy like resurrecting fish from fish soup, like having a tooth pulled, or like crossing a chasm? As anthropologist Mark Hobart has pointed out, when the metaphorical images so frequently used in development discourse to justify policies are removed, "the degree to which many theories require modification or rethinking is remarkable."[102]

These metaphors seemed especially ludicrous in light of the legacies of communism that would figure prominently in the aid story. According to Marxist theory, the state was eventually supposed to have withered away. The reality was that, under communism, Eastern European states had developed "state socialism": strong, centralized bureaucracies that maintained their power by controlling the distribution of goods and services.[103] The tradition of tight integration between politics and economics rendered separation of the spheres difficult—and made it nearly impossible to depoliticize post-1989 assistance. Because so many areas of the economy and life were under political control, the detachment of political motives from economic ones was unthinkable for many Central and Eastern Europeans. As a consequence, even after communism had been dismantled, the tradition of suspicion continued—and infected Eastern perceptions of Western motivations.

Moreover, donors' agendas were inherently political. Donors set out to tear down communism and to encourage civil society and democracy. Although these agendas were welcomed by most Eastern Europeans, they exposed the intrinsically political nature of "economic" aid. As suspicion surrounded Western motives for supplying aid and the new leaders who accepted it, the idea of the "West as demon" would also resurface in powerful ways. Many people began to believe that perhaps the communists had been partially right about Western imperialism and capitalist exploitation.

Amid the euphoria of the early months of the aid effort, these difficulties had barely started to become apparent to the Central and Eastern Europeans eagerly awaiting bounty from the West. It was not until later—into 1991, 1992, and beyond—that the East began to recognize that Western "help" meant mostly advice—and that this advice was not necessarily designed to benefit and serve the needs of its recipients. Only then could a Czech politician launch his political career by waging a campaign against a Western aid program; only then would

Polish President Lech Wałęsa angrily charge that "it is you, the West, who have made good business on the Polish revolution."[104] Most important, it was not until then that many people across Central and Eastern Europe, from factory workers and truck drivers to local bureaucrats, would begin to lose faith in the West and the system it represented, even if only temporarily. This loss of faith encouraged some groups and individuals to take matters into their own hands.

As hopes diminished, people became more suspicious of, and ambivalent toward, Western aid. Latent images of the West as "demon" that had lain dormant during the Triumphalist period began to resurface, as the phase of Disillusionment—frustration and resentment—came into its own. Just as the West as saint had written the script for Triumphalism, so the West as demon was to help set the scene for Disillusionment.

CHAPTER TWO

Consultants for Capitalism

Officials here get tired of answering the same questions
without anything coming out of it. The Western consultants
collect information, get the picture, then they go home. . . .
We are not really satisfied with this technical assistance. We
are solving the West's unemployment in this way. . . . We get
calls from ministries that receive consultants from all over
asking if aid can be reduced.

–Jarmila Hrbáčková, Slovak aid official[1]

I'm not sure we hit on the right model for technical
assistance.

–Ambassador Robert Barry,
Special Adviser for East European Assistance
to the Deputy Secretary of State[2]

IF BIG EASTERN EXPECTATIONS paired with ill-designed Western aid
presaged problems from the very beginning, the exploits of the "Marriott
Brigade" drove East and West even farther apart. The Marriott Brigade
was a term the Polish press coined for the short-term, "fly-in, fly-out"
consultants hired by aid donors who delivered technical assistance.[3] They
stayed at Warsaw's pricey new Marriott and hurtled among five-star
hotels across the region. In contrast to long-term consultants, who stayed

for months or even years, members of the Marriott Brigade appeared in the region for several days or weeks. They were nattily dressed and quick with words and promises, and Central European officials, many of whom were new at their jobs, welcomed them at first. The officials' doors were always open in those early days. But after hundreds of "first meetings" with an endless array of short-term consultants from the World Bank, the IMF, the EU, USAID, and other organizations, many host officials concluded that a certain degree of skepticism was in order. And so as early as 1991, the honeymoon was largely over in Warsaw, Budapest, and Prague. The same performance, with the same unhappy result, was repeated as the aid frontier moved east, to Russia and then to Ukraine.

What went wrong? The answer involved a complex collision of cultural and institutional realities and was rooted in the swollen responsibility that the donors bestowed on uninitiated consultants for complicated and politicized reforms such as the privatization of the region's state-owned assets.[4] Privatization involved the transfer of ownership of state enterprises or parts of enterprises to firms, individuals, or other nonstate entities. The problem, as seen on the ground, boiled down to relationships. Amid a striking lack of consensus between East and West about what had been promised and what was being delivered and about who was supposed to benefit from all the programs and reports and advice, many Marriott Brigaders failed to establish working relationships with their presumed counterparts.

On the other extreme, some consultants developed "crony relationships" with a few local elites for mutual profit. The involvement of foreign advisers in one of the most politicized processes in the transformation of Central and Eastern Europe sometimes served to rekindle the region's traditional condemnations of the imperialist West and its well-honed practice of pulling the wool over the naive foreigners' eyes. By the time the Marriott Brigade had checked out and headed home, many Western attempts designed to encourage privatization and other high-priority reforms, as defined by the donors, were well on the way to costly failure.

THE ECONOLOBBYISTS

A few high-profile economists laid the groundwork for the swarm of Marriott Brigade consultants that would follow. Although some steadfast and persistent advisers made contributions in the region, the jet-setting "econolobbyists" were more about public relations and their own publicity than they were about serious policy advice. Although not necessarily funded by government aid programs (Western foundations were frequent supporters), the econolobbyists, through their promises and illusive relationships with their hosts, created an image of Western consultants that persisted throughout the aid saga. In the West, the econolobbyists wrote op-ed pieces, delivered speeches calling for aid, and thereby helped define the "reform" agenda. They were perceived as able to effect market reforms in the East. In the East, the econolobbyists' value was seen in their ability to deliver Western money and access and to help policymakers "sell" controversial reforms in the transitioning countries.

Generally unregistered, unregulated, and unrestrained, a few highly visible econolobbyists were an integral part of the phase of Triumphalism and even gave it definition. As attention shifted from one country to another, the econolobbyists moved with, contributed to, and received attention in the period of euphoria and great expectations in whatever country they happened to be "helping to put back on track." Yet they were scarcely to be found in the subsequent phase of Disillusionment. Both at home and abroad, the econolobbyists effectively leveraged their supposed access to and influence with policymakers and money sources. And, as the public hype over one country undergoing "reform" diminished, they typically abandoned it and moved on to another.

A case in point was Jeffrey Sachs, a prominent operative on the international economic reform circuit, who, in many ways, defined the circuit. A Harvard economist, Sachs promoted "shock therapy," a popular term for austerity measures (usually associated with IMF stabilization policies) that entailed the reduction of a country's budget deficit by eliminating subsidies and price controls and tightening credit supply.[5] Sachs didn't invent shock therapy, but helped to publicize the doctrine to such an extent that he became closely identified with it in both East and West. The symbolic association was so strong that Sachs received credit or blame even for policies he did not create or help to implement.[6]

Jetting to Warsaw between trips to Prague, Moscow, and São Paulo, he appeared frequently for several days at a time in Poland during the crucial period of its initial reforms in 1989-90. While Polish economists were stressing sacrifice, Sachs peddled a vision of economic change with relatively little pain. In the summer of 1989 in Poland, Sachs predicted an end to the suffering: "The crisis will be over in six months."[7]

Sachs blossomed on prime time while other foreign advisers kept their consultations behind closed doors. His televised speech before the Solidarity Parliamentary Caucus in September 1989 galvanized public opinion, including that of some of the country's new leaders. Among his points:

1. It's necessary to take common-sense action.
2. You won't succeed if you don't.
3. If you act dramatically and make an impression, you will get money from the West.
4. Do something brave.
5. Figure out how much society can take, and then move three times quicker than that.
6. If you jump into the market economy, you will be first in line for credit—that's a promise. *Inflation will vanish and the standard of living will begin to rise within six months* (emphasis added).[8]

To people looking for simple, painless solutions, no one held more sway than a Western expert, especially one from Harvard. He appealed to a populist mood sweeping Poland. "Very seductive," Ryszard Bugaj, Solidarity economist and parliamentary representative, called Sachs's televised address. Comparing him to a faith healer, Bugaj added: "I think Sachs perceived the general mood of his listeners very well, the nature of their emotions. . . . He talked in such a smooth, confident manner that many responded as if they were hearing a revelation."[9]

Poland, perhaps unlike nations to its east, had many able economists, but in a country so long denied the gains it knew had been realized farther west, only a Westerner could galvanize public opinion and confidence. Polish officials learned to use Sachs, with his Harvard credential, American pizzazz, and boyish showmanship, to prepare their country psychologically for austerity. Stefan Kawalec, who as director general of the Ministry of Finance was intimately involved in nearly all critical economic decisions, summed up Sachs's usefulness to the government: "Sachs didn't make any new discoveries here, but he helped us in that he could make many people understand the obvious truths that they might not have understood otherwise."[10]

If Sachs had come from a non-Western country, he could not have caused such a stir. He filled a temporary vacuum during a few extraordinary months in Polish history—from Solidarity's landslide victory in June 1989 to its first term in office. His star began to fade by the summer of 1990. And by that time, the Marriott Brigade was at high tide throughout the former Soviet Bloc.

DISMANTLING THE "COMPANY TOWN"

One of the major tasks of the Marriott Brigade consultants hired by donor agencies was to aid in the privatization and economic restructuring of state-owned enterprises. In theory, at least, the donors (and certain parties and vested interests in the recipient countries) were committed to remaking entire economies according to an image of Western capitalism—which often was more a caricature than a well-informed understanding of the organization and diversity of Western economies and state-private relationships. Under the Soviet umbrella, properties throughout the region had been nationalized and, at least officially, private enterprise virtually eliminated. Entire communities of workers had been created around state-run enterprises. These "company towns," guaranteeing not only lifetime employment but also housing, social security, and health and day care, exemplified a slice of socialist life that formed part of donor images of the region.

Thus, when communism unexpectedly collapsed under its own weight,[11] a great moment of opportunity and anticipation had apparently arrived for the West. Having finally won the Cold War, the West could show that its ideology had been superior all along and put its own stamp on these formerly communist countries. It would help to create capitalist states: the "economic man" of Karl Marx was to be transformed into the economic man of Adam Smith. The fact that the collapse of communism came on the heels of a worldwide movement toward privatization headed by international financial institutions and the development community added momentum. And so the international lending institutions and the foreign aid community, often working in concert with reform-oriented indigenous elites, pressed the governments of Central and Eastern Europe to build market economies by introducing economic reforms, privatizing state-owned resources—and doing it within a few short years.[12]

It was in this spirit that privatization came to be seen as a yardstick of progress in the new democracies and that donors made it a mainstay of their aid efforts. The United States obligated more aid to "economic restructuring," including privatization and private-sector development, than to any other single effort.[13] A USAID official based in Central Europe remarked that "privatization is our first, second, and third priority." USAID's *Action Plan for U.S. Assistance to Central and Eastern Europe* of 1991 envisioned that

> [a] large portion of A.I.D.'s assistance for economic restructuring will be targeted at the privatization process which is essential to the success of overall macroeconomic reform. Assistance to individual enterprises, helping existing businesses to restructure and privatize or to improve efficiency and adapt to the new market environment will be key endeavors in the economic restructuring effort. . . . The bulk of Eastern Europe's productive capacity is in the hands of state-owned enterprises (SOEs). Large scale privatization of these SOEs is essential to the success of economic reform. The U.S. has excellent capability to provide assistance to this end, and the governments of several Eastern European countries have asked for it.[14]

Given that privatization was a leading signifier of capitalism to the donors, they often competed (and sometimes cooperated) to finance "model" and "demonstration" projects to show their political and ideological commitment to building capitalism. According to an official quoted in a report issued by the U.S. General Accounting Office (GAO), USAID "believed that privatizing a few large enterprises in the airline, steel, glass, and furniture industries would have a ripple effect on the economy."[15] The United States supported highly visible projects, notably the privatization of huge Polish enterprises employing thousands of people, such as the Huta Warszawa steel mill and the Sandomierz glass company, and national icons such as LOT, the Polish national airline.[16] Although later, the United States expanded its priorities to focus more on supporting new private enterprises and creating stock exchanges and security and exchange commissions, many of the donors' early goals focused on the privatization of company towns, with their socialist amenities such as health and day care and employee retreat centers. By transforming these "white elephants," donors aimed to drive a silver stake through the heart of socialism and bury it forever.

BIG CONTRACTS FOR THE BIG SIX[17]

The Big Six accounting firms were designated the chief agents of privatization and recipients of privatization aid. The involvement of such a firm, whether it had policy impact in a given case or not, was important to donors and to some recipient players in an intangible way. Big Six firms lent legitimacy to privatization decisions that were made both at the enterprise and the ministry levels and to the economic reforms of the Second World more generally. The Big Six were to play a critical part in cleansing communism.

And so as early as 1990, the donors turned for help to the consultants of the Big Six firms. With contracts from USAID, the EU's PHARE program, the British Know How Fund, the World Bank, the EBRD, and others, the Big Six began to establish offices in Central and Eastern Europe and to launch commercial activities. The British, given their experience with privatization under Prime Minister Margaret Thatcher in the 1980s, were seen as having special expertise in privatization and took a lead as consultants on the issue.

Coopers & Lybrand, a multinational accounting firm, was among the first of the Big Six firms to be registered in the region. By 1991, the company had offices in Warsaw, Budapest, Prague, Bucharest, Moscow, and St. Petersburg. At that time, an estimated half of the company's Central and Eastern European business was in foreign aid contracts, according to the 40-year-old David Thomas, a British national who pioneered the firm's entry into the region. The firm took on myriad aid projects, ranging from managing EcoFund, a large environmental project setup by the United States and administered by the Polish Ministries of Finance and Environment, to assessing the effects of the transition on Polish women. Coopers & Lybrand also worked on foreign aid contracts to assess Azerbaijani oil and gas reserves, a USAID-funded project to come up with a strategy for privatization in the Baltics, a PHARE-sponsored project to do the same in Albania, and a PHARE-funded project to write Romania's privatization laws. The firm was awarded contracts to privatize the Bulgarian national airline and banks and for Yugoslavian privatization projects and banking legislation. In addition, Coopers & Lybrand received funds for projects from the British Know How Fund, the World Bank, and smaller Danish, Dutch, and Swedish projects.[18]

With aid contracts to help establish itself, Coopers & Lybrand was among the most successful companies of its kind in the region. Thomas attributed this achievement in Poland to relationships he established with government officials, such as his "good buddies" Krzysztof Lis and Janusz Lewandowski. They were Poland's first heads of the Ministry of Ownership Transformation, the agency created to preside over the transfer to private wealth of the country's state-owned properties. The two men helped Thomas facilitate deals, he reported, including two of the largest joint ventures in Poland at the time, worth hundreds of millions of dollars each. One client, Unilever, a British-Dutch conglomerate that bought a soap factory in the Polish city of Bydgoszcz, entered into the country's largest joint venture, according to Thomas. Coopers & Lybrand did all the preparation for the deal, including asset valuation—an estimate of the market value of a company.[19]

While competing for, and carrying out, aid projects, the firm also had an expanding business portfolio. When asked in 1991 which areas his firm planned to move into, Thomas replied, "You could ask what areas we aren't moving into. We have clients in every sector of the economy worldwide who are looking into Eastern Europe to invest or to trade." Coopers & Lybrand's clients did business in energy, agriculture, food processing, transportation, and communications.[20] The Coopers & Lybrand story was typical of the Big Six firms: they began by winning aid contracts and setting up offices in Poland and Hungary, which then served as a base for scouting out the region and securing further contracts from aid agencies, as well as from private clients.[21]

AD HOC AID

Ideology appeared to play a role not only in the donors' efforts to break up the company town and in their legitimizing these efforts through the Big Six: The belief that "private" partners held the key to privatizing state-run enterprises and to unlocking the transition to a market economy shaped some donors' strategies for delivering aid, notably those of the United States. Three consulting consortia, chosen under "notwithstanding authority" (a directive invoked by USAID's assistant administrator that enabled competition to be waived)[22] and led by three of the Big Six accounting firms (Coopers & Lybrand, KPMG Peat Marwick, and Deloitte & Touche), formed the cornerstone of the U.S. privatization and economic restructuring aid package for Central Europe. These consortia won contracts under the Indefinite Quantity Contracts, or IQCs—a type of USAID contract that was supposed to enable a more rapid response[23]for multiple projects in privatization and related activities throughout the region that extended over a five-year period, July 1991 to July 1996, and amounted to some $60 million per consortia.[24]

U.S. officials emphasized that their philosophy was to assist the "private" sectors of Central and Eastern Europe and to accomplish their goals through it, not through any central bodies or authorities that might be "tainted" communist holdovers. Ambassador Robert Barry, special adviser for East European assistance to the deputy secretary of state, spelled it out in 1992: "We do not have government-to-government agreements. . . . Our task is to promote growth of the private sector rather than to encourage the growth of new bureaucracies."[25]

Although later in the aid effort the United States sent some consultants to work inside government ministries to help design and push privatization efforts, the focus of U.S. privatization aid in Central Europe was generally outside government bodies. Consultants were to work directly with enterprises or sectors. Because privatization aid was to be directed to private entities, it was structured to work around, rather than in coordination with, the recipients' government-run privatization programs it was supposed to help.

Donors' concepts of the private sector were drawn from Western models, rather than experience, and often failed to appreciate the complex and diverse relationships between private and state sectors that had evolved in Western societies. In addition, Central and Eastern Europe was largely lacking in one important sector: Prior to the revolutions of 1989, the countries of the region had very restricted private sectors, if any. The state had shaped the structure and workings of whatever private, small-scale business had been allowed. As there were few obvious private-sector partners in the immediate post-1989 aftermath, the U.S. preference for bypassing governments was almost entirely counterproductive when the goal was to privatize state-owned enterprises. Ignoring government agencies responsible for privatization made it virtually impossible to deliver privatization aid effectively, as the GAO also concluded.[26] Recipient officials found they had little authority to assess the work of the USAID-paid consultants, determine schedules, or terminate a contract for nonperformance or poor performance. Freelance consultants could bypass the relevant ministries and go right to the field to find and work on privatization projects. Marek Krawczuk, the official responsible for aid in Poland's Ministry of Industry, compared the situation to that of "a surgeon who comes, does his work without talking with the patient, and leaves without checking to see whether the operation was successful."[27]

This setup was also disconcerting to some of the more thoughtful consultants. In January 1992, Jeffry Baldwin, a partner at DRT International, a subsidiary of Deloitte & Touche, explained how he went about finding projects under the IQC program: He wandered around "looking for someone with the authority to be helped, even though they [Poles] don't have to spend any [of their own] money." To Baldwin's credit, he had employed more Polish staff at that point than most other consulting firms in Poland, and he had found that the best way to make contacts was through the Poles he employed, who had contacts because they "[had] worked with someone or [had gone] to school with someone." Although some useful projects may well have come out of Baldwin's approach, it highlighted the ad hoc nature of the privatization program.[28]

Further, recipient officials generally could not participate in the process once it was under way, because the IQC contracts, as well as work orders, had been signed only between consultants and Washington USAID. According to Krawczuk and other officials, consultants' reports generally were addressed to USAID in Washington, not to the local officials who supposedly were their beneficiaries (although copies were sometimes sent to the ministries). Krawczuk found that he had no authority to monitor or schedule consultants' work.[29]

Indeed, a fundamental drawback of the IQCs was that they generally afforded recipients and USAID field offices little flexibility. The circumstances under which USAID funded the IQC consortia and the working relationships under the IQCs baffled many Central European officials. A USAID-commissioned evaluation of its privatization projects concluded that the fact that USAID field offices had little authority to authorize or to amend funding of program assistance "at times, held up host country requested assistance."[30]

When the recipients had any input at all under USAID's IQC rules, it was to choose among the three Big Six contractors that Washington had selected.[31] But USAID did not always follow its own rules. For example, Slovakia's privatization ministry was first told it could choose from among the three IQC firms. But when the ministry sent a letter to the local USAID office requesting one of the firms, the ministry was told that only another firm could be made available in a timely fashion.[32] A high-level Slovak official concluded that "all this selecting [a] company seems to be only theater."

Programs under USAID contracting mechanisms were seen by many officials in the region as less effective than EU programs because the United States allowed recipients less leverage to set terms or to select experts. Indeed (again in the case of the Polish government), the recipient was not consulted about the IQC strategy or the particular firms chosen and was not officially informed even after the decisions were made. Finance Ministry official Kawalec found out about the IQC contracts only by accident. The result, Kawalec reported, was that "a number of consultants are looking for profitable assignments that may be completely unnecessary. . . . The U.S. government is paying them to provide advice to us without asking us, even without informing us."[33] When the Ministry of Finance itself tried to use the IQCs, says Kawalec, it was turned down by Washington.

SHIPS IN THE NIGHT

All these factors—the donors' misplaced emphasis on the politicized company town, their situating the Big Six firms at the helm of aid delivery in the rush to help, the ad hoc setup of much technical assistance fostered in part by some donors' ideologically driven misconceptions of the "private" sector—did not augur well for developing effective working relationships with recipients or for long-term receptiveness on the part of the host populations. On one side were the advisers, often far away, both physically and mentally, from the environment of their hosts due to the fly-in, fly-out and uncoordinated nature of much of the aid, and their lack of preparation coupled with frequent obliviousness to that deficiency. On the other side were overextended, underpaid, and sometimes corruptible officials in environments rife with lucrative opportunities. All this

portended a costly disconnection: a blatant *lack* of relationships between
donor and recipient representatives that would render much of the aid
ineffectual and sometimes even irritating to the hosts.

The scene in the halls of Central and Eastern European ministries in
the early days of the east-west encounter told much of the story. Advisers
from international lending institutions and a multitude of aid programs that
were, for the most part, working in isolation from one another descended
on the same departments in the same ministries. They were greeted by an
overburdened staff—typically political appointees or poorly paid civil
servants, most of whom could neither type efficiently nor speak English.
By 4 P.M. each day, the secretaries had gone home, but the officials, the
ones making policy and running the country, stayed much later. Life was
particularly hard for the handful of officials in any given agency who had
the information sought by the foreigners and the English-language skills
necessary to communicate with them. The same officials became responsible for meeting the hordes of visiting delegations and consultants, and
often reached a saturation point. The GAO related that "in the early stages
of reform, many consultants came to Warsaw for 1-to-2-week stays,
interviewed some officials, and then produced reports that merely repeated
everything they had been told."[34] Indeed, the hosts sometimes appeared to
be doing the educating.

Often the people and projects offered by donors were mismatched to
the needs of the hosts. For example, the GAO criticized a project in which
volunteers under a USAID program had spent four to six weeks in Poland
working on specific tasks. One volunteer charged with helping Polish
legal associations to establish a commercial law library, an American
divorce lawyer with no Polish-language skills, "had difficulty getting the
legal associations to work together effectively." In time, reported the
GAO, even "USAID officials acknowledged that the person in charge
was 'not the best person' for the job."[35] Indeed, consultants often came
with little knowledge of the countries in which they were to intervene or
the contexts of the problems they were to address. Unlike long-term
consultants, who frequently were committed to a particular country and
acquired enough knowledge of the local landscape to be genuinely
useful, the short-term consultants tended to be unfamiliar with, and even
uninterested in, local conditions.

Further, despite the pretense of treating the peoples of the Second
World as candidates for First World status, many Western consultants

applied assumptions and experience they had gleaned from their work in the Third World. These assumptions not only constituted a deep insult, but also reinforced the widely held view that Western consultants generally were unfamiliar with the institutions peculiar to postcommunist economies. Some consultants came with ready solutions that did not take into account the planned economies and state socialism of Central and Eastern Europe and the diverse experiences of the countries of the region, critical aspects of the starting point for any "reform."[36] In 1990, for example, finance official Kawalec doubted the approach of Jeffrey Sachs to the Polish economy: "There were and still are many question marks [about] how the economy will respond. In this, Sachs had no knowledge at all because he was not familiar with Communist economies. He tried to treat this economy the same as Latin American ones."[37] Indeed, a frequent complaint from Central and Eastern Europeans who came into contact with foreign advisers was that they did not know the particular needs, circumstances, and situation of the recipients and sometimes failed to take into account the level of infrastructure rebuilding that was necessary.[38]

Another complaint was that fly-in, fly-out consultants from far away were not always sensitive to the gravity of the decisions at hand. As Professor of Economics Grzegorz Kołodko, director of the Institute of Finance (and later first deputy prime minister and minister of finance) explained: "If there's a difference between Professor [Jeffrey] Sachs and myself, it's that I'm not from outside. I could have a cynical, purely professional . . . relationship, like [with] Argentina – I travel there, live in a five-star hotel, and I say 'lower real wages by 20 percent overnight. And you have to stand it because you don't have any other way out [and] this results from my economic analysis.' . . . If it works, then I'll take the credit. If it doesn't work, then I can say: 'You Argentinians, you have screwed up again.'"[39]

Recipients often perceived the consultants as arrogant, which appears to have helped them foster, in some cases, a defensive national pride. Polish minister Jacek Saryusz-Wolski, responsible for aid coordination, said in 1992 that the West's approach to assistance was "paternalistic, like a parent giv[ing] to a child."[40] One could see why such an approach offended a people whose culture and civilization were centuries old and whose educational systems typically upheld high standards.

Further, although the Marriott Brigade consultants may not have always understood important parts of their job, they did understand perks. At least that is how they appeared to their hosts in the early days of the aid effort. In contrast to their local counterparts, the Western consultants were treated well, with lush living quarters, housekeepers, and drivers. Some made exorbitant salaries (although not necessarily by Western standards). As Czech aid official Pavel Rozsypal wrote in 1994:

> The salaries paid to foreign assistance contractors advising govern-
> ment ministries are widely known by Czech officials to be strato-
> spheric in local economic terms—it is known, for example, that EU
> PHARE advisers are paid six times more (and upwards) than the
> ministers they are paid to assist. This of course causes a certain level of
> cynicism on the part of the local beneficiaries regarding just who is the
> intended beneficiary of foreign assistance; criticisms in this regard are
> widely circulated in Czech government offices.[41]

Although one could not have expected foreign consultants to be paid according to local standards, one might have hoped they would accommodate more to those standards as guests abroad. The consultants' conduct was perceived to be ostentatious and was especially off-putting to the unassuming, modest, and (if only initially) deferential local officials. While ostensibly trying to interact with their hosts in a productive way, some consultants tended to make the disparities even more evident by indulging in material excesses while they were in town that perhaps they couldn't afford at home. Local lore created a caricature of consultants that went something like this: Consultants visit Warsaw and are chauffeured around town by day to meet with a series of officials. At night, they frequent the best restaurants and then return to the marble columns, ornate chandeliers, and spacious lounges of the five-star Marriott, where they meet other foreigners for a drink. Usually in town only for a few days, their next stop is Prague or Budapest for further consulting, or Rome or Paris for vacation.

At least for a time, communist-style reactions seemed to live in the bones: As under communism, many complaints during the Disillusion-ment phase were made under the breath, while appearances were maintained in public venues. And, like the symbolic protests of oppositionists under communism, there was often much more talk than action. But over time, many host officials felt increasingly put upon and began to see little personal or professional benefit from encountering foreigners. Scenes from the Triumphalist phase, in which Eastern officials put on communist-style shows for Western visitors and in which the working understanding was "You pretend to help us, and we pretend to be helped," diminished.

By January 1992, a chorus of Polish and Hungarian officials (whose countries at that point had received the most aid) had concluded that their countries were "technically overassisted" in most areas, as Marek Kozak, a Polish official who monitored foreign aid, put it, and that the assistance was doing more harm than good. Overburdened top-level officials, often working without benefit of trained support staff, complained that they couldn't do their jobs because they had to spend so much time meeting with fact finders and consultants. Hungarian privatization official Péter Kazár called the state of affairs "ridiculous."[42] Kozak went so far as to suggest that the main benefit derived from the Marriott Brigade was not the expertise they provided, but the hard currency they contributed to the local economy.[43] Another recipient aid official stated that "foreign advisers come here and tell us what to do." He said that the technical assistance offered by the donors was designed to alleviate unemployment in the West.[44] A Price Waterhouse consultant in Poland agreed: "At the end of the day, the funding sort of ends up in the pockets of the Western governments. . . . If you're cynical . . . you could see it as a way for Western governments to pay money to Western professional firms like ours."[45]

The same complaints heard in Central Europe circa 1991 and 1992 were echoed in Russia and Ukraine in strikingly similar language several years later. As Russian economist Leonid Abalkin wrote:

> In all discussions with Russian representatives, as a rule, one can hear an opinion that the American technical aid is, by and large, directed toward satisfying the interests of Western consulting firms (creating jobs and large incomes for their employees). . . . It is more and more often mentioned by the Russian side that the Western consultants are ill-prepared for working in Russia, have poor knowledge of our economic, legal and psychological realities.[46]

And in Ukraine, because technical assistance was perceived to have gone awry, the Ministry of the Economy created a separate agency to analyze the source and destination of technical assistance and to advise the government on aid issues. According to Mykola Horkusha of the aid ministry, Ukrainian officials determined that "about 80 percent of this [technical assistance] goes for consultants. . . . During the 1993-1995 period we came to the conclusion that we don't need more consultants."[47] According to Alexander Paskhaver, an adviser on economic policy, "Western consultants need to be here for at least three months to be effective. Between 1990 and 1993 a lot of consultants came in for short periods. It was absolutely useless and expensive."[48]

A PARADISE FOR SPIES

If recipients found the advice and conduct of consultants less than ideal, another theme sometimes was voiced: that their presence and activities were suspect. Consultants who obtained access to sensitive materials, whose firms also explored business opportunities, or who worked closely with local officials perceived to be corrupt opened themselves up to such allegations.

But how the consultants were received in the host countries was not, at least initially, a question with which many donor agencies appeared to concern themselves. Donors and consultants, such as those working for the Big Six, found that they met each other's needs: Aid provided by donors helped the Big Six to gain entry to the region, and the Big Six's image of adherence to high standards of accountability and neutrality was expected to reflect positively on donors' images.

According to donors, another advantage of hiring consultants from the Big Six accounting firms was that the latter had contacts with potential Western investors. In theory, the kind of technical assistance offered by the accounting firms should have helped to create the infrastructure necessary to attract foreign investment. Some in the aid community believed that those providing technical assistance should have helped, directly or indirectly, to match companies in the recipient countries with suitable foreign investors. Yet the link between technical assistance and investment was often missing; a disconnection diffused consultants' activities at the enterprise level and activities that might have led to investment.

Further, Central and Eastern European officials frequently reported that little concrete investment activity followed from consultants' reports. Even well-conceived consultants' reports often had only the most tenuous links to the realities of implementation. The consultants' recommendations often could not be implemented and, rightly or wrongly, went "directly into the trash," as one ministry official put it. The Czech deputy minister of foreign affairs, Pavel Bratinka, reported an "overemphasis on studies and consulting work, the result of which is not immediate and in many cases doubtful."[49] Officials from the recipient Slovak privatization ministry hoped that one report, produced by a Big Six firm and funded by USAID, would provide "very concrete and tangible results" and help prepare the Slovak Republic for meeting World Bank requirements. Instead, the report turned out to be merely a "general description about the current state of privatization and some general targets."[50] As another privatization official lamented, "No enterprise wants to receive technical assistance without investment. . . . There were many studies without useful results because there were no investments [that resulted from them]."[51]

While recipient officials complained of too little matchmaking with potential investors, there could be a price if consultants got too involved with local officials—especially if those officials were perceived to be on the take. A reason often given for outsourcing government work is that outside contractors provide neutral expertise[52]—and so it was claimed in the case of the Big Six and other contractors working in the region. But the fact was that consultants working on issues such as privatization, if they were to play a role, had to work with dealmakers with insider access.

Especially in the early days of the East-West encounter, some Eastern officials and managers took advantage of lucrative opportunities. Under *nomenklatura*[53] privatization, for instance, enterprise managers acquired enterprises or parts thereof as their own private property. In one version, company insiders procured shares of newly converted companies at firesale prices. In another variant, company insiders formed spin-off private companies, some with expatriate associates. These spin-off companies then made sweetheart deals with the old state enterprises and depleted their resources by leasing state machinery at bargain-basement prices; the new company owners served as intermediaries between the state and private sector.[54]

For Eastern officials, Westerners could be a potentially useful source of contacts and more lucrative opportunities than government employment could offer. Such officials often held "side jobs"; some even owned consulting firms that did business with the very ministries in which they worked. Foreigners were routinely asked for help or subtly probed for what they might be able to provide by way of contacts, potential business partners, or clients. After interviews during which some personal rapport developed, the officials would frequently proffer their "private" business cards in addition to their official cards. Especially in the early days after the revolutions of 1989, such activity was considered "normal" in Central Europe.

With Central and Eastern European financial and regulatory institutions, banks, and government bureaucracies in flux, sensitive information, favorable deals, and speedy outcomes to any number of administrative matters could be "arranged" through contacts. Westerners who were effective in the new frontier often were those who learned to strike deals in a shadowy world of nods and winks where what counted was not formalized agreement but dependable complicity.

Information about the operations of the target ministries handling privatization and economic restructuring generally could be obtained only by knowing the right people. Privatization aid, if it was to have an impact, had to rely heavily on personal relations developed between consultants and well-placed host individuals. The result was that some employees of the consulting firms got involved in insider deals that compromised the firms' image of impartiality.

The use of Big Six firms that gathered information but often effected few palpable results rendered the donors' claims of providing help suspect. The deputy director of Poland's NIK (the Supreme Control Board, the Polish government's chief auditing agency and rough equivalent to the GAO) confirmed in 1994 that "[a] few years ago the [consulting] firms had an industrial espionage quality to them. They came and got all [the] valuable information about the enterprises—the state of the firm, the amount and cost of production, and so on—and after this they disappeared. This is also the fault of Polish officials. Today there are fewer naive officials who allow this to happen."[55]

Across the region, charges of industrial espionage were common. High-ranking officials in the region sometimes suspected advisers sent from Western bodies, ranging from the IMF and the EU to multinational corporations, of spying to assess the Central and Eastern European nations' potential competitiveness with regard to certain products. Such officials even intimated that the "advice" they received could be intended to sabotage their nation's future competitiveness. One Polish manager who worked with foreign consultants was convinced that Central and Eastern Europe had become a "paradise for [Western] spies."

The involvement of Western law firms, under contract to donor organizations to help write legislation in the region, especially gave rise to charges of dubious double dealing. *Legal Times,* a publication dealing with the activities of law firms, devoted a number of articles to the American foray into Central and Eastern Europe. Investigative reporter Sheila Kaplan observed in 1991:

> Some law firms find work [in Central and Eastern Europe] writing laws and regulations that longtime clients will soon be following. Others post advisers to Eastern European ministries, while preparing clients to do business deals with them. And it's not always clear that the U.S. firms are telling their government clients all they need to know about the firm's private clients, although many firms insist they are up front about their private client-driven agenda. . . . Nowhere is the ethics picture more murky than in the booming business of advising foreign ministries on financial matters like privatization and joint ventures.[56]

Sometimes these law firms had clients already doing business in the region or were developing clients who were potential buyers of companies at the prices set by the Western consultants. Because such a situation created an incentive to understate a property's full value, there was a built-in conflict of interest. Indeed, many of these firms appeared to be more concerned with representing the interests of their clients back home than those of the countries they allegedly came to help. The situation was so suspect that even public officials working on aid projects were inclined to air their doubts, albeit tactfully. As Polish aid official Paweł Samecki put it: "Public opinion thinks that if the British are involved in the privatization of state-owned banks that they must get something out of it, which is not *necessarily* true."[57]

WHAT'S IT WORTH?

The practice of Western consulting firms assessing the value of Central and Eastern European state-owned companies was another problematic area. Most allegations of impropriety, whether with regard to valuation or to other activities, were based in part on the fact that consultants could not value assets without being privy to sensitive data. Many short-term consultants spent what little time they had gathering information; the local people they dealt with frequently never heard from them again. This lent credence to the conviction on the part of local officials and managers who hosted the consultants that the latter engaged in industrial espionage.

The fact that the various valuation methods could produce a wide range of results opened up enormous opportunities for abuse and corruption in the free-for-all unlocked by transformation in the region. The difficulties resulting from the lack of reliability and standardization of asset valuations even in stable, well-functioning market economies were compounded in Central and Eastern Europe.[58] Many in the region believed that Western consultants continually undervalued local citizens' high degree of skill and experience, trademarks, and land. Such belittlement irritated many Central and Eastern Europeans, who, while they may have resented the socialist system, also resented the tendency of aid providers to deny national accomplishments prior to socialism and to devalue what the region's inhabitants had achieved in spite of that system's limitations.

Both consultants and local government officials had abundant opportunities for dealmaking based on insider information—the kinds of activities typically considered conflicts of interest in Western democracies. Local parties to the privatization process, including managers and workers, sometimes saw the relationship between the Western consultants' valuation of properties and their clients' investment interests as suspect. In fact, some "free-market proponents" from the West tended to seek monopolies and exclusive deals in countries legally and institutionally ill equipped to monitor their activities. A potential conflict of interest lay in the fact that Western consulting firms doing asset valuations often had clients who were potential buyers at the prices the consultants established. Clearly, this situation created incentives to understate the full value of those properties.

Outrage at such practices was directed not only at foreigners involved in local business, but also at the local elites who stood to profit, such as high officials in privatization ministries (or their family members) who set up consulting firms that did business with the ministries. Sociologist Antoni Kamiński has described this practice in Poland as "post-Solidarity-style corruption." In one case, a deputy minister who was in charge of joint ventures from 1989 to 1992 also owned and operated a consulting firm that specialized in joint ventures. When, in 1990, Prime Minister Tadeusz Mazowiecki issued a decree forbidding members of his government from owning consulting firms, the deputy minister signed the firm over to his wife. Many of his colleagues employed similar subterfuges.[59]

That local officials were thus ideally positioned to clinch deals with foreign consultants in return for sizable fees did not escape the notice of state regulatory bodies. NIK, the Polish government's auditing agency, devoted some attention to the issue. One of its classified reports found many links between representatives of local enterprises responsible for the enterprises' liquidation or privatization who also were interested in "acquiring" the enterprise, and consulting firms valuing the assets of those enterprises.[60] Lech Kaczyński, director of NIK during the crucial reform years of 1992 to 1995, identified "almost a union between a ministry [supervising privatization] and . . . three of the Big Six accounting firms involved [in asset valuations]." He added: "I expect that they [the Big Six firms] behaved differently here than in the States. There was one very reputable international firm – I couldn't open a NIK privatization [audit] report without [seeing] the name of that firm [in association with questionable practices]."[61]

In 1991, managers of Polish companies undergoing privatization were told by government officials that if they used the Western firms that the officials selected to do asset valuations, the privatization or sale of their companies would go smoothly. Industry-wide concern grew among the foreign-trading companies that made up most of Poland's export potential when the Ministry of Foreign Economic Relations, which oversaw them, pushed three USAID-supported consortia by placing them at the top of its list of approved consultants. Representatives of the companies suspected that the favored firms had paid off the ministry officials with money or perks and that the companies would receive undue benefits from doing the valuations.[62] NIK confirmed this. It also concluded that accepting the recommendations of consulting firms with respect to asset valuations sometimes resulted in significant losses for Polish enterprises and harmed the national treasury.[63]

When foreign advisers engaged in asset valuations at the enterprise level, there seemed invariably to be controversy, however inadvertent. A case in point was Monor, a large Hungarian state farm producing agricultural goods. Monor was made a priority for privatization by the Hungarian government in January 1991. Seeking to get its privatization program under way and to launch high-profile projects that would attract the attention of the international community, USAID brought in a Big Six accounting firm to help.

At the end of 1991, Monor, like many Central and Eastern European state-owned mega-firms, still was made up of small unrelated concerns producing commodities from pork and wheat to cooking oil and corn chips. One task of the State Property Agency, the government agency that was founded in January 1991 to convert state-owned property into private hands, was to break up such mega-companies into smaller ones.

Like many new managers in the region, Dr. Rozália Krizsa, an economist who was appointed the managing director of Monor, inherited a mess. A petite, brunette woman in her 50s, exuding empathy, she was at once gentle and authoritative, despite daily crises stemming from inattention and lack of investment over the years. Some 700 employees expected her to help them achieve job security. Monor, like many state-owned enterprises in the region, was entangled in a chain of debt: The company owed money to companies from which it bought raw materials. It also sold products to companies that were indebted to Monor.

In the course of working with the USAID-paid consulting firm, Dr. Krizsa and her assistants at Monor said they spent weeks compiling the information the firm requested and briefing its representatives, most of whom flew in from London. But Monor managers expressed that they were less than satisfied with the consultants' cooperation and products of their work. The short report the consultants produced provided little new information or analysis, according to management.

While the foreigners were writing their report, Monor's management, in consultation with the State Property Agency, conducted its own valuation in 1991. Management also hired an independent group of Hungarian and Western management specialists to assess the value of the company and devise a plan for its restructuring and privatization. At Monor, word circulated that the foreigners' valuation of Monor resulted in an exponentially lower figure than the two other valuations that had been conducted, and that the aid-paid firm had arranged for one of its clients to enter into a joint venture with Monor and purchase more than 50 percent of the company. "Of course," Dr. Krizsa surmised, "this is because foreign firms want to buy Monor at the cheapest price."[64]

Had the Central and Eastern European governments developed some standards for conducting valuations, such standards could conceivably have helped to allay fears that state properties were being undervalued by foreigners and their local partners. Instead, valuations continued to take place amid considerable confusion in policy, public administration, the economy, and the rule of law. Whether allegations of undervaluation were justified in any given case or not, transactions made in the absence of clear-cut valuation criteria were bound to raise eyebrows. Anatol Lawina, a former official at Poland's NIK, believed the governments of Central and Eastern Europe had to accept some of the responsibility. "We, too," he conceded, "are at fault for failing to come up with any standards and guidelines for controversial tasks such as asset valuation."[65] Why was it so difficult for Central and Eastern European officials to establish standards? Often, they lacked the requisite resources, were legally and institutionally ill equipped to monitor valuation activities, or, as indicated, stood to benefit personally from them.

MISSING THE BOAT

The story of the Polish state-owned enterprise Ursus illustrates the frequent lack of understanding of the real problems facing large, state-run enterprises in the region and the controversies to which Western consultants often contributed when they tried to assist in privatizing them. Ursus, one of the largest tractor factories in the world, located about 20 kilometers from central Warsaw, fostered both agricultural productivity and socialism. Domestic sales to private farmers accounted for most of its market. But in 1990-91, domestic demand collapsed due to a severe recession that hit agriculture especially hard. The recession was connected to administrative decisions of Finance Minister Leszek Balcerowicz's economic reform program.

Still, in 1991, Ursus, located on the dotted landscape of the great plains of Central Europe, appeared much the same as it had in its communist heyday. The roar of factory machinery was interrupted only by the occasional sputtering of shabby state buses driving past. On breaks workers milled about the grounds smoking unfiltered cigarettes. In the lobby of the administrative office building, a red tractor sat in stately splendor, a monument to the achievements of socialism. Photographs of the proud winners of workers' productivity competitions, sponsored by the factory's former communist management, adorned the walls.

But appearances of bustle were deceiving: the factory, which sold nearly 60,000 tractors in Poland in 1986 and more than 40,000 tractors in 1989, sold only about 15,000 in 1991.[66] (Nationwide, during the same recessionary period, Poland's production of agricultural machinery dropped nearly 30 percent.[67])

The workers now concerned themselves with keeping their jobs in the face of threats of mass layoffs, frozen wages, high inflation, and cutbacks in social security benefits. Many workers at Ursus had risked their livelihoods in 1976 during worker unrest, and again in the early 1980s for Solidarity, which had grown to encompass nearly two-thirds of Poland's labor force and promised to deliver on socialist guarantees of a better life for all. Following the collapse of communism, the union part of Solidarity continued the fight, this time against the radical economic reforms of the postcommunist era, and Ursus became a special outpost of radical and nationalist elements of the movement. The government wanted to see Ursus privatized, sold to foreign investors, or shut down. But because shutting down the factory or significantly reducing its workforce could cause mass dislocation and worker unrest in Warsaw, the political center, this was politically unfeasible. So while sales plummeted, Ursus continued to operate and to retain employees.

The managers of Ursus, suffering their own leadership problems, were wedged between the workers and the various government ministries and successive governments, characterized by chaos, indecision, and near bankruptcy. They wanted to find partners who could help locate new markets and put together a restructuring program in preparation for a joint venture with a Western company.[68]

In August 1991, amid allegations that the previous government had mismanaged Ursus and other state-owned giants, Henryka Bochniarz, a middle-aged no-nonsense businesswoman, was installed as minister of industry in the new government. She promptly dropped the reorganization plan that had been developed by Ursus management and the previous government. The new restructuring plan for Ursus would divide up the plant, shed labor and capacity, and put to work an international team of experts—with more clout than a Polish team or the ministry. (The new plan also disbanded the Ursus Workers' Council, which was elected by workers to represent their concerns to management and had been created following a hard-fought concession won by Solidarity.)

In September 1991, Bochniarz enlisted several companies, each of which was billed as possessing different financial and legal skills. One of them was the International Team for Company Assistance (ITCA), founded and run by Kevin McDonald, an American in his 30s with an MBA degree who had been introduced to Poland by Harvard's Jeffrey Sachs and had become known in the community of consultants advising the Polish government. With funding from the EU, the United Nations Development Program (UNDP), the German Marshall Fund, and other sources, and with a team comprised of volunteer retired executives and young, enterprising MBA graduates from Harvard and Northwestern universities, McDonald appeared at Ursus and offered his services.[69] In addition, Bochniarz hired Price Waterhouse, one of the Big Six accounting firms; Massey Ferguson, a tractor factory headquartered in the United Kingdom (Ursus had long manufactured tractors under a Massey Ferguson license); and a small Polish-owned consulting firm. The consortium leader was Larry Doyle, an Irishman. Although the government wanted to appear to be on the reform track and to use aid for this purpose, other parties to the process, such as Ursus workers and management, were not as enthusiastic.

The problems with consultants' recommendations were more than a case of some Central and Eastern Europeans reacting in a knee-jerk fashion against foreigners' advice. Rather, they represented a real fear that the consultants would say something that many of the players in the privatization process did not want to hear: that workers' jobs and their pensions were no longer secure and that the bedrock of their existence was now a pool of quicksand.

Remarking that "lots of folks want to solve Ursus's problems," Andrzej Polakowski, a deputy manager at Ursus and a charming, portly man in his mid-40s, said the managerial team put aside their misgivings and cooperated with the foreigners. Managers opened the plant's books and, according to Polakowski, turned over documents concerning sales networks, cost factors and suppliers, balance sheets, and inventories.[70]

Over several years, the consultants, whose contracts and obligations were to the outside sources that paid them, visited the enterprise. They wrote reports. The value of their reports—and the very role the consultants played—was subject to different interpretations by the many players in the enormously politicized environment. In one breath, manager Polakowski offered several criticisms frequently heard within Central European enterprises:

> A lot of people came [to Ursus] and no one especially introduced himself. . . . We found out about a lot of things only by accident. . . . It's not clear why these particular firms were chosen and what the agreements were, who pays them and how, and why Mr. Doyle was chosen [as consortium leader] above others. . . . Only some time later we found out it was Mr. Doyle . . . [who] doesn't answer to us at all. . . . Ursus had no influence on any of this, nor was it informed after the decision was made. . . . While managers are looking for advice on how to solve problems, what we get very often is only a diagnosis of what's going on in a firm, which is already known by management.[71]

Yet management often had its own problems and interests. Lisa Anne Gurr, an anthropologist who studied restructuring and labor issues at Ursus, thinks that enterprise managers sometimes simultaneously used Western consultants to accomplish their own goals and as scapegoats when restructuring plans proved to be unpopular.[72] Still, there appears to be truth in management's complaints. Polakowski and others recounted that some of the consulting firms that had come to help encountered problems of their own: Neither good management nor expertise were always in abundance, they said. McDonald's volunteers—the "friendly retired Americans"—as Polakowski called them, were new not only to Ursus, but also to Poland. Pertinent details, such as why the various consultants were chosen and what was supposed to result from the project, were shrouded in secrecy, at least at the factory level. Further, although some consultants appeared to be very motivated, overall the aid was somewhat ad hoc. According to several sources, consortium leader Doyle drew a consulting fee, called a few meetings with the consultants when he visited Poland, and circulated in the international aid community.[73]

In the end, however, much restructuring of the plant occurred in conjunction with the presence of the foreigners. Some of what they recommended came to pass. McDonald recommended, in his report, that Ursus sell off most of its divisions and that "Those employees left should [be] reduced in number by at least 50 percent."[74] And close to that number was let go during the period that the consultants were active, but not as a result of liquidation.[75] One of the consultants' most important recommendations was foreign investment, which, as of this writing, has not happened.

In 1992, Ursus Solidarity took on the government of Prime Minister Hanna Suchocka for what it saw as anti-labor policies. The trade union branch at Ursus was a major instigator and player in the nationwide strikes of August and September of 1992 and helped hasten the demise of the Suchocka government, which eventually fell in May 1993. Amid the turmoil, the former head of Ursus Solidarity was named the new manager of the enterprise.

What did not happen as a result of the work of consultants at Ursus—or anyone else—was privatization. Central European governments found that large enterprises like Ursus—the "company towns" targeted by the donors—were difficult to convert. The problem may have been that the donors (and some in-country parties) appeared to be proceeding with a rather stereotypical view of the problems of socialist firms: that their greatest need is to be privatized and modernized. The primary need of Ursus was not modernization of equipment, as evidenced by the quality of its product and the Western markets it had penetrated prior to 1989. (By the mid-1990s, although Ursus's domestic sales were still a fraction of what they had been ten years earlier, the company had expanded its exports, with the United States and Canada its primary markets.)

Ursus's main problem was that it suddenly found itself operating under conditions of severe recession. Consultant McDonald pointed out that "Anybody would have had trouble in that case."[76] Under such recession, developing new markets (or expanding existing ones), not privatizing, was the most immediate problem. The conflicting interests of managers, workers, government officials, and consultants also made quick, sensible solutions virtually impossible. A report published by NIK assessed that a 1992 program to restructure Ursus—for which the EU paid consultants 1.4 million EURO (nearly $1.5 million[77])—was wasted. While the program called for the breakup of Ursus into smaller units, another contemporaneous plan proposed a merger of production units and other recommendations that were at odds with the EU-paid advice.[78] No matter how much the donors spent on it, privatization was not the main revision that would make Ursus viable; finding new markets was.

Many years and foreign aid dollars later, Ursus appeared little closer to being privatized than when the consultants were dispatched. Ursus had gone through a succession of ministerial overseers, each one promising to privatize, reorganize, or somehow unload the enterprise. But no minister or foreign consultant had managed to surmount the political constraints.

The involvement of foreign advisers at Ursus may have contributed to the difficulties. Some within the factories perceived the consultants, who typically gained access to sensitive operations and marketing data, as suspect. Some groups felt that "foreigners have come to loot." The point is not whether such perceptions were valid in a given case, but rather that the involvement of aid-paid consultants often fed those perceptions. Consultants' involvement tended to encourage anticapitalist, anti-Western, and antiprivatization sentiments among those radical populist groups (with elements of radical nationalism) that charged that local elites involved in privatization had been corrupted by the West. The Solidarity unionists at Ursus responded to the situation by so decorating the main entrance to the factory: "A Foreign Elite Steals from Us While the Polish People Are at the Bottom" and "Polish Property for All Poles."

Such sentiment helps to explain why the privatization of large enterprises, often company towns, was so difficult. According to a report commissioned by USAID to evaluate its Central European privatization projects, of the five large firms assisted by USAID-paid consultants, only one was privatized, and that one not as a result of USAID help. The evaluation determined that

> to date, assistance to large individual enterprises has not generally been successful in bringing about privatization promptly and cost-effectively. . . . In most cases, privatizations of large enterprises are almost invariably slow in being consummated. Invariably, these enterprise-specific situations and the problems that surround them are new and complex.[79]

Yet another report commissioned by the EU on PHARE consulting in enterprises delicately addressed the subject by noting that "the impact of the consultants was less satisfactory in highly politicized cases."[80] And a NIK report, citing instances of technical assistance to large enterprises, determined that as much as 60 percent of EU funds paid to consulting companies was wasted.[81]

Eventually, even the USAID office in Poland recognized the flaws in concentrating on large-scale enterprises. As the GAO reported:

> Although USAID/Poland noted some achievements while utilizing this approach [privatizing a few large enterprises to have a ripple effect on the economy], the mission concluded that firm-specific and sectoral assistance was too time-consuming and costly. For example, the $3.7 million in USAID funding for the glass sector led to only four state-owned enterprise privatizations, a cost of more than $900,000 per enterprise privatized. In addition, as of May 1994, only four of eight targeted enterprises had been privatized under the almost completed furniture sector project.82

In addition, USAID spent more than $1 million restructuring LOT Polish Airlines in preparation for its privatization.[83] But the first stage of privatization did not take place until November 1999, and, as of this writing, more than half of the airline's shares remain in state hands.[84]

In 1995, the GAO confirmed that "the pace of privatization for larger state-owned enterprises has been slower than expected, and significant portions of Polish productive capacity and employment remain in the hands of the government."[85] As of the turn of the century, a very minor portion of the large, strategic companies (steel mills, coal mines, shipyards, defense enterprises) had been privatized.[86]

DUST IN THEIR EYES

Privatization aid was politicized not only at the level of the enterprise and of the individual consultants and officials involved. The legacy of communism's integration of politics and economics made it nearly impossible to depoliticize such aid. And so privatization and economic restructuring efforts were not as new to Central and Eastern Europeans as many donor representatives might have thought. In fact, the intrinsic natures of privatization aid and communist planning were not so very different. Citizens of the Second World had seen this play enacted on other stages. Decades of "planned change" and communist reform programs[87] had conditioned them into a cynicism that seemed well justified in light of what anthropologist John Bennett calls the "myth of planning" in development assistance.[88] Now the Western donors replaced the Communist Party in the role of enlightened planner, albeit a capitalist one. Aid, like the communist reforms before it, failed to conform to planned agendas; hence, although the roles were performed by other actors, the denouement was remarkably similar.

And, just as communist central planners set targets for production by officially mandating that firms meet fixed production quotas, so the donors specified quotas regarding the number of firms to be privatized within a given time frame. To donors, the number of firms that had been privatized served as an important indicator regarding a country's "transition" to a market economy. If a country met the donors' goals, it was regarded as being "on the reform track" and eligible for further aid. If it failed to meet these targets, it might be seen as backward and face reduction or suspension of aid.

Central and Eastern Europeans were prepared to handle this: An entire language was developed under communism to describe the practice of creating fictions to please authorities. Russians speak of *ochkovtiratel'stvo* (literally, to kick dust into someone's eyes), meaning to pull the wool over someone's eyes or to fool the observer, boss, or do-gooder. As economist James Millar has pointed out, this practice had a long history under communism, and continued unabated in postcommunist times: "The focus of official *ochkovtiratel'stvo* today on the macro level is on international organizations, such as the IMF, the World Bank . . . and others that have attempted to establish 'conditionalities' for the awarding of reform funding. Much current reporting of success in reform is, therefore, eyewash."[89] This would not come as a surprise to anthropologist Mark Hobart, who has observed that "the overlap of developers' and local discourses does not lead to improved communication, but to strain on those locals who are involved in both, and to techniques of evasion, silence and dissimulation."[90] Indeed, some recipient governments at times have tried to placate both sides by attempting to convince outsiders that they were "on the reform track" while seeking to quell internal protest by proceeding at a slower pace.

The responses of officials and managers under both regimes were similar: Just as they had engaged in certain "fictions," ranging from subtle readjusting of figures to outright falsification, to meet prespecified targets under central planning, so they employed the same kinds of fictions in the aid process to please the Western consultants and the donor community. Some so-called privatizations proved to be paper transactions only.[91]

Just as there were obvious reasons for the original development of *ochkovtiratel'stvo,* so there were reasons for its use in the postcommunist era. By unwittingly encouraging the habit of *ochkovtiratel'stvo,* aid served to reinforce some of the old communist ways. Yuriy Yakusha, economic affairs counselor at the Embassy of Ukraine in Washington, D.C., cited a "discrepancy in understanding" between donors and Ukrainian authorities as to what could be accomplished with regard to privatization in a given time frame. "They [the donors] were expecting a little unrealistic rate for privatization": 800 enterprises each month. "Technically perhaps it was possible," Yakusha conceded, but there was "real political opposition" and a property registration system was not in place. There was "definitely" a lot of pressure to deliver quick privatization, said Yakusha, "no matter [at what] expense and what outcome. It's a kind of socialist planning."[92]

Yet whether its aims were realistic or not, the donor community typically continued to press for speedy privatization, in part through its consultants in Central and Eastern Europe, who were not only engaged to assess individual companies, but later in the aid effort also worked directly with ministries responsible for planning the privatization of state-owned enterprises. Under U.S. assistance, for instance, teams of resident consultants, supplemented by short-term experts who came in for specific tasks, were placed both in Poland's Ministry of Privatization and Hungary's State Property Agency to accelerate privatization efforts. According to USAID official Mark Karns, the teams were charged with the task of helping certain divisions in the ministries responsible for mass privatization to focus more on transactions and to enable the ministries to move to the execution phase.[93] But politics could and did interfere with their work. After the change of governments in Poland in 1993, alternative projects had to be sought for the advisers who were just coming on board. There was a built-in tension between the visions and demands of donors, on one hand, and the realities and political constraints faced by local officials, on the other.[94]

No consultant or aid agency can reasonably be blamed for not predicting the twists and turns of Central and Eastern European politics. But the changing nature of privatization policies, combined with the time it took to get contracts signed and consultants into the field, made providing effective privatization aid difficult.[95] An analyst who observed efforts by Poland's Ministry of Privatization to answer objections to its mass privatization plan in 1992 holds that these efforts "indicate the ways in which it, the [Ministry of Privatization], and the foreign consultant presence all were politically sensitive and may have contributed to declining support for privatization."[96]

Donors had generally assumed that the East would accept the political, economic, and social changes recommended by donor governments and the international financial institutions. According to Jan Krzysztof Bielecki, prime minister of Poland during 1991 (and also a minister in a subsequent government), no one in the relevant policy circles, from foreign advisers sent by international institutions such as the International Monetary Fund (IMF) to local officials, considered alternatives. At that time, "nobody [in the donor community] raised the issue of a social safety net," recalls Bielecki, which he finds startling in retrospect. "We forgot, donors forgot. . . . [No Central and Eastern European aid recipient asked] the donors to insist on a social [safety] net." The fact that nobody "took it into consideration as a necessary political factor" ultimately "strengthened ex-Communist forces in these countries."[97] Bielecki was only one of a number of politicians in Poland and the region whose tenures in office were short-lived. Both Poland and Hungary have elected socialist/leftist governments, as have some nations farther south and east. Pushing reforms too hard could delay them even further because in some cases it could lead to a backlash effect that would serve to solidify opposition.

RETHINKING PRIVATIZATION AID

Clearly, one major issue in assessing technical assistance for privatization was its sensibility in the post-1989 Second World: To what degree could privatization aid—with its ideological implications on the donor side (reflected in how donors targeted, structured, and conditioned the aid) and inherently political overtones on the postcommunist (recipient) side—achieve positive results?

A related issue was corruption. With privatization inevitably came corruption – albeit to varying degrees, depending on the context and the privatization program being implemented.[98] Some privatization programs held up in the West as "success stories," at least initially, were in fact riddled with corruption.[99] Involving donors and consultants in such a messy business as privatization not only rarely achieved positive results, but also, as we shall see in the Russian case (presented in chapter 4), the involvement of foreign consultants could be counterproductive.[100]

All around, ideological, institutional, and political constraints on the part of the consultants, the donors, and the aid recipients appeared to work against the effective use of aid money for privatization. Privatization called for a complex task of institutional change, involving building basic legal infrastructure such as property rights and viable systems of banking and taxation. Working with these politicized processes was a far more challenging task than achieving macroeconomic stabilization, in which a recipient government could bring inflation under control by decree or regulation.

It is telling that Central Europeans themselves were largely responsible for the varying privatization paths and programs on which they embarked. Most privatization that did take place in Central Europe (excluding Russia) could not be linked to foreign aid expenditures. Other developments in which foreign consultants had no role, such as the sale or liquidation of smaller state-owned enterprises at the local level and the considerable growth of private sectors, tended to be the chief engines of restructuring. In Poland, for example, the government brokered joint ventures of its most attractive firms and, in small towns, handed over state-owned small shops to the municipalities, which left them in public hands, sold them, or closed them. Much privatization was accomplished through liquidation, with the major players the Ministry of Industry and company insiders.[101]

A corollary point is that foreign aid in the large factories might have been helpful had it been directed not toward privatization per se, but toward working with the various interests to help solve problems. This aspect of the failure of frontal-assault privatization has been noted by anthropologist Gurr.[102]

Privatization aid also appears to have played a marginal role in finding investment partners. It is revealing that some Central and Eastern European companies committed to undergoing privatization and to finding joint-venture partners ultimately chose to bypass foreign aid and Western consultants entirely. When help was believed necessary, the companies selected and paid their own consultants, who answered directly to the companies. Likewise, when Central and Eastern European governments deemed the privatization of a company to be a priority, they too employed their own resources and those of potential joint-venture partners to get the process under way.

Finally, whether privatization aid was worth the problems seems a fair question. As we have seen through Ursus, Monor, and other troubled enterprises in the region, the very targets (large, state-owned enterprises) and design (ad hoc or delivering aid outside local privatization bodies) of assistance could cause problems of perception, without necessarily producing favorable results in terms of restructuring or privatization. Although development agencies purport to offer impartial solutions and the expertise they provide is presented as neutral and technical, development ideologies have unintended consequences and perform sensitive political functions.[103] As anthropologist Hobart has put it, "Whatever its merits, scientific knowledge applied to development is not neutral, as is so often claimed, nor are the implications of its use."[104]

In Central and Eastern Europe, there were special causes for caution given the region's legacy of integration of politics and economics. Privatization aid there was inherently political, and, even if delivered under the guise of neutral, technical help, perceived by recipients as politically charged. Many Central and Eastern European enterprise managers and workers viewed the "neutral" technical advice they received from Western experts as anything but neutral. And so suspicion about donors' motives clung to any claim that the aid was politically disinterested or benign. In some cases, donors and their consultants may have inadvertently rekindled the kind of suspicion and collusion between politics and economics that had characterized communism.

A BETTER WAY

Another pertinent question was the extent to which technical assistance relationships were designed to be useful. If the consultants and aid representatives were such a problem, why didn't the recipient countries send them home? That was not an option that recipient officials generally entertained. Aid was, in many respects, not an end in itself, but part of a larger package of new relations between East and West. Often, aid was more a matter of maintaining good relations and contacts and of occasionally receiving useful hardware. (Equipment and technical assistance sometimes came as a package.) Some officials conceded that "occasionally, [the consultants'] advice or contacts are useful" or "we need the equipment that the consultants bring." However, often the working principle was "the donors pretend to help us, and we pretend to be helped."

The lack of overall strategy and productive working relationships between Eastern and Western agents greatly complicated technical assistance to the Second World. The limited cases of effective technical assistance were those in which *relationships* between donors and recipients made sense. In such cases, assistance was well targeted: Specific recipients identified the type of expertise they needed, handpicked the consultants, and developed effective working long-term relationships with informed oversight from aid agencies.

Some of the technical assistance rendered under the British Know How Fund fit this bill. Although small in comparison to EU and USAID programs, the Know How Fund earned a favorable reputation among many of the region's officials early in the aid effort. With few strings attached, recipient officials could select advisers of their choice to be paid by the Know How Fund. For example, several long-term, hands-on advisers from the London School of Economics were in residence in Poland's Ministry of Finance. In such cases, the Know How Fund became known for the leeway it allowed recipients, its flexibility, and its relative speed. Zdeněk Drábek, former chief aid coordinator of Czechoslovakia, says that it made decisions "very quickly" and "without much bureaucratic procedure."[105]

Another case of effective technical assistance appears to be some of the expertise provided to the region through the U.S. Treasury Department's Financial Sector Technical Assistance Program. Although funding and strategies were provided for in inter-agency agreements, Treasury hired the technical advisers. This contracting arrangement enabled flexibility in part because the agencies were not subjected to all of USAID's contracting constraints.[106] The experts, requested by officials in recipient institutions, were hired for specific tasks, usually involving taxation, budget, banking, and government debt. In 1998, in response to a growing perceived threat of international financial crime, the Treasury Department added a law enforcement program to assist foreign governments in revising their laws and reorganizing their ministries to combat financial crime, organized crime, and corruption.[107]

Under Treasury's program, short-term specialists were brought in when deemed advisable to address specific needs related to the overall agenda.[108] Treasury's Tax Advisory Program, for example, was developed by a program director who traveled to the various countries and, having conducted fieldwork for several weeks at a time, learned the identities and the needs of the relevant players. Prospective advisers were then screened and interviewed by both parties. Salvatore Pappalardo, an American adviser to Poland's chief debt negotiator, received an award from the Polish government for his help in successful debt negotiations. Pappalardo has related that Poles "like to see commitment to understanding the situation and working with them."[109]

In short, such long-term assistance was helpful because it generally was seen by the relevant host officials as impartial, professional, and able to accomplish what local firms could not—at least not early in the economic restructuring process. Long-term programs avoided the lack of continuity and follow-up that often plagued short-term ones. They could be effective if they were integrated into the institutions that they were trying to help and were well received.

To be effective, aid must be structured in a depoliticized way that can largely preclude interference in host-country politics and problems of local perception. Assistance can be helpful when consultants are seen by local officials—and a larger public—as advocates for the recipient nation. Aside from having expertise to offer, a crucial feature of effective technical assistance appears to be neutrality and the appearance of neutrality. Providing strategic support and training to key institutions was a related area where aid sometimes could help to build nonpartisan, lasting institutions independent of political whim. Some aid provided to the parliaments of the region was invaluable in this regard.

Two small programs that, according to many accounts, were most effective were the Senate-initiated Gift of Democracy program and the Frost Task Force program of assistance to the parliamentary institutions of Central Europe, which received support from the U.S. Congressional Research Service. The effort provided information technology and resources to parliaments, as well as training for parliamentary staff, including research and library personnel. For example, the Gift of Democracy program purchased computers for the Polish Parliament and Senate. This enabled them to set up a local-area network with local databases and connections to American and European databases.[110]

Wiesław Staszkiewicz, director of the Polish Parliament's Bureau of Research, said the program provided "very significant help" to his bureau, which supplied information and training for representatives (like the U.S. Congressional Research Service), expert opinions on prospective legislation, and monitoring as requested by the Parliament. Especially helpful was the training provided in Washington, where people learned how reference services and libraries could be organized effectively and where they made valuable contacts that they could continue to call upon.[111]

The Bureau of Research was developed largely on the model of the U.S. Congressional Research Service. When, in 1994, the United States ended its assistance, the European Parliament and the Council of Europe assumed some of the functions of education and training that the Congressional Research Service had previously provided. The Europeans encouraged an expansion of initiatives to "harmonize" Polish laws with those of the EU in preparation for Polish accession to it.[112]

Impartiality was a key component in the assistance offered and in the Bureau's survival and good reputation. In time, the Bureau became self-sufficient, with its operating budget funded by the Polish Parliament and Senate.[113] By 1998, it had fully convinced the Polish government of the necessity of such an impartial institution, according to director Staszkiewicz. He said the bureau had survived a succession of governments in a partisan environment because of its insistence on remaining neutral.

As of mid-1998, the Bureau of Research had issued some 19,000 expert opinions to Parliament upon request and had become one of the best operations in Europe. The Bureau has been engaged—and is expanding its efforts—to help set up similar offices in nations to the south and east of Poland. What has been most difficult to explain in Romania, Albania, and Bulgaria, observed Staszkiewicz—but is crucial—is that such an office must remain nonpartisan.[114]

Changing views about Western aid were in evidence in Poland, Hungary, and the Czech Republic by 1994. Despite mistakes, and the resentment they engendered, much of the antagonism present in Central Europe in the first years of the aid effort had dissipated. Recipients adapted as their experience with donors grew and led to another phase of aid relations: Adjustment. After early frustration and resentment about the inadequacies of foreign consultants and the help they offered, Central European officials became better at identifying their needs and more selective about foreign (and local) advisers. As consultant Pappalardo observed in 1994, there were "a lot of carpetbaggers early on. . . . At this stage of the process Poles are more aware of the things they know and, most importantly, of the things they don't know. They've learned to clarify their needs."[115]

Regardless of whether much of the technical assistance rendered was effective, a natural progression occurred. As Poles, Hungarians, and Czechs developed technical capacities, the need for foreign aid–sponsored technical assistance diminished.[116] They developed new skills for dealing with the donor community and became more realistic about what aid could (and could not) do for them. In some cases, they concluded that the costs of working with an aid program, in terms of timing and meeting donor requirements, outweighed the benefits, and they chose not to do so.

A related development was the blurring of distinctions between donor and recipient personnel. Initially, it had been possible to detect just who was who by nationality, language, style, and dress. By 1994, however, many Western consulting groups, including accounting firms, were hiring more local citizens and expatriates who spoke Polish, Hungarian, Czech, and Slovak. Donors also recruited some former high-level Central European officials who had served in the first postcommunist governments. For example, the Polish-American Enterprise Fund hired a former deputy minister of privatization and a former undersecretary in the Ministry of Industry and Trade to be vice presidents. Marek Kozak, who, two years earlier, had criticized Western aid efforts, headed a private-sector development initiative for the EU. Some Central European consultants, by then anointed "Westerners" themselves, even served as the new missionaries of the West and helped spread the gospel of reform in the East.

The extent to which these consultants, as well as those based in the donor countries, could be useful largely depended on how aid was designed and the relationships it engendered with various recipient parties. Helping to build up independent institutions was especially important in environments in which information and expertise unconnected to a political group or agenda was under constant attack. Exercising as much independence as possible was crucial precisely where it was most difficult to remain neutral and professional. At no time would this be more apparent than when the West, hoping to help create democracy, civil society, and an independent sector where none supposedly had existed for nearly 50 years, funded partisan groups. Through the weightiest years of the aid effort, many of these groups would seek to enhance their own agendas, rather than to further the noble goals of the donors.

CHAPTER THREE

A Few Favored Cliques

The various political shifts and upheavals within the
communist world all have one thing in common: the undying
urge to create a genuine civil society.

—Václav Havel, 1988[1]

WHILE DISPATCHING CONSULTANTS ACROSS THE OCEAN as its agents
of change, the West also set out to supplant communism by supporting
certain local organizations and groups as exemplars of and vehicles for
creating democracy and a civil society. This approach held that, under
communism, the nations of the Eastern Bloc never had a "civil society,"
in which citizens and groups were free to form organizations that
functioned independently of the state and that mediated between citizens
and the state.

Because this lacuna epitomized the all-pervasive communist state,
both Western and Central European opinion makers saw creating a civil
society and independent organizations as building the connective tissue
of a new democratic political culture. The experience and writings of
Central European dissident intellectuals such as Václav Havel in Czechoslovakia and Adam Michnik in Poland helped crystallize the view of an
idealized civil society[2] playing a vital reconstructive role in the former
communist states. Although the concept subsequently became central to
how donors thought about Central and Eastern European "transition," in
the recipient societies, the idea tended to be limited to certain circles. It
was not, for example, necessarily shared by large segments of the various

populations (not even by parts of the Opposition close to Poland's Roman Catholic Church).

The building blocks of civil society were thought to be nongovernmental organizations (NGOs), which donors also saw as important vehicles of technical assistance and training. Donors had high hopes for this "independent sector": It was to replace the discredited centralized bureaucratic state, decentralize services, and build democracy. And so donors made the development of a civil society and support of NGOs a primary focus, if not always as a funding priority, certainly in rhetoric.

Americans tended to talk the loudest about establishing civil societies in the region.[3] The fall of the Berlin Wall energized American efforts to try to remake Central and Eastern Europe in "our" image by exporting the can-do mentality and the tradition of citizens' initiatives and local governance. The U.S. Congress obligated some $32 million in 1990-91 to support "democratic institution building" in Poland and the other ex-communist states.[4] By the end of 1999, the United States had obligated $379 million to promote political party development, independent media, governance, and recipient NGOs.[5] Many of these projects were carried out through grants to American quasi-private organizations, notably the National Endowment for Democracy (NED) and its affiliated institutes, including the AFL-CIO's Free Trade Union Institute (FTUI), the Center for International Private Enterprise (CIPE), and the National Democratic and National Republican Institutes for International Affairs (NDI and NRI). A host of American NGOs, seasoned by USAID- and foundation-supported work in the Third World, also lobbied and competed with each other for the new business.

While bilateral donors such as the United States provided grants directly to NGOs in the region (albeit often using Western NGOs as their intermediaries), the EU's PHARE program worked through agreements negotiated with the governments and coordination units of the host countries. (In both cases, though, government bureaucracies provided relatively little oversight.) Two main initiatives in Central Europe have emerged from the PHARE program since 1991: "social dialogue" and "civil society." Social dialogue activities were designed to bolster NGOs in the region by providing information, legal services, training, and grants for projects, while under the civil society program, PHARE has supported locally administered NGOs with funds (typically totaling between 100,000 to 200,000 ECU, roughly \$119,000 to \$261,000[6]) administered through the EU delegations in the region. In addition to these initiatives, PHARE has financed NGOs working in social welfare areas through grants administered by the labor ministries in Hungary and Poland as well as financed cooperation and exchange between higher education institutions in nations of the European Union and those of Central Europe.[7] By the beginning of 1998, the EU's PHARE program had contributed nearly 158 million ECU (roughly \$194 million[8]) to support civil society, including NGOs and democracy development in Central and Eastern Europe.[9]

Yet despite lip service to democracy building throughout the aid effort, as of 1999, the United States had devoted only about 17 percent of its Central and Eastern European aid expenditures to democracy assistance.[10] With regard to Russia, the share of democracy assistance was approximately two percent as of 1999.[11] Similarly, the EU's democracy program to Central and Eastern Europe and the former Soviet Union comprised only about one percent of its assistance budget.[12]

Private donors made an equal—if not greater—contribution to democracy assistance than governments. The collapse of communism galvanized more than 60 European and North American foundations, most of which had not previously been active internationally.[13] The Hungarian American financier George Soros, who began philanthropic involvement in the region before 1989, undertook a huge effort. The "Soros network," as it is sometimes called by insiders, consists of country-specific foundations, network programs, and short-term initiatives.[14] Soros has spent more in the region than any other foundation and some bilateral donors.[15]

But, as with privatization efforts, it would be difficult, if not impossible, for any donor—public or private—to create democratic pluralism from the outside. As anthropologist Steven Sampson has observed, "NGOs in Eastern Europe are unique in that they are specific products of the communist and postcommunist political cultures, on the one hand, while being overtly influenced—if not totally financed—by foreign actors on the other."[16] Foreign financing in the form of grants meant that choices had to be made about just who the appropriate grantees were. Donors were profoundly ill equipped to make these choices. They were easily outdone by Central and Eastern Europeans skilled in the necessary arts of self-presentation and preservation through their experiences under communism.

Just who were these brokers? In Poland and Hungary, many were members of long-standing elite groups who had survived by asserting themselves against a stifling state. Where the state had tolerated pockets of "independent activity" beyond its control, tight-knit groups formed "small circles of freedom" and even pushed the limits of state tolerance in both economic and political arenas. Before 1989 in Poland, for example, many Solidarity activists had redefined reform by redirecting their efforts from political to economic activity and preaching a new philosophy: form a club or lobby to do what needs doing and finance it through entrepreneurial activities. Some people who had previously exchanged underground leaflets at private gatherings turned to trading software and financial schemes. These small circles provided identity, intimacy, trust, and pooled resources, all vital for both political and economic sustenance. Much Western assistance to Central Europe after 1989 was built on the backbone of these energized elites; they cultivated international contacts and set up NGOs and "foundations" to receive Western funds.[17] In addition to these established groups, a new class of economically active young adults came into their own in the 1990s. Although, as individuals, some played brokerage roles, they generally were not major beneficiaries of Western aid.

If a few groups had built their base on oases of "independent activity," and younger participants were forging new ground, others in the region had survived and thrived by planting themselves firmly within the Communist Party apparatus and state. Many visible new businessmen were former *nomenklatura* operatives; some also set up "foundations." Further east, in Russia and Ukraine, many intermediaries favored by the West were former communists. As anthropologist Sampson has described, many of these people in the recipient countries learned very quickly how to manipulate and maneuver the new orbit of opportunities:

> One sign of the transition is that some individuals who were very good at the "wooden language" of socialism have now mastered the jargon of democracy programmes, project management, capacity building and other catch-phrases such as "transparency" and "empowerment." Such individuals serve as brokers in the unequal relationship between the west and the east. Like brokers everywhere, they manipulate resources and thrive off the maintenance of barriers. The forum for such activity

is the world of projects, and civil society development is part of this world.[18]

The established groups, regardless of their role under communism, served as gatekeepers for aid from the West. They had carte blanche to put their irons into all fires simultaneously—policy, government, business, politics, and foundations. And so a handful of brokers made decisions and amassed resources on a large scale, by local standards, and Western funding tended to reinforce their success.

The trouble with this is that the choices the donors made were inevitably problematic, especially given one powerful and persistent communist legacy: the pivotal role of the state and its strong, centralized bureaucracy.[19] After the collapse of communism, the agendas of the donors and the new leaders of Central and Eastern Europe came together: The donors could secure the demise of the discredited communists and fill the postcommunist power vacuum where it existed;[20] the leaders could leverage the aid to consolidate their positions, just as the communists had controlled state resources. This confluence helped to create a paradoxical path for aid to take: The central role of the state under communism smoothed the way for the donors by providing a model that persisted beyond its collapse. And so demons from the past came to haunt aid programs intended to help establish democracy and civil society, just as they had privatization.

AGENDAS IN COMMUNISM'S AFTERMATH

During the period of euphoria and excitement immediately following the collapse of communism, local access to the West was the way to get ahead. One of the many places this could be seen in the spring of 1990 in the newly independent Poland was at the Polish Council of Ministers, a cabinet-level office. There, dozens of Poles were attending a "training for democracy" workshop set up for the leaders of the region's new political parties and put on by visiting American political consultants and media pollsters.

Aleksander Hall, the minister responsible for political parties, opened the workshop. Soft-spoken and looking uncomfortable in a suit with trousers hanging over the tops of his shoes, he welcomed the guests.

The leaders of the "political parties" graciously, deferentially, and profusely thanked the Westerners for coming to teach democracy. "We have so much to learn from you," said one. The consultants were equally elated to meet the maiden leaders of Poland. The leaders of so many political parties—35—had taken the time to attend the workshop. What a coup! The consultants exulted over the death of communism and said how grateful they were to have this rare opportunity to assist Poland. Listening dutifully, the Poles were treated to an explanation of the importance of fliers and mass mailings in a session entitled "How to Use the Post Office in a Political Campaign"—in a country where one of the greatest political landslides in its history had just been accomplished without the post office, which was notorious for taking days to deliver a letter across town or for simply losing it.

Over three days, the consultants did not learn that candidate-to-citizen meetings in parishes—not glitzy mailings or television ads—had mobilized Polish voters. Moreover, the consultants had little idea whom they were encountering as participants. Yes, they were representatives of "political parties." For the most part, however, these were not national political leaders but, rather, representatives of political discussion clubs that had mushroomed during the relaxation of control preceding the collapse of communism. The truly influential politicians belonged to citizens' organizations that claimed to represent the collective interests of all society, not those of politicians, who were seen as selfishly competitive. Minister Hall, one of the few real political players present, represented a long-standing, highly influential Christian democratic group, but it was not a political party at the time.

Why did the Poles care to participate in the workshop? It seemed clear that they hardly expected to glean lessons in democracy from the Americans, who could only tell them about curiosities far removed from Polish political or daily realities. The hallway conversations, especially their unspoken subtexts, exposed the gap between the foreigners—enthusiastic, well intentioned, and naive—and the quick-on-the-uptake Poles, who parroted the buzzwords of pluralism and civil society while pursuing the main goal of each of them: access to potentially useful foreigners. The Poles painted a grim picture of their circumstances, one that played to the Westerners' inflated view of their own usefulness.

A consultant (respectfully): "You were in prison, too? I admire your courage."

A politician (smiling modestly): "Yes, I was." [It didn't take any special courage. I was picked up just like all my friends.]

A consultant: "You suffered. If there's anything we can help you with now, just let us know."

A politician: "The workshop has been so enlightening. One thing just occurred to me. There's a shortage of paper and, you know, we don't have enough money to buy fax or photocopy machines." [Of course, we think you can help. Travel abroad? Funds? Other contacts? Anything that might give us visibility in the West and the prestige we need here that is associated with Western exposure. That's why we bothered to come to your workshop.]

A consultant: "Perhaps my organization could help."

A politician (humbly): "Oh, we would be most grateful!"

These encounters resembled the rituals observed under communism that had served to cushion foreigners from the real (Polish) world, which foreigners could never quite grasp because they were shielded from harsh realities. Urban Poles, especially those who came into contact with foreigners, tended to talk about things they thought foreigners respected and omitted more dubious topics, such as the wheeling and dealing nearly everyone engaged in to survive. So visitors usually did not learn how Poles obtained goods and services in a shortage economy at a time (1982 and 1983) when the rationing system allowed each citizen one pair of Polish-made shoes per year. Polish formality and reserve arose partially from an instinct to survive in a climate of fear and uncertainty. The rituals and language of public life helped to maintain a mantle of normalcy that enshrouded informal dealings and private life. In its ritual character, public life provided a stark contrast to what many people did unofficially.[21] The practice of putting on public shows, honed under communism, was thus ideal preparation for handling the onslaught of people from the West. In an article entitled "Playing the Co-Operation Game," anthropologist Marta Bruno concludes that "As long as recipients see these occasions [workshops with Western consultants] as a ritual lip-service or as 'tax,' which they have to pay in order to obtain funding, they will simply reinforce the artificiality of development projects."[22]

The artificiality could be observed on both sides. Oblivious, having had a wonderful time, and having acquired many new "friends," the consultants moved on to their next workshop in Prague or Budapest. Then they returned home from the whirlwind trip with their misconceptions intact and a stack of makeshift visiting cards. The trip would make good cocktail party conversation for some time; the consultants had made "friends" with the new leaders of Central Europe and helped them to build democracy.

Dozens of such early East-West encounters played out in Warsaw, Prague, and Budapest, and later, when aid resources moved east, in Moscow and Kiev. Deficient in cultural and historical sensibilities, consultants and aid representatives often made social fools of themselves, failing to realize that their chief source of attractiveness was in their own pocketbooks or their perceived access to others' pockets. Meanwhile, Central and Eastern Europeans—their eyes on foreign travel and access—applied to unsuspecting foreigners the persistence and sophisticated wheeling- and-dealing-skills that they had honed under communism.

A class of resourceful brokers and operators with enough energy and skill to play in the new arena was formed. Central and Eastern European businessmen needed trading partners; academic deans of depleted universities, money to make payroll and foreign trips; physicians, modern equipment and foreign trips. Westerners' visits to the region, their enthusiasm, and their money provided incentives for local people to formalize existing associations and even to create new initiatives that could attract and receive Western money. As anthropologist Sampson has observed, "Social networks can't get grants, but autonomous associations can."[23]

"Foundations" multiplied: Westerners living in the region were inundated with requests from local friends who had set up organizations and needed help writing English-language proposals to potential funders. One person created a foundation to preserve crumbling monuments, another started one to clean up the polluted environment, and yet another launched a foundation to open a school. As more and more aid money poured in, initiating a project without a Western sponsor became almost unthinkable, like running for public office in the United States after filing for bankruptcy.

The issue was not just money. The issue was, critically, "symbolic capital"—an individual's combined cultural, social, and financial power, which served to compound the power of the individual's group in the public arena[24]—that could be leveraged both in and outside the region. To get money from the West was to be blessed by it, especially in the initial period of East-West contact in each country. Securing Western—sometimes specifically American—funds greatly enhanced one's reputation and lent legitimacy that could be leveraged internally to enhance symbolic capital and accrue further political, financial, and social rewards. For this reason, even small sums of hard currency could be enormously life enhancing to the beneficiaries.

Just how did partners find each other? The ad hoc atmosphere of the early days of the aid effort was custom made for the class of well-heeled brokers that arose to take advantage of opportunities and to guide foreign partners. Having just come from a power lunch in Paris, the jet-setting American CEO in Prague needed local fixers not only to set up contacts and translate, but also to explain the ABCs of doing business in the new frontier: "Economist," "bank," "profit," "tomorrow," and "yes" didn't necessarily mean the same things as in the West. Western foundation representatives, too, needed translators, fixers, and, for the larger operations, local office staff.

The promise of Western money and access often inspired secrecy, suspicion, and competition among groups. The arrival of government and foundation delegations from the West was greeted with bursts of gossip and speculation about who was meeting with whom and who was doing and getting what. Each group developed—and guarded—its own prized Western contacts. It was not necessarily in a group's interest to share information and contacts with the outside world.

In fact, information about who was who was the most valuable—and scarcest—commodity on the East-West circuit, especially during the Triumphalist phase. Westerners were entering a previously semiclosed world, usually not knowing much, if anything, of its sophisticated legacy of reputations, cliques, and intrigue. Representatives of foundations, corporations, and government agencies typically toured the region with lists of up to a dozen or so names of the "most important people" for each country. Names often were obtained from other Westerners and by virtue of Easterners' visibility in the West. The lists became self-fulfilling prophecies; many of those whose names appeared on them in time received funding from multiple sources.

Thus, although a multitude of Western programs offered travel, training, and scholarship opportunities, there were only a few channels of selection for them. There was much to be done, but seemingly few to do it: Only a few highly skilled Easterners were adept at working in the new environment. The same groups and individuals, who tended to travel in the same circles as each other, took advantage of multiple opportunities.

Easterners, too, often had little information about Western personalities and organizations, but were quick studies in maneuvering the situation to their advantage. Many educated and astute young adults from intelligentsia backgrounds carved out a triad of business, foundation, and scholarly activities. Western partnerships facilitated all of these activities, and so such Easterners also served as consultants, brokers, and partners, and depended more on Western contacts and opportunities than on indigenous ones. Previously engaged in traditional academic careers in philosophy, philology, and physics that commanded respect, but little income, they now were involved in both the old activities that afforded the intelligentsia prestige and the new ones that offered money. Many members of Poland's bright young intelligentsia split their energies between lucrative business activities and sociology (a catch-all field under which critical discussion had been possible in communist Poland and Hungary and in which many who assumed important positions in postcommunist Central Europe had been trained). Many assistant professors of sociology and psychology set up businesses and/or foundations "on the side," all the while carrying out minimal duties at the university and collecting meager state salaries.

One such person was Grzegorz "Larry" Lindenberg, a Ph.D. sociologist in his early 30s. Lindenberg was short, slight, friendly, and, in contrast to his Western counterparts, casually dressed and often smiling behind a bushy beard. Poor after their release from martial-law internment, he and a few of his ex-cellmates had in time begun to trade in computers and electronic equipment by traveling from Singapore to Bratislava to Warsaw and Kiev. In addition, Lindenberg became the managing editor of the newly created *Gazeta Wyborcza,* which quickly became the most widely circulated newspaper in Poland. Using his access throughout Poland—starting with the Ministries of Industry and Finance—Lindenberg helped some Western investors navigate the country's complicated bureaucratic and political structures. He also played a role in promoting Harvard economist Jeffrey Sachs when Sachs first appeared in Poland in the late 1980s.

Called upon by their countrymen to be economic and political players and to help their country get back on its feet, new managers such as Lindenberg became windows to the West at a crucial time and served as invaluable assets to Western investors, attorneys, and entrepreneurial academics. As these businessmen received scores of calls and offers from Westerners, their visibility and opportunities quickly compounded. Myriad such contacts blossomed for mutual advantage, as well as to facilitate efforts that would have wider influence.

EARLY EASTERN GATEKEEPERS

Before the revolutions of 1989, important precedents for giving and receiving had been set both by donors and by Central European recipients. Individuals with name recognition in the West—often dissidents—tended to be selected as the beneficiaries of Western help. In their own social contexts, they were "more equal than others." Some on-the-scene observers contended that endowing them with resources may have reinforced existing social hierarchies. In an article entitled "The Opposition and Money," a known activist writing under a pseudonym explained the role of Western money in supporting underground operations and the very survival of the Polish Opposition in the late 1970s and 1980s:

> It is worthwhile to remember that those who carry out such lofty and noble ends are still human beings like the rest of us, who need money to live. . . . Payments for articles, books, reviews, and sometimes interviews published in the West provided Oppositionists with much-needed income. Some received awards; others were granted lucrative Western scholarships or fellowships. Activists had many opportunities to earn money at home by working for independent papers and publishing houses (that paid in *złoty)* or working for Western correspondents (for dollars) as translators or fixers. . . . Some Oppositionists were more equal than others. Well-known activists had many more opportunities to earn money than their less famous colleagues. Such genuinely eminent figures . . . could live comfortably from selling their views in the form of paid interviews with foreign press agencies. Indeed, such people had many more offers than they could accept. Western journalists worked for Western editors, who had only a vague idea about the situation in Poland, and thus always demanded the same names. Such Oppositionists often had to turn down intrusive Western correspondents.

Moreover, in such necessarily clandestine circumstances, there was a natural tendency to blur the lines between what was one's own and what belonged to the group, and thus was meant for wider benefit.

> The distinction between monies and goods designated for individual and for collective use was never clear. . . . Exact bookkeeping was often deemed impossible for security reasons, and the activists' own money easily got mixed with the "company" money. . . . It was also rather difficult at times to determine whether an activist was honored with some prize from abroad for his personal, individual achievements or on behalf of the group and the cause he represented. Did, for example, the Nobel Peace Prize simply honor the undoubtedly heroic Lech Wałęsa or also millions of less famous, more deprived, more easily suppressed workers across a defiant nation? In some cases a contributor earmarked the money for a common, opposition purpose, in others he did not. One may presume that the recipient kept some part of it for himself.[25]

However different the circumstances, the recipients that donors selected and what these recipients did with the money in the thaw years of the 1980s set patterns that persisted into the 1990s. To a large degree, assistance under the rubric of building democracy, civil society, and independent institutions was, especially in the years immediately after 1989, a continuation of the status quo; that is, donors funded the same individuals and groups they had previously supported. For example, through FTUI, NED continued its support, begun in 1984, to Solidarity with a grant of $355,000 in fiscal year 1989 to assist Solidarity activities both in and outside Poland. Through the International Rescue Committee in New York, NED renewed funding, begun in 1987, to Solidarity with a grant of $1 million in fiscal year 1989 to maintain a social services fund to assist workers and their families.[26] Through the Czechoslovak Society of Arts and Sciences, NED carried on funding that in part supported "independent scholars and writers in Czechoslovakia."[27] NED president Carl Gershman described the endowment's targets:

> Endowment funds were used to provide supplies and equipment for the independent publishing movements in Poland; to sustain independent publications as well as independent cultural, human rights, and political organizations in Czechoslovakia; to provide Hungarian dissidents

with paper and ink to publish their journals during the period before the opening; to support regional initiatives and transnational cooperation among democratic movements throughout the region through the Multinational Fund for Friendship and Cooperation in Central and Eastern Europe, a movement of democratic activists themselves; and to provide communications technology and knowledge to the emerging independent publishing and press groups in the Soviet Union.[28]

In 1989, with the collapse of communism in Central and Eastern Europe, the West affirmed its support of the new noncommunist politicians and leaders who would shape the direction of Central and Eastern European states. The flood tides that had swept away the communist regimes brought unprecedented opportunities—and obligations—into the hands of the heroes of resistance. The communists' fall from power left a vacuum in many areas of public life, from finance and foreign affairs to health and social services. (Of course, a few years later the communists had reassumed power in Poland and Hungary and also had enriched their roles in the private economy.) And a multitude of new institutions had to be created: financial and regulatory systems, ministries of privatization, and independent news organizations. With the old guard gone overnight, a small group of trusted and untainted new leaders had to staff the old posts and to identify, create, and fill the positions needed to shape the new environment. Western donors were eager to participate in this process and especially to support people who had name recognition as heroes of the revolution.

The U.S.-funded NED already mentioned, which distributed nearly all the SEED money allocated by the U.S. Congress for "democratic institution building" in 1990, was an important case in point. NED supported the new democratic leaders by funding their political parties and groups. Under NED, the NDI and the NRI, as well as the International Foundation for Electoral Systems and other organizations, provided training and assistance to political parties.[29]

In Hungary, these organizations financed emerging political parties, notably the Alliance of Free Democrats. The support was intended to "help to shape political public opinion in Hungary during this transitional period, through publications, seminars, and lectures on democracy. Communication and interaction among the alliance's network throughout the country [was] also [to] be strengthened."[30] In Poland, NED financed the Citizens'

Committees—the local and national fora under which most of the pre-1989 opposition organized itself in 1990-1991.[31] The Citizens' Committees were major recipients of U.S. political aid to the opposition in Poland and had at their disposal significant political, diplomatic, and media support, particularly from Radio Free Europe—assistance that proved pivotal.[32] And, in Czechoslovakia, NED provided organizational support for the political party Civic Forum,[33] which appears to have given it advantages vis-à-vis other groups throughout the Czech and Slovak political spectrum. A number of private funders also provided decisive support to political parties: The New York-based Freedom House, for example, provided direct assistance to political parties in Poland and Hungary, while the Andrew W. Mellon Foundation supplied funding in Czechoslovakia. The national foundations of George Soros generally were directed by his long-time associates and boards made up of former dissidents often involved in political, not only intellectual, pursuits.[34]

The groups that the West chose to fund in the early 1990s tended to include high-profile activists who had been visible in the West in the 1980s. One such individual was Adam Michnik. Under communism, Michnik was an historian and influential intellectual of a prominent Polish Opposition group. After communism, he was editor-in-chief of *Gazeta Wyborcza* and, for a short time, an active politician. Long before Solidarity existed, the youthful Michnik jeopardized his freedom to oppose the communist regime. When, in 1980, the entire nation rose up behind Solidarity, he assumed leadership and authority. And 18 months later, when General Wojciech Jaruzelski imposed martial law and outlawed Solidarity, Michnik sat in a prison cell. He wrote essays for the *New York Review of Books* that conveyed both the mean atmosphere of Poland under martial law and its undaunted spirit of hope and resistance.

Now, with communism fallen, Poland seemed like a blank slate. Michnik became involved in innumerable activities to put his country on a democratic course: Having helped select the leaders of Central Europe's first noncommunist parliament, he sat in the Polish Sejm and served as a leader of the powerful political movement Citizens' Movement for Democratic Action (ROAD), which had been started by the faction of Solidarity that grew out of the non-nationalist wing of the Opposition. Michnik was also an effective fundraiser and proved himself as an organizer not only of political action, but of institutions that had inescapably economic aspects, such as his newspaper.

Revered by Western intellectuals, Michnik met with dozens of visitors. In the early years of transformation, he became the darling of many Western foundations. Many resources went to support the projects of people in his circle. *Gazeta Wyborcza*, the first independent daily in Central and Eastern Europe, received grants from a number of Western sources, including a grant of $55,000 in 1989 from the U.S. government (through NED and the Polish American Congress Charitable Foundation).[35] Such sums went a very long way in Poland at the time.

Despite Michnik's talents and image in the West, not all of his countrymen were so admiring and impressed. At the same time he was writing essays celebrated in the West, some Polish critics said that he and those like him were building their careers on their reputations in and sponsorship from the West, and that the extensive contacts and support over the years gave them unfair advantages. Politicians outside what they perceived as the favored group, such as Piotr Wiśniewski of the Polish Socialist Party (PPS), a leftist party, were unhappy with this state of affairs. And Zbigniew Rykowski, associated with an opposing right-wing political group, characterized the Soros-created Stefan Batory Foundation as a "headquarters for ROAD."[36] Indeed, the Batory Foundation's board members were, for the most part, from the same circle and associated with business enterprises. As insider Irena Lasota herself acknowledged: "Let us not kid ourselves. Batory operates like a political party. It may be a very nice political party, with which many of us agree, but it is a political party nonetheless."[37] However, many of the critics of this circle were themselves vying for Western support.

The fact that NED financed selected political groups to the exclusion of others fed perceptions among some groups that the United States was playing partisan politics. In Poland's parliamentary election of 1991, for example, NED funded only the incumbent candidates, who already had an advantage because they had almost exclusive access to the government-owned television, radio, and press.[38] The political opposition was displeased with this. Vocal disagreement came from the ranks of the Confederacy of Independent Poland (KPN), the populist, nationalist, and traditionalist group that had participated in the formation of Solidarity and maintained some support from young workers, students, and small private businessmen. As a result of this and other funding decisions, KPN sent a spokesman to testify before a U.S.

congressional subcommittee in March 1990. In statements submitted in subcommittee hearings, KPN charged that:

> The idea to support democracy and pluralism is a very good one. But that has nothing to do with using NED funds to bolster leftist groups in Poland while the center and center-right groups receive no funds at all.[39]

A KPN spokesman further complained:

> The groups that emerged from the Communist Party and its allies and Solidarity have enormous resources and maintain an almost complete monopoly in the media while independent political parties that enjoy increasing popular support are denied resources or equal access to the media. . . . Leaving all the American assistance in the hand of one political orientation is not acceptable. It is as if in the United States all finances for political campaigns were given only to the Democratic Party, which would allocate or promise to allocate some money for the Republican Party.[40]

The pattern of providing funding to explicitly political parties and groups continued farther east. Between 1992 and 1997, USAID awarded NDI and NRI a combined sum of $17.4 million to conduct programs in Russia. From 1990 to 1992, these organizations used about $956,000 in NED funds to help the anticommunist Democratic Russia Movement establish a printing facility and disseminate literature. NDI and NRI also conducted civic education and grassroots organizing programs for Russians at the national and local levels. According to USAID, the purpose of the grants was to help reformist political parties strengthen their organizations and their role in elections, parliament, and local government.[41]

These cases reflect a larger pattern: in general, donors assisted Central and Eastern European groups associated with people whom the West identified with programs of market reform (such as that of Finance Minister Leszek Balcerowicz in Poland, where the most vocal alternatives to the Balcerowicz program were postcommunist or nationalistic populist programs). In other words, economic agendas appear to have been the decisive factor in many aid decisions said to be about democracy, pluralism, or civil society.

Significant differences characterized the structures within which aid was distributed in Central Europe, as compared with Russia. To begin with, although reform-oriented groups in Central Europe garnered much of the aid, they did not have a monopoly on it, in contrast to the Russian "clan" that we will observe in detail in chapter 4. *Moreover, very different institutional and legal frameworks developed in the 1990s in Russia as compared, for example, with Poland, where there is little evidence of criminal mafia infiltration in the political establishment, as there is in Russia.*[42] Polish recipients generally operated in a more transparent and accountable way, and their primary motivation was largely to build a political base, not self-enrichment, in contrast to some Russian recipients.

Still, citizens in Central Europe and Russia raised many of the same concerns, albeit often with different intensity. Although, from a donor's point of view, one can understand the homily that "helping someone is better than helping no one," the meddling in local politics that the "help" sometimes created puts the wisdom of this belief in doubt. Support of one group to the exclusion of others built up certain elites—indeed, helped to crystallize some in the first place. The groups with enough clout and Western contacts to get foreign money gained steadily, while others with just as much indigenous support but less visibility in the West—and, thus, less foreign monetary support—lost ground.

Arguably, this reality had both positive and negative aspects: On one hand, those supported by the West were sometimes the people best equipped to be leaders and make critical decisions. On the other hand, resentment was stirred up among those outside the networks—especially among those who would likely have been in leadership positions if people had been chosen primarily on the basis of expertise. This concentration on a select few contributed to resentment especially because the few beneficiaries tended to distribute money and favors based on group loyalties and obligations. For donors to overcome this dilemma would have required in-depth knowledge of the histories and politics of local groups—expertise they seldom sought or appreciated the value of.

Once again, then, Western donors seemed to be caught in a paradox: To achieve their stated reform goals (in this case, of pluralism, civil society, and democracy), they selected and promoted specific political parties and groups. But this strategy seemed more likely to help narrow, rather than to widen, the range of participation.

LEFT-OUT LOCALITIES

Throughout the region, the groups favored by most donors were typically located in large cities such as Budapest, Warsaw, Kraków, Gdańsk, and Prague, particularly in the immediate post-1989 aftermath. In the rush to move funds quickly in the first years of the aid effort, donors concentrated on cities that were centers of government, even when their projects had no link to government. Donors hoped that funds would "filter down" to the localities. However, without accountability and incentives for dispersal, funds typically stayed at the center.

Many local leaders, who had heard about and were eager to accept the massive foreign aid that was said to be on its way, did not view this development favorably. Tadeusz Wrona, mayor of the Polish city of Częstochowa, declared in April 1991 that foreign aid "should go to big towns and counties, not to [the] Warsaw government. . . . If it goes to Warsaw, nothing will get to us. . . . If there's to be real help from the West, you have to strengthen the counties. Because if the county goes bankrupt, we'll have to go back to the old centralized system." Nevertheless, prosperity was not far away, although not often as a result of foreign aid: During the 1990s, markets and business infrastructure developed very quickly in certain cities and areas (as described in chapter 5), including Częstochowa. The effects of these changes were soon felt in many of the smallest of towns and communities in Poland.

Some donors succeeded at providing decentralized aid. Germany, which shares borders with Poland and the Czech Republic and also is active in Hungary, took advantage of its proximity, knowledge of these countries, and issues of mutual interest to develop links and projects in an attempt to achieve influence in Central Europe. Much of Germany's aid to Central Europe went directly to the localities. In this model, aid flowed from one *land* (region) to another *land* with an emphasis on cross-border initiatives, especially between Germany and Poland. The point of departure, the delivery mechanisms, and the targets all were decentralized.[43] This *land* to *land* approach has earned a reputation for facilitating valuable cross-border cooperation in commercial and cultural exchange in many areas[44] and also has been employed farther east.

By the mid-1990s, the United States and the EU targeted much more aid to the localities. These donors invested in some projects, several of which dealt with business and infrastructure development (described in chapter 5), that effectively tapped into local knowledge and worked with the localities. Between 1994 and 1998, the EU committed 18 percent of all PHARE monies to cross-border cooperation between recipient countries and their adjacent EU neighbors and to addressing the development problems that they may face.[45] However, the instruction that might be gleaned from any effective projects was little considered farther east.

PARLOR POLITICS

A look at aid distribution in Central and Eastern Europe helps to explain why understanding the dynamics of the individual countries was so important and what happened when donors overlooked them.

The fall of communism had brought an "open historical situation"— a period of immense structural change, in which a new universe of possibilities suddenly comes into being—as historian Karl Wittfogel has termed it.[46] Such open moments encourage a free-for-all environment in which unclaimed resources and untapped opportunities are pursued. In the new East, those who were the most energetic, savvy, and, in some cases, unscrupulous were the most successful. Many others felt left behind as they watched their friends take advantage of opportunities. As an acquaintance expressed in 1995: "I feel that I'm on the dock and everyone else has taken off."

With much of the state bureaucracy still entrenched, but disoriented, and with many social institutions in disarray or being dismantled, certain elites were well placed to get whatever they wanted—from business monopolies to great advantages in privatization. Opportunities were sometimes fleeting: They opened up for weeks or months, only to close as someone cornered them, laws or other circumstances changed, or better opportunities came along. The ambitions and activities of the players were not curbed by rules and regulations, which often were nonexistent, unknown, unenforced, or simply ignored. Many prominent Central and Eastern Europeans—and equally as many of their less prominent brethren—could not be pegged simply as lawyers, businessmen, scholars, or consultants. They had their fingers in a kitchenful of pies and were adept at cultivating international contacts. Unlike in some Western countries, where control of much more of the political economy was settled and where professional differentiation and conflict-of-interest practices were highly developed, in the new East, those who legislated and implemented law were often those who regulated change and were responsible for monitoring abuse.

As discussed in chapter 2, some Polish government officials operated consulting firms that did business with their own ministries. For example, the deputy minister of privatization in the first two postcommunist governments (those of Tadeusz Mazowiecki and Jan Krzysztof Bielecki), who was responsible for joint ventures, at the same time owned a consulting firm that specialized in such ventures. According to sociologist Antoni Kamiński, "[a] distinctive mark of the post-Solidarity elite's rule was considerable tolerance of conflicts of interest."[47] And in a 1991 Polish banking scandal, speculators working with several state-owned Polish banks made off with hundreds of millions of dollars.[48]

Groups could wield extensive influence because of the *contexts* in which they were operating: where, to varying degrees, the rule of law was weakly established, "the rules were what you made them," and interpretation and enforcement of the law was subject to much manipulation. The differences in legal context in the nations of Central and Eastern Europe were not sufficiently appreciated by donors, and that lack of appreciation reduced the effectiveness of Western aid. Aid agencies involved in these environments also could fall victim to such practices.

Also underappreciated by donors was the communist upbringing of Eastern partners. Donors failed to understand that, in some Central European nations, especially those that donors considered aid priorities, a limited "civil society" had existed long before the fall of communism.[49] Central European dissidents had been only partly right about the absence of a civil society, as anthropologist Chris Hann has noted:

> I was, and remain, very sceptical of the way "society" was invoked by some "dissident" intellectuals and by various commentators outside the region to imply that Eastern European populations were united in their opposition to socialist governments. In this discourse, civil society is a slogan, reified as a collective, homogenised agent, combating a demonic state.[50]

Many Central European scholars and dissidents had seen a wide gap between "state" and "society."[51] Polish sociologist Stefan Nowak developed this argument in his theory of the "social vacuum." Nowak's theory conceived of postwar Poland as an "atomized" society, its mediating institutions destroyed by war and imposed revolution. Family endured in harsh dichotomy to the state; an overgrown public sphere pressed heavily against the private. People collided with rigid institutions. Nowak evoked this vision in a single dictum: "The lowest level is the family, and perhaps the social circle. The highest is the nation . . . and in the middle is a social vacuum."[52]

However, Nowak and his followers overlooked the degree to which their societies had evolved alternative institutions; this fact fit neither Western nor Eastern models. If Nowak were correct and there was no middle ground, it is difficult to imagine how bureaucratic systems, totally divorced from the community they allegedly served, could function at all, as clearly they did. In Central and Eastern European societies, many of the most vital institutions were intentionally nonpublic and insubstantial. The Nowak model overlooked the labyrinth of channels through which deals and exchanges were made, both between people as "themselves"— private individuals—and as representatives of economic, political, and social institutions. This complex system of informal relationships, involving personalized patron-client contacts and lateral networks, pervaded the official economy and bureaucracy and connected them to the social circle. Although not explicitly institutional, these relationships exhibited clear patterns.[53]

Under communism, the sudden and massive social changes throughout the region, notably the huge urbanization of the peasantry, contributed to the erosion of social norms. People became adept at operating in a twilight world of nods and winks, in which what counted was not formalized agreement but dependable complicity. Where organizing outside of state bodies was banned, people who dared to undertake such activities did so as part of a close-knit circle of some kind, in which enduring relationships, frequent contact, and the ability to verify reputation made trust a critical component.[54] In the Polish case, this was the social circle, or *środowisko* (among intelligentsia often called *salons),* a trusted group of friends forged through family and social background. Members of the same parlor mixed socializing with politicking. Anthropologist Jeremy Boissevain has described such groups as "cliques," made up of dense[55] and multiplex[56] networks whose members have a common identity.[57] (Clique in this social anthropological meaning should not be confused with the Polish or Russian *klika,* which has very pejorative meaning.) Boissevain has noted that the clique has both an objective existence, in that "it forms a cluster of persons all of whom are linked to each other," and a subjective one, "for members as well as nonmembers are conscious of its common identity." Members of these publicly informal but internally rigorous elite circles worked together for years and developed intricate, efficient, and undeclared networks to get things done in the face of dangers and difficulties that intensify bonds. Civil society in the 1990s would, by definition, arise from—or at least against the backdrop of—those well-established relationships and organizational capacities.

FROM COMMUNISM TO CIVIL SOCIETY?

In the late 1980s, as Central and Eastern European states weakened and exerted less control over organizations independent of them, there was an outburst of activities that challenged the state and its restrictions—especially in Poland and Hungary, the nations most tolerant of such activities. Although little organizing outside the state was officially permitted, even before the political revolutions of fall 1989, starting an organization or business had become a ticket to success in Poland.[58] As communism began to loosen its reins, some noncommunist elites began to create voluntary associations that were illegal, but sometimes tolerated, for purposes ranging from improved housing and environment to halting the construction of nuclear power plants.

Through "social self-organization," these new standard-bearers of civil society sought to revive long-suppressed civic values and grassroots organizations. But organizing itself was often more important than a group's stated purpose: The very act of bringing together like-minded colleagues and drafting a manifesto was sometimes the most essential activity of a group's entire history. Although most of these groups were not explicitly political, their very founding was a political statement in countries that, at best, shakily tolerated them.[59]

In 1989, members of these elite cliques emerged to direct their energies simultaneously into a number of arenas, including business, government, the international domain, and also politics. Because the groups operated in many arenas beyond the political, it was misleading to assume that they were just another form of interest group, faction, or coalition—conventional categories often used in the fields of comparative politics, public administration, and sociology. The potential influence of the clique was much more widespread and monopolistic than that of interest groups, factions, or coalitions. Cliques served to mediate between the state and private sectors, as well as between bureaucracy and private enterprise. Ill-equipped to deal with such a phenomenon, conventional social science could not sufficiently explain the role of cliques in changing state-private and political-administrative relations.[60]

Another feature of these cliques—and another departure from conventional models—is that they, not the individual, typically chose how to respond to new opportunities. Economists usually consider individuals as the primary unit of response to economic opportunities, but in the new East, the more correct unit of analysis of response to economic incentives was often the clique. Operating as part of a strategic alliance enabled the clique's members to survive and thrive in an environment of uncertainty.

With crumbling states and weak institutions, Central and Eastern European cliques had wide latitude and few restraints. They tended to pursue their own agendas, regardless of their connections to formal institutions. They were "institutional nomads," because circumstances demanded loyalty to the group but not necessarily to the formal institutions with which the members of the group were associated.[61] For example, a civil servant (dependent on the tenure of a specific political leadership, if not actually brought in or bought by it) was typically more loyal to his or her clique than to some weak "office." Another result of this state of affairs was that resources and decision making in economic, political, and social spheres tended to be concentrated in just a few hands.

Like the "big men" of Melanesia, whose position depends on their ability to maintain personal prestige and the prestige of the group, figures such as Adam Michnik were larger-than-life institutions in themselves. Their standing did not stem so much from formal authority or title, but from abiding informal authority and reputation. They were more than the sum of their titles, and special access to Western aid compounded the advantages. Just as Melanesian big men accumulate wealth and regularly hold feasts and shower lavish gifts upon their less eminent tribesmen, Central and Eastern European big men were expected by those in their circles to carry out certain duties, among them giving to those less privileged. They offered their members perks such as Western contacts and business clients and trips abroad sponsored by Western foundations. This arrangement enhanced the clout, internal political standing, and symbolic capital of the privileged men, which in turn served to enhance their reputations in the West. Naturally, those who were indebted to these men also sang their praises abroad and reinforced their authority and mystique. It was a self-fulfilling and self-perpetuating cycle.

The initiatives of the big men were often more informed by politics than the donors expected. Western funding reinforced the ability of certain influential groups to shape all aspects of economy, politics, and society, undeterred by the rule of law. What did this portend for the efforts of Western donors, whose stated goal was to encourage the development of a civil society? Because many funds went to groups that were exclusive, informal, de facto political clubs, they helped to reinforce the clubs rather than to widen political participation or to "build democratic institutions." Some funds empowered entrenched political and economic cliques and power brokers, in some cases undercutting legitimate state institutions and governance.

A critical civil society question concerns the capacity of these groups to expand beyond their originating circles. Would they remain exclusive or would they attract new members on the basis of common interests? Under communism, the groups and networks that made up "civil society" were, by their very creation, making a political statement. After the collapse of communism, "the public domain underwent a rapid bifurcation," as Grzegorz Ekiert and Jan Kubik describe it: "Two *separate* (at least in Poland) domains emerged: a *vibrant and growing* domain of civic associations and organizations and a more *torpid and elitist* domain of political parties and 'political' interest groups."[62]

Generally, voluntary associations and political movements form themselves around new leaders, issues, and interests, rather than around long-established relationships. Several social scientists point to the restricted capacity of voluntary associations to expand beyond their originating circles, a contention borne out by the behavior of many Central and Eastern European groups.[63] Although their inability to expand limited the creation of a more extensive civil society, organizing around common interests continued to evolve, at least in some contexts.

The case of Poland, which before the fall of communism probably had the region's most advanced "civil society," albeit based on deep-rooted associations, suggests that building a civil society based on common interests was not so easily accomplished. In the early 1990s, there was little apparent coalition building among social circles; the creation of coalition movements with national political goals seemed especially difficult. Some circles were made up of members of the old communist establishment; others comprised members of the old anticommunist one, such as the Solidarity activists drawn from Poland's intelligentsia-Opposition establishment. There was much antagonism among the latter: The divisions within Solidarity-Opposition[64] were especially visible following the deep social conflicts among circles that surfaced during the presidential campaign of late 1990. The Warsaw-Kraków Opposition circle (from which was largely drawn the government of Prime Minister Mazowiecki) confronted Solidarity leader Lech Wałęsa, and his followers in a bitter *social* conflict that smoldered long after the election.

Scant research has been done thus far on coalition building in the region and emerging patterns of social organization. However, there is little in the legacies of communism and of the fragmented nature of postcommunist political systems to suggest that significant capacities for coalition building among cliques developed in the 1990s in many Central and Eastern European settings. In Russia, for example, nearly $1 million in U.S. funding from NDI and NRI to support "reformist" political parties yielded few results, according to the GAO: "Despite the institutes' work, reformist parties have been either unwilling or unable to form broad-based coalitions or build national organizations and large segments of the Russian public have not been receptive to their political message."[65] Anthropologist Hann rightly determines that, despite multiparty elections and robust promotion of market-oriented economic policies, "it has not been easy to establish the rich network of associations outside of the state that comprises the essence of the romanticized western model of civil society."[66] Political scientists Ekiert and Kubik likewise conclude that "the postcommunist civil society represents a complex amalgam of old and new organizations and is often characterized by considerable fragmentation and political divisions."[67]

NGO SPEAK

By the time the Iron Curtain parted and exposed private groups to the West, the development community had been supporting NGOs for about a decade.[68] NGOs were, as Sampson has noted, "creatures of the global community of democratic rhetoric, of human rights, of grants, conferences, lobbies and politics, which characterizes East-West relations generally."[69] A recent Carnegie Endowment-sponsored study of foreign-funded NGOs in Central and Eastern Europe and the former Soviet Union found that "local groups proliferated in Poland, Hungary, Russia, Kazakhstan, Uzbekistan, and Kyrgyzstan often around issues that Western donors found important, but rarely around issues that locals confronted on a daily basis."[70]

The philosophy underlying the NGO movement held that recipient groups could do all sorts of good things that traditional projects attempting "development" through governments could not: build community capacity, propose solutions to local problems, and provide a social safety net. And so NGOs became a doubly attractive opportunity for donors. NGOs were a special favorite of the United States, with its emphasis on funding the "private" sectors of Central and Eastern Europe.

Amid the drive to create NGOs, however, donors often lost sight of the extent to which NGOs, like "civil society," represent *models,* that is, ideal representations of how things ought to work. Sampson has observed that "as models, they do not actually operate that way in those countries which are exporting them."[71] The same appears to be true in the countries to which NGOs are exported. The Carnegie Endowment-sponsored study concluded that "Western NGOs have played a large and important role in the *design* and *building* of institutions associated with democratic states. These same strategies used by NGOs, however, have had minimal impact on how these new institutions actually *function.*"[72] A popular handbook for Russian environmental groups translated concepts such as strategic planning, fundraising, and press releases as "strategicheskoe planirovanie," "fandraizing," and "press-relizy," an indication of their alien nature.[73]

Part of the problem was that the NGOs exported by the donors were frequently at odds with Second World legacies. Whether their ostensible purpose was social welfare, election education, or improvement of environmental conditions, NGOs were seen as furthering "transition," or at least as being important by-products of these other endeavors. This interpretation assumed that the emerging NGOs were similar to their Western counterparts, despite the very different conditions under which they developed and operated. But many of the donors' assumptions about how NGOs would operate and what they would contribute were inaccurate in the new contexts. "Voluntary," "private," and "philanthropic" initiatives were permeated by the market and politics. NGOs could play productive roles, but they were not necessarily equipped to be the building blocks of democracy that the donors envisioned.

Even the vocabulary used to describe the concept of NGOs, usually adopted from English, was confused in the context of Central and Eastern Europe. "Third sector," "independent sector," "private voluntary sector," "nonprofit sector," "charitable organization," and "foundation," defined in varying ways even in the West, all were mouthed by Eastern counterparts, often with only the vaguest notions of their meanings and of the legal-regulatory regimes from which they sprang. Jakub Wygnański, a sociologist and expert on Central European NGOs, has observed a "lack of communication" between East and West in which people used the same terms to mean different things.[74]

For instance, NGOs in Central Europe generally incorporated themselves as either foundations or associations. Registering as a foundation typically provided more favorable legal and tax advantages than registering as an association. Foundations were usually service-providing groups that did not give grants (as they would have in the West), but raised money in order to carry out activities themselves. Foundations encompassed a number of types of organizations, including larger and more stable NGOs and the region's few grant-making organizations. On the other hand, most small, grassroots-oriented NGOs organized around common interests were registered as associations.[75] By 2000, in Poland, for example, there were more than 5,000 foundations and some 21,000 associations.[76]

The Support for East European Democracy (SEED) legislation of 1989, which authorized millions of dollars to the region to "promote the private sector [and] democratic pluralism," specified that funds should go only to private entities in Central and Eastern Europe. But at the time the donors arrived, institutional arrangements between private and state sectors were shifting. Given the complex (and diverse) interrelationships of state, private, and civil societies that had emerged in the region, there was evidence to suggest that these relationships would eventually take a different shape from those generally familiar to donors. The donors' faith in the private sector also appeared simplistic in light of the complex and diverse state-private institutional arrangements that Western democracies themselves had developed. (For example, most American and British NGOs, although "private," receive some governmental funding.)[77] Given the fact that the state remained a major source of resources, demarcation between private and governmental organizations was often obscure.

As many different forms of ownership emerged in the latter days of communism, state employees such as managers "acquired" state enterprises or portions thereof, all the while maintaining some relationship with the state. After 1989, private-state institutional arrangements built on, and further developed, this model. For example, some Hungarian and Polish officials interested in attracting Western funds earmarked for NGOs had little trouble bypassing the private-sector requirement. They started "nonprofit" organizations attached to their state agencies. While state employees actually received the money, it still could be categorized as going to the private sector.

Even in Poland, which has enjoyed some success in its economic reforms, ambiguous state-private relationships appear to be institutionalized. Since 1989, legislative initiatives have enabled the creation of corporate, profitmaking bodies, which are formally nongovernmental but that use state resources and "rely on the coercive powers of the state administration," as sociologist Kamiński has analyzed it.[78] These bodies make it legally possible for private groups and institutions to appropriate public resources to themselves "through the spread of political corruption." Kamiński elaborates:

> One way of obliterating the distinction between public and private consists in the creation of autonomous institutions, "foundations" or "agencies" of unclear status, with broad prerogatives supported by administrative sanctions, and limited public accountability. The real aim of these institutions is to transfer public means to private individuals or organisations or to create funds within the public sector which can then be intercepted by the initiating parties.[79]

These state-private entities, lying somewhere between the state and the private sector,[80] are enshrouded in ambiguity. They are part and parcel of the "privatization of the functions of the state," as Piotr Kownacki, deputy director of NIK, the Polish government's chief auditing agency, puts it, and they represent "areas of the state in which the state is responsible but has no control."[81] The entities' "undefined functions and responsibilities" are a defining characteristic, as Kamiński explains: "From the government's point of view, [these entities] have the legal status of private bodies, whereas from the point of view of the collectives controlled by these bodies, these are public institutions."[82]

Given such institutional arrangements, then, it is not surprising that Central and Eastern E uropean NGOs often distributed Western perks to themselves and their peers on the basis of favoritism rather than merit. Those charged by the West with public outreach were often not equipped for that role.

Another important variance between Western NGO models and Eastern realities was the difference in attitudes and practices concerning trust in the workplace, especially in the early days of "transition." Central and Eastern European groups often were unwilling to share information or otherwise cooperate with anyone who had not reached the status of personal friend. Sampson observes that "Westerners seem to be able to cooperate successfully even when they do not know each other at all, and in spite of having diverse political opinions, lifestyles and tastes. Put another way, work colleagues in the West can work well together on the job without ever becoming friends." This ability to cooperate contrasted with the Eastern European NGOs he has observed, in which deep-rooted trust was a prerequisite to being able to work together. Along these lines, anthropologist Marta Bruno has observed the following:

> The practice of bringing together in a workshop different groups of recipients who do not know each other can also have a boomerang effect. Individuals in post-socialist societies still tend to privilege those social relations determined exclusively through personal connections. Strangers are to be trusted only if they are linked by a common acquaintance who is also trustworthy. This system operates as much in the public and work spheres as it does in the private one. Unless western project workers have good and close personal relations with the recipients and therefore can serve as a guarantee of trustworthiness, it can be counterproductive to bring together previously unacquainted recipients. Given the usually limited amount of resources of aid projects, other recipients are seen as undesirable competition and the dominant attitude is one of suspicion. Furthermore, intricate cultural attitudes stemming from ethnic, social and gender stratification may also come into play and reinforce negative reciprocal feelings. These frameworks of social relations usually escape Westerners' sensibili-

ties, unless they are project workers with extensive knowledge of local cultures.[83]

Sampson adds that, to be successful in the new environment, NGOs had "to start realizing that the essence of democracy is not cultivating friends but 'doing business' with allies. This doing business is part of civil society in the market sense. Even market competitors who hate each other—mafia gangs, for example—can often find a common interest to do business together."[84]

In the absence of sophisticated, well-conceived incentives on the part of donors to help build bridges among recipient groups, funding frequently inspired competition among groups, rather than cooperation, and served to reinforce existing hierarchies. Bruno has written that "Russians have accepted the 'given' of international aid and co-operation projects (whether wanted or not) and are weaving them into the complex system of patronage, social relations and survival strategies which are taking shape in post-socialist Russian reality. . . . Presumably involuntarily, donor agencies are offering, through development projects, new sources for reinforcing the elitist, feudal-type system of social stratification."[85]

Anthropologist Hann has likewise concluded: "The focus [on NGOs] has tended to restrict funding to fairly narrow groups, typically intellectual elites concentrated in capital cities. Those who succeed in establishing good relations with a western organisation manoeuvre to retain the tremendous advantage this gives them. The effect of many foreign interventions is therefore to accentuate previous hierarchies, where almost everything depends on patronage and personal connections."[86]

Another effect arises from dependence on foreign funding. With the outside donor as chief constituent, local NGOs are sometimes more firmly rooted in transnational networks than in their own societies. The Carnegie Endowment-sponsored study cited earlier noted that the dependence of local NGOs on Western assistance "often forces them to be more responsive to outside donors than to their internal constituencies. . . . Their dependence has the unintended consequence of removing incentives to mobilize new members and of fostering interorganizational competition for grants that breeds mistrust, bitterness, and secrecy within and between organizations."[87]

And so, while neglecting groups with laudatory goals and indigenous support, donors sometimes funded organizations that were not operating in the public interest, especially in the initial period of East-West contact.

THE GREEN JET SET

A case in point was the Regional Environmental Center. In 1989-90, Western donors targeted the environment as a top funding priority, not only for the well-being of Central and Eastern Europe but also for the benefit of Western Europe, which was near enough to be damaged by its neighbors' nuclear power plants, acid rain, or polluted waterways. So Western funders, especially foundations and bilateral donors, supported the environmental movement, largely by funding NGOs both directly and indirectly.

The antecedents of the environmental movement were Hungary's Danube Circle, Czechoslovakia's Green Circle, and other groups in the region that had challenged communism as they fought for environmental causes. Strongest from 1986 to 1989, the "environmental movement" included many people who used it as a means to engage in activities against or outside the state.

Given the movement's multipurpose nature, it was natural that, once communism fell, many of those previously involved in the movement, who now could pursue other endeavors unconstrained, abandoned it to do just that. A wave of environmentalists—leaders of the region's environmental organizations—stepped into key government posts in Central Europe. There, many abandoned environmental concerns in the name of budget cuts and helped to institute the shock therapy and other austerity measures of the day.

Meanwhile, the Western environmental and aid communities underwrote the region's elite environmentalists. In 1990, Austria, Canada, Denmark, the EU, Finland, Japan, the Netherlands, Norway, and the United States donated some $20 million to the Regional Environmental Center, housed in a charming old silk mill in Budapest. Created as a result of the SEED legislation, the center had been conceived as a catalyst for activity throughout the entire region and attracted considerable donor resources. Its mandate was to develop institutional capabilities and outreach programs and to promote public awareness and participation.

Under the leadership of Executive Director Peter Hardi, a former communist, the center had weak links to the Hungarian government as well as to the region's governmental bodies and environmental ministries. "An institution to give out money," the Center awarded grants in ways that "divided the NGO community," as István Tökés, an official in the Hungarian Ministry of the Environment, explained.[88] Having virtually no agenda of its own, the Center disbursed money to favored environmental groups throughout the region, which were supposed to conduct studies and public outreach activities. Elena Petkova, a former board member of the Center, confirms that Hardi "failed to support any kind of mechanism to make grants competitive. He didn't try to build capacity and there was no transparency. People got grants if they knew him or someone on the board."[89] Consequently, the Center fulfilled little of its public outreach mission, especially in its initial years.

In a setting in which there was little precedent for making information available to citizens, either for free or at all, the aid-funded environmental NGOs responsible for gathering and disseminating environmental information to the public often guarded the information they acquired and made it available only at a price. With resources in short supply, organizations and individuals tended to use the money and perks they received to broaden their own opportunities and enhance their résumés, rather than to develop environmental policy or support clean-up activities. It was hardly a step toward the civil society that donors thought they were underwriting.

This state of affairs was mirrored in the environmental ministries and institutes. State-run agencies that had been massively subsidized in the old system suddenly lost their funding or saw it dramatically cut. Their chief resources became their databases, such as geographical survey or monitoring information. In some scenarios, one branch of government sold to another.

Given the competitive atmosphere, it was not surprising that the NGOs often declined to share information and advantages with others and conducted little outreach. A few "environmentalists" spent their time on the international conference circuit, largely working their own contacts and opportunities. One Hungarian environmentalist spoke of herself and her colleagues as the "green jet set."[90] Moreover, according to the GAO, the Regional Environmental Center's "early operations suffered from financial management and programmatic weakness."[91] As a result,

USAID withheld approximately $1.4 million, about one-third of U.S. funding to the Center, until evidence could be provided that its operations had been improved,[92] and Director Hardi resigned after being asked to leave by the donors.[93]

Given the fact that U.S. aid's main job was to sign up projects and contractors and "to get the money out the door"—and there was considerable pressure from multiple sides to do so—intervention in problematic projects and admissions of failure were unusual. Consciously or unconsciously, project officers had incentives to go along with contractors and collude in the process. But U.S. aid officials took the uncommon step of trying to reorient the Center, an indication of the gravity of its problems. Following a financial and management audit in 1992, the Center was radically reorganized. With donors and recipients working together, the Center's management and financial practices, program direction, and criteria for giving grants to NGOs all were revamped, a finding that the GAO independently confirmed.[94]

Although the Regional Environmental Center failed initially to achieve the ambitious goal the donors had set of becoming a catalyst for environmental activism, the situation had changed substantially by mid-decade. Eventually both donors and recipients emphasized the need to fund NGOs with more indigenous public support and with track records that could be verified.[95] The earlier heavy-handed and top-down approach involved, on the recipient side, elites who knew English and had quickly learned how to write grant proposals. But by 1993, there began to be more of a "bottom-up" approach, especially to assistance provided by foundations.

Under the able leadership of Stanisław Sitnicki, a Polish scholar and environmentalist who took over the Center in 1993, and Jernej Stritih, a Slovenian who assumed control in 1996, local projects expanded. Sitnicki and Stritih involved more local people and field officers throughout Central Europe. They set up operations in Romania, Bulgaria, and other so-called second-tier countries, trained local people to serve as the directors of, and staff for, these newly established field offices, and located grassroots groups that wished to become involved in a larger network.

Under its new leadership, the Regional Environmental Center moved from merely providing money to initiating projects and policies. The Center began conducting policy research and bringing together people who were participating in regional policy issues, such as the United

Nations Economic Commission for Europe (UNECE) Convention on Public Participation in Environmental Decision-Making. The Center also became a player in regional processes such as harmonization for EU expansion.

In the same spirit, the Environmental Partnership for Central Europe, under the leadership of the German Marshall Fund, pooled the resources of several foundations (notably the German Marshall Fund, the Rockefeller Brothers Fund, and the Charles Stewart Mott Foundation) to "encourage NGOs to get started and to participate around environmental problems in their communities," according to Marianne Ginsberg, coordinator of the Partnership.[96] In 2000, the Partnership still awarded grants, "but not just to create local initiatives, but to have a strategy in transportation, the right to know, energy issues, nature conservation, and land-use issues." EU accession, and its likely impact on local environments, was a major thrust.[97] Miroslav Kundrata, country director of the Czech office of the Partnership since 1994, has detailed some of the changes in the Western-funded business of NGO environmental grantsmanship:

> The Partnership's own knowledge and skills have developed. . . . In a relatively short time, we have gone from reacting to grant proposals to initiating them. We are becoming less dependent on our Western advisors, particularly the U.S. Support Office, in running an effective, well-managed foundation. Along with this growing independence has come a realization that we hold our future in our own hands, and that the projects we support are capable of contributing to change.[98]

In this way, the changes in the Regional Environmental Center during the 1990s exemplify the evolution of many NGOs through the periods of Triumphalism, Disillusionment, and Adjustment.

AFTER ADVERSITY

The first few years of "transition" in Central Europe were not long in terms of time, but they loomed large in symbolic and psychological terms. Just as the euphoria and optimism of the phase of Triumphalism were great, so was the heavy despondency of Disillusionment. Eventually the disappointment gave way to more clear-eyed agendas and grounded expectations on the part of both East and West.

By 1994, the luster of the words "civil society" had dimmed. With that, some adjustment on the part of donors occurred with regard to their support of specific elites. Although most aid went to the national centers and was explicitly or inexplicitly political, aid sometimes helped to encourage grassroots development and decentralization of NGOs and the building of institutional infrastructure for local and national governments. As regional and local leaders became more effective lobbyists, and as donors became more experienced, pressure mounted to go outside the capitals and major cities. In time, local leaders began to receive somewhat more of the aid. And, in response to protest from Central Europe, by 1994 the United States stopped funding explicitly political groups in the Visegrád countries.

In time, some overall positive results came out of the NGO sector in Central Europe. In Poland, for example, an entire NGO-support industry has emerged: The Forum of Nongovernmental Initiatives (FIP), an informal coalition of Polish NGOs, was created in 1993, and the Network of Information and Support Center for Non-Governmental Organizations (SPLOT), in 1994.[99]

Less than a decade after the collapse of communism in Central Europe, NGOs appeared to have defined their identities more precisely as NGOs and were more inclined than previously to differentiate between their interests and those of business or the state. The "we-versus-they" approach inherited from the communist past, in which civil society was, by definition, the antagonist of the state and the representative and proponent of society, had diminished, and Polish NGOs now worked to build bridges in business and in Parliament. In a productive attempt to connect with the business sector, FIP created a "benefactor of the year" award, given to businesses for philanthropic contributions on the basis of innovation, staff involvement, amount of money, and sustained effort.[100] NGO expert Wygnański explained that "people are grasping these sectors as separate things, but connected." The donors, simply by being there, helped this process. They offered NGOs time and opportunities to identify themselves—to discover "who they were"—and to find their own way in the new contexts.

Further, the degree to which Central European NGOs conducted public outreach also changed somewhat. Wygnański has noted that, "at the beginning people were very much in need since social policy was such a disaster. Now more and more associations and foundations are being organized to help or support others."[101] An example of this is Polish Humanitarian Action, which sent convoys of relief supplies to war-torn former Yugoslavia and Chechnya. Although the organizing principle of such groups largely remained abiding relationships, people also had more access to, and were more trusting of, information provided by the media, independently of their personal contacts. The Polish media provided much information about NGOs: From 1993 to 1999, more than 19,000 articles on the subject appeared in the press. Polish Humanitarian Action, for example, received considerable attention. Wygnański relates that now, "They [Polish Humanitarian Action] don't have to look for people; people look for them."[102]

An important change in the aid process over time was the ways in which Western aid-funded organizations changed the rules of the game by introducing new processes and procedures. Jay Austin, a senior attorney and co-director of the Environmental Program for Central and Eastern Europe at the Washington-based Environmental Law Institute, with support from USAID and American foundations, worked with environmental and legal organizations in Central and Eastern Europe. "By coming in with our own set of rules," he notes, "we're in essence elevating the set of people that have skills appropriate to those goals, even if those aren't the right goals. . . . You create a process. Elevating a class of English-speaking people who can absorb enough buzzwords from an RFP [Request for Proposals] in order to put together something that looks like a Western budget may or may not be the kind of people that we'd like to most encourage in the environmental sector." In subtly changing the rules, donors also changed the politics.[103]

Aid profoundly shaped the kinds of standards that were set for management, accountability, disbursing monies, and transparency. By the mid-1990s, many NGOs were publishing their findings and their sources of funding. The Polish FIP even ran a campaign in the summer of 1998 under the slogan "Be transparent: publish an annual report," to encourage NGOs to disclose their financial and program activities.[104]

Aid-funded exchange and training eventually played an important and positive role in setting standards of transparency and teaching management skills. Aid offered many training opportunities, which gave Central European NGOs exposure that they could use on their own terms.

Even if the source of funds was or became local government, many NGO leaders and participants were trained under Western funding.

People-to-people contact was especially important. Part of the operations of many Western NGOs involved long-term, ongoing relationships and intensive exchange over a host of issues. Unlike the short-term, fly-in, fly-out consultants bearing advice, this continuous people-to-people exchange appears to have had a significant cumulative impact on the operations and positive work of NGOs.

Another important change was that donors, through their funding decisions, in time encouraged, sometimes successfully, collaboration among groups and governments in the East. The Regional Environmental Center and the Environmental Partnership developed considerable cooperative networks and projects in the East under the eye of Western donors.[105] The Soros-created Stefan Batory Foundation funded Polish NGOs to work together with Central European, Balkan, Ukrainian, Russian, Baltic, and Central Asian NGOs on projects ranging from ecology and cultural events to the development of special education programs and the training of local government officials.[106] And the United States, Poland, and Ukraine launched a trilateral initiative to facilitate cooperation between Poland and Ukraine, especially the sharing of expertise acquired in Poland's reform experience with its eastern neighbor.[107]

In Central Europe, as the new century approached, the days of simple acceptance or simple rejection of "the West" had long faded. Citizens actively debated the desired place of Western models. Aid-funded training provided to NGOs had been organized around American values, even when "training the trainers" was conducted by Central Europeans (who often had been trained by Americans). Much of the language used in conjunction with nonprofit organizations was American, even in cases in which Central European words would have sufficed. For example, the Polish NGO community spoke about "wolontariusze" (volunteers), while an indigenous word, *ochotnicy,* could have served just as well. By 1998, Polish NGOs had spurned the idea that they should simply adopt Western practices and vocabularies and had begun to discuss just how they should fit American NGO designs into the Polish context. NGOs were, as Wygnański relates, engaged in "debate about how to build the NGO sector in Poland and how to find language and symbols for the sector in the Polish framework."[108] "The whole question," he says, "is whether there has been a transfer of knowledge and skills. The first challenge is whether we can survive on our own without Western funding. The second is if we can be helpful in transferring our experiences and be used as a bridging vehicle between East and West."[109]

What would have been the alternative to the early years of donor misadventure? The assumption often underlying this question, common in the donor community, was that there were no alternatives, that any alternatives were undesirable or untenable, or that, in any event, one had to choose just a few partners. This assumption was used to justify the donors' concentration on a few elite groups and players. But there almost always were alternatives to the particular elite groups and brokers who had been especially adept at cultivating Western contacts and partners and who had received the bulk of the rewards. These alternatives—other individuals and groups—were often no less, and sometimes even more, talented than those that had been selected. The problem was not that donors had selected the wrong people, but that the funding of almost any group affected internal politics, the intricacies of which outsiders usually did not comprehend.

Finding the less vocal people was not easy. Given the prior isolation of donors and recipients, it was a process that had to take time. Still, the challenge was in enlisting the expertise of people sufficiently intuitive, informed, and committed to donor efforts in the new environment and in designing aid to foster these efforts. Nowhere would this be the case more than in Russia—and nowhere with more dire consequences.

CHAPTER FOUR

A Few Good Reformers:
The Chubais Clan, Harvard, and
"Economic" Aid*

The story . . . begins . . . when an idealistic, but pragmatic "St. Petersburg mafia" of young economists led by Mr. [Anatoly] Chubais . . . infiltrated the power structure in Moscow. . . . It is the story of how a modest amount of funding from the United States Agency for International Development enabled a handful of bright kids from Harvard and a few dozen middle-aged pros from Wall Street to help the Russian privatization agency begin to build the regulatory framework and trading infrastructure necessary to develop the new securities market.

—Briefing paper prepared for USAID
by the "Harvard Project," the chief conduit
of U.S. economic aid to Russia[1]

THE DISSOLUTION OF THE SOVIET UNION in December 1991 and the end of the Cold War paved the way for the aid story to move east. The West began a repeat performance of its efforts in Central and Eastern Europe: International lending institutions and the foreign aid community

---

* See Appendix 4 for a list of the players and the institutions, organizations, and commissions that figure prominently in this story, and a chart of institutional relationships compiled by the United States General Accounting Office.

pressed for economic reform and the privatization of state-owned resources; donors promised billions of dollars in aid to the former Soviet republics. Many aid programs set up in Central and Eastern Europe were transported to Russia and the other former republics; a host of Western consultants moved with them. By 1994, aid to Russia was in full swing.[2]

It had been damaging enough when Western donors selected a few groups in Central and Eastern Europe to receive aid, especially when the donors barely knew whom they were supporting. But in Russia (and later Ukraine), major donors—particularly the United States—took this approach to an extreme. The United States placed its economic reform portfolio—set up to help engineer the enormous shift from a command economy to free markets—into the hands of a single group of self-styled Russian "reformers." From 1992, when aid first appeared, through much of the decade, U.S. economic aid to Russia was entrusted to these men, who were dominated by a long-standing group of friends from St. Petersburg that Russians called a "clan" (here referred to as the "St. Petersburg Clan" or the "Chubais Clan," after its leader, Anatoly Chubais). This Clan worked closely with Harvard University's Institute for International Development (HIID) and its associates to establish and run a Moscow-based program that leveraged U.S. support. The program served as the gatekeeper for hundreds of millions of dollars in U.S. Agency for International Development (USAID) and G-7 taxpayer aid, subsidized loans, and other Western funds and was known simply as the Harvard Project.[3]

The Clan came to control, directly and indirectly, millions of dollars in aid through a variety of organizations that were set up to bring about privatization, legal reform, the development of capital markets, a securities and exchange commission, and other economic reforms.[4] Through these organizations, two Clan members alone became the gatekeepers for hundreds of millions of dollars in aid money and loans from international financial institutions. U.S. support also helped to propel Clan members into top positions in the Russian government and to make them formidable players in local politics and economics. U.S. support bolstered the Clan's standing as Russia's chief brokers with the West and the international financial institutions. The aid seemed to yield results, notably the transfer of a large number of state-owned companies to "private" ownership.

But was economic reform the driving agenda of the Chubais Clan? And what made it deserve the status of partner with the West more than other Russian reform groups? More important, did the strategy of focusing largely on one group further the aid community's stated goal of establishing the transparent, accountable institutions so critical to the development of democracy and a stable economy for this world power in transition? As in Central Europe, what were the long-term implications in Russia of supporting one group of reformers at the expense of others? From the very beginning, Russian observers took note of the activities and motivations of the Chubais Clan. But it would not be until the late 1990s—and the eruption of a scandal that could hardly be ignored—that many Western observers would begin to consider the implications of U.S. and Western policy and what it had wrought.

THE FORGING OF THE HARVARD—ST. PETERSBURG PARTNERSHIP

In the late summer and fall of 1991, as the vast Soviet state was collapsing, Harvard professor Jeffrey Sachs and other Western economists participated in meetings at a dacha outside Moscow where young "reformers" planned Russia's economic and political future. Boris Yeltsin, then in the leadership and undermining Mikhail Gorbachev and the Soviet Union (which would break up by year's end), was building his teams of advisers—and the men from St. Petersburg were to figure prominently in that team. Their vital Western contacts distinguished them from other groups looking to have a hand in shaping Russia's economic policy.

It was the springtime of East-West courtship. Russia seemed a blank slate ready for reform; dramatic change was in the air. The West fell in love with the new faces cast from its own ideological mold, and this cadre of "reformers" assumed the role that the West had created for them. They promised quick, all-encompassing change that would remake Russia in the Western image and eliminate the vestiges of communism.

At the dacha, Sachs and several other Westerners, some of whom were senior members in a project paid to Sachs's consulting firm, Jeffrey D. Sachs and Associates, Inc.,[5] offered their services and access to Western money. They would provide the theory and advice to reinvent the Russian economy. The key Russians present were Yegor Gaidar, the first "architect" of economic reform, and Anatoly Chubais, who was part of Gaidar's team and later would replace him as the "economic reform czar." Individual Russians paired off with their Western counterparts to work on economic policy. Chubais, with his savvy, American self-starting style, found common ground with Andrei Shleifer, a Russian-born émigré who, still in his early 30s, had climbed to the pinnacle of academic success in America as a tenured professor of economics at Harvard and who served as a senior member in Sachs's consulting project named above. Shleifer met Chubais through Sachs, according to a book co-authored by Shleifer.[6] Both Shleifer and Chubais were young, ambitious, and apparently eager to make economic policy history. They combined forces to plan the privatization of Russia's state-owned enterprises.

Supporting the Sachs-Gaidar-Chubais policies (though not at the dacha meetings) was yet another Harvard man, Lawrence Summers. In 1991, Summers was named chief economist at the World Bank. Summers would later occupy the posts of undersecretary, then deputy secretary, and, finally, secretary of the Treasury. In 1993, newly inaugurated President Clinton appointed Summers under secretary of the Treasury for international affairs. In this role, Summers was directly responsible for designing Treasury's country-assistance strategies and for the formulation and implementation of international economic policies.[7] He had deep-rooted ties to the principals of Harvard's Russia project. Shleifer credits Summers with inspiring him to study economics;[8] the two received at least one foundation grant together.[9] Summers's publicity quote for *Privatizing Russia,* a book co-authored by Shleifer, declares that "[t]he authors did remarkable things in Russia and now they have written a remarkable book."[10]

Summers had also long been connected to Sachs, his colleague from Harvard. Summers hired Sachs's protégé, David Lipton, a Harvard Ph.D. who had been vice president of Jeffrey D. Sachs and Associates (and who, together with Sachs and Shleifer, was listed as a senior member of the Sachs consulting project), to be deputy assistant secretary of the Treasury for Eastern Europe and the former Soviet Union. After Summers was promoted to deputy secretary in 1995, Lipton moved into Summers's old job and assumed "broad responsibility" for all aspects of international economic policy development. Lipton and Sachs published numerous joint papers and served together on consulting missions in Poland and Russia. "Jeff and David always came [to Russia] together," remarked Andrei Vernikov, a Russian representative at the International Monetary Fund (IMF). "They were like an inseparable couple."[11]

According to Vernikov and other sources, Sachs presented himself as a power broker who could deliver Western aid.

Sachs helped Gaidar, who served as minister of finance and the economy from November 1991 to April 1992, then as first deputy prime minister, followed by acting prime minister to December 1992, promote a policy of "shock therapy," which aimed to swiftly eliminate most of the price controls and subsidies that had underpinned life for Soviet citizens for decades.[12] Gaidar, Sachs, and their supporters believed that such a policy would lift the nation out of the doldrums of its command economy and set it on the bright road to capitalism. Shock therapy did free most prices, but it did not pay sufficient attention to the fact that the economy was monopolistic. Many experts believed that shock therapy contributed significantly to the subsequent hyperinflation of 2,500 percent. One result of the hyperinflation was the evaporation of much potential investment capital: the substantial savings of ordinary Russians.[13] By November 1992, Gaidar was under severe attack for his failed policies. He was ousted in December of that year. Despite a brief return as first deputy prime minister, Gaidar continued his policy influence primarily behind the scenes.

Chubais took over where Gaidar left off. According to some Westerners' reports, he was much more presentable than Gaidar. He seemed suave and well spoken. Then in his mid-30s, Chubais was adept at cultivating and charming his Western contacts. The British magazine *Economist* predicted a future for Chubais as Russian president by the year 2010.[14] Western politicians and investors came to see him as the only man capable of keeping the nation on the troublesome road to economic reform. Chubais was on intimate terms with some Western officials, including high officials of the World Bank, the IMF, and the U.S. government, including Deputy Treasury Secretary Lawrence Summers. In a letter of April 1997 (obtained and published by a Russian newspaper) addressed "Dear Anatoly," Summers instructed Chubais on the conduct of Russian foreign and domestic economic policy.[15]

To help him in his appointed task, Chubais assembled a group of Westward-looking, energetic associates in their 30s, many of whom were long-standing friends from St. Petersburg. From the start, the "young reformers" and their Harvard helpmates chose rapid, massive privatization as their showcase reform. The Harvard group secured awards from the U.S. Agency for International Development for work on privatization and other economic reforms and channeled them through the Harvard Institute for International Development. According to Treasury official Mark Medish, "Sachs was the one who packaged HIID as an AID consultant."[16] Harvard economist Shleifer became director of the Institute's Russia project. Another Harvard player was a former World Bank consultant named Jonathan Hay, who played a minor part in the Jeffrey D. Sachs and Associates project.[17] In 1991, while still at Harvard Law School, Hay had become a senior legal adviser to Russia's new privatization agency, the State Property Committee (GKI).[18] The following year, the youthful, hard-working Hay was made the Harvard Institute's general director in Moscow.

With aid money and Harvard's involvement, the St. Petersburg Clan, which Deputy Secretary Summers later called a "dream team"[19] (an invaluable endorsement given his position and status), came to occupy important positions in the Russian government and ran a series of aid-created and funded "private" institutions. Made significant by virtue of hundreds of millions of Western dollars, Chubais was a useful figure for Yeltsin: first as head of the GKI, beginning in November 1991, then additionally as first deputy prime minister in 1994, and later as the lightning rod for complaints about economic policies after the communists won the Russian parliament (Duma) election in December 1995. Chubais made a comeback in 1996 as head of Yeltsin's successful reelection campaign and was named chief of staff for the president. In March 1997, Western support and political maneuvering catapulted him to first deputy prime minister and minister of finance. Although fired by Yeltsin in March 1998, Chubais was reappointed in June 1998 to be Yeltsin's special envoy in charge of Russia's relations with international lending institutions.

Chubais's success at courting power on all sides placed the Chubais Clan in a unique position. As Russian sociologist Olga Kryshtanovskaya explained it, "Chubais has what no other elite group has, which is the support of the top political quarters in the West, above all the USA, the World Bank and the IMF, and consequently, control over the money flow from the West to Russia. In this way, a small group of young educated reformers led by Anatoly Chubais turned into the most powerful elite clan of Russia in the past five years."[20]

The interests of the Harvard Institute group and the Chubais Clan soon became one and the same. Their members became known for their loyalty to each other and for the unified front they projected to the outside world. By mid-1993, the Harvard-Chubais players had formed an informal, collusive and extremely influential group of "transactors" that was shaping the direction and consequences of U.S. economic aid and much Western economic policy toward Russia. "Transactors" work together for mutual gain, even while formally representing their respective parties. Transactors may genuinely share the stated goals of the parties they represent—in this case, the United States and Russia—but they have additional goals that may, advertently or inadvertently, subvert or subordinate the purposes of the parties they ostensibly represent.[21] As a new decade begins, some key transactors in this story are under investigation for corruption and other criminal activities—the consequences of their undeclared goals. Recently, the U.S. government brought a suit against four American transactors and Harvard University. It alleges that the defendants "were using their positions, inside information and influence, as well as USAID-funded resources, to advance their own personal business interests and investments and those of their wives and friends."[22]

HARVARD'S BLANK CHECK FROM UNCLE SAM

Without experience in Russia and under obligation to carry out congressional spending mandates, an insecure USAID was persuaded to largely delegate responsibility for America's role in reshaping the Russian economy to the Harvard Institute group. The Institute's first award from USAID for work in Russia came in 1992, during the Bush administration. Over the next four years, between 1992 and 1997, with the endorsement of influential proponents in the Clinton administration, the Institute received $40.4 million from USAID in noncompetitive grants for work in Russia. It was slated to receive another $17.4 million, but USAID suspended its funding in May 1997, citing allegations of misuse of funds.[23] Approving such a large sum of money as a noncompetitive "amendment" to a much smaller award (the Harvard Institute's original 1992 award was $2.1 million) was highly unusual, according to U.S. officials.[24] Also highly unusual was the citing of "foreign policy" considerations—that is, the national security of the United States—as the reason for the waiver.

Nonetheless, the waiver was endorsed by five U.S. government agencies, including the Department of the Treasury and the National Security Council (NSC), two of the leading bodies making U.S. aid and economic policy toward Russia (and Ukraine). From Treasury, the Harvard-connected David Lipton and Lawrence Summers supported the Harvard Institute projects. In his capacity as USAID's deputy assistant administrator of the Bureau for Europe and the New Independent States, Carlos Pascual signed the waiver on behalf of USAID. Pascual's support for Harvard projects continued, and he was later promoted to the NSC, where he served as director of Russian, Ukrainian, and Eurasian Affairs from 1995 to 1999.[25]

Thus, through high government directives promoted by Harvard-connected administration officials, and with competitive bidding and other standard government regulations and procedures largely circumvented, the Harvard Institute secured terms that were different from, and more advantageous than, those for many other aid contractors. Further, key Harvard-connected officials were responsible for handing the Institute not only the bulk of USAID's economic reform portfolio in Russia, but also the authority to manage other contractors. In addition to receiving tens of millions in direct funding, the Institute helped steer and coordinate USAID's $300 million reform portfolio in grants to the Big Six accounting firms and other companies such as the public relations firm Burson-Marsteller.[26] This put the Harvard Institute in the unique position of recommending U.S. aid policies in support of market reforms while being a chief recipient of the aid, as well as overseeing other aid contractors, some of whom were the Institute's competitors. Louis Zanardi, the U.S. General Accounting Office (GAO) official who spearheaded the GAO investigation of the Harvard Institute's activities, adds that the Institute's substantial influence was possible "because of its close relationship with the Chubais group and USAID."[27]

Beginning in 1992, Jonathan Hay, the Harvard Institute's general director and its public face in Moscow, served as a key link between the Chubais Clan and the aid community at large. Hay assumed large power over contractors, policies, and program specifics. He said he viewed his role as "getting policy focused right and turning that into a message for donors," which included helping Chubais and others to prepare requests to the leadership of USAID that communicated what the Russian government wanted to do.[28]

Because of their special standing with high government officials, the Chubais-Harvard transactors were able to urge contractors to use certain institutions and people. Many consultants not connected to Harvard indicated that Hay had some control over their purse strings and that he spoke on behalf of the Russian government (that is, the Chubais Clan) to USAID and other Western organizations. Thus, it is not surprising that at a meeting that the author observed among Hay, representatives of the Clan, and senior aid-paid Western consultants, the consultants treated Hay with considerable deference.[29]

Hay had easy access to the powerful Chubais Clan and often served as its spokesman. Clan principals directed donor officials, contractors, and even GAO investigators wanting to talk to Russian officials responsible for aid to Hay. The Institute sometimes spoke on behalf of the Clan, sometimes on behalf of itself as an aid contractor, and sometimes also as a contractor managing the projects of competitor contractors. From an American perspective, the Harvard Institute appeared to have a conflict of interest.

All this meant that, in practice, and under cover of economic aid, the United States delegated to the Harvard Institute, a private entity, foreign policy in a crucial area that involved complicated choices. This arrangement eventually came under scrutiny. In 1996, Congress asked the GAO to investigate the Harvard Institute's activities in Russia and Ukraine. The GAO found that "HIID served in an oversight role for a substantial portion of the Russian assistance program,"[30] that the Harvard Institute had "substantial control of the U.S. assistance program,"[31] and that USAID's management and oversight over Harvard was "lax."[32]

In 1997, as the result of yet another investigation, this time beginning with USAID's inspector general (and later referred to the U.S. Department of Justice), USAID canceled nearly $14 million of its commitments to the Harvard Institute amid allegations that Andrei Shleifer and Jonathan Hay, the Russia project's two principals, had "abused the trust of the United States Government by using personal relationships . . . for private gain."[33] In May 1997, citing evidence that the two men had used their positions and inside knowledge as advisers to profit from investments in the Russian securities markets and other private enterprises, the Harvard Institute fired them. In January 2000, a Harvard task force issued a report alluding to the financial scandal and recommending that the Harvard Institute be closed.[34]

In September 2000, in a suit brought against Harvard University, Shleifer, Hay, and their wives, the U.S. government alleged that the two men "were making prohibited investments in Russia in the areas in which they were providing advice."[35] Although acknowledging that they participated in and benefited from many of the alleged activities, Hay and Shleifer denied that their activities constituted a conflict of interest with their official positions. Tellingly, USAID Deputy Administrator Donald Pressley acknowledged: "We had even more than usual confidence in them [Harvard advisers], and that's one reason we are so distressed that this has occurred."[36]

A FEW GOOD MEN

Just what was this Chubais Clan? A core group of people who contacted one another for many purposes, the clan was a "clique," as defined in chapter 3. The clique was a strategic alliance that responded to changing circumstances and helped its members promote common interests through concentration of power and resources.[37] (As noted earlier, this use of "clique" should not be confused with the Russian *klika,* which has a decidedly pejorative connotation—that of an establishment gang.) Sociologist Olga Kryshtanovskaya explains the clique, or "clan" in the Russian context, as follows:

> A clan is based on informal relations between its members, and has no registered structure. Its members can be dispersed, but have their men everywhere. They are united by a community of views and loyalty to an idea or a leader. . . . But the head of a clan cannot be pensioned off. He has his men everywhere, his influence is dispersed and not always noticeable. Today he can be in the spotlight, and tomorrow he can retreat into the shadow. He can become the country's top leader, but prefer to remain his grey cardinal. Unlike the leaders of other elite groups, he does not give his undivided attention to any one organisation.[38]

Core members of the St. Petersburg Clan were originally brought together through university and club activities in the mid-1980s in what was then Leningrad. Most members of the Clan studied at the Leningrad

Institute of Engineering Production, where Chubais was a student; the Institute of Finance and Economics; or Leningrad State University.[39] Some also were associated with the Leningrad Shipbuilding Institute and the Leningrad Polytechnical Institute.[40] Chubais was an active participant in ECO (Economics and Organization of Industrial Production), a club, and its namesake magazine, which was published by the Russian Academy of Sciences. According to Leonid Bazilevich, vice president of the club, who was Chubais's professor and was acquainted with several members of the Clan, members were "very intensively connected" with one another at that time and "well-oriented to Western economic models."[41]

Later, in the Gorbachev years of *glasnost,* some members of the Clan became involved in explicitly political activities and established an informal club that called itself Reforma. This club organized special meetings on economic issues that sometimes attracted hundreds of people. Reforma put together lists of candidates and platforms for local and national elections, as well as drafts of legislation and a business plan for a free-enterprise zone in Leningrad.[42] Later, Chubais and other members of the Clan established a connection with the mayor of the city, Anatoly Sobchak, and became influential in its administration. In moving from academia to city government, "Chubais brought with him many of the brightest young scholars he had come to know working in Leningrad's well-developed intellectual circles," political scientist Robert Orttung has noted.[43] Before going to Moscow, several members of the Clan served as first deputy mayor under Sobchak (Chubais, Alexey Kudrin,[44] Sergei Belyaev, and Vladimir Putin—Russia's new president). Some (Chubais, Belyaev, Eduard Boure, and Mikhail Manevich[45]) headed state privatization agencies there, and still others (Dmitry Vasiliev and Alfred Kokh[46]) worked as deputies in those offices.

Although later in Moscow, the St. Petersburg Clan took on some powerful members who were not from their hometown (notably Maxim Boycko from Moscow, whom Shleifer says he introduced to the Clan), all were tied and obligated to Chubais. Chubais and the Clan depended on, and appeared to work closely with, still others, such as Ruslan Orekhov, head of the president's legal office. According to Shleifer, Orekhov's association with the group began in 1993, when its members had to work with Orekhov because decrees went through his office.[47]

Although cliques do not necessarily have a center or leader,[48] they have recognized authorities who often retain their standing and influence whether they shoulder responsibility or not. By skillfully manipulating others' interests, a clique authority builds up a following of those who are under obligation to return past favors and support.[49] According to Bazilevich, members of the Chubais Clan supported one another "in critical situations."[50]

There were powerful reasons for the Clan to stick together after the breakup of the Soviet empire in 1991. Chubais called on its members to serve in key government positions. Operating as part of a strategic alliance was crucial to the Clan's effectiveness in helping to run the country, as well as in tapping into lucrative opportunities.[51] Members of the Clan discovered that, working together, their Western contacts could help them leverage foreign support for use as a political and financial resource at home. And, indeed, the Clan did serve as a critical launching pad and resource for Chubais.

NOBLE REFORMERS IN THE SHADOWS OF SOCIALISM

The Chubais Clan was well positioned to become the group of "reformers" favored by the West. Donors tended to identify the reformer as such, not because he was a change agent in support of market reform, but because he possessed the personal attributes that Westerners responded to favorably. Although the reformer might, indeed, have embraced market reform, the identity markers that Westerners appeared to recognize most often were a pro-Western orientation; the ability to speak English and to converse in the donor vernacular of "markets," "reform," and "civil society"; established Western contacts (the more known or influential, the better); travel to and/or study in the West (a privilege generally reserved for the economic elite); and, perhaps most important, a self-proclaimed identity (at least vis-à-vis the West) as a reformer who associated with other reformers.

The most popular Russian reformers in Western political and aid circles were young, energetic, and adept in their dealings with donors. As Donald Jensen, former second secretary at the U.S. Embassy in Moscow, put it: "Absolutely, they knew how to play us. . . . And knew very consciously how to project what they wanted to an American audience and get the Americans to go along."[52]

Westerners often took members of the Clan at face value. As USAID's Thomas A. Dine stated, "If [Chubais associate] Maxim Boycko tells me that X, Y, and Z are reformers, I believe him."[53] Dine went on to note that "it's no secret that nationalists and communists don't like [Chubais], and perhaps that's the best proof of all [of his reform credentials]."[54] Western officials and the media promoted the of Chubais and the "Young Reformers" and overlooked other reform-minded groups. A self-promoting view that the only alternative to the Chubais Clan was the communists, loudly advanced by the Chubais-Harvard transactors (and by influential parts of the Western aid and political community), does not hold up under careful scrutiny. Throughout the aid story, at every step of the way, there existed viable and important alternatives to the policy choices that were made and to the West's strategy of conducting economic reform through political support of the Yeltsin government and one clan.[55]

Identifying reformers on the basis of personal attributes and declared ideological positions, as they looked in the West, clearly had a cost: It alienated and often overwhelmed other reformers and potential reformers, as well as many Russians generally. Aleksandr Lebed, Russia's national security chief, questioned Western perceptions of reformers throughout the aid effort. In 1996, his spokesman pointed to a common misperception by contrasting two governors:

> We Russians and you Americans often use the same words meaning different things. For example "the true reformer": Is it a friend of the West, as you usually think? We have two governors—one is considered by mass media to be a true liberal, reformer, market-thinker. He really uses only the market language, is West-oriented, young, has "camera appeal," is full of energy and zeal. He has all the opportunities that the title—"true reformer"—affords him: support from Moscow and the West. The second reformer is called "Red," almost communist, anti-reformer, old-thinker. No one can say that this man is the friend of the West and the central government. At first glance the picture is clear, there is no doubt: one is "the Reformer," the other "the communist." But in reality the first man can speak well and advertise himself to the West, while the other one tries to do little, slow but effective steps to achieve civilized market reform and does not care how he looks in the eyes of the mass media.[56]

In short, donors, by equating Western-oriented Russians with reform agendas and traditionalist or communist Russians with anti-reform agendas, created stereotypes. As political scientist Peter Stavrakis observes, these stereotypes made it "virtually impossible to conceive of a pro-reform Russian nationalist."[57]

An even more fundamental problem with the view that the fate of the Russian political economy was being decided by a contest between a few good reformers and everyone else was that this belief overemphasized ideology and neglected the role of communist legacies in change processes. Although such a dramatic step as the breakup of an empire might have looked like a death followed by a resurrection, in fact it was more like a messy divorce involving custody disputes over young children. The emergence of the new Russian state in 1991 did not constitute a fresh starting point: Deep-rooted groups and processes helped to shape the very nature of the Russian state.

While the chief political analyst at the U.S. embassy in Moscow, Thomas E. Graham speculated that Russia is run by rival "clans" with largely unchecked influence.[58] With unstable political, legal, and administrative structures, there were myriad opportunities for clans to penetrate public institutions and lay claim to resources. This state of affairs enabled clans to bypass other sources of authority and influence and thereby enhance their own. As the main rivalry among clans occurred within the executive branch, the Russian government could not ensure impartiality under the rule of law.

The Chubais Clan was so closely identified with particular ministries and institutional segments of government that the respective agendas of the state and the Clan sometimes seemed identical. The same was true of competing clans, which had similar ties with other government organizations, such as the Central Bank, the Ministry of Finance, and the "power ministries" (the Ministries of Defense and Internal Affairs, and federal security services). These clans depended on state authorities to stand far enough away from commercial activities so as not to interfere with the clans' acquisition and allocation of resources, but close enough to ensure that no rival clans would draw on the resources. Under these circumstances, it would be unreasonable to expect that any ambitious group would neglect its own financial and political agendas, especially when it had been designated the sole beneficiary of so much aid.

What were the effects of concentrating aid on one particular clan, if the clan system was "business as usual" as in Russia? Was it realistic to expect that any clan would operate in a vacuum, especially when it was singled out to receive resources to which competing clans would not have access? Beyond this, given the Russian self-image of a wounded superpower,[59] was it reasonable to expect that Western support of one particular clan in a highly politicized environment would not fuel charges of Western interference from other clans? Aid designed to promote a particular political group does not advance the building of institutions that are transparent and unaligned with any one clan. The goal of working toward such institutions is critical in structuring a democratic political and economic system, even if the goal is virtually impossible to achieve.

Although Western donors were inclined to view the loyalty exhibited by the Chubais Clan as part of its effectiveness, many Russians regarded the Clan as a communist-style group that was adept at commandeering resources for itself. The Chubais transactors' primary source of clout was neither ideology nor even reform strategy, but precisely their standing with and their ability to get resources from the West. Long-established loyalty might mean "They're effective" in the West, but in Russia it tended to mean "They're sharing money."

THE GREAT GRAB

The Chubais Clan's partnership with the Harvard group took shape in 1991 and 1992, when Russian economic reform activities were centralized in the GKI. It was as the engine of Russia's ongoing privatization that Chubais played his largest role—an admirable one in the eyes of international financial institutions and many Western governments; a sinister one to many Russians.

Shortly after Boris Yeltsin became the elected president of the Russian Federation in June 1991, the Federation's Supreme Soviet passed a law mandating privatization. This was two months before the August coup attempt. In the confused political environment that followed the attempt, several schemes to realize privatization were floated before the Supreme Soviet.[60]

One was the brainchild of the Chubais-Harvard team. As the first head of the new GKI beginning in November 1991, Chubais, together with his team of St. Petersburg and Western advisers, drew up plans to privatize no fewer than 15,000 state enterprises. The team designed and coordinated the signature mass-voucher privatization program, launched in November 1992, in which citizens were given shares, or "vouchers," in state-owned enterprises. USAID spent $58 million to underwrite this privatization program, including its design, implementation, and promotion.[61] Through the Harvard Institute, USAID supported about ten advisers to the GKI,[62] whose contracts added up to $7.75 million.[63]

In addition to USAID and the Harvard Institute, the Harvard group worked under other venues and funding. Project documents of Jeffrey D. Sachs and Associates state that "Professor Sachs, Dr. Lipton, and Professor Shleifer have worked with Deputy Prime Minister Chubais and the staff of the Russian State Committee on Privatization. . . . The [Sachs] team has had an extensive interaction with the [Russian] State Committee on Privatization and has helped in the design of the mass privatization program legislation recently enacted by Parliament."[64] The documents further state that Andrei Shleifer "has played a central role in the formulation of the Russian privatization program. . . ."[65]

A USAID privatization official explained that "it was essential to jump-start the mass privatization program. At that time there was enormous pressure to get things going."[66] At first blush, it indeed seems that things "got going"—the U.S. Department of State's 1996 annual report on aid to the former Soviet Union declared that "Russia's mass-privatization program was successfully completed in July 1994, with state assets having been transferred to over 40 million new shareholders. By 1996 an estimated half of Russia's workers were employed in private firms—almost three times as many as in 1992."[67]

However, the privatization of state-owned enterprises by issuing vouchers was controversial from the start, and only a small minority of Russian citizens benefited from it. The privatization program that the Supreme Soviet had passed in 1992 was structured to prevent corruption, but the program that Chubais implemented encouraged the accumulation of vouchers and property in a few hands and opened the door to widespread corruption. Sociologists Lynn D. Nelson and Irina Y. Kuzes, who have detailed the minute-to-minute proposals and politicking around privatization, explain:

> The reformers did not want to openly discuss the actual objective behind their voucher distribution proposal, because they were telling the public one thing while pursuing an entirely different goal. Whereas at the time of the parliament's June discussions Chubais had clearly stated, "The politics of the State Property Management Committee are not to further the stratification of society but to let everyone take part in people-oriented privatization," the plan that [the] GKI had secretly developed was designed to have the opposite effect. And by November, Chubais was not hesitant to advance an entirely different interpretation of voucher privatization's meaning for the Russian citizenry. Now he was not speaking about the "stratification of society," but rather about personal freedom, freedom to cash in on vouchers rather than to participate in "people-oriented privatization."[68]

Citizens could purchase shares in formerly state-owned companies by investing their vouchers directly at auctions or indirectly through unregulated voucher investment funds. Either way, managers retained control over most industries, investors wound up owning very little, and the average Russian struggled to survive amid economic hardship.[69] Economist James Millar concludes that voucher privatization was "a de facto fraud."[70]

Privatization was intended to spread the fruits of the free market. Instead, it helped to create a system of "tycoon capitalism" acting in the service of half a dozen corrupt oligarchs. The "reforms" were more about wealth confiscation than wealth creation; and the incentive system encouraged looting, asset stripping, and capital flight.[71] E. Wayne Merry, former chief political analyst at the U.S. Embassy in Moscow, observes that "We created a virtual open shop for thievery at a national level and for capital flight in terms of hundreds of billions of dollars, and the raping of natural resources. . . . "[72]

Moreover, as crime specialists Svetlana Glinkina[73] and Louise Shelley[74] point out, privatization was carried out with little concern for organized crime.[75] Yet privatization processes shaped the distribution of wealth in Russian society as well as citizens' perceptions of democracy and capitalism. Part of the public came to associate the terms "market economy," "economic reform," and "the West" with dubious activities that benefited only a few people while others experienced a devastating decline in their standard of living—a far cry from their secure lives under socialism.

Public sentiment against privatization was visceral: Russians came to call it the "great grab." Distancing himself from Chubais's policies and citing the corrupt nature of the governmental apparatus, Yeltsin derided "Chubais-style" privatization.[76] In the December 1995 Duma election in Russia, communist parties won about one-third of the popular vote and 42 percent of the seats, a strong showing that was partly attributable to anti-privatization sentiment.[77] Reform came under siege by citizens and parliamentarians, and activities of the Chubais Clan were placed under investigation by parliamentary bodies. As Russia scholar Peter Reddaway reports:

> In 1997, the Duma voted by 288 to 6 to denounce the privatization program of 1992-1996 as "unsatisfactory." According to the chairman of the Duma commission set up to examine the program, its results were "chaotic" and "criminal": Although 57 percent of Russia's firms were privatized, the state budget received only $3-5 billion for them, because they were sold at nominal prices to corrupt cliques.[78]

Chubais, one of the most hated public figures in Russia, was branded by millions of Russians as the architect of "grabitization"—the man who gave away the nation's great factories and its vast wealth of natural resources at fire-sale prices. As the executor of privatization, he had strong links with some of Russia's rising power groups and new rich, and many average people perceived him as an agent of the privileged. In 1997 nationwide public opinion polls, 70 percent of those surveyed said that Chubais's privatization policies had a "bad" effect[79]—one that was linked to Harvard and America. At a 1998 symposium entitled "Investment Opportunities in Russia" at Harvard's John F. Kennedy School of Government, Yuri Luzhkov, the mayor of Moscow, made what might have seemed to many an impolite reference to his hosts. After castigating Chubais and his monetarist policies, Luzhkov, according to a report of the event, "singled out Harvard for the harm inflicted on the Russian economy by its advisers who encouraged Chubais's misguided approach to privatization and monetarism."[80] Luzhkov said that "Harvard was in fact harmful to us by

having proposed one of the models for privatization in Russia. Moreover this was a substantive harm."[81]

DEMOCRACY BY DECREE

Beginning in 1992, Chubais acquired a broad portfolio, ranging from
privatization and the restructuring of enterprises to legal reform, the
development of capital markets, and the creation of a regulatory framework for business and securities transactions. A number of commissions
dealing with bankruptcies, tax arrears, and debt were set up under
Chubais, who also headed the GKI and in 1994 became first deputy
prime minister. The creation of the Commission on Economic Reform in
1995 was further confirmation, as the Russian newspaper *Kommersant-
Daily* states, that "a new center of economic power is being created
around First Deputy Prime Minister Anatoly Chubais." With "very
great" powers, the commission was described as "a quasi-Council of
Ministers . . . in direct competition with the bodies that have already been
vested with such powers."[82] As sociologist Kryshtanovskaya summed it
up, "Gradually, his [Chubais's] men started controlling not just privatization, but also the anti-trust policy, the bankruptcy mechanism, taxes,
relations with regions (including the organization of the gubernatorial
elections) and what was called 'the propaganda work' in Soviet times."[83]

Chubais's program was so controversial that he ultimately had to
rely largely on presidential decrees, the preferred method of many market
reformers, for implementation. Members of the Chubais Clan bragged
that, after the privatization program passed Russia's parliament, "every
subsequent major regulation of privatization was introduced by Presidential decree rather than parliamentary action."[84] And a 1996 presidential
directive dictated that only Chubais (at the time Yeltsin's chief of staff)
had the authority to decide whether presidential decrees were ready to be
signed—a directive that could be circumvented only upon receiving
direct instructions from the president.[85]

Over the years, many aid officials embraced this dictatorial modus
operandi and promoted presidential decree and the circumvention of
parliamentary authority as a means of achieving market reform. Jonathan
Hay and his associates actually drafted many of the Kremlin decrees. As
USAID's Walter Coles, a key American official in the privatization and

economic restructuring program in Russia, pointed out, "If we needed a decree, Chubais didn't have to go through the bureaucracy." Further, with U.S. funding, Western public relations firms have engaged in "public education" to promote privatization. USAID spent $18.9 million on public education for mass privatization alone, including publicity around the voucher auction.[86] Acknowledging the lack of political support for many "reform" measures, Coles said, "There was no way that reformers could go to the Duma [the parliament of the Russian Federation set up in 1993] for large amounts of money to move along reform."[87] They didn't have to. U.S. assistance policies in Russia, like some of those in Central Europe, supported specific individuals and reforms at the expense of democratic processes and institutions.

Of course, the Russians themselves are primarily responsible for the manner in which reform was carried out. But by putting its reform portfolio in the hands of the Chubais Clan, USAID alienated other parties to the reform process who clearly had to be brought on board if legal and regulatory reforms were to be implemented. Without public support or understanding, decrees constitute a weak foundation on which to build a market economy. Some reforms, such as lifting price controls, may be achieved by decree. But many others, including those of privatization and economic restructuring, depend on changes in law, public administration, or mind-sets, and require cooperation across the full spectrum of legislative and market participants, not just a clan. Without support from parties to the reform process, reforms were almost certain to be ignored or even subverted during implementation.

A case in point was USAID's showcase effort to reform Russia's tax system and to set up clearing and settlement organizations (CSOs)—an essential ingredient in a sophisticated financial system. Those efforts failed largely because they were put solely into the hands of one group, which declined to work with other market participants. In Moscow, for example, despite millions of USAID dollars, many of the Russian brokers were excluded from the process and declined to use the Moscow CSO.[88] Thus, since 1994, when consultants working under USAID contracts totaling $13.9 million set out to design and implement CSOs in five Russian cities, very little evidence of progress has emerged. The GAO's report called the CSO effort "disappointing."[89]

This did not surprise Charles Cadwell, a consultant working in Russia under USAID's legal reform program. He explained that "to the extent you want to control relationships among firms and to affect the behavior of managers, that is the last thing that can be done by decree. Managers will continue to operate in the old ways until there are incentives to operate in new ones. You have got to have people on board."[90] Responsible USAID contractors working in Russia also felt compelled to address the issue of inclusion. As Cadwell put it, "Do you access and deal with local politicians and political realities, or do you bulldoze over them?"[91]

Indeed, some influential Russians complained of just that. Leonid Abalkin, director of the Institute of Economics of the Russian Academy of Sciences, said that American aid was "given to Chubais" and that it was about "personal contacts."[92] Sergei V. Burkov, chairman of the Duma's Committee for Property, Privatization, and Economic Activity, concurred that American aid supported one particular political group. The "process needs to be opened up," he stated.[93]

It is easy to understand the donors' impulse to support a "reformer" group. As the U.S. Department of State's deputy aid coordinator (now coordinator) William B. Taylor explained, U.S. aid officials chose a narrow focus: "We have a limited amount of money. If you spread your money too thin, you probably won't have as much of an effect. As [USAID Administrator] Brian Atwood has said, you can go [in] . . . as a sprinkler and spread out over a lawn or can go in as a firehose."[94] Of course, the strategic targeting and coordination of resources are critical. But USAID went further to sustain certain firemen. As USAID's Coles proclaimed, "Reformers are the ones that are willing to take the risk. Their necks are on the line."[95]

While this approach sounds good in principle, it is less convincing when put into practice because it is an inherently political decision thinly disguised as a technical matter. As Harvard-Chubais principals Andrei Shleifer and Maxim Boycko themselves acknowledged in an American book funded by the Harvard Institute[96] and found on the desks of many USAID officials:

> Aid can change the political equilibrium by explicitly helping free-market reformers to defeat their opponents. . . . Aid can help reformers by paying for the design and implementation of their projects, which gives them a greater capacity for action than their opponents have. Aid helps reform not

because it directly helps the economy—it is simply too small for that—but because it helps the reformers in their political battles.[97]

In a 1997 interview, Ambassador Richard L. Morningstar, the Department of State's top aid official, stood by this approach: "If we hadn't been there to provide funding to Chubais, could we have won the battle to carry out privatization? Probably not. When you're talking about a few hundred million dollars, you're not going to change the country, but you can provide targeted assistance to help Chubais"[98]—an admission of direct interference in Russia's political life. [99]

Shleifer and Boycko defined the goal of U.S. assistance to "alter the balance of power between reformers and their opponents" and confirmed that "United States assistance to the Russian privatization has shown how to do this effectively."[100] In answer to the question "Did USAID help propel Chubais into top positions in Russian government?" USAID Assistant Administrator Thomas A. Dine concurred with the "reformers": "As an observer, I would say yes."[101] In other words, on its own terms, the firehose approach worked.

THE TWILIGHT ZONE OF FLEX ORGANIZATIONS

As the locus of reform shifted following the mass-privatization activities centered around the GKI, USAID set up a separate office for the Harvard Project and funded a network of private organizations run by the Harvard-Chubais transactors.

For many in the donor community, channeling money through private organizations was ideal, as that would circumvent inefficient and cumbersome bureaucracy. USAID's Walter Coles acknowledged that the organizations were "set up as a way to get around the government bureaucracy."[102] But some "private" organizations created by USAID in Russia often carried out functions that ought to have been the province of the state. The organizations helped the transactors to bypass legitimate bodies of government, such as ministries and branch ministries relevant to the activities being performed, and to circumvent the democratically elected Duma. Indeed, the transactor-run organizations frequently carried out key functions of the state (for example, negotiating loans with international financial institutions, making and executing economic policy, and implementing legal reform).

The donors' flagship organization was the "private," Moscow-based Russian Privatization Center (RPC), which was held up by many in the aid community as a model for other aid-supported organizations. The RPC was established by Russian presidential decree in November 1992 under the direction of Chubais, who was chairman of its board even while head of the GKI.[103] After reform activities expanded beyond the GKI, the RPC received its own aid-funded office in a separate building.

The RPC epitomized the operations of the aid-sustained Harvard-Chubais transactors. It was closely tied to Harvard in myriad ways, only one of which was characterized by a USAID-supplied explanation: that the Harvard Institute provided management support to the RPC.[104] RPC documents state that Harvard University was both a "founder" and "Full Member of the [Russian Privatization] Center," which was the "highest governing body of the RPC."[105] Harvard's Shleifer served on the board of directors, along with Anders Åslund, a Washington-based former Swedish diplomat, long connected to Sachs and Shleifer. Åslund helped to deliver Swedish government monies to the RPC and served as a broker between the Chubais coterie and the governments of Sweden and the United States. Members of the Clan appointed one another to serve in the founding, governing, and management structure of the RPC;[106] Chubais was chairman of the board; Maxim Boycko, managing director until July 1, 1996; Eduard Boure, managing director after July 1, 1996; and Dmitry Vasiliev, who also served as a vice chair of the GKI, deputy chairman of the board. Chubais, who recruited the RPCs board members, continued to serve on it even after Yeltsin dismissed him from government.[107]

The World Bank's Ira Lieberman, a senior manager in the Private Sector Development Department, who helped design the RPC, said that it had "become a very convenient source for multidonor funding."[108] Setting up the RPC, USAID's Coles said, "was a way . . . to get good people like Maxim Boycko . . . [and the] group of people that Chubais was managing that were sitting at the GKI." Coles thought it was beneficial that setting up the RPC took ministries and branch ministries out of the policy process and gave the green light to an "independent body"—that is, Chubais, Boycko, Vasiliev, and the Harvard Institute. Such an "independent group being financed outside government structure could be hired and paid market rates."[109]

With the Harvard Institute's help, the RPC received some $45 million from USAID[110] and millions of dollars more in grants from the EU, the governments of Japan[111] and Germany, the British Know How Fund, and "many other governmental and non-governmental organizations," according to the RPCs annual report.[112] The RPC also received loans both from the World Bank ($59 million) and the EBRD ($43 million) to be repaid by the Russian people.[113] A 1996 confidential report commissioned by the State Department's Coordinator of U.S. Assistance to the NIS called the RPC "substantially over funded and largely 'an instrument in search of a mission.'"[114] The report also said that the RPC suffered from "'imperial overstretch.'"[115]

In 1996, the World Bank committed a $90 million loan to support privatization and post-privatization activities, of which $59 million was to be managed by the RPC. The RPC was important in planning the loan, according to Lieberman. The World Bank picked up some of the overhead and operating costs that USAID previously covered.[116] Despite Finance Minister Boris Fedorov's opposition to at least some aspects of this loan,[117] the World Bank (and the RPC) proceeded, and additional loans were negotiated.[118]

The largesse that flowed through the RPC appears to have been much greater than the sum total of all these figures would indicate. The RPC's CEO and Chubais Clan principal Maxim Boycko has written that he managed some $4 *billion* dollars from the West while head of the RPC, according to Veniamin Sokolov, head of the Chamber of Accounts of the Russian Federation, Russia's equivalent of the U.S. General Accounting Office. The Chamber has attempted to investigate how some of this money was spent. According to Sokolov, a report issued by the Chamber in May 1998 shows that the "money was not spent as designated. Donors paid hundreds of thousands of dollars for nothing . . . for something you can't determine."[119]

Formally and legally, the RPC was a nonprofit, nongovernmental organization. But the "private" RPC was funded by Russian presidential decree and received foreign aid funds because it was run by the St. Petersburg "reformers," who occupied key positions in the Russian government. Was it, then, a government organization? Lending credibility to its identity as such, the RPC's tasks included helping to make policy on inflation and other major macroeconomic issues, as well as negotiating loans with international financial institutions. Even more convincing was the fact that the RPC had more control than the GKI over some secret privatization documents and directives, according to the Chamber of Accounts. Two RPC officials were authorized to sign privatization decisions (Boycko and the American Jonathan Hay).[120] So a Russian and an *American*—both representing a *private* entity—were approving major privatization decisions on behalf of the Russian Federation.

This blurring of the RPCs identity led to confusion among aid officials. USAID's Dine said that he thought USAID saw the RPC as a government organization but that he had "never considered" the question. Dine added that "Maxim [Boycko] was a government employee [when heading up the RPC]."[121] All the while asserting its nongovernmental status, the RPC was treated by USAID as a government ministry when U.S. assistance authorities asked it to nominate one person to serve on a technical evaluation panel to select a contractor.[122] According to USAID contracts officer Stanley R. Nevin, USAID normally chooses this representative from a recipient government ministry, not from private bodies.[123]

The World Bank's treatment of the RPC provides yet another example of its ambiguous status. The Bank's funding of the not-for-profit, nongovernmental RPC was unusual in that the Bank typically negotiates with governments. In this case, repayment was to be made by the Ministry of Finance, the official borrower for the Russian government, while the RPC served as the implementing agency.[124] The Bank's Lieberman maintained that "we [the Bank] didn't give [the loan] to [the RPC] as a private organization but as an agent for the government of Russia . . . the government of Russia is responsible for paying it back."[125] However, as a Russian representative to an international financial institution observed, "the same people who approve the loans use the money. This is what I don't like about it."

Concerned about conflicts of interest and questions of accountability, donors created the trappings of independent institutions. The RPC, for example, was set up with much of the usual Western apparatus of bona fide nonprofit organizations and even employed some Western administrators paid by donors. As a U.S. aid official in Moscow put it: "The RPC may be private but certainly looks political, just as the Heritage Foundation may be private but certainly supports a political constituency. The average Russian doesn't make that distinction."

The network of Local Privatization Centers, or LPCs, outside Moscow under the umbrella of the Moscow RPC illustrates this point.

The LPCs were supposed to develop restructuring plans for enterprises and advise local governments on policy questions. With Western aid concentrated in Moscow, donors endorsed aid to the provinces. By 1996, ten LPCs had been set up, each with about 12 employees and one or two satellite offices with several employees.[126] Three aid-paid consulting firms—Price Waterhouse, Arthur Andersen, and Carana—were charged with setting up the LPCs, two or three each. Representatives of all three reported that the LPCs, far from serving development, instead were steeped in political considerations, and they questioned the degree to which the LPCs were designed for sustainability.[127]

The idea of channeling technical resources beyond Moscow and setting up centers to help do so sounded promising. However, with aid as a political resource for the Chubais Clan and local leaders accustomed to looking to Moscow for favors, the Moscow RPC used its network of LPCs for its own political purposes.[128] Dennis Mitchem, a former partner at Arthur Andersen, reported that "many things revolved around political considerations. I was told by Victor Pankrashchenko [deputy director at RPC] that, for political reasons, our center in Novosibirsk would not be opened."[129] Thus, although Arthur Andersen was supposed to set up four LPCs, it was allowed to set up only three.

The USAID-funded RPC replicated Moscow's central authority in the patron-client tradition of Soviet society with regard to how central authority and local elites treated each other. Under that system, the careers of regional elites depended on high communist patrons in Moscow, and access and invitations to Moscow depended on the whim of high party officials there. Following that practice, Maxim Boycko, the RPCs managing director at the time, handpicked the directors and deputy directors of the regional centers, according to the consultants who helped to set up the LPCs and a USAID official in Moscow handling them.[130] Mitchem noted that "there were political reasons behind appointments" and that "some appointments were purely political."[131]

LPC leaders were rewarded for loyalty, even if that involved doing little or nothing, and sometimes even were reprimanded for local reform initiatives. Mitchem said that it was disconcerting to contractors that "we had some strong talents, and we made it clear to the RPC and AID that we wanted to use our talents," but were often stymied. He also said that the LPC directors were concerned mainly with pleasing the RPC: "They did what Maxim [Boycko] wanted. Maybe the RPC didn't want to accomplish anything."[132]

Robert Otto of Carana, who set up the rest of the LPCs, likewise stated that local directors were "inclined to do whatever Moscow told them to do. The central office defines the rules of the road. From the start it was clear that the RPC wanted the LPCs to facilitate the RPC's agenda." Otto recounted that "the only thing that mattered to the RPC was that the LPCs did what [the RPC] wanted doing. . . . The LPC people slid very easily into that because it was normal for them to get orders from Moscow."[133]

Under all these circumstances, were useful activities with a potentially lasting impact being accomplished? The RPC received so much money largely because of the Western clout of "reformers" Chubais and Boycko. Was an organization dependent on the clout of these two men able to spawn sustainable institutions? After a 1996 investigation into the Harvard Institute's activities in Russia, the GAO concluded that "the RPC's sustainability is in question once USAID assistance ends in 1997."[134]

In the autumn of 1994, Harvard made another institutional push by creating several more aid-funded "private" institutions. One was the Russian Federal Commission on Securities and the Capital Market, or the Federal Securities Commission, a rough equivalent of the U.S. Securities and Exchange Commission (also known by Americans as the "Russian SEC"). The Federal Securities Commission was founded by Russian presidential decree and run by Chubais Clan member Dmitry Vasiliev, who served as executive director and vice chairman of the board, while Chubais served as chairman. The commission had very limited enforcement powers and Russian funding, but USAID supplied funds through two Harvard-created and -funded organizations run by Jonathan Hay, Vasiliev, and other members of the Harvard-Chubais coterie.

One organization was the Institute for Law-Based Economy (ILBE), funded both by the World Bank and USAID. ILBE was set up to help develop a legal and regulatory framework for markets and evolved to entail drafting decrees for the Russian government. It received nearly $20 million from USAID. Like the RPC, one of ILBE's founding partners was the "President and Fellows of Harvard University."[135] The 1996 confidential State Department report referred to earlier suggests that Harvard was involved in ILBE's activities. The report states that, according to the Harvard Institute, ILBE's "founders are expected to provide political support for the activities of the ILBE."[136]

It is logical that this state of affairs led to abuse. In particular, key transactors *obstructed* reform when such initiatives originated outside their own group or when the initiatives were perceived as conflicting with the agendas of their group.[137] When a USAID-funded organization run by the Chubais-Harvard transactors failed to receive the additional USAID funds they had expected, they promptly blocked legal reform activities in the areas of title registration and mortgages—programs that were launched by agencies of the Russian government.[138] In such instances, the transactors' interference put them at cross purposes with their own purported aim of fostering markets.

Despite persistent reports of such abuse, U.S. officials for many months defended and supported the Harvard-Chubais group, though from the beginning USAID had failed to monitor the group adequately, as indicated by the GAO's 1996 finding that USAID's management and oversight of the Harvard Institute was "lax." When, in 1997, USAID's inspector received disturbing documents and began investigating the Harvard Institute, the laundry list of alleged misconduct included investments in the lucrative Russian securities markets and other "activities for personal gain."[139] For example, the U.S. government suit against Harvard University and four American transactors in September 2000 alleged that "Shleifer, [Nancy] Zimmerman [Shleifer's wife], and Hay purchased several hundred thousand dollars worth of shares in Russian oil companies, and concealed the ownership of those shares by using the name of Shleifer's father-in-law." Hay has been named in another investigation, as well.[140]

Hay allegedly also used his influence, as well as USAID-financed resources, to help his girlfriend (now wife), Elizabeth Hebert, set up Pallada Asset Management, a mutual fund, in Russia, according to government sources. A third transactor, Sergei Shishkin, appeared as needed, once as the head of ILBE, sometimes as the director of five Russian companies, among them Pallada. After U.S. investigators noticed this, new Pallada documents materialized without Shishkin's name. Pallada became the first mutual fund to be licensed by Vasiliev's Federal Securities Commission. Vasiliev approved Pallada ahead of both Credit Suisse First Boston and Pioneer First Voucher, much larger and more established financial institutions.[141] Moreover, as reported in Russia,

Vasiliev's commission entrusted Pallada—without a competitive tender and with funding from the World Bank's Investment Protection Fund— with management of a government fund to compensate victims of equities fraud. Russia's Accounting Chamber reported that an investigation had revealed that not a single kopeck had been paid to a defrauded investor in the first year and a half of the fund's existence, though the fund's Western consultants had been receiving their salaries.[142]

As the flow of Western aid diminished, Hay, Shleifer, and Vasiliev looked to keep their activities going. Using ILBE resources and funding, they established a private consulting firm, ILBE Consulting, with tax-payer money. One of the firm's first clients was Shleifer's wife, Nancy Zimmerman, who operated a Boston-based hedge fund that traded heavily in Russian bonds. According to Russian registration documents, Zimmerman's company set up a Russian firm with Sergei Shishkin, the ILBE chief, as general director. Corporate documents on file in Moscow showed that the address and phone number of the company and ILBE were the same.[143]

In August 1997, ILBE's Russian directors were caught removing $500,000 worth of U.S. office equipment from the organization's Moscow office.[144] The equipment was returned only after weeks of U.S. pressure. When auditors from the USAID's inspector general's office sought records and documents regarding ILBE's operations, the organization refused to turn them over, and the auditors left empty-handed.[145]

Thus the transactor-created, aid-funded "flex organizations"—so-called in recognition of their impressively adaptable, chameleon-like, multipurpose character—played multiple and conflicting roles: They could switch their status and identity as situations dictated. They sat somewhere between state and private, between the Russian government and Western donors, and between Western and Russian allegiance and orientation. They were sometimes private, sometimes state,[146] sometimes pro-Western, sometimes pro-Russian. Whatever their predilection at a given moment, the organizations were run by the Chubais-Harvard transactors (with financial support from USAID through Harvard and U.S. contractors)[147] and served as the transactors' domain and political and financial resource.

Flex organizations were also compatible with the Russian cultural context, in which control and influence, not ownership, were pivotal.[148]

They mimicked the dual system under communism, in which many state organizations had counterpart Communist Party organizations that wielded the prevailing influence. And they may have facilitated the development of what the author has called the "clan-state," a state captured by unauthorized groups and characterized by pervasive corruption.[149] E. Wayne Merry, the former U.S. senior political officer, regretted the U.S.-sponsored creation of "extra-constitutional institutions to end-run the legislature." He added that "many people in Moscow were comfortable with this, because it looked like the old communistic structure. It was just like home."[150]

TRANSIDENTITIES

Not only could transactor-run organizations switch status and identity according to the situation, so could some individual transactors. Key Harvard-Chubais transactors could change their national identity back and forth as convenient: sometimes as American representatives, sometimes as Russian ones, regardless of which side they came from. To suit the transactors' purposes, the *same* individual could represent the United States in one meeting and Russia in the next—and perhaps himself at a third—regardless of national origin. Such "transidentity capabilities"[151]—this ability of an individual to shift his identity at will, irrespective of which side originally designated him as a representative—lent yet another source of flexibility and influence to the transactors.

A significant example is that of the Harvard Institute's Russia project general director Jonathan Hay. Hay's transidentity was institutionalized by policies and procedures on both sides. Formally a representative of the United States, Hay interchangeably acted as an American and a Russian. As an American, Hay not only acted as Harvard's chief representative in Russia, but also exercised formal management authority over other U.S. contractors, which the U.S. government had granted to the Harvard Institute under a cooperative agreement. In addition to being one of the most influential foreign consultants in Russia, Hay was also appointed by members of the Chubais Clan to be a Russian. As a Russian, Hay was empowered to sign off on pivotal, high-level privatization decisions of the Russian government.[152] According to a U.S. official investigating Harvard's activities, Hay "played more Russian than American."

Another example of transidentities is that of Julia Zagachin, an associate of Hay's. Zagachin, an American citizen married to a Russian who was chosen by Chubais Clan principal Dmitry Vasiliev, head of the Russian Federal Securities Commission, to assume a position designated for a Russian citizen. Zagachin was to run the First Russian Specialized Depository, which holds the records of mutual fund investors' holdings and was funded by a 1996 World Bank loan. As journalist Anne Williamson, who specializes in Soviet and Russian affairs, has reported, the World Bank had established that the head of the Depository was to be a Russian citizen. But Vasiliev and other members of the Clan apparently had determined that if their associate Zagachin headed the Depository, they would retain greater control over its assets and functions, so as to evade accountability if necessary.[153] The financial arena yields many such examples of transidentity, in which Chubais transactors appointed Americans to act as Russians.

It was (and is) difficult to glean exactly who at any given time prominent consultants on the international circuit represented, for whom they actually worked, all sources of funds, and where their ambitions lay. Harvard economist Jeffrey Sachs, who served as director of the Harvard Institute from 1995 to 1999, and conducted advisory projects in the region, in the early 1990s sometimes under the umbrella of Jeffrey D. Sachs and Associates, Inc.,[154] provides a case in point.[155] According to journalist John Helmer, Sachs and his associates (including David Lipton, who later went to Treasury with Lawrence Summers) played both the Russian and the IMF sides. During negotiations in 1992 between the IMF and the Russian government, Sachs and associates appeared as advisers to the Russian side.[156] However, Helmer writes that "they played both sides, writing secret memoranda advising the IMF negotiators as well."[157]

Adding to the ambiguity was the question of whether Sachs was an *official* adviser to the Russian government. Although he maintains that he was[158]—and he certainly was often portrayed as such in the West— some key Russian economists as well as international and American officials have suggested otherwise.[159] Jean Foglizzo, the IMF's first Moscow resident representative, was taken aback by Sachs's practice of introducing himself as an adviser to the Russian government. As Foglizzo told Williamson, "[When] the prime minister [Viktor Cherno- myrdin], who is the head of government, says 'I never requested Mr.

Sachs to advise me'—it triggers an unpleasant feeling, meaning, who is he?"[160]

Whatever ambiguity surrounded Sachs in terms of whom he represented at a given time, his role as an intermediary and promoter seemed clear. In 1992, when Yegor Gaidar (with whom Sachs had been working) was under attack and his future looked precarious, Sachs offered his services to Gaidar's parliamentary opposition. In November 1992, Sachs wrote a memorandum to the chairman of the Supreme Soviet, Ruslan Khasbulatov (whose reputation in the West was that of a retrograde communist), offering advice, Western aid, and contacts with the U.S. Congress. (Khasbulatov declined Sachs's help after circulating the memo.)[161] Sachs was also adept at lobbying American policymakers, as indicated, for example, in U.S. State Department memoranda.[162] And he was visible in a promotional role in Russia, holding press conferences to explain, justify, and advocate the economic policies of the Russian government to the Russian public.

An associate of Sachs's and another ubiquitous transactor was Anders Åslund, the former Swedish envoy to Russia. Åslund was connected to Chubais and the Clan even before the dacha days. Based in Washington, he worked with Sachs and Yegor Gaidar. Like the grants Sachs secured, those that Åslund received from several sources were substantial.[163] He played a key role in promoting the Chubais group. Åslund appeared to represent and to speak on behalf of American, Russian, and Swedish governments and authorities. He was seen by some Russian officials in Washington as Chubais's personal envoy, and is known to have played a role in Swedish aid and policy toward Russia, as stated earlier. (For example, Åslund was highly influential with Sweden's Prime Minister Carl Bildt, who promoted him in Washington and included him in a high-level official delegation to the White House.[164]) Although a private citizen of Sweden, he participated in high-level, closed meetings shaping U.S. and IMF policies toward Russia in the Departments of Treasury, State, and USAID.[165]

Åslund was also involved in brokering business activities in Russia.[166] He had "significant" business investments there, according to Vyacheslav Razinkin, head of the Interior Ministry's Department of Organized Crime.[167] In addition to (or perhaps as part of) his work for the Chubais Clan, governments and business, Åslund was paid to do public relations. His assignment in Ukraine, where he also was active and funded by George

Soros's Open Societies Institute, explicitly included public relations on behalf of Ukraine, according to Soros-funded advisers who worked with Åslund in Russia and Ukraine.[168] Åslund's effectiveness in this role no doubt was enhanced by his affiliation with Washington think tanks, his frequent contributions on Russia and Ukraine to publications such as the *Washington Post* and the London *Financial Times,* and the fact that he was invariably presented as an objective analyst, despite the promotional roles he additionally played.[169]

Clearly, the most effective transactors are the ones most skilled at exploiting fragmentation and amorphous structure: flex organizations, bureaucracy, and governments. The transactors have multiple roles and identities at their disposal and are adept at working them.

ORCHESTRATED MUSICAL CHAIRS

The Chubais-Harvard transactors' near monopoly on aid in support of market reform, which they often realized through decree and "private" organizations used as political machines, made it easy for their representatives to actively pursue their own interests and to work on all sides of the table both in Russia and with the donors. The transactors worked through the donor community to influence aid policies toward Russia, to direct the allocation of technical assistance grants, and then to manage the monies themselves. Chubais signed letters requesting foreign aid while he and his associates were also the recipients of the aid.

With the backing of the United States, other donor nations, and the international financial institutions, the Chubais Clan and the Harvard Institute group were loyal and mutually dependent. Each was the other one's entree. The Clan was Harvard's avenue to Russia, key to its ability to claim clout and contacts with the Russian government. In turn, Harvard was the Clan's channel to U.S. policymakers and aid dollars, although members of the Chubais group learned to cultivate their own contacts and subsequently often spoke on their own. Jonathan Hay often spoke on behalf of Maxim Boycko, Dmitry Vasiliev, and other Chubais Clan members.[170]

In lobbying for aid contracts, the Harvard Institute group continually cited its access to Russian "reformers" as its primary comparative advantage as advisers; this access was a key part of the Harvard group's public relations efforts. Lobbying was very effective because the structure of authority was, in many ways, ad hoc and allowed to be so, because USAID's management practices were often fragmented and ambiguous. If a member of the partnership failed to get a "yes" in one place, he often went up the ladder (or around it) until a "yes" was provided. When he did not get a hearing to his satisfaction or was turned down by lower or local USAID authorities, he had the option of going directly to higher authorities, often the U.S. Department of State's coordinator of NIS assistance, Richard L. Morningstar. Jonathan Hay, Maxim Boycko, Dmitry Vasiliev, and Ruslan Orekhov all made trips to Washington to talk to Morningstar and/or lobbied him directly when they were stymied somewhere down the chain. Some officials high in the chain of command in the U.S. executive branch strongly endorsed Harvard's role in Russia.

The Chubais Clan and Harvard were not only loyal to each other, but with the backing of U.S. officials, they also employed loyalty as a key strategy for success. In the United States, the Harvard transactors touted Chubais as the voice of Russia, and he became the quintessential enlightened Russian in the eyes of many U.S. officials and commentators. After Chubais was dismissed by Yeltsin as first deputy prime minister in January 1996, he was placed on the Harvard Institute payroll, a demonstration of solidarity for which senior U.S. officials openly declared their support.[171] In response to the question "Why was Chubais put on the USAID-HIID payroll?," USAID's Dine replied that "the Harvard people said that they could use him as a consultant to them."[172]

Similarly, when Stanford University, not Harvard, was awarded a contract to work with the Clan-run Russian Federal Commission on Securities and the Capital Market, Vasiliev turned down Stanford's help. Harvard Institute director Shleifer explained that Vasiliev "had a group of people he was working with. The people at Stanford were on record [as] being extremely hostile to privatization. . . . He didn't want to work with them." Also, because Vasiliev was getting a loan from the World Bank, Shleifer remarked, the "AID loan doesn't matter as much."[173] The Clan managed to wring additional funds out of USAID for the same project that Stanford was to have worked on, now with Harvard as the partner. In September 1995, the Russian Federal Commission and the Harvard Institute received $1.7 million as an amendment to the 1992 cooperative agreement.

The Chubais-Harvard transactors arranged for themselves and their associates to be well represented on the high-level Gore-Chernomyrdin Commission, which helped to facilitate cooperation on U.S.-Russian oil deals and the Mir Space Station. The Commission's Capital Markets Forum was chaired on the Russian side by Chubais and Vasiliev and on the American side by the SEC's Arthur Levitt Jr. and Treasury Secretary Robert Rubin, a former board member of the Harvard Management Company (HMC), which oversees Harvard University's investments. In a speech at Harvard in January 1997, Deputy Treasury Secretary Lawrence Summers said that "assisting Russia in the development of its capital markets is a top priority of the Treasury Department" and that the forum's four working groups drew on "some of the best talent that the United States has to offer."[174] In an April 1997 speech before the U.S.-Russia Business Council, Summers reiterated that the U.S.-Russia Capital Markets Forum "has enlisted the participation of the best experts the U.S. can offer."[175]

Andrei Shleifer was named special coordinator of the Capital Markets Forum's working groups, the only representative to all four working groups: Investor Protection; Capital Markets Infrastructure; Collective Investment Vehicles; and Taxation, Accounting, and Auditing. Elizabeth Hebert, Hay's girlfriend and head of Pallada, also served on two of the forum's working groups, along with CEOs from Salomon Brothers, Merrill Lynch, and other powerful American-based investment houses. When a U.S. Treasury spokesman was asked who named Shleifer and Hebert to the forum, the answer was that they were appointed by the Chubais group—specifically, according to other sources, by Dmitry Vasiliev.[176] In fall 1997, Congress asked the GAO to look into Shleifer's role in the Gore-Chernomyrdin Commission. The U.S. Department of Justice, with concurrence from the U.S. House of Representatives' International Relations Committee, requested that GAO suspend its probe, pending the outcome of Justice's investigation.

Thus, the Chubais-Harvard partnership appeared to be virtually "seamless," as one observer put it. It was like a game of musical chairs, with key transactors directing when the music would be turned on and off. This game, in which roles were constantly being switched depending on the situation, facilitated deniability. As the manager of other aid contractors, the Harvard Institute could represent its own interests as an aid contractor, while as a representative of the Russian government, the Institute's Hay could represent the interests of Harvard as a contractor and/or those of the Chubais Clan. With regard to individual transactors, as pointed out earlier, if the Harvard Institute's manager in Moscow was asked by U.S. authorities to account for privatization decisions and monies, he could say he made those decisions as a Russian. If donors found themselves under fire for funding controversial privatization practices of the Russian state, they could disassociate themselves from the state because they were funding "private" organizations, even if these organizations were controlled or strongly influenced by key officials of the state.

The same was true of the Chubais Clan. Each side could publicly blame the other if they came under close scrutiny. If the Chubais Clan came under fire from countrymen for public policies or misuse of funds, the Clan could disassociate itself from the Americans. It could claim that cynical and selfish American contractors were at fault. The author's analysis of U.S. aid to the Chubais Clan[177] prompted Clan member Maxim Boycko to respond by attacking American consultants. In an article in a major Russian newspaper, Boycko wrote that "The most important thing for a [Western] firm is to secure a big government contract and report back to its own government of [having] complet[ed] it. . . . Evidently, when the American side was to account for the work done to those who gave them contracts, it was dreamed up—in order to increase their own weight and importance—that American specialists had a powerful influence on Chuba[i]s."[178]

Finally, as the manager of other aid contractors, the Harvard Institute could represent its own interests as an aid contractor, while as a representative of the Russian government, the Harvard Institute's Hay could represent the interests of Harvard and/or those of the Chubais Clan. The play of identities that transactorship affords enables maxi-mum maneuverability and deniability and also the opportunity to reduce accountability to bodies, procedures, and structures on both sides. A system that facilitates deniability by definition lacks outside accountability and precludes significant oversight on the part of authorities who are not aligned with the chosen group. As one U.S. contractor concluded, this setup "not only enabled deniability, it institutionalized it."

HARVARD BUSINESS REVIEW

The Chubais-Harvard transactors extended themselves into many important spheres and institutions, not only Russian economic reform and foreign aid. Their aid-facilitated entree, legitimacy, and resources supported their activities in other areas, including allegedly the Russian securities market, both in Russia and internationally, and may have helped some transactors enrich themselves.

Members of the Chubais Clan—the very group that Treasury Secretary Summers had called a "dream team"—were consistently under investigation in Russia. Many substantiated reports of the Chubais transactors using public monies for personal enrichment have been published. Today some of these same persons and their associates are among those under investigation for alleged involvement in laundering billions of dollars through the Bank of New York and other banks.[179]

Just how much did Anatoly Chubais profit from his aid-bolstered ventures? As an example, in February 1996, Chubais's Foundation for the Protection of Private Property received a five-year, $2.9 million unsecured, interest-free loan. According to the pro-Yeltsin, pro-reform *Izvestia,* the Stolichny Bank, a commercial bank that enjoyed lines of credit from the EBRD and World Bank, made the loan in return for a small percentage of the Sibneft oil company when it was sold at auction and for later control of one of the state's largest banks. Chubais defended himself by saying such practices were common in the West, but he failed to provide any reasonable explanation for some $300,000 in 1996 income not accounted for by his government salary.[180]

During Yeltsin's 1996 presidential campaign, security officials apprehended two close associates of Chubais as they were walking out of the Russian White House with a box containing more than $500,000 in cash for Yeltsin's campaign. According to tapes of a later meeting recorded by a member of one of Russia's security services, Chubais and his cronies strategized about burying evidence of any illegal transaction, while publicly claiming that any allegations of chicanery were the work of political enemies. Chubais was also able to engineer, through Yeltsin, the dismissal of several political competitors, including Alexander Korzhakov, head of the Kremlin security service and a longtime Yeltsin bodyguard and family friend.[181] A protracted, lackadaisical investigation began, but was eventually dropped amid the Duma's political jockeying with Yeltsin's administration.

Journalist Anne Williamson examines privatization and the development of finance capitalism in Russia in her forthcoming book, *Contagion: The Betrayal of Liberty—Russia and the United States in the 1990s.* She notes that Chubais's intimate relations with both Russian bankers and his Harvard friends provided many opportunities for ostensibly disinterested aid-funded advisers to become interested parties. A look at the "loans-for-shares" scheme that began under Chubais's direction in 1995 illustrates the coziness. The ostensible goals of loans-for-shares were to raise urgently needed revenue for the state budget and to provide large state firms with effective management. In theory, the government would auction off its shares in large corporations, banks would bid freely to hold the shares in trust with a right-to-purchase option, and winners would pay the treasury with loans.

But the opposite occurred. In the name of privatization, loans-for-shares transferred control of the nation's prime assets for token sums to seven preselected private banks. Rather than creating competition, this "privatization" transformed lucrative state monopolies into lucrative private monopolies. As Jonas Bernstein, an American journalist in Russia, wrote in the *Moscow Times:* "The loans-for-shares process looks more and more like the functional equivalent of show trials: a series of staged events designed to give predetermined outcomes the appearance of spontaneity."[182] Well-placed Russian officials admitted that these transfers were insider deals. Boris Fyodorov, former Russian finance minister, characterized loans-for-shares as "a disgusting exercise of a crony capitalism, where normal investors were not invited, where even among Russian so-called investors, only those who were friends of certain people in the government were invited. And there's a big suspicion that no real cash came to the government. . . .These loans-for-shares unleashed a wave of corruption like never before, and the West, especially the IMF, kept quiet."[183]

Williamson details the ways in which the Harvard Management Company (HMC), the university's endowment fund, and American billionaire and currency trader George Soros benefited from some of the most valuable deals under loans-for-shares. The key link here is another Chubais associate, Vladimir Potanin, chairman of United Export Import Bank (Unexim) since 1993 and in 1996 first deputy prime minister in charge of finance. Potanin, the originator of the loans-for-shares scheme, paid rock-bottom prices for shares in the nation's crown jewels: Norilsk

Nickel, the world's largest producer of nickel and producer of a glittering basket of other metals in volumes capable of setting world prices; Sidanko, Russia's fourth-largest oil company (with more oil reserves than America's Mobil Oil); and Novolipetsk Metal Factory, Russia's second-largest steel mill.[184]

Potanin was associated with the highly visible Boris Jordan, a Russian-born U.S. citizen and entrepreneur who, at age 26, pioneered the Russian equities market for Credit Suisse First Boston. There Jordan established the Icebreaker Fund. Potanin and Jordan formed the investment bank Renaissance Capital; Jordan became its CEO and set up Renaissance's Sputnik Fund, another investment fund. According to Williamson, the early investors in Sputnik were George Soros and the HMC—the only Icebreaker Fund investors who chose to keep their money with the young Jordan, rather than with the established Credit Suisse First Boston. Why? At least part of the answer, Williamson maintains, lies in the fact that by staying with Jordan, Soros and the HMC were the only foreign investors who were permitted to participate in the loans-for-shares auctions. Contrary to the rules governing loans-for-shares, under which foreigners were excluded, these two investors were able, via Jordan's close relationship with Potanin, to get in on two of Unexim's best deals, Novolipetsk and Sidanko.[185] Ostensibly to distance himself from these deals, Soros characterized privatization under Chubais as "quite repulsive" and Chubais himself as "tainted by the robber capitalist arrangements" at a 1998 Harvard-sponsored investment conference.[186] In testimony before the House Banking Committee later that year, Soros was asked how he was able to participate in the deals. He admitted: "I think that there were no foreign investors in that because we were a part of a Russian group that bid. I would say I was part of the crony stuff that was going on, and it was that [sic] still the old deal where the various groups divided this place among themselves."[187]

Jack Meyer, president of the HMC, declined to comment when asked whether Harvard had invested in Novolipetsk. Meyer denied getting any investment advice from Andrei Shleifer or Jonathan Hay, although Harvard economist Jerry Green, the university's former provost, said it was not uncommon for the HMC to solicit investment advice from Harvard professors who had special insight into certain emerging markets.[188] Jay Light, a professor at the Harvard Business School and the only Harvard academic on the HMC board, also denied any connection between the HMC and Harvard professors. But he said that Jack Meyer got to know Boris Jordan seven years ago, that Meyer has "talked about Boris for a long time," and that for the HMC's Russian investing, Meyer "runs the show."[189]

Williamson reported that Harvard has profited by trading in Russia's high-yield domestic bond market, which relies heavily on IMF lending. The U.S. official responsible for signing off on IMF lending is former Harvard professor and now Secretary of Treasury Lawrence Summers. Shleifer, Hay, and Soros, as well as Chubais and some of his cronies, invested in what was, in 1996, the most lucrative government debt market in the world, especially for holders of the short-term treasury bills (known as GKOs) issued by the Russian Finance Ministry.[190] Soros, who began supplementing his philanthropic activity in Russia with invest-ments several years ago, said, when asked at a Moscow press conference if his investments were serving to consolidate the country's oligarchy, that strengthening the oligarchy would benefit Russia.[191] In March 1998, Soros revealed that he had secretly lent the Russian government several hundred million dollars in summer 1997 to pay pensions as Yeltsin had promised. For many Russians, Soros's revelation answered the question of what, beyond a "very favorable" interest rate, he had received in return for his generosity. Weeks after making the loan, Soros was allowed to join a handful of Russian investors in bidding successfully for 24 percent of Svyazinvest, a national telecommunications holding company created by the government. (Soros later said he had "made a mistake.")[192]

Outrage over the auction of Svyazinvest grew in late summer 1997 and led to the September firing of GKI chairman Alfred Kokh, a Chubais Clan member who also served as deputy chairman of the board of the Harvard Institute-created, Western-funded RPC discussed earlier. (Kokh is currently under investigation for embezzlement charges and was denied entry into the United States in December 1999[193]). Even Boris Yeltsin noted that "some banks are apparently closer [than others] to the heart of Alfred Kokh, and this is not proper."[194] In a game of musical chairs for public consumption, Kokh was replaced by Chubais associate Boycko, former CEO of the RPC.

But Boycko would soon become a victim of another corruption scandal, involving payments of some half a million dollars to Chubais and other key members of the Chubais Clan, including himself, Kokh, Vasiliev, and Arkady Yevstafiev, who was one of the two men arrested for carrying cash out of the Russian White House.[195] Kokh had struggled to explain a book advance he received from a Swiss company affiliated with Unexim. He never wrote the book but declared $100,000 in 1996 income from the firm.[196] In 1997, several more "authors" received $90,000 each for another unpublished book on the history of Russian privatization, each from the same Swiss company, of which Chubais associate Potanin is chairman and which is run by Boris Jordan's uncle. These men did not deny the payments, which Alexander Minkin, the prominent investigative reporter who uncovered them, called a "veiled bribe." Yeltsin subsequently fired three of the culprits, including Boycko, and also harshly criticized Chubais for "unacceptable activities" in his personal financial dealings.[197]

In addition to investigating the "book scandal," Russia's prosecutor-general's office reportedly has examined the following Chubais-related activities: the GKI's activities since 1991, offers of apartments to those who moved to Moscow after accepting official posts, a land purchase by Chubais, and a bank loan he took to build a dacha. This office has also investigated whether Chubais provided the IMF with information on Russia's economy and on what terms.[198]

Chubais was forced by Yeltsin to relinquish his assignment as finance minister but continued to hold the post of first deputy prime minister until he was fired in March 1998. In June 1998, however, he was reappointed to be Yeltsin's special envoy in charge of Russia's relations with international lending institutions.

When the issue of "Russian" corruption captured American headlines in 1999, Treasury Secretary Summers began insisting that the Russian government make amends. "This has been a U.S. demand for years," he claimed, as if he had not been a crucial and steadfast sponsor of the Harvard advisors (now being sued by the U.S. government), as if he had not himself addressed letters to "Dear Anatoly" and had not continued to meet with Chubais, by then a private citizen, in the summers of 1999 and 2000.[199] This after Chubais admitted that he had "conned" from the IMF a $4.8 billion installment in July 1998.[200] The details of that deal had been worked out in Summers's home over brunch—at a meeting that the *New York Times* deemed crucial to obtaining release of the funds.[201]

Yet because their success is grounded in mutual loyalty and trust, and because of their shared record of activities, some of which may open them up to allegations of corruption and to legal actions, the transactors have some incentive to stick together or at least to cover for each other. Polish sociologist Adam Podgorecki has aptly called this phenomenon "dirty togetherness."[202]

Not surprisingly, then, in times of crisis for the Harvard-Chubais nexus—such as the ruble crisis of August 1998 and the Bank of New York money-laundering scandals—the transactors and their associates have sought to bolster their colleagues' continued clout and standing in both Russia and the United States. Thus, Treasury Secretary Summers has frequently rushed to the defense of Chubais and other key transactors. In testimony before the U.S. House of Representatives' Committee on International Relations, for example, Summers stoutly defended Chubais and asked that Chubais's prepared statement ("I Didn't Lie") be placed in the Congressional Record.[203] Similarly, Åslund serves as a staunch defender of and advocate for Chubais. He also has been arguing Vladimir Putin's cause.[204]

The Chubais transactors appear unlikely to disappear in Vladimir Putin's Russia. In fact, Putin has long been intertwined with them. An operative in the KGB and briefly head of its successor agency, Putin, like most associates of the Chubais Clan, hails from St. Petersburg and was intimately involved in the "reforms" there. After moving to Moscow to work with Chubais, Putin helped to suppress criminal investigations that implicated Yeltsin and members of his family—as well as Chubais himself.[205] Chubais, in addition to his current role as chief of the country's electricity conglomerate, helped to run Putin's spring 2000 presidential campaign.[206]

FOLLOWING IN COMMUNISM'S FOOTSTEPS

To appreciate the full implications of donors playing favorites, it is necessary to understand the effect that the legacies of communist social organization and suspicion had on the role of aid after the breakup of the Soviet Union. To legitimize themselves and increase their power at the local and national levels, the new Russian leaders needed to supply the goods and services that the former communists had provided. Because demand invariably exceeded supply in the "shortage economies"[207] of socialism, command over resources guaranteed state control and also the development of informal patronage networks to allocate resources. With the breakdown of the command economy, there were fewer resources to distribute and many more potential channels of distribution. This new scenario weakened the influence of the state at a time that people continued to expect it to provide. Aid from the West offered a way to meet these expectations: It became a political resource for Russian reformers to allocate in the communist tradition, through patronage networks like those that virtually ran various regions of the Soviet Union.[208]

Yet by following in communism's footsteps, Russian politicians and aid recipients opened themselves to a barrage of criticism and a great deal of suspicion. The fact that the chosen "reformer" group had as much to do with politics as with activities in support of market reform further contributed to the cynicism Russians felt about aid efforts. So did the narrow way in which the United States seemed to have chosen the Chubais Clan as its partner for achieving its market-reform agenda. Although members of this group occupied some key roles in government early on and were talented, they also clearly made themselves available, appealing, and apparent to influential Western contacts. Although the Chubais Clan was organized so that its members knew, supported, and promoted one another, Western decision makers tended to see individual "reformers" and often were not aware of the extent to which members of the Clan were associated with one another and the importance of the group's internal organizing in establishing itself vis-à-vis the West. By proclaiming themselves reformers, members of the Clan established a reputation as the West's most suitable Russian partners. In turn, by anointing Chubais as a chosen reformer, U.S. assistance helped him to develop an international reputation.

Because the Chubais Clan monopolized U.S. aid much earlier and more completely than any other clan, there was little direct competition among clans for aid resources. But there was much resentment. The disillusionment of those who were not young or glib or "Western" enough to be chosen was candidly expressed by a spokesman for Aleksandr Lebed, Russia's former national security chief: "We [are] disappointed by the way you Americans find friends in Russia. Criminal and corrupted men use all new opportunities with success, but men of work and honor cannot advertise themselves. If you do not want crisis in Russia, if you want [a] free, wealthy, democratic Russia, try to find friends that really can work on market reforms."[209]

By largely putting their eggs in one basket and allowing much aid to be used as the tool of one group, aid planners and politicians alienated non-Western-oriented reformers and opened themselves to suspicion and cynicism about aid programs, capitalism, and the West. Along with accusations that the West was playing colonialist politics, foreign advisers working with the Chubais Clan also were subject to criticism. "Too much" foreign involvement presented issues of credibility with the Duma. The response, both on the part of USAID and the Russian government, was to diminish USAID's visibility and to "Russify" aid projects to show that they were under Russian, not foreign, control. But because the Russians who assumed control often were linked to the Chubais group, the old suspicions were fueled.

Aid to Russia may have served to revive the old idea, nurtured under communism, of the West as an imperialist and colonialist demon. The fact that much Western aid—especially high-visibility privatization aid—led to inequitable results and was explicitly political, directed to supporting those deemed by Western and development communities to be "reformers," contributed to this perception. For instance, an article in the popular Russian daily *Komsomolskaya Pravda* alleged that Anatoly Chubais had robbed Russia of millions of dollars, that Harvard Institute's Jonathan Hay was a CIA agent, and that U.S. advisers in general "were effectively collecting economic information about the situation in the Russian economy" that "ends up in the hands of American financial-industrial corporations."[210] A USAID contractor in Russia, Ronald Childress, recounted how his Russian hosts, having gotten to know and trust him after several years, each asked: "Ron, why are you *really* here? I think *you* are sincere, but your government has something else [a hidden purpose for your presence here]. . . .Western policy was designed to break us up and to make sure we never, ever come up again."[211]

As long as suspicion of Western motives remained pervasive, politicians unfriendly to the United States were able to mobilize popular support by showing that the Russian government was subject to undue foreign influence. Members of the Duma, after an investigation, issued a report decrying the "dozens if not hundreds of American organizations operating in Russia within the framework of various assistance and cooperation programs." The report concluded that "intelligence and other operations are performed by such organizations, including the

Peace Corps, which has nothing to do with the goals proclaimed by these organizations."[212]

A REPEAT PERFORMANCE IN UKRAINE?

As Ukraine began to enjoy more Western press and political attention in 1994 and 1995, following President Leonid Kuchma's economic reforms, that nation became the target of much assistance, partially as a reward for its perceived advances. Aid to Ukraine also was seen as an alternative to aid to Russia, which was threatened to be cut back following that country's assault on Chechnya and its suspected sales of nuclear technology to Iran. By 1996, Ukraine, which faced (and at this writing still faces) severe financial crisis, was the third-largest recipient of U.S. assistance (after Israel and Egypt).

U.S. policymakers were inclined to emulate the Russian aid model in Ukraine; that is, to look for "reformers." As USAID's assistant administrator Dine has expressed it:

> The reformers are the performers. USAID supports the activities of key economic reform leaders. . . . For example, USAID staff work closely with Russia's first deputy prime minister, Anatolii Chubais. . . . Chubais and his proteges are the Adam Smiths of Russian reform economics. USAID is also working with Ukrainian economy minister Roman Shpek, whom President Kuchma tapped to help lead an independent Ukraine out of three years of decline.[213]

U.S. support for the Harvard Institute in Ukraine was steadfast. Thus, while Jonathan Hay and Andrei Shleifer were lobbying for aid dollars in Russia, their globe-trotting colleague Jeffrey Sachs, head of the Harvard Institute since the summer of 1995, turned his attention to Ukraine. Sachs's prescriptions had rendered him an anathema in Russia, but Ukraine was the new economic reform frontier.

Sachs and his associates built on methods the Harvard Institute had perfected to secure USAID funding for the Institute's operations in Russia: the backing of their Harvard colleagues now in official Washington and the claim that the Institute's work in the former Soviet Union was essential to U.S. national security. The Harvard coterie was helped by billionaire financier George Soros and his grantee Anders Åslund, the Swede.

Sachs co-authored Harvard's proposal to provide macro- and micro-economic advice to Ukraine with Åslund. As in Russia, the Harvard Institute (this time composed of a different group of players) lobbied for, and was awarded, a contract to offer macroeconomic advice and to work with high officials, notably Minister of Economics Roman Shpek. The Harvard Institute's proposal was unusual in a number of respects, beginning with its point of origin, which was not USAID. In answer to the question "Where did the HIID-Ukraine project originate?" Laurier Mailloux, director of USAID's Office of Privatization and Economic Restructuring, reported that it "did not originate here." And who made the decision to fund the HIID-Ukraine project? "That was a political decision that we [my office] weren't involved in. . . . there were a number of other actors."[214]

Indeed, the unsolicited Sachs-Åslund proposal did not prove to be an easy sell. The prospect of the Harvard Institute working in Ukraine met with resistance from USAID officials both in Washington and Kiev, as well as from the IMF and Ukrainian officials, including some in the National Bank of Ukraine, Ukraine's central bank. All opposed Harvard's project as redundant. The project "has not been without controversy"—the need for it was questioned by both the USAID mission in Kiev and by players within the Ukrainian government, including the National Bank, according to then-deputy aid coordinator William B. Taylor.[215] Further, a letter to USAID from the government of Ukraine stated that Ukraine did not need more macroeconomic advisers. USAID's Dine acknowledges that "they [the IMF] thought it would be duplicating their work."[216]

Sachs responded by launching a lobbying effort. He contacted members of the U.S. Congress and made trips to Washington to meet with State Department and USAID officials. Some of his associates in government helped set up a high-level interagency "Steering Committee" that favored Harvard and promoted the Harvard-Ukraine award, according to USAID's Thomas Dine. Stanley R. Nevin, the USAID procurement officer who signed the Harvard award, said that the Department of the Treasury was especially "involved" in the Harvard-Ukraine project.[217] A key player in the Treasury Department, David Lipton, Sachs's former business associate and co-author, and by then assistant secretary of the Treasury for Eastern Europe and the former Soviet Union, represented Treasury on the Steering Committee. Other members of the committee were Harvard graduate Richard Morningstar, head of the U.S. Department of State's Coordinator's Office, National Security Council official and Harvard graduate Carlos Pascual, and Thomas Dine and Donald Pressley from USAID. As of this writing, Pascual is the U.S. Ambassador-designate to Ukraine.

Members of the Steering Committee met a number of times with Soros and Åslund, according to committee participants. Soros hosted at least one meeting attended by Lipton, other committee members, and Sachs. And Åslund was a frequent visitor at Treasury, where he met with Lipton and his boss, Deputy Secretary Summers, Sachs's colleague from Harvard.[218] As a result of this collaboration, the considerable objections to the Harvard Institute's work in Ukraine were overruled by the U.S. executive branch. Representatives of the Steering Committee (or their deputies) signed the "foreign policy" exemptions that directed USAID to bypass the usual competition and enabled the Harvard Institute to secure funding for its Ukraine operations, albeit at a lower level than originally sought.[219]

Although the GAO investigated the Harvard Institute's Russian and Ukrainian projects in 1996, its findings were largely suppressed by the agency's timid management. The audit team concluded, for example, that the U.S. government exercised "favoritism" toward Harvard, but this conclusion and the supporting documentation were removed from the final report.[220]

POLICIES FOR A POSITIVE IMPACT

Like Central and Eastern Europeans, Russians and Ukrainians expected Western help after the fall of the Soviet Union. In Russia, reactions to Western aid had the special flavor of a superpower gone down: Many Russians experienced the loss of superpower status as a loss of identity. As one Russian analyst put it: "We are no longer one-sixth of the earth's surface. . . . But we continue to carry within ourselves one-sixth of the globe. . . . It is a scale we have become accustomed to."[221] But Western aid resonated somewhat differently in Ukraine than it had in Russia. In contrast to Russia's "power culture"[222] sense of innate superiority,

Ukraine evinced something of an inferiority complex. Ukraine was not a down-and-out superpower; it was a nation deeply frustrated by its economic and political isolation. Despite these differences, assistance met with the same phases of Triumphalism followed by Disillusionment as elsewhere in Central and Eastern Europe.

What was the alternative to supporting "reformers," charged as they were with responsibility for economic reform for the nation? And what could be wrong with creating private organizations to bypass inefficient government? The fallacy lay in thinking that lasting institutions can be built by supporting particular people, instead of helping to facilitate processes and the rule of law. A system based primarily on personal connections and handshakes did not foster the development of independent institutions that could outlive their current executives. Crucially, by singling out one group of "reformers," the United States discouraged many reforms—and encouraged anti-Western, anti-reform elements, who could point with glee to the absence of real benefits to Russia. Indeed, far from fulfilling their promise of a better life, the U.S.-sponsored "reforms" of the 1990s left many, if not most, Russians worse off.[223] And by promoting the media-savvy, polished, English-speaking Chubais Clan, and excluding other, less Westernized groups shaping Russian politics and economics, the U.S. aid establishment offended many Russians and fueled anti-Western sentiment. Many Russians today blame precisely the Western aid and advice they have received. E. Wayne Merry, a former senior political officer with the U.S. Embassy in Moscow, explains this in terms of the Russian weariness for "reform" experiments:

> I remember, in the early '90s, I think the most poignant slogan that you saw in Russia during the demonstrations was "no more experiments." The people were terribly tired of being treated like laboratory rats. This effort to build the new socialist man, scientific socialism had left people feeling completely alienated from their authorities. And the one thing the Russian people wanted was not to be treated like experimental material.
>
> And unfortunately, what they got in the 1990s was another series of experiments, where many of the scientists conducting the experiments were not even Russians, but were people sitting in offices in Washington, in the U.S. Treasury and the IMF. And I think much of the

disillusion with the West, much of the hostility that Russians now feel, particularly towards the United States, is reaction to what they feel was another series of failed experiments.[224]

Thomas E. Graham, also formally of the U.S. Embassy in Moscow, sees a connection in the "growing anti-Western, anti-Americanism" in Russia and Western advice: "Political elites began to question the type of advice that the West was passing on. Many of them drew the conclusion that the West had achieved what it wanted, which was the weakening of the Russian state."[225] How Russian elites perceived the efficacy of Western aid programs and the motives of donors should have been a source of concern to donors, especially because many Russians already questioned U.S. motivations. According to one public-opinion survey carried out in the spring of 1995, two-thirds of the Russian people believed that the United States had a calculated anti-Russian foreign policy.[226] Opinion polls conducted by the Department of State's Office of Research have tracked a downslope in favorable opinion of the United States from more than 74 percent in 1993 to 65 percent in 1994 to 54 percent in 1999 and 48 percent in mid-2000.[227] In one poll, 41.1 percent of the respondents said that Western countries wanted Russia to be a "Third World" state, 37.5 percent supposed that their goal was to destroy Russia as an independent state, and only 3.7 percent felt that the West was trying to help.[228]

Still, many U.S. officials have argued that the most effective method of implementing market reform is through a committed group with intimate access to both sides (and to many activities in both countries). Yet this mode of organizing relations has served to undermine democratic processes and the development of transparent, accountable institutions in Russia. By systematically bypassing the democratically elected parliament, U.S. aid flouted a crucial feature of democratic governance: parliamentarianism. Operating by decree was clearly anti-democratic and contrary to the aid community's stated goal of building democracy. Further, setting up flex organizations to supplant the state and indeed, an entire informal parallel executive further weakened the message to the Russians that the United States stood for democracy. Finally, providing a small group of power brokers with a blank check inevitably encouraged corruption on both sides, precisely at a time when the international community should have been demanding the development of a legal and regulatory framework that protected property rights and the sanctity of contracts.

There were other, more constructive scenarios possible in this story, had the donors chosen to devote the bulk of their efforts to working with and helping make government more effective, rather than simply bypassing it through top-down decrees and chameleon-like organizations, and had donors attempted to broaden their base of recipients and supported structures that all relevant parties could participate in and effectively own. A leading American university might have played a more positive role toward this end.

Building lasting, nonaligned institutions is a tough assignment in any context, and all the more so in Russia, especially given the time frame in which some legislative bodies like to see "results." The major challenge in the post-Soviet environment is to work out how to help build bridges in such a conflict-laden environment, with many groups but few center coalitions. There has been a growing realization on the part of some U.S. aid officials that aid was not just a technical matter, but a complex task with political challenges that had to be faced. As Keith Henderson, head of USAID's rule-of-law program for Eastern Europe and the former Soviet Union, has said, "We realized in Russia that it was important to work with many different players and one way to do that was to work with different [U.S. and European] contractors who worked with different players. We knew it was important to have all of these different people in the process."[229] Choosing one group was merely the path of least resistance, which promised toutable short-term results but with troublesome long-term outcomes.

To foster reform, donors need to work to develop a market infrastructure that all relevant parties can support—not just one political faction. As one aid-paid consultant expressed it: "One of the hardest parts of Western aid . . . was figuring out how to build member-owned, member-driven organizations that are neutral third parties and don't have a vested interest in the success of one or several parties. . . . The hardest thing to get people over is political ties . . . to get leaders of organizations to seek opinion and perform for people who aren't political buddies." It is by no means an easy job, but the task of aid workers is to build contacts and work with all relevant groups toward the creation of transparent, nonexclusive institutions. There must be pressure to build institutions and against concentrating so much influence in the same hands, even if this goal is difficult to achieve. Only by truly encouraging such changes—not by depending on "reformers" who prevent them from taking the steps that must be taken—can the aid community make a genuine contribution to enduring positive change.

CHAPTER FIVE

A Few Good Financiers:
Wall Street Bankers and *Biznesmeni*

> It's typical of every fund that they set out to do something
> with small and medium sized enterprises and then it became
> clear that it's not so easy.
> —Marek Kozak, head of an aid-funded
> program to foster business development in Poland[1]

IF DONORS CONFRONTED A TRADE OFF between the latitude they
conferred upon consultants and recipients to design and implement aid
programs and their own control and oversight of these programs (as seen
in the types of aid discussed in chapters 2 through 4), there was equally
a balance to be struck in yet another area of aid to the Second World:
assisting private business in diverse and rapidly changing business
environments.

The disintegrating Eastern Bloc ushered in a new era of what the
Poles called *biznes*—mom-and-pop service industries and traders
hawking everything from bananas to computers. An important stated
goal for Western donors—and a key to creating competitive markets—
was to provide support for new small and medium-sized businesses and
especially to help foster stronger, more highly developed business
sectors as a prerequisite to the development of a market economy and
democracy.

In lending support to this sector, donors employed a combination of
aid approaches—sending Western consultants and funding indigenous

groups—described in chapters 2 through 4. The consultants were loan officers or advisors on such issues as how to write a business plan; the groups were newly emerging "businesses"—often family members or partners of previous acquaintance.

Like the privatization of state-owned companies, the creation of a new business sector carried symbolic weight for the donors. Under socialism, business had been either heavily restricted, or, as in the Soviet Union, totally outlawed and pushed into an underground economy. The creation of a flourishing business sector was an integral part of entombing the socialist state and creating a capitalist one.

However, Central and Eastern Europe was a diverse landscape of fluctuating business conditions and of changing politics and domestic and external economic constraints. It would be very difficult to strike a balance between incorporating knowledge of local business practices, conditions, and needs of a given time and place and imposing donor standards and oversight.

FAMILY BUSINESS

Just what was the "private sector" in Central Europe circa 1990, and in what fields could foreign aid programs play a useful role? This question could not be answered once and for all: given that *biznes* practices and conditions varied considerably over time and place, there were differences in the need and demand for any kind of business support. In the immediate post-1989 aftermath in Central Europe, new opportunities for trade seemed to open up for a few weeks or months, only to close again. Legal infrastructure and enforcement and financial terms were in flux.

The communist legacies that shaped the emergent business sectors, and the effects of those legacies on further development, however, were steady. Part of the private sector was comprised of formerly state-owned companies that private people—often former *nomenklatura* managers— had simply "made one's own." Put another way, these companies had been "privatized" by virtue of state managers having acquired them. (See chapter 2 for discussion of the privatization of state-owned enterprises.) The other, more dynamic, part of the private sector consisted of new business.

In Poland under communism in the 1980s, the legal private sector—which included much of agriculture, construction, small shops, restaurants, handicrafts, and taxis—was the largest in the region. It generated nearly one-fifth of the national income and employed nearly one-third of the work force in the early 1980s.[2] Despite the considerable risks entrepreneurs still had to assume to operate in 1990, the number of businesses increased from 805,879 on January 1, 1990, to 1,028,484 on August 8, 1990.[3] Such activity was grounded primarily in trading, not acquisition of state resources and property.

Throughout the 1990s, Poland saw an explosion of new businesses. Most of these were domestic or household enterprises: in 1992, the average number of employees in new businesses was 1.7, including owners, according to a World Bank study.[4]

The family as a unit of business was not a new invention. Under the informal economies that flourished with communism, the family was the focus of work and consumption and the starting point for the exchange of information, which at that time was critical to the success of many activities. The family was the survival unit of pooled scarce goods and services.[5] Trust was essential in informal economies: it simply did not make sense in most cases to hire outside of one's social circle. Although such behavior may appear irrational to outsiders, family relationships facilitated certain understandings that did not require legal contracts. Being outside on one's own—without networks—was like being on a sinking ship without a life jacket. Both trust and the use of family networks figured prominently in the evolution of *biznes* in the 1990s.

The idea of formal labor markets—in which employers advertise jobs and people apply for them—was problematic when applied to Central and Eastern Europe. Polish employers of new businesses, for example, seldom hired in a meritocratic way; instead, they chose workers from the ranks of those already in their networks. Someone working at the university would receive a call from a member of his social circle now in public office who was "looking for someone from our circle" to head up a project in the government civil service. A study by sociologist Barbara Heyns found that the use of such friendship and family networks to find jobs persisted even when factors that typically predicted employment in the private sector (such as being male, young, urban, and educated) were taken into account,[6] although, in Central Europe, the trend, at least among some groups and the younger generation, appears to be toward professionalization and the adaptation of Western "professional standards."

Another important dynamic of the emergent private sector (and one that casts doubt on some Western models) involved the relationship of two spheres of activity and employment: state and private. Some economists studying household strategies tended to assume that the two spheres were separate and distinct.[7] Yet, in reality, they may not be so easily separable. Household strategies and patterns defied the neat ideological categories of planned versus market economy and state versus private sector.

In fact, some evidence suggests that families throughout the region tended to pursue diversified choices.[8] In a common pattern, one member of the family would be employed in the more stable state sector while another would work in the private sector, which provided more opportunities but at greater risk. In Tula, Russia, men worked at reduced salaries in munitions factories, the main industry in a city with a population of about 600,000, while their wives traveled to Moscow to buy goods to sell in the Tula bazaars. When trading became too risky, families could fall back on the low but reliable salaries and benefits provided by state jobs, which included "side earnings"—trading or additional work opportunities available by virtue of the job. This was an insurance strategy: families pursued reasonable options in the context of the constraints and the enabling features of their environment. Their behavior was logical, not ideological.

It was also typical throughout the region, especially among certain groups, for a member or members of the family to work in *both* the state and private sectors. In Central Europe, as well as in Russia and Ukraine, many scholars on leave from the academies of science (which continued to provide long-term guarantees and some benefits) also were employed by Western-funded organizations. Many people with their own private consulting firms kept one foot in the government sector, thus staying on government payrolls. In Central Europe circa 1990-91 (but rarely much later) as well as further east quite consistently, visitors who interviewed officials in their official capacities frequently were offered "private" business cards from the officials' side businesses, which sometimes had business dealings with the ministries for which they worked. This indicated that the host officials were looking for other opportunities.

Such other opportunities would introduce, by many Western standards, a "conflict of interest" or potential conflict of interest with their government jobs. However, one of the few advantages of working at low-wage civil-service jobs was the opportunity for Western contacts and contracts that the jobs sometimes could provide. Thus, someone from the region might see a fringe benefit where an outsider saw a conflict of interest. One government official in Kiev gave the author three business cards: two for his own private consulting firms and one for his state job as an adviser to the president.

These 1990s relationships between "private" *biznes* activities and "state" sectors were deeply rooted in socialism. Given that such patterns were likely to continue to influence business development, what were the needs of the evolving business sectors, and where could foreign aid programs play a useful role?

PROGRAMS

The United States was among the first of the donors to begin to find out. Authorized under the SEED Act in 1989,[9] the U.S. Enterprise Funds were designed to promote the development of Central and Eastern European private sectors, including loans, equity investments, grants, technical assistance, and joint ventures. Although the SEED legislation provided an overall framework for the funds, it allowed them substantial latitude in how they actually would operate.[10] This portfolio was deemed so important that the $240 million authorized for the Polish-American Enterprise Fund and the $60 million for the Hungarian-American Enterprise Fund—the first to get under way in 1990—consumed a substantial portion of the initial U.S. aid package.[11] Enterprise Funds accounted for some 28 percent of the SEED assistance for the region between fiscal years 1990 and 1993.[12] The funds received considerable publicity, both at home and in the recipient countries. A USAID-commissioned evaluation affirms that "The funds became one of the most visible manifestations of the U.S. pledge to support the transformation."[13]

From the perspective of the aid community, the hallmark of the funds was their independence of operation and the limited government oversight to which they were subject. As originally structured, they were accountable only to their boards of directors. In 1993, however, Congress charged USAID with greater oversight responsibility but maintained USAID's very limited approval authority over program decisions.[14] With little competition from other donors for loans or grants to support Central and Eastern European business, the Enterprise Funds were seen by many as a premier assistance program, and one that constituted a new kind of public-private partnership: a less-regulated type of foreign aid that would encourage private enterprise mainly through loans and direct investments rather than traditional grants. The management of the Polish-American Enterprise Fund described it as a "bold experiment—a new way for the U.S. government to deliver economic assistance to Poland, tapping into private sector expertise unencumbered by the bureaucratic constraints normally associated with governmental organizations."[15] The funds often were cited as an aid "success story" and held up by the U.S. Congress and critics of traditional aid programs as a template for future aid. In 1995, the funds had disbursed nearly $270 million in investments to 3,305 companies. By 2000, the funds had obligated more than $1 billion to 18 countries in Central and Eastern Europe and the former Soviet Union.[16]

The often slow, bureaucracy-laden EU, which, in contrast to the United States, channeled its aid to governments, was not prepared to start up a substantial business-aid program so quickly. However, in time, the EU's PHARE program introduced an innovative concept conceived by Polish specialists. Beginning in 1993, as the EU broadened its portfolio to include small- and medium-sized enterprises and infrastructure support, it launched the "Struder" program for development in selected regions of Poland. Largely designed by Poles with EU support, Struder was administered by the Polish Agency for Regional Development, a government agency established in 1993 to support regional development. Struder was to spur development in six (later, under Struder II, fourteen) *voivodships* (provinces) that suffered from the costs of economic restructuring but were deemed to have significant growth potential. The program provided grants, equity capital, guarantees, training, and advisory services in an effort to stimulate profitable investments and infrastructure development.[17] By the end of 1997, when Struder was phased out, the EU had provided 76.7 million ECU (about $85 million[18]) to the program. Other small EU-funded programs followed (primarily for infrastructure, with limited resources available for technical assistance and training), bringing the figure up to more than 100 million ECU in

2000.[19] However, largely a local invention, Struder never expanded into other countries.

Other donors and programs also launched business-development programs: a host of mostly small initiatives, such as microcredit lending, was funded by Western foundations, governments, or some combination thereof. Still, the U.S. Enterprise Funds were held up as a model, especially among some European donors that worked solely through governments and felt constrained by that practice. The funds were relatively unencumbered by government regulation on the donor side, and, in some recipient countries, on the recipient side as well. One independent evaluation of the funds noted that "Other donor agencies in the region were envious of the speed with which the funds became operational, and the flexibility and independence allowed in the programs."[20]

Yet nearly all business-support programs faced daily dilemmas that reflected a larger trade-off: to what extent to impose donor standards of paper trails and accountability and to what extent to take into account the knowledge and business conditions of the hosts.

MISSION AND MOTIVATIONS

The U.S. Enterprise Funds appear to have had differing answers to that question, depending largely on the context in which a specific fund was operating and the leadership of that fund. The major challenge facing the Enterprise Funds was an inherent conflict between "aid" and "business" orientations—an identity crisis typical of some development banks. Should they support risky business activities that could produce big results or less risky activities that would demonstrate "success," especially to the U.S. Congress? And was their mission to give aid liberally or to make sound business decisions using stringent Western loan criteria? And so this fundamental—and probably unavoidable—dilemma enveloped their mission: were they in the aid business or were they in business?

The question arose forcefully in Central Europe where the Enterprise Funds got off to a rough start. Central Europeans often were introduced to the Enterprise Funds through publicity surrounding the visits of President George Bush and other American dignitaries who announced their launch. The Enterprise Funds fell into the rhapsodic phase of Triumphalism. A USAID-commissioned report notes that

The funds became one of the most visible manifestations of the U.S. pledge to support the transformation. As such, they have brought considerable political good-will to the United States.[21]

However, the phase of Disillusionment was not far behind. The same report goes on to say that

> this political dimension created two serious problems. First the announcement of the funds created an avalanche of requests for money from would-be business owners, putting a great strain on the funds during their start-up phase. Second, there was a great deal of disappointment and negative publicity in the countries when people discovered that the funds were requiring repayment of the capital with interest.[22]

Indeed, the high profile of the Enterprise Funds helped to raise peoples' expectations—expectations that were greatly out-of-step with the funds' possibilities for delivery. In the first weeks and months following the launching of a fund, the local offices—which often at the time had only skeleton staffs—received hundreds of applications, which often were little more than handwritten requests for money. The Polish Fund, for example, was announced before it was up and running, creating a huge backlog of applications that led to frustration and resentment.[23]

Greatly contributing to the problem was the fact that Central and Eastern Europeans generally had little background for understanding just what fund managers expected by way of documentation and collateral. They had scant understanding of the necessity of a business plan, let alone how to put one together. Further, there had been little clarification explaining that the funds would not be disbursed in the form of grants, but were loans that had to be repaid—and with interest. Former Czechoslovak aid coordinator Zdeněk Drábek said that people had understood that the funds would consist of grants to small businesses. "[There was] a lot of disappointment," he said, "when they [people] discovered that money was not to be given away freely."[24]

There was also a perception among some recipient officials that the needs of Central and Eastern European business were not necessarily foremost among the concerns of the Enterprise Fund managers. Each fund was a private, nonprofit corporation. Boards were headed by prominent financiers and venture capitalists, and board members, such as AFL-CIO president Lane Kirkland and former national security adviser Zbigniew Brzezinski, donated their time. The funds embarked on a three-pronged investment strategy: (1) direct investments involving equity or debt-equity combinations to joint ventures or privatized enterprises; (2) joint bank lending programs designed to direct credit in the range of $20,000 to $200,000 to small businesses; and (3) small-loan programs for small businesses and lending programs to specific industries.[25]

Funds operating in Central Europe generally took a conservative approach to lending money, to achieve the goal of self-sufficiency. They did not dispense monies easily or quickly, requiring loan applicants to produce much of the same kind of financial documentation that typically was required for loans in the United States. For most businesspeople in the former communist countries this was nearly impossible at least in the immediate postcommunist aftermath: they lacked a paper trail and credit track record (audited financial statements and tax returns were typically unavailable) and were unaccustomed to Western loan-application procedures. Further, as the managing director of the Hungarian-American Enterprise Fund, Charles Huebner, related, given their lack of such experience under communism, Hungarians had little sense of obligation to pay back loans. As stealing from the state had been a key survival strategy under communism, why should repaying a banking institution be expected?[26] However, within a few years Central European businessmen had generally become familiar with acceptable Western business practices.

More often than not, Enterprise Fund managers opted to devote their efforts not to the small businesses requiring just a little capital that typified the region, but to big, visible deals and joint ventures that promised rewards in prestige and cash. Joint ventures, which the SEED legislation listed as an option,[27] were easy to create, lucrative, yielded incentive funds for the partners, and looked good to Congress because they helped U.S. business—even though smaller, indigenous businesses were the ostensible primary targets of the funds' attentions.

The Polish Fund was known for its profits. To bypass the $150,000-a-year salary ceiling for fund officers set by Congress, some officers devised enterprising ways to augment their salaries. In Poland, fund managers created a "clone," the Polish Private Equity Fund, which was financed partly by foreign private investments and partly by the original Enterprise Fund. Unlike the Enterprise Fund, a share of the profits of the Equity Fund went to the managers. It made both equity and loan investments but did not take part in the fund's small loans program, high-risk agricultural investments, or join in technical assistance efforts.[28] Fund managers also discovered that one way of getting in on potentially lucrative deals was to enlist the help of former Polish government operatives. By 1994, the fund resembled a Washington revolving door, with several former high privatization officials having been hired to manage fund portfolios. The Polish Fund, unlike others in Central Europe, maintained costly executive and investment offices in the United States.[29]

Similarly, the Hungarian-American Enterprise Fund set up, and invested $4 million in an investment services company, nearly all of its paid-in capital, which earned some of its partners twice (or higher) the fund's salary ceiling. This deal violated fund policies, which restricted investments to $3 million and required substantial contributions by co-investors.[30] In addition to questions about the salaries of fund partners and staff, the GAO found cases of potential conflicts of interest or the appearance thereof. For example, a Polish fund director served as president of a fund-supported foundation, as well as a professor at the university where the foundation was established. He was paid for serving in all three capacities at the same time.[31]

All this led to criticism that the funds, being too risk averse, failed to fulfill their primary mission of supporting small and medium-sized indigenous businesses.[32] As Henryka Bochniarz, a former Polish privatization official (not working for the fund) charged: "They [the funds] want to have very good investments without headaches. . . . They behave like a demanding commercial institution. . . . This was not the idea of the Enterprise Funds. . . . When you talk to the [fund] people, you have the feeling that the windows program [of small loans] is totally not important. . . . But from the point of view of Polish society, the windows program was very important."[33]

Similar views were expressed elsewhere in Central Europe. Zdeněk Drábek, former aid coordinator of Czechoslovakia, said, "The idea was that it [the fund] would go to small firms. . . . The reality was that it went to finance companies that had 500 to 1,000 employees."[34] When the Hungarian Fund invested in companies that had access to other sources of capital (representing 12 percent of its invested capital), the GAO questioned "whether such investments were consistent with the fund's mandate to develop small- and medium-size businesses." Hungarian Fund officials countered with trickle-down economics, asserting that these investments in publicly traded companies "leveraged additional investment capital by (1) encouraging other investors to invest and (2) helping to stabilize the stock market, which was not very efficient in pricing stock offerings." Fund officials added that the investments helped to balance the portfolio and enabled the fund to invest in other, riskier businesses.[35] But Zbigniew Brzezinski, a member of a board of the Polish Fund, seconded the judgment of GAO, remarking, "These funds should promote native private enterprises. They were not set up to establish foreign private investment."[36] However, compared with the development banks operating in the region, the Enterprise Funds maintained a favorable track record, as reported in a USAID-commissioned evaluation:

> Enterprise funds are helping to broaden access to capital for entrepreneurs by investing in enterprises that have few alternatives. The funds have invested more than $267 million, a high percentage of which has gone to small and medium-sized enterprises. Enterprise funds are more effective at providing capital to private businesses than are other international organizations such as EBRD, World Bank, and EC Phare. Nevertheless, even under the best of circumstances, enterprise funds are able to help only a small percentage of the newly emerging private enterprises in the region.[37]

And, with such a large gap between the expectations created and the ultimate results, the fact that the funds failed to concentrate on small targets was not lost on the recipients, especially given the publicity the funds had generated in the host countries. As Bochniarz reported, "Today [the Polish Fund is] one of many financial institutions coming here and trying to make money. Nobody considers this part of American aid."[38]

The Polish Fund's profitability eventually created a dilemma: What to do with some $300 million (generated by fund loans and investments) left over when the fund declared its mission fulfilled and went out of business? After some controversy,[39] it was decided in 1999 that $120 million would be returned to the U.S. Treasury, while the remainder would be used to set up the Polish American Freedom Foundation.[40] The foundation has begun its work by subsidizing local educational programs and enterprise development projects in local communities, according to

Poland's former Ambassador to the United States and foundation president Jerzy Kozminski.[41]

In time, some fund-sponsored programs made important contributions. The Polish Fund pioneered mortgage banking, a form of financing previously unavailable in Poland. Aiming to encourage residential construction and home ownership, the Polish-American Mortgage Bank operated by first financing residential construction projects and later furnishing mortgage loans to buyers of the units.[42] Mortgage programs are being tried in some countries further east.[43]

Nowhere was the tension between taking risks and playing it safe, between smaller and larger investments, more pronounced than in Russia, where the business environment generally presented tougher obstacles than in Central Europe. Robert Towbin, who served as president of the Russian-American Enterprise Fund during 18 months in 1994 and 1995, said that, when he set up the office in Russia and hired staff, he envisioned that the fund would invest in small and medium-sized companies.[44] But finding such companies was not easy. Racketeers and government-favored monopolies stacked the deck against newcomers and forced many of them out of business. As Towbin put it, "You had to go out to the countryside and find investments. . . . That's a lot harder than it looks." The most successful program, in Towbin's view, was the small-loans program, a program under which Russian banks found the client and serviced the loan, and the fund put up the money. The bank received half the interest; the fund, the other half. Most of the loans were repaid. Towbin said that "Of all the things the fund has done, the small loans program was probably the most successful."[45]

However, the bulk of the fund's lending ended up consisting of direct equity investment. In this portfolio, Towbin invested in small and medium-sized companies in basic industries such as machinery equipment, dress manufacturing, supermarkets, and finance. Each of these investments was a three- to four-year project. Towbin and other foreigners who worked successfully in the Russian environment underscored the necessity of working with such companies as partners. According to Towbin, "You've got to really work with companies who don't understand the profit motive . . . to keep expenses down, prices up, and make up the difference in the middle. In contrast to the old days, where the more people you employed, the better you were doing, . . . you have to take risks and hopefully you'll get rewards."[46]

But other decisionmakers thought that the Russian fund should speculate in vouchers, buy into investment funds, and invest in American companies doing business in Russia. When Towbin resigned over this difference of opinion, many of the commitments he had made were simply dropped and some funding that had been promised never provided. In any case, operating in Russia was far from easy, especially given the amount of corruption in Russian business (including banks), as shown in chapter 4. The Russian fund, generally operating under much more difficult conditions than those in Central Europe, walked a perpetual tightrope between making conservative and risky judgments.

Some business-support programs failed *both* to make profit and take risks, as the Czech and Slovak Fund demonstrates. A USAID-commissioned evaluation wrote that the fund "is failing to achieve either commercial success or development impact. The investments are suffering major losses, and are generally marginal both in market and in development terms."[47] A member of the fund's board, which was encouraged to resign following a scandal involving its director,[48] emphasized the ambiguity of the funds' mission. "They are neither fish nor fowl," he said.[49]

LOCUS OF LOANS

The tension between the stated mission of the Enterprise Funds and the disbursement of loans also appeared in the geographical concentration of monies. The funds tended to focus on the most developed areas of the recipient countries, where investment already was concentrated, rather than underdeveloped ones. Yet the greater need was often in the latter, where there was little investment.

For example, the Czech Republic experienced "an emerging regional polarisation along the east-west axis," according to sociologist Michael Illner. Regions with the highest developmental potential were those with higher levels of private business and foreign capital investment and also with many trans-border linkages. The two largest urban centers of Prague and Brno enjoyed especially favorable developmental potential.[50]

Likewise, in Poland, very low unemployment and a high degree of private-sector development, privatization, and investment characterized a few favored regions. High unemployment, a virtual stalemate in privatization and the development of business infrastructure, and scant foreign investment all were concentrated in certain other regions.[51] The Warsaw province accounted for about 41 percent of all foreign capital invested in Poland and about 33 percent of the total number of joint-venture companies in March 1993.[52] The pattern of regional disparities (of weak and strong regions) was much the same at the turn of the century.[53]

This trend holds across the landscape of Central and Eastern Europe: diversity characterizes not only individual countries of the region, but also communities and regions within each country. Summing up a volume of work dealing, in part, with the increasing accentuation of regional, ethnic, and other historical differences after 1989, anthropologists Frances Pine and Sue Bridger state:

> The economic prospects of villagers living in beautiful mountain areas near western borders may be very different from those of industrial workers in areas highly polluted by crumbling and archaic factories. For the former, the new order may open opportunities for local developments such as tourism and cross-border trade; for the latter, unemployment and increasing privation has been a more common experience.[54]

Jacek Szlachta, a specialist in regional development, has a similar assessment: "The leaders of the transformation are the capitals and western portions of countries. The problem areas are the eastern and rural areas. This means efficiency and also means there are areas like Appalachia."[55]

Two important experiments designed to narrow this gap were attempted in Poland as the period of Adjustment came into its own: a microlending program under the Enterprise Fund and the EU's Struder program. These programs had as their goal to provide small loans and/or capital-equity grant support in underdeveloped areas.

The microlending program, a subsidiary of the Polish American Enterprise Fund, funded by the U.S. Congress, got under way in 1995 with a fraction of the operating budget of its parent fund. The program was distinctive in that it served clients with little or no access to bank lending. It provided loans to very small businesses: the average size of its loans was only 7,000 *złoty*—roughly $2,887[56]—and the average number of employees in the businesses funded was one to five people. Most firms supported were involved in trading, services (hair dressers, plumbers, construction services, repair shops), and production (bicycles, car parts, toys). As of mid-2000, the program had given more than 34,000 loans, operating through 30 branch centers in Poland.[57]

The microlending program was designed mostly by Poles familiar with the record of microlending programs elsewhere. The program's design was an innovative combination of features adapted from other contexts to the Polish environment and grounded in knowledge of Polish cultural practices. For example, prospective recipients of loans first had to find other firms that also needed loans. A system of interdependencies with these firms, building on models tried in Bolivia and Bangladesh, was then established to ensure loan repayment.[58] The microlending program has been seen by many as contributing valuable support to Poland's small businesses.[59]

The Struder program also made headway toward the goal of supporting small businesses in problem areas. Struder funds sustained some regional institutions and operations, including support for investment projects that created new jobs in the small-business sector. Funds also were provided for the development of small infrastructure projects that were deemed of direct benefit to small and medium-sized enterprises. These programs for regional development were within the framework of Poland's accession to the EU.[60]

Fluctuating business conditions in the recipient countries also meant that needs for dollar-denominated loans would change over time and place. The need for Enterprise Funds in the host countries had to be periodically reconsidered due to changing financial conditions. Whereas, for example, in the early 1990s in Poland there was demand for loans under the Enterprise Fund, demand later diminished due to the fact that the fund's dollar-denominated loans lost attractiveness to borrowers as the Polish inflation rate went down and bank interest rates in *złoty* declined accordingly. Businesses generally preferred to take credit in local currency. In addition, the Polish banks became increasingly reluctant to refer credit-worthy borrowers to the fund's program as the banks became more experienced in credit analysis and risk assessment. By 1994, the banks began extending loans to those borrowers themselves.

Thus, to be useful in a given business environment, funds needed to constantly adapt themselves to the vagaries of that environment.[61] A USAID-commissioned evaluation concluded that the "Funds must establish an investment philosophy based on a clear understanding of the host country's business, legal, and policy environments and not simply mirror the approach of other funds."[62] USAID Enterprise Fund adviser Timothy Knowlton put it simply: "Before you start lending money and investing, you should know where you are."[63]

LOCAL ADAPTATION,
LEADERSHIP, AND THE LIMITS OF WALL STREET

The quality of leadership was a critical factor that determined the demand for, and effectiveness of, the development funds in a given setting. Many fund principals exhibited problems noted earlier with consultants: lack of long-term commitment to their jobs and lack of knowledge about and interest in the realities and business conditions of the countries in which they were operating. As with the consultants discussed in chapter 2, those fund leaders who made extended commitments, grounded themselves in the conditions in which they were working, and developed good working relationships with local people tended to be effective. The tenures of those who did not show respect for the region were often short. Indeed, the funds became noted for a tremendous amount of turnover in leadership.

The relative success of the Slovak Fund versus the Czech Fund—despite the fact that the former operated in a less propitious region— was attributed to its leadership's commitment and adaptation to local business and cultural practices. Many more deals were finalized in the Slovak Republic than in the Czech Republic according to the GAO.[64] The leadership of the Slovak Fund exhibited much more continuity and interest in local business dynamics than did the leadership of the Czech Fund, which was marked by turnover and exhibited little adaptation to the local business climate.[65] A USAID-commissioned evaluation concluded that "the Czech fund has not established a viable program. . . . [It] has been plagued by an inordinate degree of staff turnover, and has failed to put an effective investment team in place. . . . The Czech Republic has perhaps the most conducive country conditions in all of Eastern Europe, yet the CAEF [Czech American Enterprise Fund] has one of the worst performance records."[66] In 1995, the U.S. government intervened in the fund, closing the Washington and Prague offices, replacing management, and selling the Czech investment portfolio (at a 92 percent loss of its invested capital). Henceforth the fund focused on Slovakia.[67]

Further east, astute leadership also was often lacking, although even more crucial. Barry Thomas, who previously had worked for the International Executive Service Corporation and Arthur Andersen under USAID contracts in Russia, explained what happened when he served as the chief financial officer for a company in which the U.S.-Russia Investment Fund (which was created in 1995 from the Russian-American Enterprise Fund and another similar fund) invested $5 million in return for a 50 percent ownership interest. This initial "ill-conceived" investment, reported Thomas, "was made without doing conventional planning and future cash flow expectations. . . . Certain basic things didn't seem to be part of the investment process: the assessment and development of a business plan, the expectation of future cash flow. Things were pretty loose." Furthermore, when the company was "disappearing in an insolvent condition with capital having been consumed and no sources of capital, and major problems with one investment, there didn't seem to be a reaction of the Russian Investment Fund," despite the company's preparation of quarterly reports and budgets specifically for the fund.[68]

The identity crisis of the Enterprise Funds was reflected in, and appears to have been encouraged by, a lack of clarity as to the desired expertise of fund leadership. The funds generally opted to hire investment bankers, but many of those involved in the funds at various levels suggested that people with straightforward business backgrounds were much more needed. Fund overseers and some principals tended to be enamored of a highflying, seemingly sophisticated "investment" approach, involving finance people with major Wall Street reputations. Barry Thomas, who had dealings with the Russian Fund, explained that those hired were "people maybe knowledgeable in Wall Street but not about business—a lot of people from the young MBA marketplace— aspiring investment bankers [whose] business knowledge and background was limited."[69]

Yet taking risks in a tough environment such as Russia did not mean that investments and decisions should be made without calculation, business sense, or preparation. The wrong kind of expertise was emphasized: success in such an environment required strong business skills, knowledge of Russian business conditions, and the ability to work closely with local partners to resolve issues. Instead, as Thomas reported, the fund "got enamored with something, put money into something, and didn't do proper diligence."[70]

Financial and marketing skills alone were not sufficient to run a successful Enterprise Fund operation. Paul Gibian, president of the Czech and Slovak Fund further explained:

> I don't think that sophisticated deal structures that investment bankers have created almost as an art form is what is ultimately most important. . . . The Morgan Stanleys—the numbers people—that may still have a valid role if you talk to airline or utility or energy or [the Czech automobile manufacturer] Skoda because there you have somewhat sophisticated companies that have a market track record. . . . But the sector that we are trying to support . . . has less history, so that's where the operating experience and management evaluation of local companies become much more important. . . . We need to end up not only with Western financial wizards, but also to develop local operating experience.[71]

Indeed, the record of the Enterprise Funds demonstrates that financial and marketing skills alone were not sufficient to run a successful operation. A USAID-funded evaluation of the funds concluded:

> The most successful funds are those that have built a strong, capable investment staff in the country. Ideally, the staff should be headed by an investment manager from the host country who also has extensive training and experience in business investing. . . . The presence of a knowledgeable and competent professional investment staff in the host country, combined with an investment strategy that matches the evolving market conditions, is the most important precondition for success. . . . As new Funds are started, greater effort should be made to understand local market conditions in those countries and to tailor a program that is consistent with market needs and of an appropriate scale.[72]

A MORE PROMISING APPROACH?

Aid programs to encourage business and infrastructure development suffered from many of the same problems as the other approaches outlined in chapters 2 through 4. Startup was strained and expectations were created that could not be met. Fund representatives were the targets of much of the same kinds of local criticism as were the consultants featured in chapter 2. Like the previous approaches, the effectiveness of the funds in a given case depended largely on the aid workers' (in this case, the loan officers') level of adaptation to local conditions, their knowledge of the local players, the quality of their leadership, and their long-term commitment to the effort. The identity crisis of the funds contributed to the problems: tensions between the goals of small, local businesspeople and those of fund managers (including some local elites) who wanted to look good on balance sheets and also to make money fostered frustrated relations between donors and recipients.

However, a major advantage of loan and equity programs to support business was that they did not have to rely on any one group to implement a program. They were more diversified in terms of whom they worked with, and they cooperated with a broader range of recipient individuals and groups. Thus, although the funds achieved uneven results across time and place, as a model they appeared to be more promising than many other aid strategies pursued in Central and Eastern Europe. As USAID Enterprise Fund adviser Knowlton expressed it: "We have spent a gazillion dollars starting stock exchanges as part of privatization. This was premature because value was difficult to determine and there was no transparency and people had nothing to trade. Programs that encourage local private business are the best way we've found to achieve our own goal of sustainability."[73]

CHAPTER SI X

Insights from the Second World

> Before the century ends, I believe the results in Central and
> Eastern Europe—as well as in the N.I.S. [Newly
> Independent States]—will match, if not exceed, the results of
> the eleven-year Marshall Plan.
> —Thomas Dine, Assistant Administrator, USAID, 1995[1]

IN LIGHT OF MANY FAILED RELATIONSHIPS—of misperception, collusion, corruption, and blindness to realities and needs—what were the
alternatives to the aid that Western Europe and the United States offered
the East? For the West to send none at all? It is hard to imagine that this
would have been politically acceptable in the West or satisfactory to the
East amid the euphoria of the fall of the Berlin Wall. In the still highly
polarized political environment of 1989-90, the radical rejection of
communism left the West with a newly manifest destiny. It had little
choice but to applaud the efforts of Central and Eastern Europe's freedom
fighters and promise support that it could not always supply. The West
was predisposed to give aid, just as the East was predisposed to accept it,
enthusiastically.

If the first phase of aid relations—Triumphalism—was predestined
by the prior isolation of East and West occasioned by the Cold War, what
about Disillusionment? Was it also inevitable? Emerging from the
isolation of the Cold War, both West and East were perhaps destined to

have great expectations that could not be fulfilled. Some degree of disappointment seems inevitable given the end of the Cold War and the coming into contact of two profoundly isolated worlds. Triumphalism and Disillusionment were so intense at least partly because of the isolation of the Cold War and the great expectations that its demise created. Both phases were, to a large degree, predictable aftereffects of the Cold War and communism.

Still, many findings here have shown that the donors did their part to exacerbate the tensions of Disillusionment. Had donors designed aid more thoughtfully and grasped the importance of taking into account the legacies of communism—its mindsets and political-institutional frameworks—they might have structured aid differently and thus avoided some of their mistakes. Had they not sent such an ill-suited cast of characters to the aid table, some of these legacies might have been overcome. Instead, the West's misguided aid efforts opened the door to misunderstandings and ill will on a massive scale. The central role of the state—a powerful legacy of communism—played a large part in shaping aid relations and results. The West as symbol, whether as saint or demon, was also an enduring concept that aid reinforced. If donors had treated the East less as if the blackboard of communism could be wiped clean, donor efforts might have achieved more of their stated goals.

The devil was often in the details and in administrative and political processes. The broad strokes of policy and funding typically failed to incorporate the particulars of implementation: who participated, how they were tasked, what their relationships were to each other as well as to the public and to the law. The pressure from government agencies responsible to legislatures in the donor countries to show quick results and visible benchmarks of reform often stood in the way of working toward lasting positive institutional change. The future holds the possibility of equally large failures if these issues are not addressed.

RELATIONSHIPS AND PARADOXES

The aid story in Central and Eastern Europe has entered a new stage: by 1998, nearly all U.S. aid programs to Central Europe were being "graduated," as U.S. aid officials characterized it, and aid programs to Russia and Ukraine were coming under closer scrutiny. By 1998, PHARE had reoriented its Central European program toward helping prepare the countries of the region for prospective membership in the European Union. And, as the new century approached, Poland, Hungary, the Czech Republic, Slovenia, and Estonia were much immersed in pre-accession negotiations with the EU and appeared likely to enter it within the coming decade.[2] In 2000, the United States, the EU, and other donors continued to provide assistance to nations further east but with less energy than that which characterized donor efforts in earlier years.

The aid story cannot be relived, but it may provide insights for future aid efforts. As the Cold War ended, many of its categories disappeared. The representation of the nonaligned nations as "Third World" and that of the communist East Bloc as "Second World" no longer have much analytic relevance to the political and economic world system. Anthropologists have demonstrated "how the 'Third World' has been produced by the discourses and practices of development since their inception in the early post–World War II period," as Arturo Escobar put it.[3] Limited development assistance to at least some of these countries is likely to continue, and several critical conclusions arise from the aid experience to the Second World.

The means by which donors found and connected with their foreign partners were critical to the success or failure of aid efforts, yet were critically flawed. Donors' choices could—and did—shape aid outcomes. Because the Western aid community failed to appreciate the importance of the partners chosen in both West and East, and also did not take into account relationships in the East, it actually helped to replicate some communist-style patterns—in both informal and formal relationships. The more that relationships between West and East, as well as within the East, were ill chosen and ill considered, the more likely that old patterns were replicated by Western assistance. In general, the more problematic the relationships, the more the patterns were reinforced.

In the case of technical assistance sent to Central and Eastern Europe (chapter 2), for example, it was the lack of real working relationships between Eastern and Western representatives in many cases, that tended to replicate relationships reminiscent of communism. Easterners put on communist-style shows for Western visitors (especially during the

Triumphalist phase). And, despite some overt complaining during Disillusionment, reminiscent of symbolic protest under communism, the code of conduct largely remained "You pretend to help us, and we pretend to be helped." Effective technical assistance was limited to cases in which relationships between donors and recipients made sense. These cases typically involved long-term, targeted assistance, in which recipients who were to use the advisers identified the specific type of expertise they needed and donors provided resources and oversight. With few exceptions, it appears, donors and recipients did not work this out in the Triumphalist and Disillusionment phases. Adjustment took place in some contexts after a considerable period of learning.

Such learning did not take place in relationships involving the econolobbyists, who were typically present only during Triumphalism. A version of Triumphalism appeared to be a near-universal feature of the beginnings of "reform" and the involvement of econolobbyists and international financial institutions. The econolobbyists' advice was notable for its generic quality: prescriptions offered in Bolivia were repeated in Poland and later in Russia, with little modification for country-specific conditions. The mode of operation of the econolobbyists—and the damage they did—is by now clear: they went to a country, made unrealistic promises to mostly unsuspecting citizens about such things as improvements in living standards, and pledged international aid—which usually failed to materialize in the amounts and forms expected, and which they might or might not have had access to, and which might or might not have helped. Then they typically disappeared, moving on to another country, another playground for "reform." The defining feature of the involvement of econolobbyists was that they were mostly about public relations. And they rarely were to be found in a country once the phase of Disillusionment was in full swing.

Potential recipients of econolobbyists' involvement would be well served to study the records of the prospective advisers in the countries where they have been active and to be circumspect about whose purposes the econolobbyists ultimately serve. It is potentially misleading to take the econolobbyists' accounts of their records in the various countries at face value: assessments are best made by gathering firsthand information from people with whom the econolobbyists have dealt in the recipient countries. Economists concerned with the record and professional standards of their profession might also discuss standards of conduct and monitor such activities.

In the case of Western support of NGOs that set out to do public service and outreach and help to build civil society (chapter 3), Western aid often enhanced the social, political, and economic standing of informal groups that had formalized themselves as NGOs. This reinforced the informal networks that had formed under communism, giving informal, semiclosed groups still other resources (money, information, and access to Western contacts and opportunities) to be guarded and used only for the group. Communist-style public displays were staged for the consumption of the funders, as in letters signed by an Eastern NGO (but written by its Western counterpart) extolling the virtues of projects already supported and asking for more money, much like the propagandists of old.

On the brighter side, there were cases in which supporting NGOs did not make a mockery of donor intentions. Again, these cases generally involved early error and a conscious process of learning on both sides. Such projects achieved their goals because the donors, as well as the recipients, eventually understood the patterns of informal relationships in the recipient countries and how best to work within them. The Regional Environmental Center is an example of this process of learning.

The aid model of loans to recipient businesses (chapter 5) exhibited many features of the model of supporting NGOs (chapter 3). In the NGO case, donors gave money for public outreach to be used for the greater good; in the case of business loans, donors lent money so that business-people could make money. In the latter case, there was less replication of communist-style theatrics because there was no need to hide self-interest: That people made money was expected. But, like support for NGOs, business loans could reinforce long-standing bureaucratic "arrangements" because of the lack of institutions of governance and financial infrastructures.

The case of the West's giving one "clan" or power group in Russia a blank check and free rein (chapter 4)—the logical extreme of giving to several elite groups as discussed in chapter 3—deserves special attention. This approach served to reinforce many communist-type practices: it strengthened the interdependence between the Russian economic and political systems, and reinforced the practice of inventing fictions to please authorities (in this case, the donors), in part by encouraging the viewing of a Western-selected power group as selfless "reformers." The Russian case was a disaster from beginning to end in part because Western policies helped to politicize and deform relationships. It was unlike the other models of assistance, in which donors and recipients came to some mutually workable adjustment, allowing some projects to be effective. Political scientist Peter Reddaway likens the U.S. support of the Chubais group to America's involvement in Iran, which led to the taking of American hostages in 1979.[4] Such a political or foreign aid strategy *cannot be reformed or amended.* Using "development assistance" as political assistance to one political group or leader was a feature of the Cold War—an attempt to buy loyalties—which continued in the post–Cold War period in the form of new elite-elite relations. However, as shown in Iran and Russia, the potential for political backlash is significant, serious, and has potentially grave consequences, especially in a country with nuclear weapons.

The central role of the state under communism, and its continuing aftereffects, highlights a dilemma for the donors—a dilemma that was never debated in policy and aid circles but which ultimately shaped many aid relations and results. Privatization aid to many Central and Eastern European enterprises appeared almost uniformly to yield few favorable results: operating on an ad hoc basis outside local authorities was largely ineffective and, in some cases, even counterproductive because relevant indigenous organizations and authorities were overlooked. On the other hand, as the Russian case shows, aid projects that were "successful" in donors' eyes often were fruitful because they worked through well-connected local people who "could get things done" through relationships. These "successful" aid projects relied upon a small clique to circumvent, override, or otherwise reorganize political and economic institutions and authorities, ostensibly in the service of the donors' goals, but especially those of the clique. Such relationships appeared to replicate the closed systems of informal relationships upon which the functioning of communist bureaucracies depended.

Some aid providers who found themselves in an environment dominated by informal relationships felt they had to work through those relationships to be effective. To do so, however, lent resources and legitimacy to communist-style organization, thereby both undermining the donors' celebrated attempts to build "independent institutions" and fomenting resentment against the elite cliques that benefited. Either way, donors' strategies—whether they ignored local social organization or worked through it—in crucial ways recalled and encouraged communist legacies. When donors implemented standardized aid programs, they risked being bureaucratic and ineffective; when they were more flexible, they risked reduced accountability. The paradox for donors was that, either way, aid efforts resulted in less-than-optimal aid outcomes.

As the Russian case shows, it is essential that aid policies encourage the building of legal infrastructures and participatory mechanisms, and that they take into account local perceptions, realities, and responses. At the very least, donors must discontinue support of noninclusive "private" organizations and reform by decree. Rather, donors should broaden their base of recipients and support structures to include all relevant parties. Indeed, much of the evidence here presented, from Russia as well as from Central Europe, shows that aid projects that implicate sensitive political processes are very difficult to administer effectively without engendering negative consequences for recipients and/or donors.

COLLISION, COLLUSION, AND CONSEQUENCES

This story has been about efforts to nurture relations between nations (or blocs of nations) using aid as a "bridge"[5] built by certain representatives of each side. As we have seen, a crucial factor shaping aid outcomes is just which actors or groups on each side served as bridge builders and the relationships and "chemical reactions" among them.

Perhaps just as important are the actors and influences that resolved just who would represent both donors and recipients. Their role in casting this story would not have achieved such prominence were it not for the fact that the cast (as outlined in the introduction and chapter 1) consisted of distant, if mutually fascinated, nations and peoples. Cultural ignorance—coupled with the idea that cultural knowledge is either irrelevant or easy to achieve—configured the first phases of the aid story. For example, without a good deal of cultural innocence on the U.S. side about the recipient sides, the econolobbyists could not so easily have created the image in the Western press of playing decisive policy roles. Econolobbyists could create such images only in the absence of processes that would help interpret information for one side with the benefit of cultural knowledge of the other side.

Two overall scenarios can be observed in the story of aid to Central and Eastern Europe. The first scenario is best seen in the case studies focusing mostly on Central Europe presented in chapters 2, 3, and 5 in which recipients were influenced by the donors in some important respects. In time, and usually after both collision and collusion with donor standards, procedures, and representatives, recipients responded in various ways. In some cases they incorporated standards and procedures emphasized by some donor programs and representatives (such as those regarding conflict of interest and accountability) into their own frameworks, albeit often in their own renditions. For example, the Polish NGO community instituted innovative measures to foster "transparency," as described in chapter 3. In other cases, notably the "Marriott Brigade" syndrome detailed in chapter 2, contact with donor organizations confirmed and solidified recipients' differences with the donors—sometimes unconsciously, other times rather consciously. In this first scenario, contact between donor and recipient sides was a process of back and forth, of frequent and often routine contact among many members of the "sides." It was relatively inclusive of many regions and peoples in the recipient nations, as shown in chapter 5.

The second scenario, that of economic aid to Russia (chapter 4), involved a very few pivotal people on both donor and recipient sides who formed one group that, working as a unit, played a decisive role in making and executing policy. These donor and recipient representatives created the Harvard-Chubais partnership and an identity *as a group.* Members of the group typically acted in concert, regardless of whether they formally represented the donor or recipient side. The main loyalty, at least for purposes of getting, using, and portraying aid was to the group and not to either side.

Members of the Harvard-Chubais partnership created a framework in which key members of the partnership had "transidentity" capabilities. These members could draw on the identity of either (donor or recipient) side, regardless of which side they came from. Each side could represent the other and interchange these identities depending on what was called for in a given situation.[6] The same individuals played interchangeable roles, once as representatives of the donors, once as representatives of the recipients. For example, donor representative Jonathan Hay often spoke on behalf of Maxim Boycko, Dmitry Vasiliev, and other recipient representatives from the Chubais Clan. Hay, formally a representative of the United States, interchangeably acted as a Russian (for example, as a "Russian" official empowered to sign off on pivotal high level privatization decisions) and as an American (for example, with formal management authority over other U.S. contractors). In Hay's case, this transidentity was actually institutionalized by the policies, procedures, and dictates of both sides. Likewise, Maxim Boycko, formally a representative of Russia, who to key American officials literally personified the Russian "reformer,"[7] acted as an American in some operations.

In this second scenario, the actors that represented both donor and recipient sides emerged mostly as a result not of choices made by their own sides, but by those made by the *other* side. Just who would represent the recipient side was largely decided by the self-appointed representatives of the donors whose offering of Western money, connections, and clout was readily accepted and monopolized by the Chubais Clan early in the East-West encounter. The Clan's comparative advantage in Russia, as laid out in chapter 4, was its standing in Western political and aid circles. The Clan used its claims on this access to successfully promote itself as *the legitimate representative* of the recipient side.

Similarly, on the Western side, the Harvard group cited its prior access to "reformers" in both Russia and Ukraine as its primary comparative advantage in applying and lobbying for aid contracts; this access was a key plank of Harvard's public relations efforts. These decisions were then institutionally reified by both sides, although not without substantial manipulation of procedures on both sides.

This structure of relationships among people institutionalized flexibility and afforded maximum leeway for its "transactors"[8] to play on their transidentities. It facilitated the ability of a transactor, formally representing the donor side, to arrange entrée of a fellow transactor, formally representing the recipient side, to the donor side. It enabled transactors to represent institutions on both sides, regardless of which side they came from. The most effective transactors were the ones most skilled at playing on their identities and exploiting this flexible structure.

It is conceivable that such latitude could raise questions about the legitimacy of an actor's claims to represent the side from whence he came. However, in many cases, the opposite happened: in the United States, Harvard reinforced Chubais as a signifier for Russia while Chubais's association with Harvard lent him credibility and clout in Russia, at least in some circles at some times. Likewise, in Russia,

Chubais reinforced Harvard as a signifier for the United States. In this way, transactors from different sides reinforced each other's identities *as a member of the other*.[9] Moreover, the process by which transactors reinforced the other to each other's sides served to fortify the influence and identity of the transactors *as a group*. Therefore, transidentity could simultaneously strengthen the distinctive identity of an actor, the identity of that same actor as the "other," and the identity of the group as such.

These two scenarios, then, can have very different consequences for the donors and recipients and the larger societies they represent. In the first scenario, the recipients are influenced by the donors and the process but typically continue to represent the side of their origin. In the second (Russian) scenario, one group interchangeably represents both sides and thus is empowered by transidentity capabilities. This scenario raises a question: What are the implications of a state of affairs in which the choice of who represents one side is shaped to a significant degree by self-selected representatives of the other? The play of identities that this social structure affords enables maximum flexibility and deniability, as well as the opportunity to *reduce accountability* by bodies, procedures, and structures on both sides.

In this increasingly globalized economy with snappy technology, we have the persistent illusion that transferring information is the same as communicating. But fundamental disconnects between cultures and civilizations persist. Thus, opportunities for transidentity and transactor groups to play significant roles may be growing. This phenomenon—and its implications—warrant further exploration.

ADJUSTMENT

Over a number of years of foreign assistance, something of a "learning curve" on the part of both donors and recipients evolved within each recipient country, though often after damage was done, and with the recipients, rather than the donors, doing most of the learning. The redundant and inexperienced consultants that donors sent in the first years of an aid effort to a particular country were sometimes replaced later on by more carefully chosen and useful advisers.

But despite the learning experienced among aid officials and contractors, progress was rarely transferred from one country to another. As assistance moved east, the same lessons had to be relearned (or not) in each new recipient country. Local officials in Ukraine (circa 1994-95) voiced complaints almost identical to those that Central European officials had expressed years earlier (circa 1990-91): that donors send burdensome fly-in–fly-out advisers who stay in expensive hotels and know little about the host country. Only after local criticism or lack of receptiveness to further aid in a recipient country did donors tend to alter their approaches. And in many ways, after initial contact, true change became more difficult because the legacies of communism tended to be more entrenched the farther east the donors went.

This is not to say that the outcome of the aid effort has been entirely negative, or that donor efforts invariably resulted in permanent alienation. Despite the mistakes that were made, and the resentments they engendered, much of the antagonism present a few years earlier has dissipated, at least in Central Europe. In these countries, even if both sides initially came away from the aid table disappointed, person-to-person contact has helped to reduce the isolation stemming from the Cold War. Despite its mixed legacy, aid to Central Europe has been part of a broader process of establishing "normal" relationships between West and East, and aid programs have contributed to the interchange of people and ideas. To a significant degree, these relationships mostly were between elites and on Western terms, but some relationships that were more inclusive and balanced also flourished.

Today, as some Central Europeans match and even outdo their Western counterparts in extravagance and inattention to their neediest citizens, it is sometimes hard to remember the time when the excesses of the Marriott Brigade were universally perceived as offensive. This is not to say that all potential for antagonism toward "the West" has dissipated, especially not in regions and nations where large segments of the population perceive themselves as doing poorly. But the lines of polarization appear different now, because they are primarily between those who have become wealthy with the collapse of communism and those who have not. The same, however, cannot quite be said for Russia or Ukraine.

These lines are partly drawn between countries that are seen as viable candidates to join "the West"—that is, to join multistate economic and political organizations—and those that are not. The most important of these organizations in political, economic, and social terms is the European Union, composed, at this writing, of 15 states of Western and

Southern Europe. Three new members—Austria, Finland, and Sweden—joined the EU in 1995, and since the fall of the Berlin Wall, Europeans have been weighing issues of expansion to the east. To become a member, each country must meet four EU-defined political conditions (establishing a rule of law, supporting democracy, recognizing human rights, and protecting minorities), and one economic condition (the creation of an internationally viable market economy). Ten Central and Eastern European countries have applied for EU membership. The European Commission, the central body of the EU headquartered in Brussels, selected the Czech Republic, Estonia, Hungary, Poland, and Slovenia for negotiations in the first round.

The most important aspect of EU membership is the institutionalization of relations across a range of levels and domains, economic, political, and cultural. Because of its multifaceted nature, membership in the EU is regarded as much more significant than membership in other international and regional organizations.[10] But it is important to keep in mind that memberships in international organizations are long-term relations and processes—as we have seen with the original EU members of Western Europe—and not ends in themselves. EU influences can help shape the relations and processes of its new members, but "joining the West" will not cause people to automatically forget history.

Just as the relationship between Easterner and Westerner is of paramount importance as the century closes, so is the relationship between Easterner and Easterner. This polarization is nowhere more in evidence than in Russia, where frustration and resentment toward the West may well linger. The Russian self-image of a down-at-the-heels superpower created the conditions for charges of Western interference—charges that were often linked to foreign aid. In Russia and Ukraine the perception of the West as a demon has lingered and even been reignited. In contrast to the Visegrád countries, where aid relations entailed uneasy contact but eventually resulted in some selective learning and working together, in Russia, aid resulted in adaptations detrimental to the West.

Whether as saint or demon, the West will continue to play an important role in Central and Eastern Europe's emergence from communism. The lines of polarization between East and West now appear different because at least Central Europeans are increasingly claiming a place in European and international organizations and activities. The term "Marriott Brigade" no longer resonates so harshly for local people because, more and more, some local people have adopted—and even elaborated—the lifestyle characterized by the Brigade. Polish, Hungarian, and Czech consultants now represent the West as part of EU delegations in Romania and Ukraine, and many represent donor organizations as well. More often than not they are treated as partners, if not with deference. And that is what any aid efforts, in the future, should strive to create: cooperation with partners.

If nothing else, the story of aid to Central and Eastern Europe shows how consideration of relationships must be a significant part of any aid strategy. The issues the Central and Eastern European aid story has raised—the expectations, terms, and relationships through which the West connects with the East—will endure. The means of connecting with one's foreign "partners" will continue to be crucial, and not only in situations where the West is sending aid or trying to help. Indeed, relationships are pivotal in diplomacy, international agreements, and business.

In recent years, development anthropologists have focused on the "discourses" of development. The Central and Eastern European aid story is rife with colorful metaphors of transition—of turning fish soup back into an aquarium, having a tooth pulled, or crossing a chasm. The fact that these metaphors were used not just to explain, but actually to *justify,* policies further confirms the importance of studying aid discourses.

The analysis of discourse also, critically, reveals power relations. The U.S. aid community talks about curtailing aid programs by "graduating" the recipient countries. "Graduation" implies that the pupils went to "our" school and succeeded to the extent that "we" assessed their readiness for graduation. At the very least, this view implies that "we" had more influence in most cases than we did; that "our help" was decisive. Clearly, a close look at the language of aid is warranted.

Finally, a return to the work of anthropologists in the powerful areas of social organization and political and economic links is called for in a major way—both to explain the effects of aid strategies and relations between donors and recipients, and, more important, to assess how aid affects relations on many levels in the recipient countries. It is only through a grounded, real-world focus on political, economic, and social relationships that we can understand the "chemical reactions" of the development encounter and make progress toward disentangling—and changing—the world system we know as development.

Tables

TABLE 1*

G-24 COMMITMENTS** TO CENTRAL AND EASTERN EUROPE
(JANUARY 1990 TO DECEMBER 1996)
(IN MILLIONS OF US$‡)

DONORS	PERCENTAGE OF GRANT AID	GRANT AID	CREDITS/OTHER	TOTAL
EU‡‡	51.8	9,117.5	8,496.2	17,613.7
Germany	23.6	4,526.9	14,653.5	19,180.4
United States	57.7	7,064.8	5,174.2	12,239.0
France	35.2	2,542.7	4,679.3	7,222.0
Japan	23.1	1,336.5	4,460.8	5,797.3
Austria	24.3	1,061.9	3,311.0	4,372.8
United Kingdom †	23.4	227.4	745.1	972.5
Other G-24 countries ††	38.4	25,877.7	41,520.1	67,397.8
Total	39.2	31,714.9	49,107.7	80,822.6

SOURCE: *SEED Act Implementation Report Fiscal Year 1997*, p. 224. These are the latest figures available from the G-24. See Table 2 for updated figures from these countries.

*   Figures in Table 1 are based on "G-24 Scoreboard" as reported by individual donors to the G-24. The author would like to acknowledge the help of Janet Ice of the Office of Program Assessment and Coordination, USAID (May 1998), and Isabella Meijer of the Office of External Relations with Central and Eastern Europe, European Union (May 1998). She is also grateful to Hayley Hendrickson for compiling this table.

**   A commitment "is a firm obligation expressed in an agreement or equivalent contract and supported by the appropriation or the availability of public funds, undertaken by the government or an official agency of the reporting country, to furnish resources of a specified amount under specified financial terms and conditions and for specified purposes for the benefit of a recipient country (or multilateral agency)." Source: Isabella Meijer, personal communication, 1998.

*** In this table only, Central and Eastern Europe consists of Albania, Bosnia, Bulgaria, Croatia, Czech Republic, Estonia, Hungary, Latvia, Lithuania, Former Yugoslav Republic of Macedonia, Poland, Romania, Slovak Republic, Slovenia, and Yugoslavia.

‡   The scoreboard is kept in million ECU on a calendar year basis. With the appreciation of the dollar, figures appear lower than in previous years. Figures use conversion rate of $1.10 per ECU.

‡‡ Combined figures for EU Commission and EU Other.

†   Several countries committed larger amounts than the UK. However, UK figures are presented because some UK projects were highly visible.

†† Figures presented are calculated from totals including: Belgium, Denmark, Finland, Greece, Ireland, Italy, Luxembourg, Netherlands, Portugal, Spain, Sweden, Iceland, Norway, Switzerland, EFTA Secretariat, Australia, Canada, New Zealand, and Turkey.

TABLE 2*

TOTAL OFFICIAL AID TO CENTRAL AND EASTERN EUROPE**
FROM BILATERAL AND MULTILATERAL SOURCES
1990-98***

(IN MILLIONS OF US$)

	1990	1991	1992	1993	1994	1995	1996	1997	1998	TOTAL
All Donors	8551.86	9185.38	4735.18	3587.43	5599.28	7334.59	4638.31	4338.11	5259.27	53229.41
European Commission	837.87	1269.44	1452.33	862.75	1085.19	1268.64	1182.95	1179.4	2017.74	11156.31
EU Members	6078.96	3935.11	2230.43	1268.64	1011.88	3699.49	1160.56	1042.84	1091.62	21519.53
Germany	5523.73	2634.71	479.2	320.71	264.97	2878.03	425.18	320.23	331.54	13178.3
Austria	79.14	252.73	433.48	435.48	274.38	236.04	175.68	140.75	135.77	2163.45
France	195.86	129.14	444.12	320.91	306.52	333.87	371.7	270.9	360.83	2733.85
Japan	153.13	11.14	99.69	206.31	280.24	411.44	277.79	209.09	201.64	1850.47
United Kingdom†	123.01	32.48	44.55	45.97	44.9	52.74	54.56	56.63	43.33	498.17
United States	1168	3728	273	100	908	28	106	45	68.66	6424.66

SOURCE: Compiled from the Organization for Economic Co-operation and Development's *Development Assistance Committee Online Database,* Total Official Flows, www.oecd.org (July 8, 2000). The author is grateful to Christina Hertzler for compiling this table.

*   These figures represent actual disbursements rather than commitments or obligations. Official aid compromises financial resource flows from official state or local agencies that are both administered to promote economic development and concessional in character conveying a grant element of a least 25 percent (*OECD Geographical Distribution of Financial Flows To Aid Recipients 1994-98,* Annex).

**   For the purpose of this table, Central and Eastern Europe consists of Albania, Bulgaria, Czech Republic, Hungary, Poland, Romania, and Slovak Republic and excludes the successor states of the former Yugoslavia and the Baltic states.

***   These are the latest figures available from the OECD.

†   Several countries disbursed larger amounts than the UK. The UK figures are presented because some UK projects were highly visible.

TABLES 3.1-3.2

CUMULATIVE OBLIGATIONS* OF THE UNITED STATES
TO CENTRAL AND EASTERN EUROPE THROUGH THE SEED** ACT
(IN MILLIONS OF US$)

TABLE 3.1 (FISCAL YEAR 1990-92)

Sector	Poland	Hungary	Czech Republic	Slovak Republic	Other CEE countries***	TOTAL
Economic Restructuring (includes privatization and private-sector restructuring)	454.24	85.60	48.26	38.00	71.26	697.36
Democracy Building	10.05	5.67	2.39	1.77	19.21	39.09
Improving the Quality of Life	42.58	17.18	13.81	9.04	37.88	120.49
Other	11.92	.18	.26	.14	.89	13.39
TOTAL	516.79	105.28	63.80	48.95	129.24	864.06

SOURCE: U.S. Department of State, SEED Act Implementation Report: Fiscal Year 1997, Washington, D.C.: U.S. Department of State, February 1998, Tables. The author is grateful to Christina Hertzler for compiling this table.

TABLE 3.2 (FISCAL YEAR 1990-99)

Sector	Poland	Hungary	Czech Republic	Slovak Republic	Other CEE countries***	TOTAL
Economic Restructuring	525.57	173.23	89.49	130.79	490.70	1409.78
Strengthening Democratic Institutions	121.70	36.53	17.17	34.49	169.95	379.84
Improving the Quality of Life	32.28	13.04	8.64	10.91	60.66	125.53
Other	247.15	24.67	17.98	14.79	79.42	384.01
TOTAL	926.70	247.47	133.27	190.99	800.66	2299.16

SOURCE: U.S. Department of State, SEED Act Implementation Report: Fiscal Year 1999, Washington, D.C.: U.S. Department of State, March 2000, Tables. The author is grateful to Christina Hertzler for compiling this table.

* An obligation "is an amount of money awarded to a particular activity." This definition of "obligations" is very similar to the definition of "commitments" given by the EU (see Table 1, note**). Personal communication with Janet Ice of the Office of Program Assessment and Coordination, USAID (May through July 1998).

** SEED is an acronym for Support for East European Democracy.

*** Other CEE countries consist of Albania, Bulgaria, and Romania and exclude the successor countries of Yugoslavia and the Baltic states.

COLLISION AND COLLUSION

TABLES 4.1-4.2*

GRANT AID FROM THE EU'S PHARE PROGRAM
TO CENTRAL AND EASTERN EUROPE

(IN ECU MILLIONS)**

TABLE 4.1 (1990-92)

Sector	Poland	Hungary	Czech Republic	Slovak Republic	Other CEE Countries***	TOTAL
Administrative Reform	26.7	22.5	0	0	0	49.2
Agricultural Restructuring	135	38	0	0	132	305
Civil Society, Democratization	0	0	0	0	0	0
Critical Aid	0	0	0	0	156.8	156.8
Education, Training, Research	59.3	45.5	0	0	37.2	142
Environment and Nuclear Safety	75	47	0	0	44.3	166.3
Infrastructure	42.4	8.3	0	0	39.4	90.1
Private and Financial Sectors	191.2	111.5	0	0	132.5	435.2
Social Development	45.2	29	0	0	57.5	131.7
Other	3	5	0	0	46.4	54.4
TOTAL	557.8	306.8	0	0	646.1	1530.7

SOURCE: Commission of the European Communities, *The Phare Programme Annual Report 1996*, Brussels, Belgium: Commission of the European Communities, September 1997, Tables. The author is grateful to Christina Hertzler for compiling this table.

* Figures in Tables 4.1-4.2 only include funds for the Phare program and thus are smaller than the EU figures listed in Tables 1 and 2. Additionally, in Table 1, the G-24 definition of Central and Eastern Europe includes the former Yugoslavia and the Baltic states, which are excluded from Tables 4.1-4.2.

** For Table 4.1, the average 1992 exchange rate was 1.2968 dollars per ECU. For Table 4.2, the average 1998 exchange rate was 1.1200 dollars per ECU (*International Financial Statistics Yearbook, 1999*, International Monetary Fund, pp. 924-5).

*** Other CEE countries consist of Albania, Bulgaria, and Romania and exclude the successor countries of Yugoslavia and the Baltic states.

**** According to the EU's Phare Information Center, Phare program data for 1990-98 by country for each sector are not available. The sector categories have also changed from the 1990-92 data to the 1990-98 data.

TABLE 4.2 (1990-98)

Sector	Poland	Hungary	Czech Republic	Slovak Republic	Other CEE countries***	TOTAL
Administrative Reform	****	****	****	****	****	761.23
Agricultural Restructuring	****	****	****	****	****	562.60
Civil society and Democratization	****	****	****	****	****	104.84
Education, Training, Research	****	****	****	****	****	1012.09
Financial	****	****	****	****	****	268.68
Humanitarian, Food, and Critical Aid	****	****	****	****	****	533.02
Infrastructure, Energy, Transport, and Telecommunications	****	****	****	****	****	2,145.59
Approximation of legislation	****	****	****	****	****	84.07
Consumer Protection	****	****	****	****	****	12.91
Private Sector, Privatization, and Restructuring SMEs	****	****	****	****	****	1,156.02
Integrated Regional Measures	****	****	****	****	****	340.15
Social Development and Employment	****	****	****	****	****	272.84
Public Health	****	****	****	****	****	105.57
Other	****	****	****	****	****	778.15
TOTAL	1731.51	864.04	389.74	253.23	2211.92	8890.88

SOURCE: Commission of the European Communities, *The Phare Programme Annual Report* 1998, Brussels, Belgium: Commission of the European Communities, March 2000, Tables. The author is grateful to Christina Hertzler for compiling this table.

TABLE 5

TOTAL OFFICIAL AID* TO THE FORMER SOVIET UNION
FROM BILATERAL AND MULTILATERAL SOURCES
1990-98**

(IN MILLIONS OF US$)

Country	1990	1991	1992	1993	1994	1995	1996	1997	1998	TOTAL
Russia	254.0	933.04	3418.25	8557.95	7487.84	9186.53	3743.9	5351.66	8391.32	47324.49
Ukraine	289.0	368.3	654.98	416.16	403.15	771.13	1047.77	560.54	920.32	5431.35
Other FSU***	0.0	4276.78	838.52	1598.47	2742.79	2892.44	2706.33	2632.20	3921.68	21609.21
TOTAL	543.0	5578.12	4911.75	10572.58	10633.78	12850.1	7498.00	8554.40	12903.36	74045.09

SOURCE: Compiled from the Organization for Economic Co-operation and Development's *Development Assistance Committee Online Database, Total Official Flows,* www.oecd.org (July 8, 2000). The author is grateful to Christina Hertzler for compiling this table, and also would like to acknowledge the help of Rick Wu from the OECD Washington Center.

* These figures represent actual disbursements rather than commitments or obligations. Official aid compromises financial resource flows from official state or local agencies that are both administered to promote economic development and concessional in character conveying a grant element of a least 25 percent (*OECD Geographical Distribution of Financial Flows To Aid Recipients 1994-98,* Annex).
** These are the latest figures available from the OECD.
*** Other FSU countries include Kazakhstan, Uzbekistan, Kyrgyz Republic, Georgia, Armenia, Azerbaijan, Tajikistan, Turkmenistan, Belarus, Lithuania, Estonia, Moldova, and Latvia.

TABLE 6

TOTAL OFFICIAL AID* TO RUSSIA AND UKRAINE FROM BILATERAL AND MULTILATERAL SOURCES 1990-98**

(IN MILLIONS OF US$)

Donor	Russia	Ukraine
European Union Members	29167.72	1975.17
European Commission	1260.95	459.31
United Kingdom †	324.69	73.92
Germany	23608.28	1768.72
United States	5034.88	685.21
Japan	1480.83	205.45

SOURCE: Compiled from the Organization for Economic Co-operation and Development's Development Assistance Committee Online Database. Total Official Flows, www.oecd.org (July 8, 2000).
The author is grateful to Christina Hertzler for compiling this table.

*   These figures represent actual disbursements rather than commitments or obligations. Official aid
compromises financial resource flows from official state or local agencies that are both administered to promote economic development and concessional in character conveying a grant element
of a least 25 percent (*OECD Geographical Distribution of Financial Flows To Aid Recipients
1994-98*, Annex).
** These are the latest figures available from the OECD.
†   Several countries disbursed larger amounts than the UK. The UK figures are presented because
some UK projects were highly visible.

TABLE 7

U.S. ASSISTANCE TO THE FORMER SOVIET UNION: CUMULATIVE FUNDS BUDGETED FY 1992-99

(IN MILLIONS OF US$)

Funding Category	Russia	Ukraine	Other FSU*	TOTAL FSU
FSA**	2498.75	1468.18	2784.16	6751.09
as % of total FSU	37.01%	21.17%	41.24%	100.00%
Non-FSA***	5172.74	847.11	2804.07	8823.92
as % of total FSU	58.62%	30.21%	31.77%	100.00%
TOTAL	7671.49	2315.29	5588.23	15575.01
as % of total FSU	49.25%	14.86%	35.87%	100.00%

Source: U.S. Department of State, Office of the Coordinator of U.S. Assistance to the NIS. *U.S. Government Assistance to and Cooperative Activities with the New Independent States of the Former Soviet Union, FY 1999 Annual Report,* Washington, DC: U.S. Department of State. January 2000, Tables. The author is grateful to Christina Hertzler for compiling this table.

*   Other FSU states consist of Armenia, Azerbaijan, Georgia, Kazakhstan, Kyrgyz Republic, Tajikistan, Uzbekistan, Belarus, and Moldova.
**   Freedom Support Act funds consist of: NIS Special Initiatives, Energy Efficiency and Market Reform, Environmental Policy and Technology, Healthcare Improvement, Private-Sector Initiatives, Food-Systems Restructuring, Democratic Reform, Housing Sector Reform, Economic Restructuring and Financial Reform, Eurasia Foundation, Enterprise Funds, Exchanges and Training, Russia Energy & Environment Commodity Import Program, Administrative Expenses and transfers to other agencies such as Department of Commerce, Department of Energy, Department of State, Department of Justice, the Overseas Private Investment Corporation, U.S. Trade and Development Agency, Peace Corps, Environmental Protection Agency, National Science Foundation, Customs, Nuclear Regulatory Commission, Department of Agriculture, and Department of Treasury.
*** Non-Freedom Support Act funds consist of transfers to the following: Department of Defense, Department of Agriculture, Department of Energy, National Science Foundation, Department of Commerce, Export-Import Bank, Trade and Development Agency, Department of State and the Peace Corps.

TABLE 8*

EUROPEAN UNION TACIS FUNDS ALLOCATED TO
THE FORMER SOVIET UNION BY SECTOR 1991-97†
(IN ECU MILLIONS)**

Sector	Russia†	Ukraine†	Other FSU***	TOTAL FSU
Restructuring state enterprises and private sector development	255.53	72.16	151.09	478.78
Public administration reform, social services and education	247.66	36.31	204.62	488.59
Agriculture	141.74	41.02	124.83	307.59
Energy	140.6	55.38	121.73	317.71
Transport	102.67	17.37	103.32	223.36
Telecommunications	26.53	1.38	11.2	39.11
Policy Advice	18.95	0	184.26	203.21
Nuclear Safety and environment	23.39	100.54	524.57	648.5
Other	46.82	33.62	559.82	640.26
TOTAL	1003.89	357.78	1985.44	3347.11

SOURCE: European Commission, Tacis Funds Allocated By Sector 1991-97, *Tacis Annual Report 1997*, Brussels, Belgium: European Union Directorate General 1A.

*   The EU figures in Table 7 do not coincide with those in Table 5 because Table 7 shows the funds allocated through the TACIS program and Table 5 shows all funds allocated through the EU and the EIB.

**   In 1997, the average exchange rate was 1.1341 dollars per ECU (*International Financial Statistics Yearbook, 1999*, International Monetary Fund, pp. 924-5).

*** Other FSU states consist of Armenia, Azerbaijan, Georgia, Kazakhstan, Kyrgyz Republic, Tajikistan, Uzbekistan, Belarus, Moldova, and monies allocated for regional programs.

†   Tacis program data for 1991-98 by county for each sector are not available. However, from 1991-98, Russia and Ukraine were allocated total Tacis funding of 1200.5 million ECU and 422.2 million ECU respectively (European Commission, Allocation of Tacis Resources from 1991-98, *Tacis Annual Report 1998*, Brussels, Belgium: European Commission, June 2000).

Methodology

This study is an *ethnography across levels and processes,* as set forth in the introduction. To capture the aid story, I have followed aid issues through actors and processes on both donor and recipient sides, with aid as the common thread. Interactions between donors and recipients occur on (and between) several levels and over time. In conducting an ethnography of foreign aid across levels and processes, I worked in multiple settings and charted the interactions among parties to the aid process. I employed a technique that some anthropologists have called "studying through." As Cris Shore and Susan Wright explain it, studying through "entails multi-site ethnographies which trace policy connections between different organizational and everyday worlds even where actors in different sites do not know each other or share a moral universe."[1]

Studying through has enabled me to examine interactions among aid discourses, actors, and institutions across place and time. It has enabled me to follow donors' discourses, policies, and projects all the way through to recipients' responses to them, and, in turn, back to donors' responses, and so on. It has enabled me to chart the "chemical reactions" that are produced in the interface among parties to the aid process and that shape aid outcomes. Ultimately, studying through has enabled me to track interactions not only between actors on the ground (donor and recipient representatives and other parties to the aid process), but also between the larger systems they represent. (See introduction, section titled "Chemical Reactions.")

Studying through builds on a longtime development in anthropology. Some 30 years ago, Laura Nader appealed to the discipline to "study up"—that is, to analyze powerful institutions and elites of complex societies—as an antidote to the traditional focus on poor, colonized, and marginalized peoples. "A reinvented anthropology," Nader wrote, "should study powerful institutions and bureaucratic organizations in the United States, for such institutions and their network systems affect our lives and also affect the lives of people that anthropologists have traditionally studied all around the world."[2] Likewise, Eric Wolf urged anthropologists to "spell out the processes of power which created the present-day cultural systems and the linkages between them."[3] A growing number of anthropologists are doing so. [4]

Today, given the ever greater influence of international financial and policy institutions, global elites, and globalization processes, such studies are even more compelling. No approaches or methods are better suited to studying these issues than ethnographic research across levels and processes and studying through. Such ethnographies should enable us to capture political and economic policies and globalization processes on the level(s) where they are experienced—whether a community, company, social network, cluster of networks, "clan," family, city, social strata, or public opinion.

Although many of those units are taken to be the "local" level and anthropological tradition lies in studying that level (often on-the-ground communities), an ongoing discussion in anthropology questions the nature of the local. Akhil Gupta and James Ferguson suggest that "the idea of locality is not well thought out" and call for its reexamination.[5] Sherry Ortner observes that "we can no longer take communities to be localized, on-the-ground entities, or at least that their local, on-the-ground form is only one moment and site of their existence."[6] And Jean and John Comaroff conclude that "'Locality' is not everywhere, nor for every purpose, the same thing; sometimes it is a family, sometimes a town, sometimes a nation, sometimes a flow or a field, sometimes a continent or even the world; often it lies at the point of articulation among two or more of these things."[7] Indeed, as we see in the cases presented in chapters 2 through 5, the aid story provides examples of diverse points of articulation.

FIELD RESEARCH

It is difficult to capture the process of conducting an intensive fieldwork project over ten years in multiple locations (including Washington, D.C., Brussels, London, Bonn, Warsaw, Budapest, Prague, Bratislava, Moscow, and Kiev) and so many more specific sites. To follow issues in which actors in multiple locations and sites are involved has required frequent shifts between donor and recipient societies. Moreover, the aid story unfolded over many years. For these reasons, the process of studying it was far from linear.

If a back-and-forth feel characterized the research process, the foci of my fieldwork were, by contrast, enduring. My field research focused mainly on interviewing and observation at four organizational levels: (1) at donor agencies, with individuals responsible for establishing policy guidelines and administering projects (for instance, U.S., EU, German, and UK officials located at donor headquarters as well as in donor offices in recipient countries); (2) at recipient institutions, with key officials directly involved in aid programs, including officials at the core institutions of aid coordination (for example, the [Polish] Council of Ministers; the [Hungarian] Assistance Coordination Secretariat of the Ministry of International Economic Relations; the [Czech] Centre for Foreign Assistance of the Ministry of the Economy; and the [Slovak] Department of Foreign Assistance of the Ministry of Foreign Affairs); (3) at meetings where donors and recipients came together; and (4) at selected institutions that received consultants and/or funds, including enterprises, consulting firms, nongovernmental organizations, and such recipient ministries as privatization, industry, finance, and environment.

With multiple donors, multiple recipients, and myriad projects, the subject might indeed appear overwhelming, and indeed, at times it felt so. The study was ambitious, but I was able to narrow its scope. It helped, for example, that a limited universe of relevant agencies and individuals was involved in efforts on the recipient side. In the privatization ministries of Central Europe, for example, typically two, at most three, officials in each particular aid effort principally worked directly with the privatizing enterprises and the foreign consultants sent to advise them. It was possible therefore to talk with each of them.

To select projects for close study from among hundreds of potential sites, I conducted an exploratory survey of priority projects in the priority countries, *as seen by the donors*. I began my empirical research in Poland, Hungary, and Czechoslovakia, which were viewed as most likely to succeed among the transitional countries and which received the most donor attention and funding, at least initially.[8] Later, as donors moved into Russia, I worked there as well. (See introduction, section titled "In the Field.")

In scouting around potential projects, I cast a wide net. Many of the cases I then chose to examine in depth were considered by donors to be "model projects," with several or many donors concentrating resources on them. These projects included the Ursus tractor factory near Warsaw, the Regional Environmental Center in (later, near) Budapest, and the Russian Privatization Center in Moscow. Extensive study of these projects provided much information about the overall results of the particular aid strategies they represented.

I found that the economic, political, and social impacts of grant aid could be accurately assessed on a broad scale only after studying specific cases of aid implementation. For example, the economic impact of privatization assistance would be extremely difficult, if not impossible, to establish without first evaluating individual cases. Many variables enter into privatization, including the political environment and the political and economic interests of parties to the privatization process, such as ministry officials, factory managers, and workers. Establishing a sound causal relationship between aid and a specified economic outcome (by looking, for example, at the number of technical advisers or the number of privatized companies), is highly problematic. Further, equating economic success or "development" simply with the number of factories privatized also is highly problematic. My approach, therefore, was to assess the effects of aid in individual cases.

To gather firsthand information, I have employed two methods in particular: The first is the long-tested "extended case method" detailed by anthropologist J. Van Velsen, which "requires the ethnographer's close acquaintance with individuals over a lengthy period of time and a knowledge of their personal histories and their networks of relationships."[9] I found this technique particularly appropriate to studying the unfolding aid story. It enabled me to follow individuals and groups through a series of decisions, events, and problems and was especially useful as a tool for studying relationships among individuals and groups representing donor and recipient sides. Although the individuals and groups involved in a particular "case" sometimes were located in different sites, they always were connected by the policy or aid implementation process and/or by actual social networks.

I conducted many open-ended interviews and compared and assessed people's responses to the same questions over time.[10] The open-ended format allowed people to define their own issues and to explain in their own terms. I asked people about their own activities, perspectives, and networks, as well as about those of others in their circle or organization. In following particular circles and organizations, I also talked with those outside them, but having direct experience with them.

The information I sought (for example, Western perspectives on Central and Eastern European problems, and Central and Eastern European views of Western projects) could best, and in many cases only, be gleaned through in-depth fieldwork and related interviewing and observation. The networks and interrelationships I explored (for example, among a group of Western consultants, a Russian clan, and certain donor officials) could be obtained only through access to and trust among a variety of informants familiar with the same project. By traveling to the region at regular intervals and following up interviews conducted earlier as much as possible, I was able to track changes in policy implementation and in responses on the Central and Eastern European side.

The second method I employed to gather firsthand information, though less established as a method used by anthropologists, appears to be particularly called for in an ethnography across levels and processes. My research entailed hundreds of interviews and informal conversations with officials, notably aid principals in donor countries. This required using methods and ethics from journalism, which involve techniques such as formal interviewing. It also required cross-checking critical information and confirming key points with multiple sources. Again, it was necessary to move back and forth among field sites to cross-check and verify, if sometimes only by telephone or e-mail once contact had been established.

Because anthropologists increasingly study the powerful, I believe that the anthropological ethic ordaining that "our first responsibility is to those whose lives and cultures we study" ought to be reexamined. The dilemma is about how to proceed when a study examines both those controlling the funding and defining the problems (donors) and those with typically much less influence and recourse (recipients). What of the anthropologist's responsibility to the more powerful (donor) end? Does an anthropologist have the same responsibility to an agency that employs a public relations staff as it does to a tribe facing extinction? I have concluded that studying powerful institutions and actors binds anthropologists to the ethical code and practices of journalism with regard to treatment of "sources." Therefore, I protect the confidentiality of sources when they have so requested.[11] Anthropologists engaged in research in government agencies on sensitive issues may find it difficult to proceed without employing ethics from journalism because it will be expected of them by their sources.[12]

In addition to firsthand interviewing and observation, I have consulted reports and internal memoranda of donors and recipients, project documents, studies by other scholars and analysts, investigative reports and reporters, materials obtained under the Freedom of Information Act, and evaluations carried out by donors and independent organizations. The U.S. General Accounting Office and the EU Court of Auditors conducted a number of valuable investigations that served to confirm and broaden my findings. More and more, anthropologists are consulting such works. As Akhil Gupta and James Ferguson write: "Talking to and living with the members of a community are increasingly taking their place alongside reading newspapers, analyzing government documents, observing the activities of governing elites, and tracking the internal logic of transnational development agencies and corporations."[13]

FURTHER THOUGHTS

As I have learned, studying programs and policies in which powerful institutions and actors are involved can spur much-needed public debate. It also can generate attack from individuals whose troubling conduct has come to light as a result of the research. For example, after publication of the first edition of this book and articles on the subject, two advisers involved in the aid story sought to discredit my work and to portray me as a conspiracy theorist "going after leading advocates of radical market reform."[14] Confirmation of my findings from sources such as investigatory bodies helped to firmly establish the credibility of the study.

In the course of this study, I have found common ground not only with fellow anthropologists but also with political scientists, economists, lawyers, investigators, and journalists working on pieces of the same issues. The world of the anthropologist, especially one studying across levels and processes, may no longer be so isolated. Perhaps this is an indication that cross-fertilization of approaches and methods increasingly may be called for in anthropological studies of global issues and interactions. By bringing to bear anthropological approaches and methods such as studying through, anthropologists can take the lead.

Interviews

HOW TO INTERPRET THIS LIST

In conducting research for this book I interviewed some 1,855 people during the period of 1991 to 2000, of which about 690 were on-the-record. The following list is *illustrative* of categories of people with whom I did formal on-the-record interviews. Many of these people were interviewed several times, and/or are people with whom I had ongoing conversations throughout the aid story.

However, this list does *not* represent, or underrepresents, several major categories of interviewees with whom conversations were typically "off-the-record" or "on background," and therefore may not be included here. I had numerous such meetings and conversations with staff members of congressional and parliamentary bodies, staff members of investigatory bodies (including U.S., international, Central European, and Russian), and mid- and high-level actors. This list also underrepresents Western consultants. I had numerous meetings with consultants who provided valuable information but did not wish to be named.

Titles and affiliations are given *for the time during which the interview took place.* As much as possible, I took titles from business cards provided by interviewees. However, when cards or specific titles were not provided, I instead give a brief description.

Aanenson, Chuck. Program Officer, USAID, Poland.

Abalkin, Leonid. Director, Institute of Economics, Russian Academy of Sciences.

Artemiev, Igor. Private Sector Development Specialist, World Bank.

Austin, Jay. Senior Attorney and Codirector of the Environmental Program for Central and Eastern Europe, Environmental Law Institute, Washington, D.C.

Baldwin, Jeffry. Partner, DRT Poland (subsidiary of Deloitte & Touche), Poland.

Banque, Robert. Director, Office of Technical Assistance, U.S. Department of Treasury.

Barry, Ann R. Deputy Chief of Mission, U.S. Delegation, Organization for Economic Cooperation and Development, Paris.

Barry, Robert. Ambassador and Special Adviser for East European Assistance to the Deputy Secretary of State, United States.

Bazilevich, Leonid. Professor, Department of Management and Engineering Management, Stevens Institute of Technology.

Bejger, Peter. Media Advisor, USAID-funded Ukraine Market Reform Education Program.

Bernard, Richard P. Executive Director, Resource Secretariat for the Russian Federation Commission on Securities and the Capital Market.

Bernstam, Michael. Economist, Hoover Institution, Stanford University.

Bielecki, Jan Krzysztof. Former Prime Minister, Poland, and Executive Director, European Bank for Reconstruction and Development, London.

Bochniarz, Henryka. Former Minister of Industry, Poland.

Bogutyn, Tomasz. Manager, Corporate Development Department, LOT Polish Airlines.

Bonwitt, Bob. SIGMA, Organization for Economic Cooperation and Development, Paris.

Borodziej, Włodzimierz. Director General, Parliament Bureau of Research, Poland.

Bosnjakovic, Branko. Development and Outreach Manager, Regional Environmental Center, Hungary.

Boure, Eduard. Head, Russian Privatization Center.

Bovt, George G. Director, International Department, *Kommersant Daily*, Russia.

Boycko, Maxim. Head, Russian Privatization Center.

Bratinka, Pavel. Deputy Minister, Ministry of Foreign Affairs, Czech Republic.

Brodsky, Olexandr. First Deputy to Head of the Agency, Agency for Coordination of International Technical Assistance, Ukraine.

Brooks, Michael. USAID official, working on Enterprise Funds.

Brunat, Eric. Resident Expert, Institute for the Economy in Transition, EU - TACIS - PROMETEE, Russia

Brzezinski, J. Ian. Director, National Security Programs, Council of Advisors to the Parliament of Ukraine.

Brzezinski, Zbigniew. Board member, Polish-American Enterprise Fund.

Bugaj, Ryszard. Representative to *Sejm*, Poland.

Bujak, Zbigniew. Representative to *Sejm*, Poland.

Bulkley, Jonathan A. Managing Director, KPMG Peat Marwick, Moscow.

Burisch, Michael. Team leader, Programme and Evaluation Adviser, Ministry of International Economic Relations, PHARE Secretariat, Hungary.

Burkov, Sergei V. Chairman of the Committee for Property, Privatization and Economic Activity of the State Duma of the Federal Assembly of the Russian Federation.

Burns, Richard. Chief, Division of Privatization and Finance, Office of Economic Restructuring, Bureau for Europe, USAID.

Burton, Phil. Consultant, DRT, Czechoslovakia.

Cadwell, Charles. Consultant, USAID's legal reform program, Russia.

Cenková, Jitka. Head of G24 Unit, Centre for Foreign Assistance of the Ministry of the Economy of the Czech Republic.

Childress, Ronald. Former director of Rule of Law Consortium, ARD/ Checchi Joint Venture in Russia.

Ciepiela, Cecilia. Official, Office of Private Enterprise and Economic Restructuring, USAID Moscow.

Clifford, Deirdre. Official on privatization, USAID.

Coles, Walter. Official on privatization, USAID.

Cordet-Dupouy, Annie. Principal Operations Officer, World Bank, Poland.

Cybert, Piotr. Former employee, DRT, Poland.

Czerniawski, Jan. Consultant, Price Waterhouse, Poland.

Dąbrowski, Marek. CASE (consulting firm), Warsaw, Poland.

Davenport, Michael H. Second Secretary, British Embassy, Poland.

Dean, Steve. Division Chief, Contracts Division for Eastern Europe and the New Independent States, USAID's procurement office.

Dempsy, David. USAID-funded Financial Adviser - Privatization, State Property Agency, Hungary.

Di Carlo, Rosemary A. Cultural Attache, U.S. Embassy, Moscow.

Dine, Thomas A. Assistant Administrator, USAID.

Drábek, Zdeněk. Former aid coordinator, Czechoslovakia.

Edwards, Joan. Senior Commercial Officer, United States Foreign Commercial Service, Warsaw, Poland.

Egermayer, Petr. Employee, USAID, Czechoslovakia.

Eubank, Lawrence. Vice President, National Operations, Russian American Enterprise Fund.

Fargas, Paweł. International Relations department, Ministry of Finance, Slovakia.

Foley, John. Consultant, Price Waterhouse, Moscow.

Frankel, David P. Legal Consultant, Ministry of Administration and Privatization of National Property, Slovak Republic.

French, Barry. Bozell SMG, Moscow.

Garai, Eugen. Official, Czechoslovak Embassy, Warsaw.

Ghazanfar, Agha. Consultant in Ukraine.

Gibian, Paul. President, Czech and Slovak American Enterprise Funds.

Ginsberg, Marianne. Coordinator, Environmental Partnership for Central Europe, and Senior Program Officer, German Marshall Fund.

Glinkina, Svetlana. Deputy Director, Institute for International Economic and Political Studies, Russia.

Głowacki, Jacek. Deputy Director, Parliament Bureau of Research, Poland.

Gold, Michael. Managing Director of the Crimson Capital project in the Ministry of Privatization, Czech Republic.

Gomm, Jean. Principal Administrator, Centre for Co-Operation with the Economies in Transition, Organization for Economic Cooperation and Development.

Goodwin, Penny. Senior Vice President, Bozell SMG, Moscow.

Graham, Thomas. Former Chief Political Analyst, U.S. Embassy in Moscow, and Senior Associate, Carnegie Endowment for International Peace.

Guilford, Richard. Coopers & Lybrand and Hungarian Foundation for Enterprise Promotion, Hungary.

Gurr, Lisa Anne. Anthropologist and expert on Ursus, the Polish tractor factory, Wayne State University.

Gyebnár, István. Third Secretary, Ministry for Foreign Affairs, Department of International Economic Relations, Hungary.

Gyözö, Antalfi. Head of department, Monor (enterprise), Hungary.

Hadley, Stephen J. Official, USAID–Kiev.

Hardi, Peter. Executive Director, Regional Environmental Center, Hungary.

Hartelius, Dag. Director, Department of Central and Eastern Europe, Ministry for Foreign Affairs, Sweden.

Haško, Viliam. Assistant to the State Secretary, Ministry of Administration and Privatization of National Property of the Slovak Republic.

Hay, Jonathan. General Director, Harvard Institute for International Development (HIID) program in Russia.

Heba, Bogusław. President, Foundation for Privatisation in the Republic of Poland.

Henderson, Keith. Head, USAID rule-of-law program for Eastern Europe and the former Soviet Union.

Hines, Mary. Consultant, Price Waterhouse, Poland.

Hodík, Jiří. Coordinator, PHARE privatization program, Czech Republic.

Horkusha, Mykola. Deputy chair of the Department for Business Support, Ministry of the Economy, Ukraine.

Hrbáčková, Jarmila. Department of Foreign Assistance of the Ministry of Foreign Affairs of the Slovak Republic.

Huebner, Charles. Managing Director, Hungarian-American Enterprise Fund.

Huger, Greg. Director, private sector initiative in NIS, USAID.

Hume, Ian. Head, World Bank, Poland.

Humphreys, Michael B. Counsellor, European Commission Delegation in Ukraine.

Hunter, John. Consultant, Coopers & Lybrand, Czechoslovakia.

Ichord, Robert. USAID official working on energy issues.

Ivanov, Vadim V. Director, Institute of Economic Policy, Moscow, and Member, Board of Directors, Institute for the Economy in Transition, Moscow.

Ivantchenko, Igor A. Deputy Director for Cooperation with International Organizations and Foreign Countries, Ukraine.

Jacoby, Ruth. Former Director, Secretariat for Cooperation with Central and Eastern Europe, Sweden.

Jenkins, Gary. Official, British Know How Fund.

Jensen, Don. Former Second Secretary at the U.S. Embassy in Moscow, and Associate Director of the Broadcasting Division for Radio Free Europe/Radio Liberty.

Johnson, Harold J. Director, National Security and International Affairs Division, U.S. General Accounting Office.

Johnson, Susan Rockwell. Senior Advisor to the Ambassador for Technical Assistance and Cooperation, U.S. Embassy, Moscow.

Jolez, George. Director of Consulting, Coopers & Lybrand, Hungary.

Joslin, William. Representative, USAID, Poland.

Kacprowicz, Grażyna. President, Foundation for Public Administration Development, Omega-PHARE, Poland.

Kaczyński, Lech. Former Director of NIK (Supreme Control Board), Poland.

Kádár, Béla. Minister, Ministry of International Economic Relations, Hungary.

Kalabiński, Jacek. Washington Correspondent, *Gazeta Wyborcza* (Warsaw, Poland).

Kaliakin, Boris. Deputy Executive Manager, Coordinating Unit for EC Technical Assistance, Moscow.

Kamiński, Antoni. Sociologist and Consultant, Adam Smith Centre, Poland.

Kaplan, Sheila. Investigative reporter.

Karns, Mark. Privatization official, USAID.

Kawalec, Stefan. General Director, Ministry of Finance, Poland; Head, National Bank of Poland.

Kazár, Péter. Deputy Director, Policy and Asset/Portfolio Management Unit, State Property Agency, Hungary.

Kinnear, Ralph. Social Development Adviser, Overseas Development Administration, British Know How Fund.

Kittel, Walter. State Secretary, Germany.

Kjaer, John. Principal Coordinator, PHARE program, Brussels.

Klevana, Leighton. President, Slovak American Enterprise Fund.

Klimova, Rita. Former Czechoslovak Ambassador to the United States.

Knowlton, Timothy. USAID Enterprise Fund Adviser (personal services contractor), Washington, D.C.

Kobelinski, Mitchell. Former Administrator, Small Business Administration, United States.

Koch, Thomas. Bundesministerium für Wirtschaft, Bonn, Germany.

Kołodko, Grzegorz. Professor of Economics and Director, Institute of Finance; former First Deputy Prime Minister and Minister of Finance, Poland.

Kopátsy, Sándor. Economist and former member, State Property Agency, Hungary.

Kopińska, Grażyna. Program Director in Poland, Polish-American Enterprise Clubs.

Kováts, Kornél. Assistance Coordination Secretariat of the Hungarian Ministry of International Economic Relations.

Kowalski, Piotr. Vice President, The Enterprise Credit Corporation, Polish American Enterprise Fund.

Kownacki, Piotr. Deputy director, Zespol Analiz Systemowych, Najwyższa Izba Kontroli (NIK) (the Supreme Control Board), Poland.

Kozak, Marek. Official (aid coordination unit), Council of Ministers, Poland; General Director, Polish Agency for Regional Development.

Krawchenko, Bohdan. Director, Institute of Public Administration and Local Government, Cabinet of Ministers, Ukraine.

Krawczuk, Marek. Official, Agency for Industrial Development, Ministry of Industry, Poland.

Krizsa, Rozália. Managing director, Monor (enterprise), Hungary.

Król, Stanisław. Director, Economic Portfolio, Huta Warszawy, Warsaw, Poland.

Krowacki, Krzysztof. Minister, Ministry of Finance, Poland.

Kryvenko, Oleksandr. Editor-in-Chief, International Media Center, Internews, Ukraine.

Kucheriv, Ilko. Executive Director, Democratic Initiatives Research and Educational Center, Kiev, Ukraine.

Kutcherenko, Elena. Deputy Director of the Department for Cooperation with the U.S.A. and Canada, Agency for Coordination of International Technical Assistance.

Lawina, Anatol. Official, Najwyższa Izba Kontroli (NIK) (the Supreme Control Board), Poland.

Lewicki, Zbigniew. Official, Ministry of Foreign Affairs, Poland.

Lieberman, Ira. Senior Manager in the Private Sector Development Department, World Bank.

Light, Jay. Professor, Harvard Business School and member of board of directors of Harvard Management Company (HMC).

Lipson, Clara. Polish American Enterprise Funds.

Lipton, David. Vice President, Jeffrey Sachs and Associates, Inc.

Lom, Paul. Managing Partner, KPMG, Czechoslovakia.

Long, Dennis. USAID official working in environment, energy, technology.

Lubina, Lubo. Slovak Ministry of Foreign Affairs.

Ludwiczak, Zdzisław. Deputy Director, Department of the Americas, Ministry of Foreign Affairs; Senior Advisor in the Ministry of Foreign Affairs, Poland.

Lukács, Erzsébet. Director, Directorate of International Relations, State Property Agency, Hungary.

Mailloux, Laurier. Director, USAID's Office of Privatization and Economic Restructuring.

Maj, Waldemar. President, Foundation for the Development of the Financial Sector, EC PHARE Financial Sector Development Programme, Poland.

Makkay-Chambers, Adrienne. Deloitte & Touche, Budapest, Hungary.

Martinec, Ivo. Federal Ministry of the Economy, Bureau for Coordination of Foreign Assistance, Czechoslovakia.

Matiaszek, Petro. Executive Director, Council of Advisers to the Parliament of Ukraine

Matisová, Andrea. Slovak Ministry of Foreign Affairs.

Maund, Jim. Official, British Know How Fund.

Mayhew, Alan. Former head, EU PHARE program.

McCaffrey, Gregory A. Business Manager/Consultant, Policy Economics Group, KPMG Peat Marwick, Moscow.

McCuaig, Leslie. Project Officer, New Business Development, USAID-Moscow.

McDonald, Kevin. International Team for Company Assistance (ITCA).

Medish, Mark. Official, U.S. Department of Treasury.

Meiklejohn, Dominic. Second Secretary, British Know How Fund, British Embassy, Poland.

Merry, E. Wayne. Former Chief Political Analyst at the U.S. Embassy in Moscow, and Director, Program on European Societies in Transition, The Atlantic Council of the United States.

Merzlikin, Konstantin. President, Cash Union, Moscow.

Mientka, Walter. Secretary of the International Mathematical Olympiad Advisory Board.

Miles, Richard. Deputy Chief of Mission, U.S. Embassy, Moscow.

Mirel, Pierre. Deputy-Head of Unit, Commission of the European Communities, Directorate-General for External Relations, PHARE Operational Service.

Misiuna, Piotr. Head of the Privatisation Unit, Ministry of Foreign Economics Relations, Poland.

Mitchem, Dennis. Former consultant in Russia and former partner, Arthur Andersen.

Möller, Matthias. Bundesministerium für Wirtschaft, Bonn, Germany.

Montag-Girmes, Ralf-Dieter. Director of post-privatization support with the Russian Privatization Center.

Morningstar, Richard L. Ambassador, Special Advisor to the President and Secretary of State (Coordinator, U.S. Assistance to the NIS).

Mosner, Matt. Official, USAID - Moscow.

Müller, Jan. Chairman, Czech Securities Commission, Czech Republic.

Nádházi, Ágnes. Assistance Coordination Secretariat of the Hungarian Ministry of International Economic Relations.

Náthon, István. Director General for International Economic Relations, Ministry of Foreign Affairs, Hungary.

Nelson, Lynn D. Sociologist and expert on Russian privatization, Virginia Commonwealth University.

Nestor, Stilpon. Official working on Central and Eastern European privatization, Organization for Economic Cooperation and Development, Paris.

Nevin, Stanley R. Contracts officer, USAID.

Ng, Renae. Official, European Bank for Reconstruction and Development, London.

Nicol, Bill. Official, Organization for Economic Cooperation and Development, Paris.

Nuti, Mario. Economist, London Business School, United Kingdom.

Nyiri, Lajos. General Director, Head of Department of International Relations, Department of International Relations, National Committee for Technological Development, Hungary.

Okraska, Adam. Project Manager, Foundation for the Development of the Financial Sector, EC PHARE Financial Sector Development Programme, Poland.

Otto, Robert. Consultant, Carana, Russia.

Palacka, Gabriel. State Secretary of the Slovak Ministry of Administration and Privatization of National Property.

Pappalardo, Salvatore. Adviser to the Minister of Finance, Office of Commercial Debt Negotiations, Ministry of Finance, Poland.

Pascual, Carlos. Director for Russian, Ukrainian, and Eurasian Affairs, National Security Council.

Paskhaver, Alexander. Advisor of the President of Ukraine on Economic Policy and Ukrconsulting-Ukrainian Consulting Firms Association, Senior Partner, the Kiev Consulting Group, Ukraine.

Penoyar, William. Procurement Officer, USAID.

Peters, Gary. Associate Director for Enforcement in the U.S. Treasury Department's Office of Technical Assistance.

Peterson, Åke. Former Deputy Director, Secretariat for Cooperation with Central and Eastern Europe, Sweden.

Petkova, Elena. Former board member, Regional Environmental Center.

Pistor, Katharina. Harvard Institute for International Development.

Polakowski, Andrzej. Deputy Manager, Ursus, Poland.

Poletayev, Yuri. Head, Market Research Department, Russian Centre for Public Opinion and Market Research.

Pomorski, Adam. Russia specialist and former Expert to Batory Fund's East-East Commission.

Porvazník, Ján. Director, privatization section for industrial branches, Ministry of Administration and Privatization of National Property of the Slovak Republic.

Poznański, Jacek. Official, Polish Council of Ministers.

Pressley, Donald. Representative, USAID, Poland.

Przybytkowski, Kazimierz. Secretary, Ursus-Solidarity, Poland.

Radwanski, Witold. Deputy Director, European Bank for Reconstruction and Development, Poland.

Rasbash, Andrew. Economic Advisor, Commission of the European Communities Delegation, Poland.

Reczek, Tony. Consultant, Coopers & Lybrand, Poland.

Repa, Antoni. Supervising Project Manager, Mass Privatization Department, Ministry of Privatization, Poland.

Richter, William L. Official, Industry and Financial Sector Reform, USAID-Moscow.

Rishoi, Thomas L. Project Development Officer, USAID-Moscow.

Rogers, John. Official, USAID, Czechoslovakia.

Rosinski, Zbigniew. Representative, Ursus-Solidarity, Poland.

Roussel, Lee. USAID Representative, Czechoslovakia.

Rozsypal, Pavel. Director of the Centre for Foreign Assistance of the Ministry of Economy, Czech Republic.

Rykowski, Zbigniew. Sociologist, Warsaw University; Director, parliamentary information office, Poland.

Sachs, Jeffrey. Economist, Harvard University, and director, Harvard Institute for International Development.

Sadowski, Andrzej. President, Adam Smith Centre, Poland.

Sakharov, Victor. Head, Vladivostok Stock Exchange, Russia.

Samecki, Paweł. Director of the Bureau for Foreign Assistance, Polish Council of Ministers; Undersecretary of State, Ministry of Finance.

Saryusz-Wolski, Jacek. Minister (responsible for foreign aid), Council of Ministers, Poland.

Schmidt, Klaus. Counsellor, Commission of the European Communities Delegation, Poland.

Schulze, Loren L. Project Development Officer, USAID, Slovak Republic.

Schwartz, Jeffrey. Consultant in Russia, Price Waterhouse.

Seymour-Smith, Charlotte. Programme Manager for Hungary, Bulgaria, Czech Republic, and Slovakia, Know How Fund, United Kingdom.

Shalnev, Alexander. Foreign News Analyst, *Izvestiya,* Moscow.

Shishkin, Sergei. Deputy Director, Russian Privatization Center.

Shleifer, Andrei. Project Director, Harvard Institute for International Development (HIID) program in Russia and economist, Harvard University.

Shpakovych, Vasyl. Vice President, International Business Services, S.A., Ukraine.

Sieracki, Jakub. Deputy Director, *Polska Agencja Rozwoju Regionalnego.*

Sipko, Juraj. Director, International Relations, Ministry of Finance, Slovak Republic.

Siwicki, Jacek. Vice President, Enterprise Investors, Poland.

Snelbecker, David. Associate Director, Project on Economic Reform in Ukraine (PERU).

Sokolov, Veniamin. Head, Chamber of Accounts of the Russian Federation.

Stamp, Penny. Senior Manager, Coopers & Lybrand, Poland.

Starozhitskaya, Matiya. Journalist, News Broadcasts of IMC, Internews, Ukraine.

Staszkiewicz, Wiesław. Director, Bureau of Research Chancellery of the *Sejm,* Poland.

Stefaniak, Jolanta Dorota. Director, Foundation for Privatisation in the Republic of Poland.

Stefanowicz, Jan. Attorney at Law and Vice President, Juris, Poland.

Stepankova, Tetyana. Adviser to the National Bank of Ukraine and to Victor Pynzenyk, vice minister for economic reforms, and deputy chair for technical aid for the Council of Ministers, Ukraine.

Sterbanz, Richard. Consultant, Deloitte & Touche, Poland.

Subbotin, Dmitry. Federal Commission on Securities and Capital Markets, Moscow.

Sullivan, Gavin. Project Manager, Russian Privatization Center.

Szilárd, Imre. Head of Secretariat of the Secretary of State, Ministry of International Economic Relations, Hungary.

Szlachta, Jacek. Deputy Director, Poland's Central Office of Planning, Regional Policy Department, Poland; Professor, Główna Szkoła Handlowa (Warsaw School of Economics).

Szostek, Agata. International Relations and Credit Director, *Fundusz Mikro.*

Szövényi, Eszter. Senior Officer, Department for International Relations, Ministry for Environment and Regional Policy, Hungary.

Szwajkowski, Witold. Chief Operations Officer, Microloans Program, Enterprise Fund, Poland.

Szwarcewicz, Dariusz. Senior Consultant, Policy Economics Group, KPMG Peat Marwick, Poland.

Taylor, William B. Deputy Coordinator of NIS Assistance, U.S. Department of State.

Thomas, Barry F. Former CEO, Plyko, Russia.

Thomas, David. Consultant, Coopers & Lybrand, Poland.

Thomas, Scott. Former USAID official, at OECD.

Tikhomiroff, Sacha. Senior Project Manager, Russian Privatization Center.

Titov, Vladimir. Chief of Staff to Aleksandr Lebed, Russia.

Tökés, István. Head of the Department of International Relations in the Ministry of the Environment, Hungary.

Torp, Kristian. Co-ordination Advisor, Ministry of International Economic Relations, Assistance Coordination Secretariat, Hungary.

Toth, Magda. Employee, Regional Environmental Center, Hungary.

Towbin, Robert. Former president, Russian-American Enterprise Fund.

Trzeciakowski, Witold. Former Minister of Central Planning, Poland.

Uchimura, Motomu. First Secretary, Embassy of Japan, Warsaw, Poland.

Ushanov, Yury A. Deputy Director, Center for Conversion and Privatization, Institute of the USA and Canada Studies, Russian Academy of Sciences.

Vásárhelyi, Judit. Independent Ecological Center and former board member, Regional Environmental Center, Hungary.

Vernikov, Andrei. Russian representative to International Monetary Fund.

Viacheslav, Shironin. Center for Business Information, Business Development Program, USAID-Moscow.

Vishny, Robert. Professor of Finance, University of Chicago.

Vitez, Andrew. Consultant, DRT Hungary.

Von Muenchow-Pohl, Bernd. First Secretary - Economics, Embassy of the Federal Republic of Germany, Warsaw, Poland.

Wahlbäck, Krister. Former Head of Department of Security Policy Analysis, Ministry for Foreign Affairs, Sweden.

Wassersug, Stephen. Program Manager, Regional Environmental Center, Hungary.

Wasylyk, Myron. Advisor to the Chairman, State Property Fund of Ukraine.

Weingarten, Bill. Member, U.S. delegation to OECD.

Wesseldijk, Enie. Executive Secretary, International Institute for Democracy, Strasbourg, France.

West, Gordon. Head, Office of Economic Restructuring, USAID.

Wickland, Brian. Official, USAID, Washington, D.C.

Williamson, Anne. Journalist specializing in Soviet and Russian affairs.

Wittkowsky, Andreas. Journalist, Kiev, Ukraine.

Wrona, Tadeusz. Mayor, Częstochowa, Poland.

Wülker, Margitta. Official, Bundesministerium für Wirtschaft, Bonn, Germany.

Wygnański, Jakub. Director of database on Polish NGOs, KLON; Board member, Forum on Nongovernmental Initiatives, and board member, Batory Foundation.

Yakusha, Yuriy. Economic Affairs Counselor, Embassy of Ukraine, Washington, D.C.

Yeatman, Perry. Representative, Burson-Marsteller, Moscow.

Zanardi, Louis H. Staff member, National Security and International Affairs Division, U.S. General Accounting office.

Zieliński, George. Deputy Director, Coopers & Lybrand, Poland.

Zienchuk, Michael. Advisor, Ministry of Foreign Affairs, Ukraine.

Economic Aid to Russia

PLAYERS

JONATHAN HAY: on-site general director of the Harvard Institute for International Development (HIID) program in Russia; a graduate of Harvard Law School who was fired from HIID's Russia project in May 1997 for alleged "activities for personal gain by [HIID] personnel placed in a position of trust in Russia," and later sued by the U.S. government, Hay has denied that his activities constituted a conflict of interest. Hay, along with Dart Management, Inc., also has been named in a civil suit under U.S. racketeering laws filed in the U.S. District Court of New Jersey by Avisma Titano-Magnesium Kombinat alleging that Hay and Dart skimmed at least $50 million from its profits. Hay currently runs an on-line food delivery service in Moscow.

JEFFREY SACHS: well-known Harvard economist: came to symbolize "shock therapy;" helped lead the publicity effort to deliver Western aid and advice to Poland, Russia, Ukraine, and other countries in the region, sometimes under the umbrella of Jeffrey D. Sachs and Associates, Inc.; served as director of HIID from 1995 to 1999; currently director of Harvard's new Center for International Development.

ANDREI SHLEIFER: Russian-born American and Harvard economist: served as project director of HIID's program in Russia and on the board of directors of the HIID-created, Western-funded Russian Privatization Center (RPC), which received millions of Western aid dollars; together with Jonathan Hay, was fired from the project in May 1997 for alleged conflicts of interest (he has denied) and later sued by the U.S. government; remains a Harvard professor of economics.

LAWRENCE SUMMERS: Harvard professor of economics and close associate of Andrei Shleifer; served as chief economist at the World Bank from 1991 to 1993, as under secretary of international affairs at the Treasury Department from 1993 to 1995, as deputy secretary from 1995 to 1999, and as secretary of the Treasury beginning in July 1999.

HARVARD-CONNECTED

ANDERS ÅSLUND: Washington-based Swedish economic historian active in Russia and Ukraine: long-connected to the Chubais Clan, worked with Jeffrey Sachs and Yegor Gaidar (Boris Yeltsin's first architect of economic reform) in Russia, served on the board of directors of the HIID-created, Western-funded RPC, and has been funded by billionaire George Soros; currently senior associate at the Carnegie Endowment for International Peace.

ELIZABETH HEBERT: investor and girlfriend (now wife) of Jonathan Hay: allegedly used USAID-paid access and favors to benefit her mutual fund, Pallada Asset Management, and also allegedly misused a World Bank loan to set up a government fund to compensate victims of equities fraud; named in civil suit filed by U.S. government.

DAVID LIPTON: Harvard-trained Ph.D. economist, IMF employee from 1981 to 1989, and vice president of Jeffrey D. Sachs and Associates, Inc. from 1989 to 1992; worked with Sachs in Poland, Russia, and other countries in the region; served as deputy assistant secretary of the Treasury for Eastern Europe and the Former Soviet Union from 1993 to 1995, and as assistant secretary for international affairs from 1995 to 1999; senior associate at the Carnegie Endowment for International Peace; currently managing director of Moore Capital Strategy Group; continues to participate in international meetings to discuss aid strategies in an unofficial position as a "Russia expert."

CARLOS PASCUAL: Harvard graduate: served as U.S. Agency for International Development (USAID) deputy assistant administrator of the Bureau for Europe and the New Independent States; served in the National Security Council as director for Russian, Ukrainian, and Eurasian affairs from 1995 to 1999; currently U.S. Ambassador-designate to Ukraine.

JULIA ZAGACHIN: Russian-born American HIID consultant, associate of Jonathan Hay and coworker of Elizabeth Hebert, and handpicked by Jonathan Hay and Chubais Clan member Dmitry Vasiliev to set up a World Bank and USAID-funded depository.

NANCY ZIMMERMAN: investor and wife of Andrei Shleifer connected through business deals to Elizabeth Hebert and Julia Zagachin, who allegedly used USAID-paid access and favors to benefit her investments in Russia; named in civil suit filed by U.S. government.

CHUBAIS CLAN

MAXIM BOYCKO: CEO from 1993 to 1996 of the HIID-created, Western-funded Russian Privatization Center, which received millions of Western aid dollars; later served as chairman of the State Property Committee (GKI) for several months in 1997 before being fired by Boris Yeltsin for accepting a thinly veiled $90,000 payment from a company that had received advantages in privatization.

ANATOLY CHUBAIS: chief figure in the St. Petersburg or Chubais Clan; underwritten by the West, led economic reform and privatization efforts and wielded tremendous influence (both in and out of government) from 1992 to the present; although fired by Boris Yeltsin in March 1998 from his post as first deputy prime minister, was reappointed in June 1998 to be Yeltsin's special envoy in charge of Russia's relations with international lending institutions; at times the second most powerful man in Russia after Yeltsin; served as chairman of the board of the "private" RPC; made his mark as the first chairman of the State Property Committee (GKI) and deputy prime minister beginning in late 1991, was promoted to first deputy prime minister in 1994 only to be dismissed by Yeltsin in 1996, made a comeback as head of Yeltsin's reelection campaign in 1996, later that year was named Yeltsin's chief of staff, and was promoted to minister of finance and first deputy prime minister in 1997; most recently CEO of Russia's electricity monopoly, United Energy Systems (UES), since 1998, helped to run Vladimir Putin's spring 2000 presidential campaign, and continues to be received by high Washington officials even as a private citizen.

ALFRED KOKH: served as deputy chairman of the board of the Chubais Clan–HIID-run RPC, named State Property Committee Chairman after Maxim Boycko was fired by Boris Yeltsin, accepted a thinly veiled $100,000 payment from a company that had received advantages in privatization, and was himself fired by Yeltsin in 1997 for favoritism; under investigation in Russia for embezzlement charges, and denied entry into the United States in December 1999.

DMITRY VASILIEV: deputy chairman of the board of the Chubais Clan–HIID-run RPC; served as head of the Federal Commission (the Russian version of the SEC), and worked closely with Jonathan Hay to manage millions of Western aid dollars.

SERGEI SHISHKIN: deputy director in 1996 of the U.S.-created and -funded Institute for Law-Based Economy (ILBE), later ILBE director;

listed as director for several Russian companies, two of which were owned by Elizabeth Hebert and Nancy Zimmerman.

BANKERS

BORIS JORDAN: American entrepreneur of Russian heritage, pioneered the Russian equities market for Credit Suisse First Boston, and, together with Vladimir Potanin, formed the investment bank Renaissance Capital and also set up Renaissance's Sputnik Fund, which attracted investors such as billionaire George Soros and Harvard Management Company (HMC).

VLADIMIR POTANIN: Chubais associate and chairman of Unexim (United Export Import) Bank since 1993 and also served as deputy prime minister in 1996; owns significant stakes in Russian banks, oil, metals, natural gas, and telecommunications.

GEORGE SOROS

GEORGE SOROS: Hungarian-born billionaire financier, known both for his currency speculating and philanthropic activities, who is tied to at least one person in each of the above categories: Jeffrey Sachs and Anders Åslund are his grantees, he meets with U.S. officials Lawrence Summers, David Lipton, and Carlos Pascual, and connections with Anatoly Chubais, Boris Jordan, and Vladimir Potanin facilitated his entree into Russian business.

INSTITUTIONS, ORGANIZATIONS, COMMISSIONS

U.S. DEPARTMENT OF TREASURY: a leading agency making U.S. policy toward Russia and Ukraine, which supported Anatoly Chubais and the Chubais Clan and HIID projects in both Russia and Ukraine.

NATIONAL SECURITY COUNCIL (NSC): a leading agency making U.S. policy toward Russia and Ukraine, which supported Anatoly Chubais and the Chubais Clan and HIID projects in both Russia and Ukraine.

U.S. DEPARTMENT OF STATE, OFFICE OF THE AID COORDINATOR: a leading body carrying out U.S. policy toward Russia and Ukraine, which supported Anatoly Chubais and the Chubais Clan and HIID projects in both Russia and Ukraine.

U.S. AGENCY FOR INTERNATIONAL DEVELOPMENT (USAID): the U.S. government agency through which foreign aid flows.

GORE-CHERNOMYRDIN COMMISSION: a high-level, bilateral commission set up by U.S. Vice President Albert Gore and Russian Prime Minister Viktor Chernomyrdin; formally the US-Russia Joint Commission on Economic and Technological Cooperation after Chernomyrdin's dismissal by Yeltsin, the commission has continued between Gore and the new prime ministers.

WORLD BANK: the development bank funding some projects in Russia run by Anatoly Chubais and members of the Chubais Clan.

HARVARD INSTITUTE FOR INTERNATIONAL DEVELOPMENT (HIID): Harvard University's institute specializing in international development, founded in 1974 and slated for dissolution (and the integration of its projects into other university programs) in 2000, following allegations of mishandling of USAID funds.

HARVARD MANAGEMENT COMPANY (HMC): Harvard's endowment fund, which has invested in Russia through Renaissance Capital's Sputnik Fund since the early 1990s.

RUSSIAN PRIVATIZATION CENTER (RPC): a "private" organization set up in 1992 to further privatization and economic reform. The RPC was run by Chubais Clan members, substantially funded by USAID, and also received hundreds of millions of dollars in grant aid and credits from the United States, the governments of Germany, the United Kingdom, and Japan, the European Union, the World Bank, the European Bank for Reconstruction and Development, and others.

INSTITUTE FOR LAW-BASED ECONOMY (ILBE): an HIID-created, U.S.- and World Bank–funded "private" organization run by the Harvard–Chubais coterie, which was set up to help develop a legal and regulatory framework for markets and evolved to entail drafting decrees for the Russian government.

STATE PROPERTY COMMITTEE (GKI): the Russian state's privatization agency founded in 1991, which, under the leadership of Chubais Clan members, carried out the privatization of some 15,000 state enterprises.

FEDERAL SECURITIES COMMISSION: rough equivalent of the U.S. Securities and Exchange Commission (SEC), known by some Americans as the "Russian SEC," established by presidential decree and run by Chubais Clan member Dmitry Vasiliev.

ORGANIZATIONAL PROFILE OF THE HARVARD INSTITUTE FOR INTERNATIONAL DEVELOPMENT
(AS OF JUNE 30, 1996)

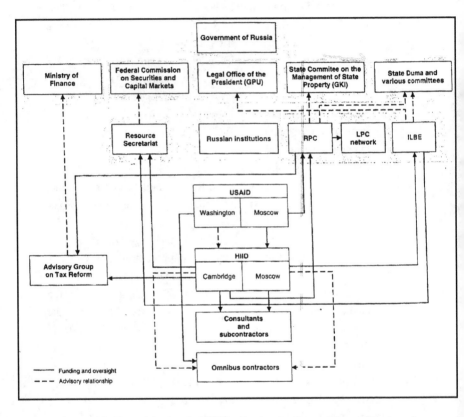

Source: U.S. General Accounting Office, *Foreign Assistance: Harvard Institute for International Development's Work in Russia and Ukraine,* Washington, D.C., GAO: National Security and Affairs Division, November 1996, p. 62.

Legend:
HIID= Harvard Institute for International Development
ILBE= Institute for Law-Based Economy
LPC= local privatization center
RPC= Russian Privatization Center
USAID= U.S. Agency for International Development

NOTES

INTRODUCTION

1. Interview with Grzegorz Kołodko, March 13, 1990.
2. This perspective is informed by a joint research proposal with David A. Kideckel, "Foreign Aid as Ideology and Culture: The Case of Transitional Eastern Europe," submitted to (and funded by) the National Science Foundation, 1993.
3. Anthropologist Philip C. Parnell has conducted pioneering ethnography across levels and processes in the Philippines and Mexico. See Philip C. Parnell, "The Composite State: The Poor and the Nation in Manila," *Ethnography in Unstable Places,* Carol Greenhouse, Elizabeth Mertz, and Kay Warren, eds., Duke University Press, forthcoming, and *Escalating Disputes: Social Participation and Change in the Oaxacan Highlands,* Tucson, AZ: University of Arizona Press, 1989.
4. Anthropologist Arjun Appadurai provides an important treatment of processes of "globalization" from the angle of actors who are profoundly affected by global processes (Arjun Appadurai, *Modernity at Large: Cultural Dimensions of Globalization,* Minneapolis, Minnesota: University of Minnesota Press, 1996).
5. Because aid is seldom conceptualized as a process and interface between social systems, the problem is little examined in much of the theory on foreign assistance, which has been formulated mainly by non-anthropologists from donor societies. (See, for example, the following economists' critiques of the economic development field: Benjamin Higgins [*A Path Less Travelled: A Development Economist's Quest,* National Centre for Development Studies 2, Australian National University, Canberra, 1989]; Tony Smith ["The Underdevelopment of Development Literature: The Case of Dependency Theory," *The State and Development,* Atul Kohli, ed., Princeton, NJ: Princeton University Press, 1986]; and Judith Tendler [*Inside Foreign Aid,* Baltimore, MD: Johns Hopkins University Press, 1975].)
6. Anthropologist Michael Herzfeld has explored how the outcomes of nation-state policies are influenced by actors in semi-closed environments (Michael Herzfeld, *A Place in History: Social and Monumental Time in a Cretan Town,* Princeton, NJ: Princeton University Press, 1991).
7. See, for example, C. M. Hann (*Tazlar: A Village in Hungary,* London, United Kingdom: Cambridge University Press, 1980; *A Village Without Solidarity,* New Haven, CT: Yale University Press, 1985), David A. Kideckel ("The Socialist Transformation of Agriculture in a Romanian Commune, 1945-1962," *American Ethnologist* vol. 9, no. 2, 1982, pp. 320-340; *The Solitude of Collectivism: Romanian Villagers to the Revolution and Beyond,* Ithaca, NY: Cornell University Press, 1993), Martha Lampland (*The Object of Labor: Commodification in Socialist Hungary,* Chicago, IL: University of Chicago Press, 1995), Carole Nagengast

(*Reluctant Socialists, Rural Entrepreneurs: Class, Culture, and the Polish State,* Boulder, CO: Westview Press, 1991), Steven Sampson ("The Informal Sector in Eastern Europe," *Telos,* no. 66, winter 1986, pp. 44-46), and Janine R. Wedel (*The Private Poland: An Anthropologist's Look at Everyday Life,* New York, NY: Facts on File, 1986; *The Unplanned Society: Poland During and After Communism,* New York, NY: Columbia University Press, 1992).

8. A. F. Robertson proposes that development agencies themselves are as worthy of study as the peasant groups with which anthropologists typically are concerned (*People and the State: An Anthropology of Planned Development,* Cambridge, United Kingdom: Cambridge University Press, 1984). Michael Cernea, "Sociological Knowledge for Development Projects," Conrad Kottak, "When People Don't Come First," and Norman Uphoff, "Fitting Projects to People," suggest that development ideologies affect the implementation of development projects (*Putting People First: Sociological Variables in Rural Development,* Michael M. Cernea, ed, New York, NY: Oxford University Press, 1985). Wolfgang Sachs *et al* discuss "knowledge as power" (ed., *The Development Dictionary: A Guide to Knowledge and Power,* London, United Kingdom, Zed Books, 1992) while Michael J. Watts analyzes the history of development and its language ("Development I: Power, Knowledge, Discursive Practice," *Progress in Human Geography,* vol. 17, no. 2, 1993, pp. 257-272) and Arturo Escobar discusses its "invention" ("The Invention of Development," *Current History,* vol. 98, no. 631, November 1999, pp. 382-386). Mark Hobart (ed., *An Anthropological Critique of Development: The Growth of Ignorance,* New York, NY: Routledge, 1993) establishes a relationship between development and the "growth of ignorance," while R. D. Grillo and R.L. Stirrat (eds., *Discourses of Development: Anthropological Perspectives,* Oxford, United Kingdom: Berg, 1997) explore discourses of development and the relationships that arise between power, politics, and ideology in the practice of development.

9. Arturo Escobar ("Anthropology and the Development Encounter: The Making and Marketing of Development Anthropology," *American Ethnologist,* vol. 18, no. 4, November 1991; *Encountering Development: The Making and Unmaking of the Third World,* Princeton, NJ: Princeton University Press, 1995) and James Ferguson (*The Anti-Politics Machine: "Development," Depoliticization, and Bureaucratic Power in Lesotho,* Cambridge, United Kingdom: Cambridge University Press, 1990) provide important illustrations of this point.

CHAPTER ONE

1. William Pfaff, "Redefining World Power," *Foreign Affairs,* vol. 70, no. 1, 1990/ 1991, p. 47; cited in the address of John Brademas, former U.S. congressman and president of New York University, at the conference "Economies in Transition: Management Training and Market Economies Education in Central and Eastern Europe" cosponsored by the White House and the Treasury Department, The Cash Room, United States Department of the Treasury, Washington, D.C., February 26, 1991.

2. The idea of joining Europe is by no means new in the region. As anthropologist Susan Gal has pointed out, "Debates about the meanings of Europe were important elements in the 18th- and 19th-century construction of national identities throughout the peripheral regions of capitalist Europe." Although there are important

political, cultural, and historical differences shaping debates among elites within different nations, common features of the debates include, according to Gal: "the elites' painful recognition of their regions' economic and political backwardness under peripheral capitalism" and "the consequent attempt to adopt western (European) models of material and technological advancement, 'civilization,' bourgeois life, and liberal democracy." (Susan Gal, "Bartok's Funeral: Representations of Europe in Hungarian Political Rhetoric," *American Ethnologist,* vol. 18, no. 3, August 1991, p. 443.)

3. Michal Illner, "Post-Communist Transformation Revisited," *Czech Sociological Review,* vol. 4, no. 2, 1996, p. 161.

4. As political sociologist Claus Offe points out, ideas of a "third road"—a more democratic and efficient socialism—or of a course that might replace the Soviet-style economic regime (such as those floated during the Prague Spring of 1968) were "conspicuously absent in the post-1989 events." (*Varieties of Transition: The East European and East German Experience,* Cambridge, MA: MIT Press, 1997, p. 107.)

5. Cited in John Lukacs, "The Legacy of the Marshall Plan," *Washington Post,* May 25, 1997, p. C3.

6. American President Harry Truman signed the European Recovery Program, later known as the Marshall Plan (after Secretary of State George C. Marshall), on April 3, 1948.

7. According to the U.S. Department of State, Office of the Historian, "The initial response of several East European nations to the Marshall Plan was positive. Both the Polish and Czechoslovak Governments expressed their intentions to send delegations to the organizational meeting to open in Paris on July 12, 1947." (U.S. Department of State, Public Affairs, Office of the Historian, "The Marshall Plan: Origins and Implementation," June 1982, p. 24.)

8. Quoted in John Robinson and Michael Kranish, "In Speech to Congress, Walesa Presses Case for Aid," *Boston Globe,* November 16, 1989, p. 12.

9. PHARE's name, which means "lighthouse" in French, reflects the EU's initial focus on Poland and Hungary. After its first year of operation the PHARE program broadened its target to include other countries in Central and Eastern Europe, but the old acronym was retained.

10. The countries of the G-24 are Canada, the United States, Japan, Australia, New Zealand, Austria, Belgium, Denmark, Finland, France, Germany, Greece, Iceland, Ireland, Italy, Luxembourg, the Netherlands, Norway, Portugal, Spain, Sweden, Switzerland, Turkey, and the United Kingdom.

11. For further details on this issue, see Stephen Haggard and Andrew Moravcsik, "The Political Economy of Financial Assistance to Eastern Europe, 1989-1991," *After the Cold War: International Institutions and State Strategies in Europe, 1989-1991,* Robert O. Keohane, Joseph S. Nye, and Stanley Hoffman, eds., Cambridge, MA: Harvard University Press, 1993, pp. 247, 258-261.

12. Public Law 101-179, *Support for East European Democracy (SEED) Act of 1989,* November 28, 1989.

13. Public Law 101-179, *Support for East European Democracy (SEED) Act of 1989,* November 28, 1989. For authorization and allocation amounts, see U.S. General Accounting Office, *Eastern Europe: Donor Assistance and Reform Efforts,* November 1990, pp. 14-15.

14. By the end of 1992, the United States had committed $4.6 billion, followed by Germany ($3.6 billion) the EC Commission ($3.2 billion), and Canada ($1.6 billion). These figures, which are based on the April 1993 G-24 Scoreboard, cover

the period from January 1990 through December 1992 (U.S. Department of State, *SEED Act Implementation Report: Fiscal Year 1993*, Washington, D.C.: U.S. Department of State, January 1994, pp. 278 and 279).

15. European Commission, "G-24 Assistance Commitments: Assistance by Sector," Brussels, Belgium: European Commission, January 1990-December 1992.

16. With regard to U.S. assistance, the U.S. Department of State reported $6.98 billion in cumulative obligations to Russia and $2.21 billion in obligations to Ukraine as of September 30, 1999 (U.S. Department of State, *U.S. Government Assistance to and Cooperative Activities with the New Independent States of the Former Soviet Union, FY 1999 Annual Report*, prepared by the Office of the Coordinator of U.S. Assistance to the NIS, Washington, D.C.: Department of State, January 2000, tables).

17. The sum appropriated under the Marshall Plan, $13.3 billion over four years in 16 countries (U.S. Department of State, Public Affairs, Office of the Historian, "The Marshall Plan: Origins and Implementation," June 1982, p. 30), is equal to approximately 87.5 billion in 1997 dollars (Elizabeth Neuffer, "Marshall Plan Legacy Thrives Abroad" *Boston Globe*, June 3, 1997, pp. A-8).

18. Pascal Bruckner, *The Tears of the White Man: Compassion as Contempt*, New York, NY: Free Press, 1983, p. 80.

19. With a few exceptions, what "underdeveloped" or "Third World" countries have in common is receipt of official foreign aid, not hunger, poverty, stagnation, exploitation, or race. Economists P. T. Bauer and B. S. Yamey and Pascal Bruckner (Ibid.) make this case. Bauer and Yamey explain that: "Official foreign aid has been the unifying characteristic of this huge, variegated, and utterly diverse collectivity ever since its components began to be lumped together from the late 1940s onward as, successively, the 'underdeveloped world,' the 'less developed world,' the 'non-aligned world,' the 'developing world,' the 'Third World,' and now, the 'South.' These expressions never made any sense except as references to a collectivity of past, present, or prospective aid recipients." (P. T. Bauer and B. S. Yamey, "East-West/North-South: Peace and Prosperity?" *Commentary*, September 1980, p. 58.)

20. While Poland, Hungary, and the Czech Republic relied to a large degree on industry, Romania, Bulgaria, and Albania were more dependent on agriculture. While Poland and Hungary had substantial private sectors prior to 1989, Romania, Bulgaria, and Czechoslovakia had very limited private sectors; Albania had none. Ethnic and political turmoil also contributed to perceptions of developed versus less developed nations. For example, Romania was regarded somewhat as a "black sheep," as David Kideckel has observed, due to "its violent revolution, the questionable commitment of its leaders to democracy and the market, and its persistent ethnic difficulties." (Janine R. Wedel and David A. Kideckel, "Foreign Aid as Ideology and Culture: The Case of Transitional Eastern Europe," proposal submitted to [and funded by] the National Science Foundation, 1993, p. 4).

21. Quoted in Janine Wedel, *The Private Poland: An Anthropologist's Look at Everyday Life*, New York, NY: Facts on File, 1986, p. 163.

22. See, for example, OECD, *Aid and Other Resource Flows to the Central and Eastern European Countries and the New Independent States of the Former Soviet Union (1990-1995)*, January 29, 1998, p. 36. Not all situations were clear: Kazakhstan and Uzbekistan, although Central Asian, were rich with oil and minerals, respectively.

23. The publications, *Transition: The Newsletter about Reforming Economies* and *Transitions: Changes in Post-Communist Societies*, have tracked the long-standing debates on this issue.

24. Quoted in George M. Taber, "Rx for Russia: Shock Therapy," *Time*, January 27, 1992, p. 37. (Cited in Walter Adams and James W. Brock, *Adam Smith Goes to Moscow*, Princeton, NJ: Princeton University Press, 1993, p. 40.)

25. Quoted in János Kornai, *Road to a Free Economy*, New York, NY: Norton, p. 161. (Cited in Walter Adams and James W. Brock, *Adam Smith Goes to Moscow*, Princeton, NJ: Princeton University Press, 1993, pp. 17-18.)

26. Jeffrey Sachs, "The Economic Transformation of Eastern Europe: The Case of Poland," *American Economist*, vol. 36, Fall 1992, pp. 3-11.

27. This assessment was shared by many analysts of Central and Eastern European aid, including the GAO (*Poland and Hungary: Economic Transition and U.S. Assistance*, Washington, D.C.: United States General Accounting Office, May 1, 1992, pp. 30-31) and the Institute for East West Studies (Raymond Barre, William H. Luers, Anthony Solomon, and Krzysztof J. Ners, *Moving Beyond Assistance*, New York, NY: Institute for East West Studies, June 1992).

28. Gerald Creed, "Second Thoughts from the Second World: Interpreting Aid in Post-Communist Eastern Europe," with Janine R. Wedel, *Human Organization*, vol. 56, no. 3, Fall 1997, p. 253.

29. C. M. Hann, *The Skeleton at the Feast: Contributions to East European Anthropology*, Canterbury, United Kingdom: University of Kent at Canterbury, Centre for Social Anthropology and Computing, 1995, p. 19.

30. Interview with Rita Klimova of September 1992, cited in Janine R. Wedel, "The Unintended Consequences of Western Aid to Post-Communist Europe," *Telos*, no. 92, Summer 1992, p. 132.

31. Cargo Cults are movements in colonial New Guinea and Melanesia based on the belief that large loads of European luxury goods would accompany the return of ancestral spirits. See, for example, Eleanor Smollett, "America the Beautiful: Made in Bulgaria," *Anthropology Today*, vol. 9, no. 2, 1993, p. 12; David Lempert, "Changing Russian Political Culture in the 1990s: Parasites, Paradigms, and Perestroika," *Comparative Studies in History and Society*, vol. 35, 1993, p. 643; Katherine Verdery, *What Was Socialism and What Comes Next?* Princeton, NJ: Princeton University Press, 1996, p. 189; and David Ellerman, "Voucher Privatization with Investment Funds: An Institutional Analysis," Policy Research Working Paper 1924, Washington D.C.: The World Bank, Office of the Senior Vice President, Development Economics, May 1998, p. 7.

32. U.S. Bureau of the Census, *1990 Census of Population, Supplementary Reports, Detailed Ancestry Groups for States* (1990 CP-S-1-2).

33. David A. Kideckel, "Us and Them: Concepts of East and West in the East European Transition," *Cultural Dilemmas of Post-Communist Societies*, Aldona Jawlowska and Marian Kempny, eds, Warsaw, Poland: IFiS Publishers, 1994, p. 135.

34. Václav Havel, "The Power of the Powerless," *The Power of the Powerless: Citizens Against the State in Central-Eastern Europe*, John Keane, ed., Armonk, NY: M. E. Sharpe, 1985, pp. 23-96.

35. Cited in Janine Wedel, *The Private Poland: An Anthropologist's Look at Everyday Life*, New York, NY: Facts on File, 1986, p. 129.

36. Gerald Creed, "Second Thoughts from the Second World: Interpreting Aid in Post-Communist Eastern Europe," with Janine R. Wedel, *Human Organization*, vol. 56, no. 3, Fall 1997, p. 32.

37. Tadeusz Wróblewski (a pseudonym to protect identities), "The Opposition and Money," *The Unplanned Society: Poland During and After Communism*, Janine R. Wedel, ed., New York, NY: Columbia University Press, 1992, p. 239.

38. U.S. General Accounting Office, *Eastern Europe: Status of U.S. Assistance*, Washington, D.C.: General Accounting Office, February 26, 1991, appendix 1.

39. Interview of October 31, 1996, with Steve Dean, division chief, Contracts Division for Eastern Europe and the New Independent States of USAID's procurement office.

40. The responsibilities of the G-24 were assumed by other bodies in 1991; the G-24 did not become involved in coordinating aid efforts to the former Soviet Union. For details, see Stephan Haggard and Andrew Moravcsik, "The Political Economy of Financial Assistance to Eastern Europe, 1989-1991," *After the Cold War: International Institutions and State Strategies in Europe, 1989-1991,* Robert O. Keohane, Joseph S. Nye, and Stanley Hoffman, eds., Cambridge, MA: Harvard University Press, 1993, pp. 258-261.

41. Interview with Andrew Rasbash, January 29, 1992.

42. Interview of October 31, 1996, with Steve Dean, division chief, Contracts Division for Eastern Europe and the New Independent States of USAID's procurement office. Note that on July 1, 1998, long after the period of intense aid efforts in Central and Eastern Europe, two of the "Big Six" accounting firms merged: Price Waterhouse and Coopers & Lybrand became Price Waterhouse Coopers.

43. Several donor officials also emphasized this point at the working conference co-organized by the author in April 1995 and cosponsored by the Woodrow Wilson International Center for Scholars and the Friedrich Ebert Stiftung. See report of the Conference by John Harper and Janine R. Wedel, *Western Aid to Central and Eastern Europe: What We Are Doing Right, What We Are Doing Wrong, and How We can Do it Better,* East European Studies Occasional paper: Woodrow Wilson International Center for Scholars, no. 41, September 1995, p. 24.

44. Interview with Richard L. Morningstar, September 30, 1996.

45. Interview with U.S. procurement officer Steve Dean, January 7, 1998, (Also Katrina Greene interview of July 19, 1995, with Steve Dean, division chief, Contracts Division for Eastern Europe and the New Independent States of USAID's procurement office.)

46. Interview with U.S. procurement officer Steve Dean, January 7, 1998, and interview with U.S. procurement officer William Penoyar, January 16, 1998.

47. Interview with Stanley R. Nevin, August 24, 1996.

48. EU guidelines, and interview with British Know How Fund official Charlotte Seymour-Smith, December 8, 1995.

49. Officials who acknowledged this in public include U.S. Deputy Secretary of State Lawrence Eagleburger and U.S. Secretary of Commerce Robert Mossbacher at a meeting of Western leaders. (Reported by Mary Brasier in "Clash Over Aid for Eastern Europe," *Guardian,* May 24, 1990.)

50. Interview with Witold Trzeciakowski, May 10, 1997.

51. Figures on Marshall Plan were provided by David Patterson, deputy historian, Department of State Public Affairs, Office of the Historian (conversations of May 8 and May 12, 1997). Figures on aid to the former Eastern Bloc were cited in a study by Polish economist Krzysztof Ners (William Drozdiak, "E. Europeans Say West Fails in Aid Pledges," *Washington Post,* June 17, 1992, p. A33).

52. See James B. Silberman and Charles Weiss, Jr., *A History of the Technical Assistance Programs of the Marshall Plan and Successor Agencies, 1948-1961,* Washington, D.C.: World Bank, Industrial Policy Group, November 1992.

53. Interview with Witold Trzeciakowski, May 10, 1997.

54. Cited in Janine R. Wedel, "Beware Western Governments Bearing Gifts," *Wall Street Journal Europe,* January 14, 1992.

55. Reported by Blaine Harden, "Poles Sour on Capitalism," *Washington Post*, February 5, 1992, p. A1.

56. Béla Kádár, "Where Have all the Dollars Gone?" *Transition: The Newsletter about Reforming Economies*, Transition Economics Division Policy Research Department, World Bank, vol. 4, no. 5, June 1993, p. 5.

57. This figure represents average disbursement rates for nine G-24 countries and the EU for total committed assistance to Central and Eastern Europe (Raymond Barre, William H. Luers, Anthony Solomon and Krzysztof J. Ners, *Moving Beyond Assistance*, New York, NY: Institute for East West Studies, June 1992).

58. *Former Soviet Union: U.S. Bilateral Program Lacks Effective Coordination*, Washington, D.C.: U.S. General Accounting Office, February 1995, p. 5.

59. *Former Soviet Union: U.S. Bilateral Program Lacks Effective Coordination*, Washington, D.C.: U.S. General Accounting Office, February 1995.

60. Robert L. Hutchings, "Statement of Ambassador Robert L. Hutchings, Special Adviser for East European Assistance, Department of State, before the Subcommittee on Foreign Operations, House Committee on Appropriations," April 19, 1993, p. 4.

61. Several participants emphasized this point at the working conference co-organized by the author in April 1995 and cosponsored by the Woodrow Wilson International Center for Scholars and the Friedrich Ebert Stiftung. See report of the conference by John Harper and Janine R. Wedel, *Western Aid to Central and Eastern Europe: What We are Doing Right, What We are Doing Wrong, and How We can Do it Better*, East European Studies Occasional Paper: Woodrow Wilson International Center for Scholars, no. 41, September 1995, p. 24.

62. Kirsty Hughes, Philip Taylor, and Ian Christie, "Evaluation of Technical Assistance to Hungary," Policy Studies Institute (PSI), published by the Department for Education and Employment as Research Series no. 70; excerpts republished in C. M. Hann, *The Skeleton at the Feast: Contributions to East European Anthropology*, Canterbury, United Kingdom: University of Kent at Canterbury, Centre for Social Anthropology and Computing, 1995, p. 228.

63. Interview with Alan Mayhew, May 15, 1996.

64. Institute for East West Studies, *Annual Report, 1992-93*, New York, NY: Institute for East West Studies, p. 23.

65. *CCET Register Statistics*, published by the Centre for Co-operation with Economies in Transition, Paris, France: OECD, June 1994.

66. See John Harper and Janine R. Wedel, *Western Aid to Central and Eastern Europe: What We are Doing Right, What We are Doing Wrong, and How We can Do it Better*, East European Studies Occasional Paper no. 41: Woodrow Wilson International Center for Scholars, September 1995, pp. 24-25.

Some donor representatives offered the view that there were relatively few projects worth funding (for example, interview with Witold Radwanski, deputy director of the European Bank for Reconstruction and Development in Warsaw, April 6, 1994). But once a project got under way, there were sometimes opportunities for coordination and division of tasks among donors.

67. Interview with Alan Mayhew, May 15, 1996.

68. Participants at the working conference of April 1995 addressed organizational barriers to flexibility and risk and generally agreed that "Although successful aid programs require informed risk taking and flexibility, administrative and evaluation procedures tended to discourage, rather than encourage, risk taking" (John Harper and Janine R. Wedel, *Western Aid to Central and Eastern Europe: What We are Doing Right, What We are Doing Wrong, and How We can Do it Better*, East

European Studies Occasional Paper no. 41: Woodrow Wilson International Center for Scholars, No. 41, September 1995, p. 24).

69. The system of contracting was born with the "outsourcing" of defense contracts during World War II in the United States. As outsourcing expanded during the Cold War (both in the United States and in Western Europe), so did a body of regulations and procedures for hiring and holding accountable contractors, as well as ideas about the merits of employing contractors versus civil servants (Daniel Guttman, *Contracting for Government,* Washington, D.C.: Distributed by the National Academy of Public Administration, January 1997; and conversations with Daniel Guttman, an expert on government contracting for the performance of public functions).

70. "Wspólczesny Plan Marshalla?" *Nowa Europa,* April 4, 1994.

71. John Harper and Janine R. Wedel, *Western Aid to Central and Eastern Europe: What We are Doing Right, What We are Doing Wrong, and How We can Do it Better,* East European Studies Occasional paper: Woodrow Wilson International Center for Scholars, no. 41, September 1995, p 24.

72. Confirming these findings, the GAO reported that "a U.S. official in Poland told us that decisionmakers in Washington did not seek advice on projects from in-country staff, even though these staff members have first-hand knowledge of the country's conditions and monitor U.S. assistance efforts. In some cases, decisionmakers in Washington have ignored recommended actions from in-country staff." (*Poland and Hungary: Economic Transition and U.S. Assistance,* Washington, D.C.: U.S. General Accounting Office, May 1992, pp. 33-34.)

73. House of Representatives, *Foreign Operation, Export Financing, and Related Programs Appropriations Bill,* report 102-585, June 18, 1992, pp. 34-36.

74. Further frustrating in-country input was the "regional approach." Under this approach, aid to Central and Eastern Europe was targeted to a region, rather than to an individual nation, thereby suggesting the dominance of political goals over developmental ones. This approach maximized Washington's control: regional, rather than country-specific, allocations meant that Washington could shift focus from one country to another when American domestic pressures changed or when a country failed to curry sufficient favor. The chief justification for the regional approach—that many problems such as environmental ones cross national boundaries and therefore should be addressed regionally—overlooked the fact that each country designed and implemented its own policies. Indeed, some recipient aid officials complained that the regional approach encouraged competition among Central and Eastern European nations and complicated planning and monitoring.

75. General Accounting Office, *Poland and Hungary: Economic Transition and U.S. Assistance,* Washington, D.C.: U.S. General Accounting Office, May 1992, p. 34; Janine R. Wedel, "Beware Western Governments Sending Gifts," *Wall Street Journal Europe,* January 14, 1992.

76. General Accounting Office, *Poland and Hungary: Economic Transition and U.S. Assistance,* Washington, D.C.: U.S. General Accounting Office, May 1992, p. 34.

77. *Biuletyn Z Posiedzenia Komisji do Spraw Układu Europejskiego,* nr 7, Warsaw, Poland: Kancelaria Sejmu, Biuro Informacynje, nr. 311, II kad., February 16, 1994, p. 15.

78. For further discussion of recipient input, see Janine R. Wedel, "U.S. Aid to Central and Eastern Europe, 1990-1994: An Analysis of Aid Models and Responses," *East-Central European Economies in Transition: Study Papers submitted to the Joint Economic Committee Congress of the United States,* November 1994; republished in *East-Central European Economies in Transition,* editors John P. Hardt and

Richard F. Kaufman, for the Joint Economic Committee Congress of the United States, New York, NY: M. E. Sharpe, 1995.

79. Interviews with Klaus Schmidt and Andrew Rasbash of the EU delegation in Poland, April 7, 1994, and April 22, 1994, respectively; and interviews with John Kjaer and Pierre Mirel of the PHARE program in Brussels, May 4, 1994. In addition, the "Conclusions of the Presidency" document, Copenhagen, June 21-22, 1993, Brussels, European Union, p. 14 states: "Part of the resources under the PHARE programme may be used for major infrastructural improvements." A report released by the PHARE information office states that "At the Copenhagen Council it was decided to allow the allocation of up to 15 percent of the total Phare budget to co-finance major infrastructure developments with international financial institutions. The first project was an ECU 30 million contribution to a railway development programme in Poland." (*What is Phare?* Brussels, Belgium: European Commission, Phare Information Office, May 1994, p. 11.)

80. Interview with Klaus Schmidt of the EU delegation in Poland, April 7, 1994.

81. *The Phare Programme Annual Report, 1995,* Brussels, Belgium: European Union, September 25, 1997, p. 7.

82. The "Accession Partnership" countries consist of Bulgaria, Czech Republic, Estonia, Hungary, Latvia, Lithuania, Poland, Romania, Slovakia, and Slovenia. Albania, Bosnia-Herzogovina, and Macedonia participate in the PHARE program but are not candidates for EU membership. European Commission, *The Phare Programme Annual Report 1998,* Brussels, Belgium: European Commission, March 2000, p. 2.

83. To improve institution-building, PHARE introduced "twinning," which pairs member state officials with corresponding officials in candidate states to help implement the Community *acquis* (the body of common rights and obligations of all EU member states). In investment support, the EU has designated 70 percent of the PHARE budget to bring industry and infrastructure up to EC standards. European Commission, *The Phare Programme Annual Report 1998,* Brussels, Belgium: European Commission, March 2000, p. 9.

84. One exception was a small-business program with a little money for investment in a cross-border initiative to link Ukraine with PHARE countries. Interview with Michael B. Humphreys, counselor, European Commission delegation in Ukraine, August 22, 1995.

85. Interview with Michael B. Humphreys, August 22, 1995. See also European Commission, *Tacis: European Commission: The Tacis Programme Annual Report 1997,* Brussels, Belgium: European Commission, 1998.

86. Interview with Michael B. Humphreys, August 22, 1995.

87. Robert L. Hutchings, "Statement of Ambassador Robert L. Hutchings, Special Adviser for East European Assistance, Department of State, before the Subcommittee on Foreign Operations, House Committee on Appropriations," April 19, 1993, p. 3.

88. General Accounting Office, *Poland and Hungary: Economic Transition and U.S. Assistance,* Washington, D.C.: U.S. General Accounting Office, May 1, 1992, pp. 34, 31-36. This approach changed very little and was reiterated by the State Department Coordinator of U.S. assistance to the NIS. (See these strategy papers for Russia and the former Soviet Union: U.S. Department of State, *United States Assistance and Economic Cooperation Strategy for the Newly Independent States,* approved January 14, 1994, by the coordinator of U.S. assistance to the New Independent States, Washington, D.C.; and U.S. Department of State, *United States Assistance and Economic Cooperation Strategy for Russia,* approved May 19, 1994,

by the coordinator of U.S. assistance to the New Independent States, Washington, D.C.)

89. Interviews with Ágnes Nádházi and Kornél Kováts of the Hungarian Ministry of International Economic Relations, April 27, 1994, and Pawel Samecki, director of the Bureau for Foreign Assistance, Polish Council of Ministers, July 26, 1994.

90. Although crucial, the historical legacies that would distinguish problems of transformation in postcommunist Europe from those in apparently comparable nations in both First and Third World regions were overlooked by many pundits of the day. In *Varieties of Transition,* political sociologist Claus Offe details the differences between the "transition" to democracy in Latin America and Southern Europe in the 1970s and 1980s and in post-1989 Central and Eastern Europe, as well as between post–World War II and post–Cold War transformations. In the former case, Offe argues that two main differences—massive migration and the necessity of economic (not just political and constitutional) reform in the case of postcommunist Europe—distinguish these cases from each other. In comparing post–World War II and post–Cold War transformations, Offe suggests that "the post-1989 case poses the more difficult problems of transition." (*Varieties of Transition: The East European and East German Experience,* Cambridge, MA: MIT Press, 1997, pp. 31-32, 187-188.) See also Valerie Bunce, "The Political Economy of Postsocialism," *Slavic Review,* vol. 58, no. 4, Winter 1999, pp.756-793.

91. From 1959 through 1975, Hungary ranked in the top three each year. Romania also scored in the top three until 1965. From 1982 to 1985, at least two Eastern Bloc countries or the Soviet Union ranked in the top five. (Murray S. Klamkin, *International Mathematical Olympiad, 1978-1985,* Washington, D.C.: Mathematical Association of America, 1986, appendix B, pp. 11-117 and 121-124.)

92. Interview with Walter Mientka, May 20, 1997.

93. Interviews with and/or documents provided by Zbigniew Lewicki and Zdzisław Ludwiczak of the Polish Ministry of Foreign Affairs; Jitka Cenková of the Centre for Foreign Assistance of the Ministry of the Economy of the Czech Republic; Jarmila Hrbáčková, Andrea Matisová, and Lubo Lubina of the Slovak Ministry of Foreign Affairs; and Kornél Kováts and Ágnes Nádházi of the Assistance Coordination Secretariat of the Hungarian Ministry of International Economic Relations.

94. Interview with Czech official.

95. The cable stated that "at this time only Albania has signed the draft bilateral transmitted . . . and we have no hard information (other than possibly re the CSFR) that we are close to signing anywhere else. . . . The time has come for all posts to make a serious overture to the appropriate host government officials involved at the highest appropriate level and to agree on an imminent timetable for execution of these agreements, so that the program can continue without interruption." Cable from Lawrence Eagleburger, acting secretary of state, August 10, 1992.

96. Interviews with Zdzisław Ludwiczak, deputy director, Department of the Americas, Polish Ministry of Foreign Affairs, August 31, 1995, and May 12, 1997.

97. As discussed earlier, the very concept of the Third World is tied to foreign assistance; see note 19.

98. Václav Klaus, "Foreign Aid for a Post-Communist Country—Experience and Prospects," speech given before the Bretton Woods Committee, World Bank, Washington, D.C., October 15, 1993.

99. Interview with Zdeněk Drábek, July 7, 1994.

100. Marianne Gronemeyer, "Helping," *The Development Dictionary: A Guide to Knowledge as Power,* Wolfgang Sachs, ed., London, United Kingdom: Zed Books, 1992, p. 55.

101. Jánoś Kornai, "The Health of Nations: Reflections on the Analogy Between the Medical Science and Economics," *Kyklos,* vol. 36, 1983, Fasc. 2, pp.191-192.

102. Mark Hobart, "Introduction: The Growth of Ignorance?" *An Anthropological Critique of Development,* Mark Hobart, ed., London, United Kingdom: Routledge, 1993, p. 6.

103. Katherine Verdery, "Theorizing Socialism: A Prologue to the Transition," *American Ethnologist,* vol. 18, no. 3, 1991, pp. 419-439; and *What Was Socialism, And What Comes Next?* Princeton, NJ: Princeton University Press, 1996.

104. Reported by Blaine Harden, "Poles Sour on Capitalism," *The Washington Post,* February 5, 1992, p. A1.

CHAPTER TWO

1. Interview of July 4, 1994, with Jarmila Hrbáčková of the Department of Foreign Assistance of the Ministry of Foreign Affairs of the Slovak Republic.

2. Talk before the American Committee for Aid to Poland (ACAP), Washington, D.C., March 12, 1992.

3. See, for example, Jacek Kalabiński, "The Marriott Brigade in Action," *Gazeta Wyborcza,* June 21, 1991, and "The Misfortune of the Marriott Brigade," *Gazeta Wyborcza,* October 18, 1991.

4. For insight into the collision between high-level Central and Eastern European officials and their foreign advisers, especially with regard to macroeconomic agenda, see *Adam Smith Goes to Moscow: A Dialogue on Radical Reform* (Walter Adams and James W. Brock, Princeton, New Jersey: Princeton University Press, 1993). Though fictionalized, the account rings true in its depiction of the disconnect between a foreign economist, unencumbered by knowledge of the realities of the context to which he hopes to apply his theories, and the recipient of his advice: a prime minister who must implement—and take the blame for—economic policies.

5. For a detailed definition of "shock therapy," see, for example, David M. Kotz with Fred Weir, *Revolution from Above: The Demise of the Soviet System,* London, United Kingdom: Routledge, 1997, pp. 161-163.

6. Poland is a significant example of this. Sachs has maintained that "I advised the Polish Government at the invitation of Deputy Prime Minister Leszek Balcerowicz. My advisory work extended to several Ministries, and to the Council of Ministers. I also organized many workshops on behalf of various parts of the Polish Government" (letter to Janine Wedel of March 12, 1998). However, in 1991, the Polish government issued this disclaimer in the *Financial Times* ("Professor Jeffrey Sachs," June 15-16, 1991): "Professor Jeffrey Sachs of Harvard is not an economic adviser to the Polish Government. Professor Sachs visits Poland often and his visits are welcome but he has no official role with the government." The Poles who engineered the Polish stabilization plan of January 1, 1990 ("shock therapy") in which Sachs says he had a hand, including high-level officials in the Ministry of Finance, the head of the National Bank of Poland, and the director of the Institute of Finance, said in 1990 that Sachs was one of many advisers and that his ideas tended to replicate the conventional wisdom of the IMF. Well-placed observers in the U.S. State Department and Congressional Research Service, as well as the director of the European department of the World Bank, said the same thing. Further, Sachs, not the Poles, largely initiated his Polish venture. His funders

included George Soros, the Hungarian American philanthropist and investor, and the United Nations University in Helsinki. (For specific sources and details, see Janine R. Wedel, "The Economist Heard 'Round the World, Part II," *World Monitor,* October 1990, pp. 33-42.)

While associating himself with reform efforts in countries perceived as successful—Poland, for example—Sachs tends to distance himself from failed reform efforts in countries where he also was active, such as Russia, Ukraine, and Mongolia. (On Russia, see, for example, Sachs's reply to the author's article in *The National Interest* ("Tainted Transactions: Harvard, the Chubais Clan and Russia's Ruin,"no. 59, Spring 2000, pp. 23-34) published in "Tainted Transactions: An Exchange" [*The National Interest,* no. 60, Summer 2000, pp. 98-99].)

7. Cited in Janine R. Wedel, "The Economist Heard 'Round the World, Part II," *World Monitor,* October 1990, p. 38.

8. Ibid.

9. Interview with Ryszard Bugaj, March 10, 1990. (For details, see ibid., pp. 33-42.)

10. Interview with Stefan Kawalec of March 8, 1990 and April 16, 1990. This quote is from March 8, 1990. (For details, see ibid.)

11. Sociologists Michael Burawoy and Pavel Krotov are among those who argue that the Soviet state disintegrated from within: It was not a "'revolution,' but the (long-anticipated!) *withering away of the state."* (Michael Burawoy and Pavel Krotov, "The Soviet Transition from Socialism to Capitalism: Worker Control and Econom-ic Bargaining in the Wood Industry," *American Sociological Review,* vol. 5, February 1992, p. 17.)

12. For example, the GAO reported that "USAID's initial privatization strategy in Poland was based on the assumption that the privatization process would take only a few years" (United States General Accounting Office, *Poland: Economic Restruc-turing and Donor Assistance,* Washington, D.C.: GAO, August 1995, p. 57).

13. With regard to U.S. assistance to Central and Eastern Europe, nearly three-quarters of all obligations consistently fell under economic restructuring (U.S. Department of State, *SEED Act Implementation Report, Fiscal Year 1996,* Washington, D.C.: U.S. Department of State, February 1997, tables; U.S. Department of State, *SEED Act Implementation Report, Fiscal Year 1998,* Washington, D.C.: U.S. Department of State, March 1999, tables). See appendix 1, table 3.

With regard to the former Soviet Union, as of 1995, about one-fourth of U.S. obligations to the region were for private-sector development, economic restructur-ing and finance, and market reform. (United States General Accounting Office, *Former Soviet Union: U.S. Bilateral Program Lacks Effective Coordination,* Washington, D.C.: GAO, February 1995, p. 48.) As of 2000, about one-third of U.S. obligations to the former Soviet Union, under the Freedom Support Act, were for energy efficiency and market reform, private-sector initiatives, and economic restructuring and financial reform. With regard to Russia and Ukraine specifically, the portion obligated to Russia was 30 percent between 1992 and 1999, while that to Ukraine was 23 percent. Private-sector initiatives comprised the single largest category of U.S. assistance to both countries. (U.S. Department of State, Office of the Coordinator of U.S. Assistance to the NIS, *U.S. Government Assistance to and Cooperative Activities with the New Independent States of the Former Soviet Union, FY 1999 Annual Report,* Washington, D.C.: Department of State, January 2000, tables.)

With regard to EU assistance to Central and Eastern Europe, the EU consistently committed about one-fourth of its PHARE program to economic restructuring and private-sector development, including privatization, enterprise support, and aid to the financial and agricultural sectors. (European Commission, *The Phare Programme: An Interim Evaluation,* Brussels, Belgium: European Commission, 1997, annexes: table A.7, p. 66; and European Commission, *The Phare Programme: Annual Report 1998,* Brussels, Belgium: European Commission, 2000, p. 85.) See appendix 1, table 4.

    With regard to EU assistance to Russia and Ukraine, between 1991 and 1997, TACIS allocated 40 percent of its funds to Russia for restructuring state enterprises and private-sector development and for agriculture, and 32 percent of its funds to Ukraine for the same two categories ("Tacis Funds Allocated by Sector 1991-97," *Tacis Annual Report 1997,* European Union Directorate General 1A: http://europa.eu.int/comm/external_relations/nis/tar97/index.htm [May 2000].)

14. United States Agency for International Development, *Action Plan for U.S. Assistance to Central and Eastern Europe,* 1991, Washington, D.C.: USAID, p. 12.

15. United States General Accounting Office, *Poland: Economic Restructuring and Donor Assistance,* Washington, D.C.: GAO, August 1995, p. 57.

16. Ibid.

17. On July 1, 1998, long after the period of intense aid efforts in Central and Eastern Europe, two of the Big Six accounting firms merged: Price Waterhouse and Coopers & Lybrand became PriceWaterhouseCoopers.

18. Interview with David Thomas (director), January 13, 1992, and interview with David Thomas and George Zielinski (deputy director), January 27, 1992.

19. Ibid.

20. Ibid.

21. This pattern challenges a claim often made about government outsourcing and competitive bidding. Although competitive bidding was believed to provide flexibility because the government could easily terminate contractors if dissatisfied, this was truer in theory than in practice. Contractors often gained access to information and contacts and acquired expertise that made them valuable to government and much more likely to continue to win contracts. In contrast to the flexibility that outsourcing was supposed to provide, the consultants came to be seen as indispensable, and often became attached to a particular portfolio for the duration of its existence. Thus, under the banner of competition, the Big Six and the Washington "Beltway Bandits" often became entrenched. Further, although contractors were perceived as outsiders who could be used as levers against bureaucracy, they quickly became part of the system of supporting aid programs from which they benefited. (Daniel Guttman, *Contracting for Government,* Washington, D.C.: distributed by the National Academy of Public Administration, January 1997; and numerous conversations with Daniel Guttman, an expert on government contracting for the performance of public functions, 1998-2000.) The EU's Alan Mayhew recounts how, as head of the PHARE program, he tried to press for more investment, only to encounter resistance from British and Irish providers of technical assistance who had done well in contract competitions and expected to continue to do so. (Interview with Alan Mayhew, May 15, 1996.)

22. Conversation with U.S. procurement officer Steve Dean, January 7, 1998. Some details of "notwithstanding authority" are presented in chapter 1.

23. According to USAID, its purpose in setting up the IQC structure was to develop a rapid-response capability to handle requests from recipients. Although it took an estimated 8 to 18 months from the time the IQC mechanism was conceived in 1990 to the actual placing of consultants in the field (one source within USAID estimated the period between conceptualization of the program to be 12 to 18 months; another source estimated the same period to be 8 months), once the mechanism was in place

projects could get under way more quickly than they could under some other USAID contracting mechanisms. The idea was that time-consuming RFPs (requests for proposals) and open competitive bidding would be conducted only once. Once the firms had won IQCs, they did not have to go through the process of open competitive bidding again. A work order could simply be completed for individual projects, short-term assignments set up, and personnel dispatched to the field. (Conversations with Scott Thomas, former USAID official, May 2, June 3, and June 6, 1994; and with USAID official Mark Karns, June 7, 1994.) Indeed, the IQC mechanism typically enabled consultants to be sent to the field more quickly than under the EU's PHARE program.

24. Information provided by USAID procurement officer Steve Dean, November 7, 1996.

25. Talk before the American Committee for Aid to Poland (ACAP), Washington, D.C., March 12, 1992.

26. United States General Accounting Office, *Poland and Hungary: Economic Transition and U.S. Assistance,* Washington, D.C.: GAO, 1992, especially pp. 31-36.

27. Interview with Marek Krawczuk, January 31, 1992.

28. Interview with Jeffry Baldwin, January 14 1992.

29. Interview with Marek Krawczuk, April 8, 1994.

30. Development Economics Group/Louis Berger International, Inc., and Checci and Company Consulting, Inc., *Final Report: Privatization Phase II Program Evaluation,* submitted to USAID, Washington, D.C., July 30, 1993, p. 11.

31. There were ways of skirting this. For instance, in the Czech Republic, a non-IQC firm that wanted to receive funding from USAID to advise Czech privatization bodies was hired as a subcontractor to a firm that already had obtained an IQC contract. (Interview with Michael N. Gold, managing director of the Crimson Capital project in the Ministry of Privatization, July 8, 1994.)

32. Interviews with and documents provided by Slovak officials and American consultants, summer and fall 1994.

33. Interview with Stefan Kawalec, October 28, 1991.

34. United States General Accounting Office, *Poland: Economic Restructuring and Donor Assistance,* Washington, D.C.: GAO, August 1995, p. 66.

35. Ibid., pp. 43-44.

36. Of course, the economic histories of the countries of Central and Eastern Europe under communism, as well as the economic reform and privatization strategies undertaken after 1989, were diverse. For a comprehensive analysis of economic reforms, performance, policies, and outcomes in Central and Eastern Europe and the former Soviet Union, see Valerie Bunce, "The Political Economy of Postsocialism," *Slavic Review,* vol. 58, no. 4, Winter 1999, especially pp. 763-772. With regard to privatization, see, for example, David Stark, "Path Dependence and Privatization Strategies in East Central Europe," *East European Politics and Societies,* vol. 6, no. 1, Winter 1992, pp. 17-54; and Katharina Pistor and Joel Turkewitz, "Coping with Hydra-State Ownership after Privatization," *Corporate Governance in Central Europe and Russia,* Transitions Economics Division, Policy Research Department, The World Bank: A Joint Conference of the World Bank and the Central European University Privatization Project, December 15-16, 1994. Stark identifies the property forms resulting from Hungarian privatization as neither private nor collective but "recombinant" property.

37. Interview with Stefan Kawalec, March 8, 1990, and April 16, 1990. This quote is from April 16, 1990. (For details, see Janine R. Wedel, "The Economist Heard 'Round the World, Part II," *World Monitor,* October 1990, pp. 33-40.)

38. Central and Eastern European participants at the working conference co-organized by the author further confirmed this point. See John Harper and Janine R. Wedel, *Western Aid to Central and Eastern Europe: What We Are Doing Right, What We Are Doing Wrong, and How We Can Do It Better*, East European Studies Occasional Paper no. 41: Woodrow Wilson International Center for Scholars, September 1995, p. 25.

39. Interview with Grzegorz Kołodko, March 13, 1990.

40. Interview with Jacek Saryusz-Wolski cited in Janine R. Wedel, "Beware Western Governments Bearing Gifts," *Wall Street Journal Europe*, January 14, 1992.

41. Letter from Pavel Rozsypal, director of the Centre for Foreign Assistance of the Ministry of the Economy, Czech Republic, August 2, 1994.

42. Interview with Péter Kazár cited in Janine R. Wedel, "Beware Western Governments Bearing Gifts," *Wall Street Journal Europe*, January 14, 1992.

43. Interview with Marek Kozak cited in Janine R. Wedel, "The Unintended Consequences of Western Aid to Post-Communist Europe," *Telos*, no. 92, summer 1992, p. 133.

44. Cited in John Harper and Janine R. Wedel, *Western Aid to Central and Eastern Europe: What We Are Doing Right, What We Are Doing Wrong, and How We Can Do It Better*, East European Studies Occasional Paper, no. 41: Woodrow Wilson International Center for Scholars, September 1995, p. 25.

45. Interview with Jan Czerniawski, January 13, 1992.

46. Leonid Abalkin, "Evaluation of USA Technical Aid in the Course of Democratic and Economic Transformations in Russia," paper presented at The George Washington University, February 26, 1996, pp. 12-13.

47. Interview with Mykola Horkusha, deputy chair of the Department for Business Support, Ministry of the Economy, August 22, 1995.

48. Interview with Alexander Paskhaver, August 18, 1995.

49. Pavel Bratinka, "Assistance Brings Greater Understanding," *G24 Newsletter*, Prague Centre for Foreign Assistance of the Ministry of the Economy, Prague, Czech Republic, December 1993.

50. Interview with State Secretary Gabriel Palacka of the Slovak Ministry of Administration and Privatization of National Property, July 4, 1994.

51. Interview with Jiří Hodík, coordinator of the PHARE privatization program in the Czech Ministry of the Economy, cited in Janine R. Wedel, "The Unintended Consequences of Western Aid to Post-Communist Europe," *Telos*, no. 92, summer 1992, p. 136.

52. Daniel Guttman, *Contracting for Government*, Washington, D.C.: distributed by the National Academy of Public Administration, January 1997; and numerous conversations with Daniel Guttman, an expert on government contracting for the performance of public functions, 1998-2000.

53. Under the system known as *nomenklatura*, responsible positions in all spheres of government had to be approved by the Communist Party, creating a tangle of loyalties and favoritisms that precluded broader political and social participation. The *nomenklatura* had the power to accept or veto candidates for any state job and asserted a final voice over responsible positions in all spheres, from police and army posts to factory management and school principalships, on the basis of Party loyalty, not ability or qualifications.

54. For further description of such arrangements, see, for example, Connie Squires Meaney, "Privatization and the Ministry of Privatization in Poland: Outsiders as Political Assets and Political Liabilities," University of California at Berkeley, Center for German and European Studies Working Paper, April 1993; Jadwiga

Staniszkis, "Political Capitalism in Poland," *Eastern European Politics and Societies,* vol. 5, no. 1, winter 1991, pp. 127-141; and Anthony Levitas and Piotr Strzałkowski, "What Does 'Uwłaszczenie Nomenklatury' (Propertisation of the *Nomenklatura*) Really Mean?" *Communist Economies,* vol. 2, no. 3, 1990, pp. 413-416.

55. Interview with Piotr Kownacki, deputy director of NIK, April 29, 1994.

56. Sheila Kaplan, "Conflicting Signals," *Legal Times,* February 25, 1991, p. 22.

57. Interview with Paweł Samecki, July 26, 1994.

58. Any standard Western method applied in Eastern Europe can produce a huge range of estimates. One method, for example, assesses the book value, or cost, of a firm's property. Even if the firm's equipment is state of the art (which often is not the case), the supporting infrastructure—transportation and telecommunications systems—might not be. A factory in Indiana might be worth much more than a comparable one in Bulgaria because it is integrated into a well-developed infrastructure.

59. Antoni Kamiński, "The New Polish Regime and the Spector of Economic Corruption." Summary of paper presented at the Woodrow Wilson International Center for Scholars, April 3, 1996.

60. Najwyższa Izba Kontroli (NIK), Zespól Analiz Systemowych, *Informacja o Wynikach Kontroli Procesów Prywatyzacji Przedsiębiorstw Panstwowych:* Częsz I, Warsaw, Poland: Najwyższa Izba Kontroli (NIK), Zespól Analiz Systemowych, June 1991.

61. Interview with Lech Kaczyński, July 14, 1999.

62. NIK (1991) report; "List of Firms Recommended by the MWGZZ for Analysis and Asset Valuations of Privatizing Firms," document produced by the Polish Ministry of Foreign Economic Cooperation (Ministerstwo Wspólpracy Gospodarczej z Zagranica, or MWGZ), Economics Department; and interview with Jan Piotrowski of the Institut Koniunktur i Cen, Handlu Zagranicznego, November 25, 1991.

63. Najwyższa Izba Kontroli (NIK), Zespol Analiz Systemowych, *Informacja o Wynikach Kontroli Procesow Prywatyzacji Przedsieborstw Panstwowych:* Czesz I, Warsaw, Poland: NIK, Zespól Analiz Systemowych, June 1991, p. 31.

64. Interviews with Rozália Krizsa and deputy Antalfi Gyözö at Monor, November 7, 1991.

65. Interview with Anatol Lawina, April 28, 1994.

66. Polish government sources and conversations of January and July 1998 with anthropologist Lisa Anne Gurr, who spent two years studying restructuring and labor issues at Ursus. See also Lisa Anne Gurr, "The Unmaking of the Polish Working Class: Reform and Protest in the Ursus Mechanical Works, 1991-93," Ph.D. dissertation, Northwestern University, 1998.

67. Polish government sources.

68. Interview of January 24, 1992 with Andrzej Polakowski, a deputy manager at Ursus; and conversations of January and July 1998 with anthropologist Lisa Anne Gurr.

69. Connie Squires Meaney, "Privatization and the Ministry of Privatization in Poland: Outsiders as Political Assets and Political Liabilities," University of California, Berkeley, Center for German and European Studies Working Paper, April 1993, p. 27; and conversation with Kevin McDonald, July and August 1998.

70. Interview with Andrzej Polakowski, January 24, 1992.

71. Ibid.

72. Conversations with Lisa Anne Gurr, January and July 1998.

73. Sources include Andrzej Polakowski, interview of January 24, 1992.

74. Conversation with Kevin McDonald, July 2, 1998.

75. Conversations with Lisa Anne Gurr, January and July 1998.

76. Conversation with Kevin McDonald, July 2, 1998.

77. The average value of the EURO during 1999 was approximately 1.0653 (see *International Financial Statistics Yearbook 1999*, Washington, D.C.: International Monetary Fund, 1999).

78. "Znikające Euromiliony: Jak Wykorzstywano Pomoc UE dla Polski" ("Disappearing Euromillions: How EU Aid to Poland is Used"), *Wprost*, May 30, 1999, pp. 38-39; NIK, *Informacja o Wynikach Kontroli Wykorżystania Pomocy Unii Europejskiej dla Polski, Realizowanej ze Srodków PHARE*, Warsaw, Poland: Najwyższa Izba Kontroli: Department Gospodarki I Integracji Europejskiej, November 1998.

79. Development Economics Group/Louis Berger International, Inc., and Checci and Company Consulting, Inc., *Final Report: Privatization Phase II Program Evaluation*, submitted to AID, Washington, D.C., by Development Economics Group/ Louis Berger International, Inc., and Checci and Company Consulting, Inc., July 30, 1993, pp. 31-33.

80. Christine A. Bogdanowicz-Bindert, *Interim Report: IDA Assessment*, commissioned by the European Union's PHARE program, December 1993, p. 1.

81. "Znikające Euromiliony: Jak Wykorzstywano Pomoc UE dla Polski" ("Disappearing Euromillions: How EU Aid to Poland is Used"), *Wprost*, May 30, 1999, pp. 38-39; NIK, *Informacja o Wynikach Kontroli Wykorżystania Pomocy Unii Europejskiej dla Polski, Realizowanej ze Srodków PHARE*, Warsaw, Poland: Najwyższa Izba Kontroli: Department Gospodarki I Integracji Europejskiej, November 1998.

82. United States General Accounting Office: *Economic Restructuring and Donor Assistance*, Washington, D.C.: GAO, August 1995, pp. 57-8.

83. Ibid., p. 58.

84. For details of pending privatization plans for LOT, see "LOT na Giełde," *Rzeczpospolita*, June 30, 2000. Abstracted in World Reporter. (Obtained through Dow Jones Interactive.)

85. United States General Accounting Office, *Poland: Ecomonic Restructuting and Donor Assistance*, Washington, D.C., GAO, August 1995, p. 6.

86. Data provided by Grzegorz Kołodko, former first deputy prime minister and minister of finance of Poland (letter from Grzegorz Kołodko, June 20, 2000, and conversations of August 1998). See also Grzegorz Kołodko, *From Shock to Therapy: The Political Economy of Postsocialist Transformation*, Oxford and New York: Oxford University Press, 2000; and Mario Nuti, Mass Privatisation: Costs and Benefits of Instant Capitalism, London, United Kingdom: CIS—Middle Europe Centre, London Business School, Discussion Paper Series, no. 9, May 1994, p. 15.

87. There is a considerable body of work on how "planned economies" actually worked in practice. Political sociologist Claus Offe, for example, who calls planned economies a "misleading euphemism," writes: "These were admittedly economies in which there was planning; but precisely for that reason they were economies which did not function according to plan, but were instead susceptible (and vulnerable) to unpleasant surprises 'from below'—to the friction that resulted from the fact that it was not possible to coordinate actions 'on site' effectively or discipline them sufficiently." (Claus Offe, *Varieties of Transition: The East European and East German Experience*, Cambridge, MA: MIT Press, 1997, p. 5.)

88. John W. Bennett, "Anthropology and Development: The Ambiguous Engagement," *Production and Autonomy: Anthropological Studies and Critiques of Development*, John W. Bennett and John R. Bowen, eds., Lanham, MD: University Press of America, 1988, p. 16.

89. James Millar, *From Utopian Socialism to Utopian Capitalism: The Failure of Revolution and Reform in Post-Soviet Russia,* Washington, D.C., The George Washington University: 175th Anniversary Papers, 1996, Paper 2, p. 13.

90. Mark Hobart, "Introduction: The Growth of Ignorance?" *An Anthropological Critique of Development,* Mark Hobart, ed., London, United Kingdom: Routledge, 1993, p. 16.

91. See, for example, Yudit Kiss, "Privatization Paradoxes in East Central Europe," *East European Politics and Society,* vol. 8, no. 1, winter, 1994, pp. 141-152; and James Millar, *From Utopian Socialism to Utopian Capitalism: The Failure of Revolution and Reform in Post-Soviet Russia,* Washington, D.C., The George Washington University: 175th Anniversary Papers, 1996, Paper 2, pp. 13-15.

92. Interview with Yuriy Yakusha, April 16, 1996.

93. Conversations with Mark Karns, June 7, 1994.

94. A report commissioned by the EU on PHARE consulting in enterprises independently concluded that the "work of the consultants is often complicated by a management reluctant to introduce changes" (Christine A. Bogdanowicz-Bindert, "Interim Report: IDA Assessment," report commissioned by the European Union's PHARE program, December 1993, p. 3).

95. A report commissioned by USAID to evaluate USAID privatization projects in Central and Eastern Europe independently arrived at the same conclusion (Development Economics Group/Louis Berger International, Inc., and Checci and Company Consulting, Inc., *Final Report: Privatization Phase II Program Evaluation.* Submitted to AID, Washington, D.C., by Development Economics Group/Louis Berger International, Inc., and Checci and Company Consulting, Inc., July 30, 1993, pp. 1617).

96. Connie Squires Meaney, "Privatization and the Ministry of Privatization in Poland: Outsiders as Political Assets and Political Liabilities," University of California, Berkeley, Center for German and European Studies: Working Paper, April 1993, p. 30.

97. Interview with Jan Krzysztof Bielecki, December 14, 1995.

98. For discussion of corruption in Central European privatization, see, for example, Antoni Z. Kamiński, "Corruption Under the Post-Communist Transformation," *Polish Sociological Review,* vol. 2, no. II8, 1997, pp. 91-117; Grzegorz Kołodko, *From Shock to Therapy: The Political Economy of Postsocialist Transformation,* Oxford and New York: Oxford University Press, 2000, chapter 9; David Stark and Laszlo Bruszt, *Postsocialist Pathways: Transforming Politics and Property in East Central Europe,* Cambridge, United Kingdom: Cambridge University Press, 1998; and Janine R. Wedel, "Clans, Cliques, and Captured States: How We Misunderstand 'Transition' in Central and Eastern Europe and the Former Soviet Union," presented to the National Council for Eurasian and East European Research and the National Institute of Justice, 2000, and forthcoming as National Council Working Paper (section entitled "The Social Organization of the State").

99. Czech privatization appears to be one such case. Responding to the question "Were there any privatizations that weren't corrupt?" Chairman of the Czech Securities Commission Jan Müller could name only two notable examples. He added: "We are very much worried about criminal activities against shareholders that will be privatized this year or next" (interview of January 19, 2000). Also see, for example, David Ellerman, "Voucher Privatization with Investment Funds: An Institutional Analysis," *Policy Research Working Paper 1924,* Washington D.C.: The World Bank, Office of the Senior Vice President, Development Economics, May 1998.

100. For discussion of corruption in Russian privatization, see chapter 4, section entitled "The Great Grab."

101. See, for example, Connie Squires Meaney, "Privatization and the Ministry of Privatization in Poland: Outsiders as Political Assets and Political Liabilities," University of California, Berkeley, Center for German and European Studies Working Paper, April 1993, p. 29.

102. Conversations with Lisa Anne Gurr, January and June 1998.

103. See the works of anthropologists Arturo Escobar and James Ferguson. (Arturo Escobar, "Power and Visibility: Development and the Invention and Management of the Third World," *Cultural Anthropology,* vol. 3, no. 4, 1988, pp. 428-443; Arturo Escobar, "Anthropology and the Development Encounter: The Making and Marketing of Development Anthropology," *American Ethnologist* vol. 18, no. 4, 1991, pp. 658-682; and James Ferguson, *The Anti-Politics Machine: "Development," Depoliticization, and Bureaucratic Power in Lesotho,* Cambridge, United Kingdom: Cambridge University Press, 1990.)

104. Mark Hobart, "Introduction: The Growth of Ignorance?" *An Anthropological Critique of Development,* Mark Hobart, ed., London, United Kingdom: Routledge, 1993, p. 6.

105. Interview with Zdeněk Drábek, July 7, 1994.

106. For further discussion of this issue, see Janine R. Wedel, "U.S. Aid to Central and Eastern Europe, 1990-1994: An Analysis of Aid Models and Responses," *East-Central European Economies in Transition: Study Papers submitted to the Joint Economic Committee Congress of the United States,* November 1994, pp. 299-335; republished in *East-Central European Economies in Transition,* John P. Hardt and Richard F. Kaufman, eds., for the Joint Economic Committee Congress of the United States, New York, NY: M. E. Sharpe, 1995.

107. Information provided by Gary Peters, assistant director for enforcement in Treasury's Office of Technical Assistance, conversations of July 1, 2000.

108. Between FY 1990 and FY 1993, the U.S. government spent $42 million on the Treasury technical assistance program. As of June 1, 1994, the department had 28 long-term resident advisers in Eastern Europe (interview with Treasury Department official Robert Banque, June 4, 1994). Between FY 1994 and FY 2000, the program received some $126.5 million in additional funding. An estimated 20 advisers were in residence in the region at any given time, according to G. Edwin Smith, III, director of the Treasury's Office of Technical Assistance (letters of June 9, 2000, and July 10, 2000).

109. Interview with Salvatore Pappalardo, April 13, 1994.

110. Conversations with Wiesław Staszkiewicz (July 29, 1994 and August 2, 1994), Włodzimierz Borodziej (July 28, 1994), and Jacek Głowacki (July 29, 1994) of the Parliament's Bureau of Research. The Frost Task Force provided similar assistance to parliaments throughout Central and Eastern Europe.

111. Conversations with Wiesław Staszkiewicz, July 29, 1994 and August 1, 1994.

112. Interview with Wiesław Staszkiewicz, June 17, 1998; and conversation with Enie Wesseldijk, executive secretary, International Institute for Democracy, Strasbourg, France, June 15, 1998. For an evaluation of programs assisting parliamentary development in Central and Eastern Europe, see International Institute for Democracy, *Parliamentary Development Programmes: Evaluation and Beyond,* Conference Report, Berlin, Germany, May 30-31, 1997.

113. Interview with Wiesław Staszkiewicz, June 17, 1998.

114. Ibid.

115. Interview with Salvatore Pappalardo, April 13, 1994.

116. A number of donor and recipient officials, as well as an OECD report on technical assistance, support this view. (OECD, *Comparative Assessment of Key Technical Assistance to the Partners in Transition and Four New Independent States of the Former Soviet Union,* Paris, France: OECD, 1994, pp. 6-7.)

CHAPTER THREE

1. Václav Havel, publicity blurb for book jacket, John Keane, *Democracy and Civil Society,* London, United Kingdom: Verso, 1988.

2. The definition of "civil society" and its appropriate empirical application has been the subject of much study and debate among scholars. See, for instance, Jean Cohen and Andrew Arato, *Civil Society and Political Theory* (Cambridge, MA: MIT Press, 1992); Ernest Gellner, Keynote Address, Conference entitled "The Anthropology of Politics in Eastern Europe," Zaborów, Poland, October 1990; and *Conditions of Liberty: Civil Society and its Rivals* (New York, NY: Allen Lane/Penguin Press, 1994); John Hall, ed., *Civil Society: Theory, History, Comparison* (Cambridge, United Kingdom: Blackwell, 1995); John Keane, *Democracy and Civil Society* (London, United Kingdom: Verso, 1988); Adam B. Seligman, *The Idea of Civil Society* (Princeton, NJ: Princeton University Press, 1992); Keith Tester, *Civil Society* (London, United Kingdom: Routledge, 1992).

3. For insightful analysis of American democracy promotion abroad, see Thomas Carothers, *Aiding Democracy Abroad: The Learning Curve,* Washington, D.C.: Carnegie Endowment for International Peace, 1999.

4. These figures consist of funding to Poland, Hungary, Czechoslovakia, Romania, Bulgaria, and Albania, as well as to regional projects. (U.S. Department of State, "U.S. Assistance for Central and East Europe: Obligations FY 1990, 1991," *SEED Act Implementation Report: Fiscal Year 1991,* Washington, D.C.: U.S. Department of State, January 31, 1992, p. 71.)

5. U.S. Department of State, *SEED Act Implementation Report: Fiscal Year 1999,* Washington, D.C.: U.S. Department of State, March 2000, tables.

6. The average value of the ECU during 1994 was approximately 1.1886. (See *International Financial Statistics Yearbook 1999,* Washington, D.C.: International Monetary Fund, 1999, p. 925.)

7. For further information, see Krzysztof J. Ners and Ingrid T. Buxell, *Assistance to Transition Survey 1995,* Warsaw, Poland: Institute for EastWest Studies, Pecat, 1995, pp. 81-84.

8. The average value of the ECU during 1991-1997 was approximately 1.2305. (See *International Financial Statistics Yearbook 1999,* Washington, D.C.: International Monetary Fund, 1999, p. 925.)

9. Evaluation Unit of Common Service for External Relations of the European Commission, "Table 2: Phare Programmes in Favor of Civil Society Development 1991-97," *Evaluation of the Phare Partnership Programme: Final Report,* prepared by Local and Regional Development Planning for the Evaluation Unit of Common Service for External Relations of the European Commission, November 1998, pp. 31-32.

10. U.S. Department of State, *SEED Act Implementation Report, Fiscal Year 1999,* Washington, D.C.: U.S. Department of State, March 2000, tables. This figure

consists of funding to Poland, Hungary, Czechoslovakia, Romania, Bulgaria, and Albania. See appendix 1, table 3.

11. U.S. Department of State, *U.S. Government Assistance to and Cooperative Activities with the New Independent States of the Former Soviet Union, FY 1999 Annual Report,* Washington, D.C.: U.S. Department of State, prepared by the Office of the Coordinator of U.S. Assistance to the NIS, January 2000, tables.

12. The program focuses on the following eight areas: (1) parliamentary practice and procedures; (2) transparency of public administration and management; (3) development of NGOs and representatives structures; (4) independent media: (5) civic education; (6) promoting and monitoring human rights; (7) civilian monitoring of security structures; and (8) minority rights. The category of democracy promotion excludes funding for education and training, administrative reform, and social development and employment. (ISA Consult, *Final Report: Evaluation of PHARE and TACIS Democracy Programme [1992-1997],* Prepared by ISA Consult, European Institute at Sussex University, and GJW Europe, November 1997, pp. 10-11.)

13. Kevin F. F. Quigley, *For Democracy's Sake: Foundations and Democracy Assistance in Central Europe,* Washington, D.C.: Woodrow Wilson Center Press, 1997, p. 1 and appendix, table 1.

14. The 24 foundations in nearly each nation of the former Soviet world are usually called either the Soros Foundation or the Open Society Institute, although sometimes a different name is used, such as the Stefan Batory Foundation in Poland and the International Renaissance Foundation in Ukraine. (Kim Lane Scheppele, "The Soros Empire," *American and German Cultural Policies in Eastern Europe: Assessing Developments in the 1990s,* Washington, D.C.: American Institute for Contemporary German Studies, October 1999, pp. 28-29.) Soros network programs, which are directed from the Open Society Institutes (OSI) either in New York or Budapest, sponsor activities on specific topics such as higher education or media. With regard to short-term initiatives, some notable enterprises have consisted of the creation of the Central European University (CEU), currently based primarily in Budapest and Warsaw, and the International Science Foundation set up to provide grants to Russian scientists when state subsidies crumbled. (Ibid., pp. 30-34.)

For detailed information about the history, operations, and style of Soros's philanthropy in Central and Eastern Europe and the former Soviet Union, see Ibid., pp. 27-39; and Kevin F. F. Quigley, *For Democracy's Sake: Foundations and Democracy Assistance in Central Europe,* Washington, D.C.: Woodrow Wilson Center Press, 1997, chapter 7: "George Soros: Leader of the Band," pp. 87-102.

15. Kevin F. F. Quigley, *For Democracy's Sake: Foundations and Democracy Assistance in Central Europe,* Washington, D.C.: Woodrow Wilson Center Press, 1997, p. 87.

16. Steven Sampson, "Romanian Political Culture and NGOs," presented at Sinaia NGO Conference, March 1994, p. 1.

17. Thomas Carothers also makes this point for Poland and the Czech Republic (*Assessing Democracy Assistance: The Case of Romania,* Washington, D.C.: Carnegie Endowment for International Peace, 1996).

18. Steven Sampson, "The Social Life of Projects: Importing Civil Society to Albania," *Civil Society: Challenging Western Models,* Chris Hann and Elizabeth Dunn, eds., London, United Kingdom: Routledge, 1996, p. 141.

19. Katherine Verdery, "Theorizing Socialism: A Prologue to the 'Transition,'" *American Ethnologist,* vol. 18, no. 3, 1991, pp. 419-439 and *What Was Socialism, And What Comes Next?* Princeton, NJ: Princeton University Press, 1996.

20. In some countries of the region, such as Poland, "communists" were categorically purged from municipalities in the first postcommunist local elections. This was not the case, however, in other countries, such as Bulgaria and Romania.

21. The rituals of public life are further described in Janine Wedel, *The Private Poland: An Anthropologist's Look at Everyday Life,* New York, NY: Facts on File, 1986, chapter 1, "Private and Public Worlds".

22. Marta Bruno, "Playing the Co-Operation Game: Strategies Around International Aid in Post-Socialist Russia," *Surviving Post-Socialism: Local Strategies and Regional Responses in Eastern Europe and the Former Soviet Union,* Sue Bridger and Frances Pine, eds., London, United Kingdom: Routledge, 1998, p. 180.

23. Steven Sampson, "The Social Life of Projects: Importing Civil Society to Albania," *Civil Society: Challenging Western Models,* Chris Hann and Elizabeth Dunn, eds., London, United Kingdom: Routledge, 1996, p. 141.

24. The concept of "symbolic capital" is explained by Pierre Bourdieu ("What Makes a Social Class? On the Theoretical and Practical Existence of Groups," *Berkeley Journal of Sociology,* vol. 32, 1987, pp. 1-17) and Pierre Bourdieu and J. C. Passeron (*Reproduction in Education, Society and Culture,* trans. R. Nice, London, United Kingdom: Sage, 1977).

25. Tadeusz Wróblewski, "The Opposition and Money," *The Unplanned Society: Poland During and After Communism,* Janine R. Wedel, ed., New York, NY: Columbia University Press, 1992.

26. Senate Foreign Relations Committee, "Programs of the National Endowment for Democracy in Poland," *The Future of Europe: Hearings before the Committee on Foreign Relations and the Subcommittee on European Affairs,* 101st Cong., 2nd Session, December 13, 1989, January 17, February 1 and 22, March 1, 7, 21, 22, 28, and 29, May 9, and June 12, 1990, pp. 424-425. (Hereafter cited as *The Future of Europe.*)

27. Ibid., p. 426.

28. Senate Foreign Relations Committee, "Prepared Statement of Carl Gershman, President, National Endowment for Democracy, Washington, D.C.," in ibid., p. 419. (Hereafter cited as "Prepared Statement of Carl Gershman.")

29. Ibid., p. 423.

30. Senate Foreign Relations Committee, "Programs of the National Endowment for Democracy in Poland." Ibid. 429.

31. For analyses of the development of the Citizens' Committees, see Sergiusz Kowalski, ed., *Pierwszy Krok do Europy: O Komitetach Obywatelskich, Partiach Politycznych i Wyborach* (Warsaw, Poland: Ośrodek Prac Społeczno-Zawodowych przy KK NSZZ "Solidarność," 1990); and Zbigniew Rykowksi, "Narodziny Demokratycznego Systemu Władzy. O Komitetach Obywatelskich w Latach 1989-92," in *A Miało Być Tak Pięknie: Polska Scena Publiczna Lat Dziewięćdziesiątych,* Barbara Lewenstein and Wojciech Pawlik, eds., (Warsaw, Poland: Uniwersytet Warszawski, Instytut Stosowanych Nauk Społecznych, 1994).

32. Marek Ruszczynski, American representative of KPN, congressional testimony.

33. Senate Foreign Relations Committee, "Prepared Statement of Carl Gershman," p. 423.

34. Kim Lane Scheppele, "The Soros Empire," *American and German Cultural Policies in Eastern Europe: Assessing Developments in the 1990s,* Washington, D.C.: American Institute for Contemporary German Studies, October 1999, pp. 28-29.

35. Senate Foreign Relations Committee, "Prepared Statement of Carl Gershman," p. 426.

36. Conversations with Zbigniew Rykowski, January 1991.

37. Quoted in Kevin F. F. Quigley, *For Democracy's Sake: Foundations and Democracy Assistance in Central Europe*, Washington, D.C.: Woodrow Wilson Center Press, 1997, p. 92. Irena Lasota was president of the Institute for Democracy in Eastern Europe.

38. For additional reference, see *The Future of Europe*, pp. 674-78.

39. Senate Foreign Relations Committee, "Socialist Bias" (KPN documents submitted as part of statement of Marek Ruszczynski, American representative of the Confederacy of Independent Poland [KPN], New York, NY), *The Future of Europe*, pp. 442-443.

40. Senate Foreign Relations Committee, "Responses of Mr. Ruszczynski to Questions by Senator Helms," *The Future of Europe: Hearings before the Committee on Foreign Relations and the Subcommittee on European Affairs*, 101st Cong., 2nd Session, December 13, 1989, January 17, February 1 and 22, March 1, 7, 21, 22, 28, and 29, May 9, and June 12, 1990, pp. 674-675.

41. United States General Accounting Office, *Promoting Democracy: Progress Report on U.S. Democratic Development Assistance to Russia*, Washington, D.C.: GAO, February 1996, pp. 6-7.

42. The extent to which informal groups and networks penetrate, or "capture," the state is one of the most crucial issues of Eastern European democracy and development. The author has identified two distinct patterns of relationships between informal groups and the state in Central and Eastern Europe and the former Soviet Union: the "partially appropriated state" and the "clan-state." Under the "partially appropriated state," based largely on Polish material, informal groups clearly work with some relevant state authorities, but the groups are not synonymous with the authorities. The "clan-state," on the other hand, a state captured by unauthorized groups and characterized by pervasive corruption, is based on Russian and Ukrainian data. With little separation of clans from the state, a clan's influence typically can be constrained only by a rival clan, as judicial processes often are politically motivated. (See Janine R. Wedel, *Clans, Cliques, and Captured States: How We Misunderstand "Transition" in Central and Eastern Europe and the Former Soviet Union*, presented to the National Council for Eurasian and East European Research and the National Institute of Justice, 2000, and forthcoming as a National Council *Working Paper*.)

43. Interviews with Thomas Koch, Margitta Wülker, and Matthias Möller, representatives of the Bundesministerium für Wirtschaft, March 30, 1994; and with Bernd von Muenchow-Pohl, German government representative in Poland, April 11, 1994.

44. Sources include conversations of June 8, 1998, with members of Parliament of the German *land* of Hesse who are involved in exchanges and initiatives with certain areas in the east.

45. Court of Auditors, *Special Report No. 5/99 Concerning Phare Cross-border Cooperation (1994 to 1998), Accompanied by the Replies of the Commission*, Brussels, Belgium: Official Journal of the European Communities, February 21, 2000, p. C48/2-C48/3.

46. Karl A. Wittfogel, *Oriental Despotism: A Comparative Study of Total Power*, New York, NY: Vintage Books, 1981, pp. 8, 15ff, 437, 447f.

47. Antoni Kamiński, "Corruption under the Post-Communist Transformation," *Polish Sociological Review*, vol. 2, no. II8, 1997, p. 104. Also see Antoni Z. Kamiński and Jan A. Stefanowicz, "Jak Buduje Się III Rzeczpospolita: Ułomne Reguły Gry," *Zeszyty Centrum im. Adama Smitha*, November 1995.

48. For details, see press reports (for example, Tomasz Swiackiewicz, "Głowa w Mur," *Polityka,* September 7, 1991) and materials available from the Adam Smith Centre, Warsaw, Poland.

49. A number of scholars have discussed pre-1989 Central European (often specifically Polish) opposition groups and activities under the rubric of "civil society." See, for example, Andrew Arato, ("Civil Society Against the State: Poland 1980-81," *Telos* no. 47, Spring 1981, pp. 23-47); Andrew Arato, ("Empire vs. Civil Society: Poland 1981-82." *Telos* no. 50, Winter 1981-82, pp. 19-48); Michael H. Bernard, (*The Origins of Democratization in Poland.* New York, NY: Columbia University Press, 1993); Václav Havel et al., (*The Power of the Powerless: Citizens Against the State in Central-Eastern Europe,* ed. John Keane, Armonk, NY: M. E. Sharpe, 1985); Zbigniew A. Pelczynski ("Solidarity and 'the Rebirth of Civil Society,'" in *Civil Society and the State,* ed. John Keane, London, United Kingdom: Verso, 1988, pp. 361-381); Jacques Rupnik ("Dissent in Poland, 1968-78: The End of Revisionism and the Rebirth of Civil Society," *Opposition in Eastern Europe,* Rudolf L. Tokes, ed., Baltimore, MD: Johns Hopkins University Press, 1979, pp. 60-112); and Gordon H. Skilling (*Samizdat and an Independent Society in Central and Eastern Europe* Basingstoke, United Kingdom: Macmillan, 1988); Janine R. Wedel, ed., *The Unplanned Society: Poland During and After Communism,* New York, NY: Columbia University Press, 1992).

50. Chris Hann, "Introduction: Political Society and Civil Anthropology," *Civil Society: Challenging Western Models,* Chris Hann and Elizabeth Dunn, eds., London: Routledge, 1996, p. 7.

51. See, for example, Arato, "Civil Society against the State," pp. 23-47; Arato, "Empire vs. Civil Society," pp. 19-48; Bernard, *The Origins of Democratization in Poland;* Havel, *The Power of the Powerless;* Pelczynski, "Solidarity and 'the Rebirth of Civil Society,'" pp. 361-381; Rupnik, "Dissent in Poland," pp. 60-112; Skilling, *Samizdat and an Independent Society;* and Janine R. Wedel, ed., *The Unplanned Society: Poland During and After Communism* (New York, NY: Columbia University Press, 1992).

52. Stefan Nowak, "System Wartości Społeczenstwa Polskiego," *Studia Socjologiczne,* vol. 4, no. 75, 1979, p. 155-174.

53. For further analysis of Eastern European social organization, see Janine R. Wedel, introduction to *The Unplanned Society: Poland During and After Communism,* Janine R. Wedel, ed., New York, NY: Columbia University Press, 1992, pp. 1-20.

54. Richard Rose has observed that distrust is "a pervasive legacy of communist rule" (Richard Rose, "Rethinking Civil Society: Postcommunism and the Problem of Trust," *Journal of Democracy,* vol. 5, no. 3, July 1994, pp. 18-30). See also "Getting Things Done in an Anti-Modern Society: Social Capital Networks in Russia," *Studies in Public Policy* No. 304, Glasgow, United Kingdom: Centre for the Study of Public Policy, University of Strathclyde, Studies in Public Policy Number 304, 1998.

55. The networks that constitute the clique are "dense" in that members of a person's network are in touch with one another independently of that person.

56. Members are connected to each other for multiple purposes. Thus, the networks that constitute the clique are "multiplex" (rather than "single stranded"), in that members relate to each other in multiple capacities—political, economic, and social.

57. Jeremy Boissevain, *Friends of Friends: Networks, Manipulators and Coalitions* (Oxford, United Kingdom: Basil Blackwell, 1974), p. 174.

58. In Poland, organizers sought, and many received, government registration enabling them to operate openly—to raise money, hold public meetings, and publish independently of the state. In post-1989 Poland, laws on association were liberalized; a group was required only to register its name and statute with the court.

59. For a description of these developments, see these works by Janine R. Wedel, "The Polish Revolution Turns Economic," *The Christian Science Monitor,* February 13, 1989; "Solidarity in Decline," *The Christian Science Monitor,* September 21, 1989; "The Grass-Roots Revolution in Poland," *The Christian Science Monitor,* September 28, 1989; and "Polish Survivors of the Gulag," *The Christian Science Monitor,* October 31, 1989. See also "Lech's Labors Lost?" *World Monitor,* November 1989, pp. 44-54.

60. As anthropologist Madeline Landau has pointed out, these tendencies derive from the classical social theories of the nineteenth century and from the structural-functionalist "integration" models of sociological theory employed by many fields. The models reinforce the tradition of dichotomous thought through their assumption that effective institutionalization of a new system requires a tight and standardized mode of integration.

61. Polish sociologists Antoni Z. Kamiński and Joanna Kurczewska describe this phenomenon in "Main Actors of Transformation: The Nomadic Elites," *The General Outlines of Transformation,* Eric Allardt and W. Wesołowski, eds., Warsaw, Poland: IFIS PAN Publishing, 1994.

62. Grzegorz Ekiert and Jan Kubik, "(Post)totalitarian Legacies, Civil Society, and Democracy in Post-Communist Poland, 1989-1993," Institute for European Studies Working Paper no. 97.4, pp. 20-21.

63. See, for example, Jacek Kurczewski, "Shared Privacy," *The Unplanned Society: Poland During and After Communism,* Janine R. Wedel, ed., New York, NY: Columbia University Press, 1992, pp. 158-172.

64. Solidarity-Opposition was composed of two somewhat connected groups: the long-standing Opposition—the close-knit circles of dissenting political discussion and activity mostly evolved between 1968 and 1979 (above all in intelligentsia circles)—and the great body of Solidarity activists who forced their way to the forefront of the workers' resistance when Solidarity was born in 1980.

65. United States General Accounting Office, *Promoting Democracy: Progress Report on U.S. Democratic Development Assistance to Russia,* Washington, D.C.: GAO, February 1996, p. 37.

66. Chris Hann, "Introduction: Political Society and Civil Anthropology," *Civil Society: Challenging Western Models,* Chris Hann and Elizabeth Dunn, eds., London, United Kingdom: Routledge, 1996, p. 8.

67. Grzegorz Ekiert and Jan Kubik, "(Post)totalitarian Legacies, Civil Society, and Democracy in Post-Communist Poland, 1989-1993," Institute for European Studies Working Paper no. 97.4, p. 24.

68. NGOs became a focal point of the development community in the 1980s. According to Samuel Paul, "World Bank's official cooperation with NGOs began in 1981, when the NGO–World Bank Committee was established. . . . In the mid-1980s, the practical importance of development country NGOs in some sectors was increasingly recognized within the Bank." (Samuel Paul, "Nongovernmental Organizations and the World Bank: An Overview," *Nongovernmental Organizations and the World Bank: Cooperation for Development,* Samuel Paul and Arturo Israel, eds.,Washington, D.C.: World Bank, 1991, p. 5.) See also Michael M. Cernea, "Nongovernmental Organizations and Local Development," *World Bank Discussion Papers,* Washington, D.C.: World Bank, 1988.

69. Steven Sampson, "Romanian Political Culture and NGOs," presented at Sinaia NGO Conference, March 1994, p. 5.

70. Sarah E. Mendelson and John K. Glenn, "Democracy Assistance and NGO Strategies in Post-Communist Societies," *Carnegie Endowment Working Papers,* Democracy and Rule of Law Project, no. 8, Washington, D.C.: Carnegie Endowment for International Peace, February 2000, p. 19.

71. Steven Sampson, "Romanian Political Culture and NGOs," presented at Sinai NGO conference, March 1994, p. 5.

72. Sarah E. Mendelson and John K. Glenn, "Democracy Assistance and NGO Strategies in Post-Communist Societies," *Carnegie Endowment Working Papers,* Democracy and Rule of Law Project, no. 8, Washington, D.C.: Carnegie Endowment for International Peace, February 2000, p. 17.

73. Ibid., p. 48.

74. Interview with Jakub Wygnański director of database on Polish NGOs, KLON, July 15, 1994.

75. For a more detailed description of the legal and fiscal framework of Central and Eastern European NGOs, see Daniel Siegel and Jenny Yancey, *The Rebirth of Civil Society: The Development of the Nonprofit Sector in East Central Europe and the Role of Western Assistance,* New York, NY: Rockefeller Brothers Fund, Inc., 1992.

76. Interviews of February 18, 1998 and August 3, 2000, with Jakub Wygnański, board member, Forum on Nongovernmental Initiatives, and board member, Batory Foundation. For figures charting the growth of NGOs in Central Europe, see Krzysztof J. Ners and Ingrid T. Buxell, *Assistance to Transition Survey 1995* Warsaw, Poland: Institute for EastWest Studies, Pecat, 1995, pp. 75-76.

77. Alan Ware's *Between Profit and State* documents the interdependency between "intermediate organizations" and both the state and the for-profit sector of the economy. Ware's analysis shows that U.S. nonprofit human-service agencies depended on government sources for between 41 and 90 percent of their income. Alan Ware, *Between Profit and State: Intermediate Organizations in Britain and the United States,* Cambridge, United Kingdom: Polity Press, 1989, pp. 2, 106, 109, 113, and tables on pp. 74, 110, and 111.

78. Antoni Kamiński, "The New Polish Regime and the Spector of Economic Corruption." Summary of paper presented at the Woodrow Wilson International Center for Scholars, April 3, 1996, p. 4.

79. Antoni Kamiński, "Corruption under the Post-Communist Transformation," *Polish Sociological Review,* vol. 2, no. II8, 1997, p. 100. For further discussion of these entities of unclear status, see also Janine R. Wedel, "Clans, Cliques, and Captured States: How We Misunderstand 'Transition' in Central and Eastern Europe and the Former Soviet Union," presented to the National Council for Eurasian and East European Research and the National Institute of Justice, 2000, and forthcoming as National Council *Working Paper.*

80. Legal analyst Jan Stefanowicz estimates that some 30 percent of the economy falls into this category (interviews of July 14 and 15, 1999).

81. Interview with Piotr Kownacki, July 26, 1999.

82. Antoni Kamiński, "Corruption under the Post-Communist Transformation," *Polish Sociological Review,* vol. 2, no. II8, 1997, p. 100.

83. Marta Bruno, "Playing the Co-Operation Game: Strategies Around International Aid in Post-Socialist Russia," *Surviving Post-Socialism: Local Strategies and Regional Responses in Eastern Europe and the former Soviet Union,* Sue Bridger and Frances Pine, eds., London, United Kingdom: Routledge, 1998, pp. 181-182.

84. Steven Sampson, "Romanian Political Culture and NGOs," presented at Sinaia NGO Conference, March 1994, pp. 4 and 6.

85. Marta Bruno, "Playing the Co-Operation Game: Strategies Around International Aid in Post-Socialist Russia," *Surviving Post-Socialism: Local Strategies and Regional Responses in Eastern Europe and the Former Soviet Union,* Sue Bridger and Frances Pine, eds., London, United Kingdom: Routledge, 1998, pp. 171 and 179.

86. C. M. Hann, "Foreword," *Surviving Post-Socialism: Local Strategies and Regional Responses in Eastern Europe and the former Soviet Union,* Sue Bridger and Frances Pine, eds., London, United Kingdom: Routledge, 1998, p. xiii.

87. Sarah E. Mendelson and John K. Glenn, "Democracy Assistance and NGO Strategies in Post-Communist Societies," *Carnegie Endowment Working Papers,* Democracy and Rule of Law Project, no. 8, Washington, D.C.: Carnegie Endowment for International Peace, February 2000, p. 44.

88. Interview with István Tökés, head of the Department of International Relations in the Ministry of the Environment, June 7, 1994.

89. Interview with Elena Petkova, February 10, 1998.

90. Interview with Judit Vásárhelyi, former board member of the Regional Environmental Center, April 26, 1994.

91. U.S. General Accounting Office, *Environmental Issues in Central and Eastern Europe: U.S. Efforts to Help Resolve Institutional and Financial Problems,* Washington, D.C.: GAO, May 1994, p. 55.

92. Ibid., pp. 54-57.

93. Interview with Elena Petkova, February 10, 1998, other sources connected with the Center.

94. U.S. General Accounting Office, *Environmental Issues in Central and Eastern Europe: U.S. Efforts to Help Resolve Institutional and Financial Problems,* Washington, D.C.: GAO, May 1994, pp. 54-57.

95. Interviews with Judit Vásárhelyi, former board member of the Regional Environmental Center, April 26, 1994, and with István Tökés, head of the Department of International Relations in the Ministry of the Environment, June 7, 1994.

96. Conversations with Marianne Ginsberg, senior program officer, German Marshall Fund, Spring 1998, July 5, 2000, and July 10, 2000.

97. Ibid.

98. Quoted in "The Environmental Partnership for Central Europe, Report 1995/96," Washington, D.C.: German Marshall Fund, 1997, p. 5. See also *A Decade of Nurturing the Grassroots: The Environmental Partnership for Central Europe 1991-2000,* Environmental Consortium Partnership for Central Europe: Czech Republic: Staré Město, 2000.

99. Interview with Jakub Wygnański, June 17, 1998.

100. Interview with Jakub Wygnański, June 17, 1998.

101. Interview with Jakub Wygnański, February 18, 1998.

102. Interviews with Jakub Wygnański, February 18, 1998 and August 3, 2000.

103. Interview with Jay Austin, January 15, 1998.

104. Interview with Jakub Wygnański, June 17, 1998.

105. Conversation with Elena Petkova, March 30, 1998.

106. Interview with Adam Pomorski, Russia specialist and former expert to the Batory Foundation's East-East Commission, July 4, 2000.

107. Conversations with USAID official Brian Wickland, April 15, 1999 and December 21, 1999; and "Poland-American-Ukraine Cooperation Initiative (PAUCI): Secretariat Scope of Work," March 17, 1999, USAID document.

108. Interview with Jakub Wygnański, February 18, 1998.

109. Interview with Jakub Wygnański, June 17, 1998.

CHAPTER FOUR

1. *Briefing for the U.S. Agency for International Development,* prepared by Richard P. Bernard, executive director, Resource Secretariat for the Russian Federation Commission on Securities and the Capital Market, entitled "Regulation, Training and Infrastructure Development: Current Resources and 1995-96 Projects," March 29, 1995, p. 1.

2. With regard to cumulative obligations as of September 30, 1999, the U.S. Department of State reported $14.5 billion to the former Soviet Union, including $6.9 billion to Russia and $2.1 billion to Ukraine (*U.S. Government Assistance to and Cooperative Activities with the New Independent States of the Former Soviet Union, FY 1999 Annual Report,* prepared by the Office of the Coordinator of U.S. Assistance to the NIS, January 2000, tables).

3. It is worth noting that Harvard's eminent Russia scholars, such as those associated with the Davis Center for Russian Studies, were *not* involved in the Harvard projects and activities here discussed. Indeed, some of these scholars have expressed skepticism about them.

4. U.S. General Accounting Office, *Foreign Assistance: Harvard Institute for International Development's Work in Russia and Ukraine,* Washington, D.C.: GAO, November 1996, p. 4.

5. Sources include project documents submitted by Jeffrey D. Sachs and Associates Inc. to the Finnish government (project entitled "Transformation of Centrally Planned Economies: The Lessons for Developing Countries," final statement of income and expenditures, June 1990-June 1992; and Finnish Ministry of Foreign Affairs documents, including internal audit of the project, March 22, 1993).

6. Maxim Boycko, Andrei Shleifer, and Robert Vishny, *Privatizing Russia,* Cambridge, MA: MIT Press, 1995, p. viii.

7. Lawrence Summers's biography, as supplied by the U.S. Treasury Department.

8. Karen Pennar and Peter Galuszka, "Privatization Expert and Cheerleader," *Business Week,* July 19, 1993.

9. Vita of Andrei Shleifer on file at HIID, Harvard University.

10. Book jacket, Maxim Boyco, Andrei Shleifer, and Robert Vishny, *Privatizing Russia,* Cambridge, MA: MIT Press, 1995.

11. Interview with Andrei Vernikov, November 22, 1997.

12. Project documents submitted by Jeffrey D. Sachs and Associates Inc. to the Finnish government state that "The [Sachs] team has worked closely with the Gaidar team offering advice on the design and implementation of stabilization policies." ("World Institute for Development Economic Research Project on the Transformation of Centrally Planned Economies: Report on Activities, First Half of 1991," p. 6.)

13. For a detailed analysis of how shock therapy was applied in Russia, and the results, see David M. Kotz and Fred Weir, *Revolution from Above: The Demise of the Soviet System,* London, United Kingdom: Routledge, 1997, chapters 9 and 10. See also Anne Williamson, *Contagion: The Betrayal of Liberty—Russia and the United States in the 1990s,* forthcoming, chapter 7.

14. "A Survey of Russia's Emerging Market: A Silent Revolution," *Economist,* April 8, 1995.

15. Summers's dictates included the Russian tax code, oil industry prospects, and how Russia should prepare itself to join the World Trade Organization and deal with U.S. trade laws.

16. Interview with Mark C. Medish, deputy assistant secretary for Eurasia and the Middle East, U.S. Department of Treasury, November 26, 1997.

17. Project documents submitted by Jeffrey D. Sachs and Associates, Inc. to the Finnish government state: "Jonathan Hay, a Harvard law student and Rhodes Scholar, traveled to Moscow to conduct a study of the prospects for mass privatization in Russia. He quickly became a trusted advisor to Deputy Prime Minister Anatoly Chubais, and has provided important economic, legal, and logistical analysis to the staff of the State Committee on Privatization. In March, Mr. Hay also joined the team sponsored by the Ford Foundation and will continue his work in Russia over the coming year." ("World Institute for Development Economic Research Project on the Transformation of Centrally Planned Economies: Report on Activities, First Half of 1991," p. 9).

18. Vita of Jonathan Hay on file at HIID, Harvard University.

19. Lawrence Summers's speech printed in *Russia Business Watch,* vol. 5, no. 2, Spring 1997, p. 19.

20. Olga Kryshtanovskaya, "The Real Masters of Russia," *Argumenty i Fakty,* no. 21, May 1997, reprinted in *Johnson's Russia List,* by David Johnson, Washington, D.C: internet newsletter.

21. In coining this use of "transactor," the author purposefully draws on the original meaning of the term: someone who carries through or does business. The author's theory of transactorship is presented in "Tainted Transactions: Harvard, the Chubais Clan and Russia's Ruin," *The National Interest,* no. 59, Spring 2000, pp. 23-34, and in "Rigging the U.S.-Russian Relationship: Harvard, Chubais, and the Transidentity Game," *Demokratizatsiya: The Journal of Post-Soviet Democratization,* vol. 7, no. 4, Fall 1999, pp. 469-500.

22. For information on this suit, see United States Attorney District of Massachusetts, "United States Sues Harvard and Others For False Claims Relating to USAID Programs in Russia," Press Release, U.S. Department of Justice, September 26, 2000.

23. According to USAID's Deirdre Clifford (interview of June 1996), since 1992 HIID received $40,373,994 in noncompetitive grants under the First Cooperative Agreement. Another $17,423,090 was designated for Harvard under the Second Cooperative Agreement (a three-year agreement that began on September 30, 1995), of which $4.5 million was obligated. (USAID documents and interview, June 11, 1996) .

Much U.S. economic aid, notably the so-called technical assistance in such areas as privatization and economic restructuring (accounting for about two-thirds of USAID expenditures in Russia as of March 31, 1996 and remaining at that level through September 30, 1999), went to pay Western consultants. (Calculated from figures published by the U.S. Department of State [*U.S. Government Assistance to and Cooperative Activities with the New Independent States of the Former Soviet Union: October 1995-March 1996;* and *U.S. Government Assistance to and Cooperative Activities with the New Independent States of the Former Soviet Union: FY 1999 Annual Report]* prepared by the Office of the Coordinator of U.S. Assistance to the NIS), with input by Deputy Coordinator of NIS Assistance

William B. Taylor as to which categories consist largely of technical assistance, interview of August 9, 1996.)

24. U.S. government procurement officers and GAO officials, including Louis H. Zanardi, who spearheaded GAO's investigation of HIID activities in Russia and Ukraine offered this pronouncement.

25. Biography and information supplied by Pascual's office. As of this writing, Pascual is the U.S. Ambassador-designate to Ukraine.

26. U.S. General Accounting Office, *Foreign Assistance: Harvard Institute for International Developments Work in Russia and Ukraine,* Washington, D.C.: GAO, November 1996, p. 18.

27. Interview with Louis H. Zanardi, April 4, 2000.

28. Interview with Jonathan Hay, June 17, 1994.

29. The author placed numerous calls to Jonathan Hay in Moscow to obtain a response to these issues during the weeks of August 5 and August 12, 1996. Hay was reportedly in the office but did not take or return any calls.

30. U.S. General Accounting Office, *Foreign Assistance: Harvard Institute for International Developments Work in Russia and Ukraine,* Washington, D.C.: GAO, 1996, p. 17.

31. Ibid., p. 3.

32. Ibid., p. 43.

33. Letter from USAID to HIID director Jeffrey Sachs, May 20,1997. See also USAID press release, "USAID Suspends Two Harvard Agreements in Russia," Washington, D.C.: USAID Press Office, May 20, 1997.

34. The report recommended that HIID be dissolved and that selected programs be integrated into other university programs. HIID's website (www.hiid.harvard.edu) states as follows: "In July 2000, many of HIID's projects will be absorbed and integrated into other faculties within Harvard University." An inspired Harvard University spokesperson, Joe Wrinn, spun the story thus: "It's a vote of confidence for the study of international development and its permanent integration into Harvard University." Beth McMurtrie, "Report Advises Harvard to Dismantle its Institute for International Development," *Chronicle of Higher Education,* January 12, 2000, chronicle.com/daily/2000/01/2000011204n.htm.

35. For details, see, United States Attorney District of Massachusetts, "United States Sues Harvard and Others for False Claims Relating to USAID Programs in Russia," *Press Release,* U.S. Department of Justice, September 26, 2000.

36. Interview aired on Monitor Radio, May 22, 1997.

37. "Clique" appears to better convey the character of the Chubais group than other terms in the lexicon of informal organization and social networks. The clique is, of course, constituted of networks, and its members exchange with one another. But the clique is much more than a collection of networks. Networks that make up the clique are "dense" in that members of a person's network are in touch with one another independently of that person; each member of the clique is linked to every other member. Also, networks in the clique are "multiplex" (rather than "single stranded"), in that clique members are connected to one another for multiple purposes, often political, economic, and social. This feature of operating in many spheres—not only political—shows that cliques cannot be reduced to interest groups, factions, or coalitions. In the study of political anthropology, approaches within "action theory," which concentrates on face-to-face interactions within given sociopolitical contexts, have emphasized the importance of such informal groups as cliques. Also see Dawn Ryan, "Cliques, Factions, and Leadership among the Toaripi of Papua," *Adaptation and Symbolism: Essays on Social Organization,*

Karen Ann Watson-Gegeo and S. Lee Seaton, eds., Honolulu, HI: East-West Center/ University Press of Hawaii, 1978, p. 41.

38. Olga Kryshtanovskaya, "The Real Masters of Russia," *Argumenty i Fakty,* no. 21, May 1997, reprinted in *Johnson's Russia List.*

39. For detailed discussion of the backgrounds of the university's students and how the university was run, see David H. Lempert, *Daily Life in a Crumbling Empire: The Absorption of Russia into the World Economy,* vol. 1, book 2, *Life in a Russian and Soviet Institution: "The School for Useless Things,"* Boulder, CO: East European Monographs, distributed by Columbia University Press, New York, 1996.

40. Documents and conversations with Russian sources, including Leonid Bazilevich, on May 23, May 27, June 14, and August 7, 1996.

41. Interviews with Leonid Bazilevich, June 14 and August 7, 1996.

42. Conversations with Leonid Bazilevich on May 23 and 27 and June 14, 1996; and Robert W. Orttung, *From Leningrad to St. Petersburg: Democratization in a Russian City,* New York, NY: St. Martin's Press, 1995, p. 201.

43. Robert W. Orttung, *From Leningrad to St. Petersburg: Democratization in a Russian City,* New York, NY: St. Martin's Press, 1995, p. 201.

44. Kudrin currently serves as deputy finance minister in President Vladimir Putin's government.

45. In an apparent contract killing, Manevich was assassinated in August 1997. At the time, he was deputy governor of St. Petersburg and head of the State Property Committee.

46. Alfred Kokh later served as deputy chairman of the board of the Chubais-Harvard transactor-run Russian Privatization Center and also as chairman of the State Property Committee (GKI).

47. Interview with Andrei Shleifer, September 5, 1996.

48. Jeremy Boissevain, *Friends of Friends: Networks, Manipulators and Coalitions,* Oxford, United Kingdom: Basil Blackwell, 1974, p. 177; and Dawn Ryan, "Cliques, Factions, and Leadership among the Toaripi of Papua," *Adaptation and Symbolism: Essays on Social Organization,* Karen Ann Watson-Gegeo and S. Lee Seaton, eds., Honolulu, HI: East-West Center/University Press of Hawaii, 1978, p. 41.

49. Dawn Ryan, "Cliques, Factions, and Leadership among the Toaripi of Papua," *Adaptation and Symbolism: Essays on Social Organization,* Karen Ann Watson-Gegeo and S. Lee Seaton, eds., Honolulu, HI: East-West Center/University Press of Hawaii, 1978, p. 41.

50. Interview with Leonid Bazilevich, August 7, 1996.

51. This is a different unit of economic analysis and decision making from what is usually considered. Although *individuals* are often thought of as the primary units to take advantage of economic opportunities, in the environments in which the transactors operate, the unit of analysis of responses to economic incentives is not necessarily the individual; it is often the transactor *group.* Individual players must take the interests of their fellow transactors into account when making choices.

52. *Frontline* "Return of the Czar" interview with Donald Jensen, PBS website www.pbs.org\wgbh\pages\frontline\shows\yeltsin\interviews\jensen.html.

53. Interview with Thomas A. Dine, August 16, 1996.

54. Ibid.

55. For the definitive history of Russian reform efforts, see Lynn D. Nelson and Irina Y. Kuzes, *Property to the People: The Struggle for Radical Economic Reform in Russia,* Armonk, NY: M.E. Sharpe, 1994 and their *Radical Reform in Yeltsin's*

Russia: Political, Economic and Social Dimensions Armonk, NY: M.E. Sharpe, 1995.

56. Letter to Janine R. Wedel from Vladimir Titov, chief of staff to Aleksandr Lebed in the State Duma, August 28, 1996.

57. Peter J. Stavrakis, "Bull in a China Shop: USAID's Post-Soviet Mission," *Demokratizatsiya: The Journal of Post-Soviet Democratization,* vol. 4, no. 2, Spring 1996, p. 16.

58. Thomas E. Graham, "Russia's New Non-Democrats," *Harper's Magazine,* vol. 292, no. 1751, April 1996, p. 26.

59. See, for example, John W. R. Lepingwell, "The Soviet Legacy and Russian Foreign Policy," *RFE/RL Research Report,* vol.3, 1994, pp. 1-8.

60. For details, see Lynn D. Nelson and Irina Y. Kuzes, *Property to the People: The Struggle for Radical Economic Reform in Russia,* Armonk, NY: M. E. Sharpe, 1994, pp. 26-56.

61. Interview with Walter Coles, June 5, 1996; figure verified at Coles's request by Deirdre Clifford, July 24, 1996.

62. Interview with Deirdre Clifford of USAID, June 11, 1996.

63. Figures provided by Deirdre Clifford, June 11, 1996.

64. Project documents submitted by Jeffrey D. Sachs and Associates Inc. to the Finnish government: "World Institute for Development Economic Research Project on the Transformation of Centrally Planned Economies: Report on Activities, First Half of 1991," pp. 4 and 7.

65. Ibid., p. 2.

66. Interview with Deirdre Clifford, June 11, 1996.

67. U.S. Department of State, *U.S. Government Assistance to and Cooperative Activities with the New Independent States of the Former Soviet Union: FY 1995 Annual Report,* prepared by the Office of the Coordinator of U.S. Assistance to the NIS, April 1996, p. 54.

68. Lynn D. Nelson and Irina Y. Kuzes, *Radical Reform in Yeltsin's Russia: Political, Economic, and Social Dimensions,* Armonk, NY: M. E. Sharpe, 1995, pp. 50- 51.

69. See, for example, Lynn D. Nelson and Irina Y. Kuzes, *Property to the People: The Struggle for Radical Economic Reform in Russia,* Armonk, NY: M. E. Sharpe, 1994, pp. 70-74.

70. James R. Millar, "From Utopian Socialism to Utopian Capitalism: The Failure of Revolution and Reform in Post-Soviet Russia," Washington, D.C.: George Washington University 175th Anniversary Papers, paper 2, 1996, p. 8.

71. For details, see Lynn D. Nelson and Irina Y. Kuzes, *Property to the People: The Struggle for Radical Economic Reform in Russia,* Armonk, NY: M.E. Sharpe, 1994, and their *Radical Reform in Yeltsin's Russia: Political, Economic and Social Dimensions,* Armonk, NY: M. E. Sharpe, 1995; Stefan Hedlund, *Russia's "Market" Economy: A Bad Case of Predatory Capitalism,* London, United Kingdom: UCL Press Limited, 1999; Fritz W. Ermarth, "Seeing Russia Plain: The Russian Crisis and American Intelligence," *The National Interest,* Spring 1999, pp. 5-14; and "Whither Reform" speech by World Bank chief economist Joseph Stiglitz, worldbank.org/ knowledge/chiefecon/; Matt Bivens and Jonas Bernstein, "The Russia You Never Met," *Demokratizatsiya: The Journal of Post-Soviet Democratization,* vol. 6., no. 4, Fall 1998, pp. 613-647; and Anne Williamson, *Contagion: The Betrayal of Liberty–Russia and the United States in the 1990s,* forthcoming, chapter 8.

72. *Frontline* "Return of the Czar" interview with E. Wayne Merry, PBS website www.pbs.org\wgbh\pages\frontline\shows\yeltsin\interviews\merry.html.

73. Svetlana P. Glinkina, "Privatizatsiya and Kriminalizatsiya: How Organized Crime Is Hijacking Privatization," *Demokratizatsiya: The Journal of Post-Soviet Democratization* vol. 2, 1994, pp. 385-391; Glinkina, *Kriminelle Komponenten der Russischen Wirtschaft: Typen und Dimensionen,* Köln, Germany: Berichte des Bundesinstituts für Ostwissenschaftliche und Internationale Studien, 1997; and Glinkina, "The Ominous Landscape of Russian Corruption," *Transitions,* March 1998, pp. 16-23.

74. Louise I. Shelley, "Privatization and Crime: The Post-Soviet Experience," *Journal of Contemporary Criminal Justice,* vol. 11, 1995, pp. 244-256.

75. For discussions of the role and pervasiveness of organized crime in Russia, see Robert J. Kelly, Rufus Schatzberg, and Patrick J. Ryan ("Primitive Capitalist Accumulation: Russia as a Racket," *Journal of Contemporary Criminal Justice,* vol. 11, no. 4, 1995, pp. 257-275), Louise I. Shelley ("Statement on Post-Soviet Organized Crime for House Committee on International Relations," April 30, 1996; "Privatization and Crime: The Post-Soviet Experience," *Journal of Contemporary Criminal Justice,* vol. 11, no. 4, 1995, pp. 244-256; "Post-Soviet Organized Crime: Implications for Economic, Social and Political Development," *Demokratizatsiya: The Journal of Post-Soviet Democratization,* vol. 2, no. 3, summer, 1994, pp. 341-358), J. Michael Waller ("Organized Crime and the Russian State: Challenges to U.S.-Russian Cooperation," *Demokratizatsiya: The Journal of Post-Soviet Democratization,* vol. 2, no. 3, summer, 1994, pp. 364-385) and Michael J. Waller and Victor J. Yasmann ("Russia's Great Criminal Revolution: The Role of the Security Services," *Journal of Contemporary Criminal Justice,* vol. 11, no. 4, 1995, pp. 276-297).

76. "New Round of Yeltsin Decrees Spurs Reform," *Current Digest,* vol. 46, July 13, 1994, pp. 7-8.

77. Glenn Bryant, "State Duma Election Returns, 1995," *Demokratizatsiya: The Journal of Post-Soviet Democratization,* vol. 4, no. 3, summer 1996, pp. 420-421.

78. Interfax, June 5, 1997, reported in Peter Reddaway, "Questions about Russia's 'Dream Team,'" *Post-Soviet Prospects,* vol. 5, no. 5, Washington, D.C.: Center for Strategic and International Studies, September 1997.

79. Data from the Centre for International Sociological Research, Moscow (based on 1,000 respondents across Russia), reported in *The Economist,* March 15, 1997.

80. Letter from Graham Allison, professor at Harvard's John F. Kennedy School of Government, addressed "Dear Colleague," summarizing the proceedings of the Second Annual U.S.-Russia Investment Symposium, titled "Financial and Direct Investment Opportunities in Russia," held January 9-11, 1998, at Harvard's John F. Kennedy School of Government.

81. "Remarks of Moscow Mayor Yuri Luzhkov," U.S.-Russian Investment Symposium, Kennedy School of Government, Harvard University, transcript of the simultaneous translation, January 11, 1998, p. 3.

82. Vladislav Borodulin, "Rebirth of the Commission on Economic Reform: Chubais Becomes Fully Empowered Symbol of Economic Reforms," *Kommersant-Daily,* January 20, 1995, p. 2, translated in *Current Digest,* vol. 47, no. 3, February 15, 1995, p. 23.

83. Olga Kryshtanovskaya, "The Real Masters of Russia," *Argumenty i Fakty,* no. 21, May 1997, reprinted in *Johnson's Russia List.*

84. Maxim Boycko, Andrei Shleifer, and Robert Vishny, *Privatizing Russia,* Cambridge, MA: MIT Press, 1995, p. 5.

85. Published in *Rossiiskie Vesti* on August 15, 1996, cited in "Chubais Controls Presidential Decree Process," *OMRI Daily Digest,* vol. 148, August 15, 1996.

86. Information provided by Walter Coles, June 5, 1996. For further information about the "public education" program, as well as the story of how the Chubais Clan used it to promote Chubais's political party, see Janine R. Wedel, "Clique-Run Organizations and U.S. Economic Aid," *Demokratizatsiya: The Journal of Post-Soviet Democratization,* vol. 4, no. 4, Fall 1996, pp. 580-581; and Mark Ames and Matt Taibbi, *The Exile,* New York, NY: Grove Press, 2000, pp. 54-56.

87. Interview with Walter Coles, June 6, 1996.

88. For details of this case, see Janine R. Wedel, "Clique-Run Organizations and U.S. Economic Aid: An Institutional Analysis," *Demokratizatsiya: The Journal of Post-Soviet Democratization,* vol. 4, no. 4, fall 1996, pp. 592-593.

89. U.S. General Accounting Office, *Foreign Assistance: Harvard Institute for International Development's Work in Russia and Ukraine,* Washington, D.C.: GAO, November 1996, p. 8.

90. Interview with Charles Cadwell, September 5, 1996.

91. Ibid.

92. Interview with Leonid Abalkin, February 27, 1996.

93. Interview with Sergei V. Burkov, chairman of the Committee for Property, Privatization, and Economic Activity of the State Duma of the Federal Assembly of the Russian Federation, June 20, 1994.

94. Interview with William B. Taylor, August 9, 1996.

95. Interview with Walter Coles, June 6, 1996.

96. The authors acknowledge that HIID "supported" the writing of the book. The *New Republic* (Stephen Kotkin, "Stealing the State," April 13, 1998, p. 30) reports that this support was provided by USAID through HIID. However, the author was unable to confirm direct USAID support for the project.

97. Maxim Boycko, Andrei Shleifer, and Robert Vishny, *Privatizing Russia,* Cambridge, MA: MIT Press, 1995, p. 142.

98. Interview with Ambassador Richard L. Morningstar, U.S. aid coordinator to the former Soviet Union, February 11, 1997.

99. For details of U.S. unequivocal support of Boris Yeltsin and the "Reformers," see *Frontline* "Return of the Czar" interviews with former officials at the U.S. Embassy in Moscow, Thomas Graham, E. Wayne Merry, and Donald Jensen, PBS website www.pbs.org\wgbh\pages\frontline\shows\yeltsin\interviews\merry.html.

100. Maxim Boycko, Andrei Shleifer, and Robert Vishny, *Privatizing Russia,* Cambridge, MA: MIT Press, 1995, p. 128.

101. Interview with Thomas A. Dine, August 16, 1996.

102. Interview with Walter Coles, July 25, 1996.

103. Information provided by USAID's Deidre Clifford, September 22, 1996.

104. Interview with USAID's Cecilia Ciepiela, August 5, 1996.

105. U.S. General Accounting Office, *Foreign Assistance: Harvard Institute for International Development's Work in Russia and Ukraine,* Washington, D.C.: General Accounting Office, November 1996, p. 60.

106. For example, while the supervisory board nominated Maxim Boycko, a member of the Chubais Clan, to run the RPC, Boycko chose its directors, of which Vasiliev is one. (Based on information provided by Ralf-Dieter Montag-Girmes of the Russian Privatization Center, July 26, 1995.)

107. Interview with Ira Lieberman, July 23, 1996.

108. Ibid.

109. Interview with Walter Coles, June 6, 1996.

110. U.S. General Accounting Office, *Foreign Assistance: Harvard Institute for International Development's Work in Russia and Ukraine,* Washington, D.C.: GAO, November 1996, p. 57.

111. As of June 1996, Japan was the largest contributor among the G-7, according to Ralf-Dieter Montag-Girmes, director of postprivatization support with the Russian Privatization Center, in an interview of June 12, 1996.

112. Russian Privatization Center, *1994 Annual Report,* pp. 5 and 24.

113. The World Bank figure was provided by Ira Lieberman (interview of July 23, 1996), while the EBRD figure was supplied by Renae Ng (conversation of September 24, 1996).

114. Mark C. Medish, *Confidential Report on USAID Programs Supporting Commercial Law and Other Legal Reform in the Russian Federation,* Washington, D.C., September 1996, p. 6.

115. Ibid., p. 17.

116. Interview with Ira Lieberman, July 23, 1996.

117. According to Ira Lieberman in his July 23, 1996, interview, Fedorov objected to items of the loan on professional grounds.

118. Shortly before the Russian presidential election of 1996, Eduard Boure, the new managing director of the RPC, said, "It's better if we get the loan before [communist presidential candidate Gennadii] Zyuganov gets too far." Interview with Eduard Boure, June 25, 1996.

119. Documents and information from Veniamin Sokolov, head of the Chamber of Accounts of the Russian Federation (interview of May 31, 1998 and talk at American University of June 2, 1998). In 1994, both the Duma and the head of the GKI requested a detailed accounting from the RPC. They got nothing. Sergei Zavorotnyi, "The Traces of 'Privatization' Go Overseas," *Komsomolskaya Pravda,* April 8, 1997.

120. Interview and documents provided by Chamber of Accounts auditor Veniamin Sokolov, May 31, 1998.

121. Interview with Thomas A. Dine, August 16, 1996.

122. U.S. General Accounting Office, *Foreign Assistance: Harvard Institute for International Development's Work in Russia and Ukraine,* Washington, D.C.: GAO, November 1996, pp. 26, 27, and 60.

123. Conversation with Stanley R. Nevin, September 24, 1996.

124. Conversation with Ira Lieberman, August 27, 1996.

125. Ibid.

126. Interview with USAID's Cecilia Ciepiela, August 5, 1996.

127. Interviews with a representative of Price Waterhouse, July 18, 1996; Dennis Mitchem of Arthur Andersen, August 18 and 19, 1996; and Robert Otto of Carana, August 27, 1996.

128. Interview with a representative of Price Waterhouse, July 18, 1996.

129. Interview with Dennis Mitchem, August 19, 1996.

130. Interview with Cecilia Ciepiela, August 5, 1996.

131. Interview with Dennis Mitchem, August 18, 1996.

132. Interview with Dennis Mitchem, August 19, 1996.

133. Interview with Robert Otto, August 27, 1996.

134. U.S. General Accounting Office, *Foreign Assistance: Harvard Institute for International Development's Work in Russia and Ukraine,* Washington, D.C.: GAO, November 1996, p. 52.

135. Mark C. Medish, *Confidential Report on USAID Programs Supporting Commercial Law and Other Legal Reform in the Russian Federation,* Washington, D.C., September 1996, p. 16.

136. Ibid.

137. GAO sources confirm this observation (conversations of October 28, 1997, and April 23, 1998 with Louis H. Zanardi). One example of this involves RPC interference with efforts by the U.S.-funded Senior Executive Service Corps.

138. Interviews with USAID-paid contractors and U.S. government sources. A member of the GAO audit team confirms this observation (conversations of October 28, 1997 and April 23, 1998 with Louis H. Zanardi).

139. Letter of May 20, 1997, to HIID director Sachs from USAID suspending further payments to HIID.

140. For the U.S. Government suit, see United States Attorney District of Massachusetts, "United States Sues Harvard and Others for False Claims Relating to USAID Programs in Russia," *Press Release,* U.S. Department of Justice, September 26, 2000.

In a separate investigation, Hay, together with Dart Management, Inc., is the subject of a civil suit (under U.S. racketeering laws) filed in the U.S. District Court of New Jersey brought by Avisma Titano-Magnesium Kombinat over an alleged fraud and money-laundering scheme. Avisma is seeking $150 million in damages. (In the United States District Court for the District of New Jersey, Civil Action no. 99-CV-3979 [JWB], filed on December 13, 1999.) The suit alleges that a group of American investors who took over the company from the Russian bank Menatep skimmed at least $50 million from profits over a period of two years. The suit also alleges that Hay arranged the purchase from Menatep through the Moscow Institute for Law Based Economy, the USAID- and World Bank-created and funded organization. According to documents presented by Avisma, Hay "assisted in structuring the transfer of the illegal scheme from Menatep to the investors" ("*Avisma* Court Case Filing Targets More Banks," *Metals Week,* January 3, 2000, vol. 71, no. 1, p. 2).

The suit also alleges that Natasha Garfinkel Kagalovsky, wife of Menatep executive Konstantin Kagalovsky and Bank of New York employee, arranged accounts at the bank to help channel funds that Menatep had diverted. According to *Metals Week,* "the deal . . . included back-door payoffs to the investors through the same network of bank accounts and offshore entities as Menatep had used." (For further details, see "*Avisma* Court Case Filing Targets More Banks," *Metals Week,* January 3, 2000, vol. 71, no. 1, p. 2; John Helmer, "Deliberate Blindness to Fraud," *The Moscow Tribune,* December 17, 1999, p. 3; and Padraic Cassidy, "From Russia with Suit: Russian Factory Files RICO Suit Against U.S. Investor and Company," *New Jersey Law Journal,* August 30, 1999.)

141. This episode is detailed in Anne Williamson, *Contagion: The Betrayal of Liberty,* chapter 13. See also United States District Court, District of Massachusetts, Civil Action no. OOCV11977DPW, United States of America, Plaintiff, v. The President and Fellows of Harvard College, Andrei Shleifer, Jonathan Hay, Nancy Zimmerman, and Elizabeth Hebert, Defendants.

142. Matt Taibbi, "Picked Clean: How a Small Clique of Americans Scavenged the Remains of Defrauded Russians," *Exile,* January 15, 1998, reprinted in *Johnson's Russia List,* no. 2021, January 16, 1998.

143. Carla Anne Robbins and Steve Liesman, "How an Aid Program Vital to New Economy of Russia Collapsed," *Wall Street Journal,* August 13, 1997.

144. Ibid.

145. U.S. sources close to the investigation.

146. The uncritical application to Russia of Western dichotomies of state and private is analytically problematic. For detailed discussion of the applicability to Central and Eastern Europe and the former Soviet Union of conventional models of institutional change (often used in comparative politics, public administration, and sociology), see the author's "Informal Relations and Institutional Change: How Eastern European Cliques and States Mutually Respond," presented at the World Bank, Social Development Group, Washington, D.C., April 20, 1998; and "Clans, Cliques, and Captured States: How We Misunderstand 'Transition' in Central and Eastern Europe and the Former Soviet Union," prepared for the National Council for Eurasian and East European Research and the National Institute of Justice, Washington, D.C., 2000, and forthcoming as a National Council *Working Paper* (section titled "Dichotomies that Distort").

147. For example, HIID paid the salaries of expatriates in executive positions.

148. For further analysis, see, for example, Anne Williamson, *Contagion: The Betrayal of Liberty,* chapter 2, and commentaries on *Johnson's Russia List* by Jerry F. Hough (no. 3051, February 11, 1999), S. Lawrence (no. 3072, February 28, 1999), and Edwin G. Dolan (no. 3073, March 1, 1999).

149. See the author's "Informal Relations and Institutional Change: How Eastern European Cliques and States Mutually Respond," presented at the World Bank, Social Development Group,Washington, D.C., April 20, 1998; and "Clans, Cliques, and Captured States: How We Misunderstand 'Transition' in Central and Eastern Europe and the Former Soviet Union," prepared for the National Council for Eurasian and East European Research and the National Institute of Justice, Washington, D.C., 2000, and forthcoming as a National Council *Working Paper* (section titled "The Social Organization of the State").

150. Interview with E.Wayne Merry, May 23, 2000.

151. The concept of "transidentities" draws on anthropologist Fredrik Barth's work exploring "repertoires" of identities and how actors employ different identities depending on the situation. See Fredrik Barth, ed., *Ethnic Groups and Boundaries: The Social Organization of Culture Difference,* Boston, MA.: Little, Brown, 1969.

152. Documents provided by and interview with auditor Veniamin Sokolov, May 31, 1998.

153. For greater detail, see Anne Williamson, *Contagion: The Betrayal of Liberty,* chapter 13.

154. Sachs writes that his work in Russia with Anders Åslund "was supported mainly by the Ford Foundation and the Swedish Government. I was not paid by the Russian Government" (letter to Janine Wedel, March 12, 1998). In a later exchange in *The National Interest,* Sachs writes: "I received my academic salary for my work in Russia, with my leave time from Harvard University covered mainly by the United Nations University in Helsinki in early 1992, and thereafter by the advisory project supported by the Ford Foundation and the Swedish government during 1992-93." ("Tainted Transactions: An Exchange," *The National Interest,* no. 60, Summer 2000, p. 99.) The correspondence does not mention that Sachs's WIDER Institute-sponsored project, for which he received $322,728 in salary and fees (not including expenses), was paid to Jeffrey D. Sachs and Associates Inc., according to project documents. The project, the total cost of which was $2,036,122, was funded by the Finnish Ministry of Foreign Affairs and the Sasakawa Foundation (project entitled "Transformation of Centrally Planned Economies: The Lessons for Developing Countries" final statement of income and expenditures, June 1990-June 1992; and Finnish Ministry of Foreign Affairs documents, including internal audit of the project above, March 22, 1993).

155. Sachs makes much of the distance between his work and that of his Harvard colleague Shleifer, who is now being sued by the U.S. Department of Justice. Yet Sachs, Lipton, *and Shleifer* are listed as the "three senior members" of a Russia advisory project paid to Jeffrey D. Sachs and Associates, Inc. In time, Sachs and Shleifer emerged as rivals and ran largely separate operations in Moscow. However, they shared the transactorship mode of operating and many contacts in the Chubais Clan, as well as many crucial Western contacts.

156. See, for example, project documents submitted by Jeffrey D. Sachs and Associates, Inc., to the Finnish government stating that "The [Sachs] team has helped the authorities prepare for negotiations with international financial institutions." ("World Institute for Development Economic Research Project on the Transformation of Centrally Planned Economies: Report on Activities, First Half of 1991," p. 7.)

157. See John Helmer, "Russia and the IMF: Who Pays the Piper Calls the Tune," *Johnson's Russia List*, no. 3057, February 17, 1999. Sachs, in his reply to the author's article in *The National Interest* ("Tainted Transactions: Harvard, the Chubais Clan and Russia's Ruin," no. 59, Spring 2000, pp. 23-34) seems to deny that he was in correspondence with the IMF while at the same time advising Gaidar. However, one memorandum in the author's possession was written by Sachs and David Lipton, dated May 11, 1992, and directed to key Russia decisionmakers at the IMF. It shows that Sachs and Lipton were privy to internal discussion within the Fund and were proffering advice within that context without any mention of their role advising the Russian side. (See "Tainted Transactions: An Exchange," *The National Interest*, no. 60, Summer 2000, pp. 98-110.)

158. While providing no documentation for his role, Sachs writes: "I was an official adviser of the Russian Government from December 1991 to January 1994. Together with Anders Åslund I directed the Macroeconomics and Finance Unit (MFU) of the Russian Ministry of Finance, housed within Government offices." (Letter to Janine Wedel, March 12, 1998). In later correspondence in *The National Interest*, Sachs further writes: "President Yeltsin officially designated us as advisers during a meeting with us on December 13, 1991 and we received offices in the Council of Ministers during 1992 and in the Ministry of Finance during 1993." ("Tainted Transactions: An Exchange," *The National Interest*, no. 60, Summer 2000, p. 98.)

159. For example, in response to Sachs's and Åslund's "resignation" from their advisory role to the Russian government in January 1993, Prime Minister Victor Chernomyrdin, when asked to comment, said (through his spokesman) that he had not used their services, nor had he had any foreign advisers (TASS, "ITAR-TASS Highlights of January 21," The Russian Information Agency, ITAR-TASS, January 21, 1994). Chernomyrdin added that "The mechanical transfer of Western economic methods to Russian soil has done more harm than good" (Steven Erlanger, "Two Western Economists Quit Russia Posts, *The New York Times*, January 24, 1994, p. 4).

Similarly, Gaidar Institute deputy head Alexei V. Ulyukaev told journalist Anne Williamson that "Sachs was never an official adviser to the government, that's his own illusion." Gaidar, too, described Sachs and Åslund as "insignificant figures." Williamson reports that "Even Gaidar's archrival, [Grigory] Yavlinsky, insisted, 'What we did was not based on even 10 percent of their [Sachs's and Åslund's] advice. Gaidar was using those people as loudspeakers for the West, but, in fact, Gaidar did as he wished'" (Anne Williamson, *Contagion: The Betrayal of Liberty*, Chapter 7).

In addition, U.S. Treasury official Mark Medish said that Sachs and Åslund never had an official position in Russia (Interview with Mark C. Medish, Deputy Assistant Secretary for Eurasia and the Middle East, U.S. Department of Treasury, November 26, 1997).

160. Anne Williamson interview with Jean Foglizzo, February 1, 1994. For further detail, see Anne Williamson, *Contagion: The Betrayal of Liberty,* chapter 7.

161. Memorandum from Jeffrey Sachs to Ruslan Khasbulatov of November 19, 1992; interviews with Stanford University economist Michael Bernstam of August 21, 1997 and October 17, 1997.

162. See, for example, an Action Memorandum of February 4, 1993 from a State Department official to the secretary of state, in which Sachs requests an appointment with the secretary of state. The memorandum notes that Sachs also has sought appointments with National Security Adviser Anthony Lake, Treasury Under Secretary-designate Larry Summers, and Ambassador designate Strobe Talbott.

163. For example, an Åslund advisory project was awarded $642,857 in 1991-92 from the Swedish government (letter from Swedish Ministry for Foreign Affairs Dag Hartelius, April 7, 2000). Ruth Jacoby, director from 1990 to 1994 of Sweden's Secretariat for Cooperation with Central and Eastern Europe, reported that the Åslund project "wasn't particularly transparent. I'm not sure exactly where the money went to." She further clarified that "It is very difficult to say how this advice took place. Money was accounted for, but the question is what did they do for one and a half years in Moscow?" (Interview with Ruth Jacoby, April 17, 2000.)

164. Sources include Bildt Ministry for Foreign Affairs official Krister Wahlbäck, interview of April 6, 2000, and Swedish Ministry for Foreign Affairs Dag Hartelius (director, and former deputy director, Department of Central and Eastern Europe, Foreign Ministry), interview of April 6, 2000. Carl Bildt acknowledged in the Swedish Parliament, April 21, 1994, that "Anders Åslund is one of my advisors" (Prot. 1993/94:93, April 21, 1994, pp. 31, 37). See also Dan Josefsson, "The Art of Ruining a Country with Some Professional Help from Sweden," *ETC* (English Edition), no. 1, Stockholm, Sweden, 1999.

165. Interviews with U.S. officials in the Departments of Treasury and State. Treasury official Mark Medish said, for example, that Åslund was "not an infrequent visitor to both Dick [Morningstar] and Tom [Dine]" (Interview with Mark C. Medish, deputy assistant secretary for Eurasia and the Middle East, U.S. Department of Treasury, November 26, 1997).

166. For example, Åslund has long been linked to Brunswick, which began as a Moscow-based brokerage firm and evolved into an investment bank, the Brunswick Group. While Åslund claims that he only gives "lectures and briefings" ("Tainted Transactions: An Exchange," *The National Interest,* no. 60, Summer 2000, p. 101), he attended an April 1997 banking conference in New York sponsored by Brunswick Securities Ltd. *as a representative of Brunswick.* He promoted the Russian stock market to institutional investors and money managers, according to Michael Hudson, who also participated in the conference. (Anne Williamson communication with Michael Hudson May 16, 1999; and Wedel interview with Hudson, September 8, 1999.) Hudson adds (April 3, 2000) that the minimum acceptable investment was between $400,000 and $500,000.

With regard to the founding of Brunswick, Åslund introduced two of his Swedish associates to Chubais, and they then worked for Chubais at the GKI, where they helped to design and implement voucher privatization (Anne Williamson interview with Martin Andersson, February 1995). Later, "with still good relations

to Chubais," they started Brunswick Brokerage to participate in voucher privatiza-
tion and to help sell these and other assets to Western investors (Sven-Ivan
Sundqvist, "Svenska Rad Biter Pa Ryssen: Svenska Finansman i Ledningen for
Brunswick Group, Foretaget Som Ska Hjalpa Ryska Staten Att Privatisera Indus-
trin," *Dagens Nyheter,* June 15, 1997). Åslund's current wife, Anna Viktorevna
Åslund, Gaidar's former press secretary, has listed an affiliation with Brunswick-
Warburg. (Brunswick entered into an association with Warburg, effective in
November 1997.) Additional sources for Åslund's business activities in Russian and
Ukraine include those specified in the previous endnotes, as well as a number of
additional reports and sources in Russia, Ukraine, Sweden, and Washington. For
further details, see Anne Williamson, *Contagion: The Betrayal of Liberty,* chapter
13.

167. Interview with Vyacheslav Razinkin by author Anne Williamson, February 23,
1995, cited in Ibid.

168. Åslund denies that his role in Ukraine included public relations ("Tainted Transac-
tions: An Exchange," *The National Interest,* no. 60, Summer 2000, p. 101). The
author's sources include (but are not limited to) Marek Dąbrowski, conversations of
May 9, 1995 and November 27, 1997. Dąbrowski stated (November 27, 1997) that
Åslund's "kind of advertising" and "campaigning" creates a "conflict of interest."
Contrary to what Dąbrowski now alleges ("Tainted Transactions: An Exchange,"
The National Interest, no. 60, Summer 2000, p. 102), the author's conversations
with him were friendly and, indeed, *on the record.* The author has cited Dąbrowski
as a source before in print on this subject, and he has never previously disputed its
accuracy. It is unclear why he has responded so belatedly, but it is a fact that
Dąbrowski's center has received substantial funding from USAID, some of which
has been channeled through HIID. Both Sachs and Åslund are also listed as
members of the advisory council of Dąbrowski's center.

169. Åslund claims that, in writing articles, he "always mentioned" his work for the
Russian or Ukrainian governments ("Tainted Transactions: An Exchange," *The
National Interest,* no. 60, Summer 2000, p. 101). That is simply not the case. For
example, in his article "Russian's Success Story" in *Foreign Affairs* (September-
October 1994), Åslund presents himself as a senior scholar at the Carnegie
Endowment and makes no mention of any relationship he has had with the Russian
government.

170. One feature of transactorship is that the transactors on each side lobby for and
promote the transactors on the other side. Each side's transactors become the
mechanisms and funnels through which the sides gain access to the other as a
whole. In fact, a key source of legitimacy and clout of each side's transactors is their
supposed access to transactors on the other side, whose reputations they help
promote on their side. Each side's representatives must wield influence to ensure
that their partners on the other side continue to have clout and standing on both
sides. Otherwise, the opportunities and advantages that the transactor group enjoys
could be greatly compromised.

171. Interviews with William B. Taylor, then deputy coordinator (now coordinator) of
NIS assistance August 9, 1996; and Thomas A. Dine, August 16, 1996.

172. Interview with Thomas A. Dine, August 16, 1996.

173. Interview with Andrei Shleifer, September 5, 1996.

174. Lawrence H. Summers, "Russia's Stake in Capital Market Development," speech at
the Kennedy School of Government, *Treasury News,* Washington, D.C., Department of the Treasury, Office of Public Affairs, January 9, 1997, p. 30.

175. Lawrence H. Summers, "The Global Stake in Russian Economic Reform," speech before the U.S.-Russia Business Council, *Treasury News,* Washington, D.C., Department of the Treasury, Office of Public Affairs, April 1, 1997, p. 4.

176. Interview with a U.S. Treasury spokesman by Bill Mesler of *Nation,* summer 1997.

177. Janine R. Wedel, "Clique-Run Organizations and U.S. Economic Aid: An Institutional Analysis," *Demokratizatsiya: The Journal of Post-Soviet Democratization,* vol. 4, no. 4, Fall 1996, pp. 571-602.

178. Maxim Boycko, "Chubays Has Chosen Reforms," *Obshchaya Gazeta,* no. 10, March 13-19, 1997 (signed to press March 12, 1997), translated and circulated in *Johnson's Russia List.*

179. In August and September 1999, newspapers reported that billions of dollars had been laundered through the Bank of New York. (See Raymond Bonner with Timothy L. O'Brien, "Activity at Bank Raises Suspicions of Russia Mob Tie: Billions Thought to Be Laundered Through Bank of New York," *New York Times,* August 19, 1999, p.A1.) Anatoly Chubais and other members of Yeltsin's government are alleged to have been involved in money laundering. (See Jack Kelly, "Russia Fraud Case at $15 B," *USA Today,* August 26, 1999, p.1.)

180. Reported in Peter Reddaway, "Questions about Russia's 'Dream Team,'" *Post-Soviet Prospects,* vol. 5, no. 5, Washington, D.C.: Center for Strategic and International Studies, September 1997.

181. Russian Public Television, June 20, 1996, reported in ibid.

182. Jonas Bernstein, "Loans for the Sharks?" *Moscow Times,* December 19, 1995, p. 1.

183. *Frontline* "Return of the Czar" interview with Boris Fyodorov, former Russian Finance Minister, PBS web site www.pbs.org/wgbh/pages/frontline/shows\yeltsin\interviews\fyodorov.html.

184. See Williamson, *Contagion: The Betrayal of Liberty,* especially chapters 11 and 13.

185. Ibid.

186. George Soros, "Remarks by George Soros," U.S.-Russia Investment Symposium, Kennedy School of Government, Harvard University, January 9, 1998, p. 2-3.

187. Soros, "International Economic Turmoil," U.S. House of Representatives, Hearings Before the Committee on Banking and Financial Services, Washington, D.C., U.S. House of Representatives, September 14, 15, 16, 1998, p. 9798.

188. Interview with Jack Meyer by *Nation* reporter Bill Mesler, August 1997.

189. Interview with Jay Light, December 5, 1997.

190. See Williamson, *Contagion: The Betrayal of Liberty,* chapter 13. See also United States District Court, District of Massachusetts, Civil Action no. 00CV11977 DPW, United States of America, Plaintiff, v. The President and Fellows of Harvard College, Andrei Shleifer, Jonathan Hay, Nancy Zimmerman, and Elizabeth Hebert, Defendants.

191. *Interfax in English,* October 20, 1997.

192. Peter Henderson, "Russia Oligarchy Risks Peril in Asset Fight, Soros," Reuters, March 4, 1998, reported in *Johnson's Russia List,* no. 2093, March 5, 1998.

193. *Radio Free Europe/Radio Liberty Newsletter,* January 4, 1999, www.nupi.no.

194. *RFL/RL Newsline,* vol. 1, no. 99, part 1, August 20, 1997.

195. One of these men was Arkady Yevstaviev, who also was a key player in an earlier scandal involving the USAID-paid public relations firm Sawyer Miller. Under a USAID-paid contract to Sawyer Miller, the Chubais Clan used USAID-funded "public education" efforts to further their political agendas. According to Sawyer Miller representatives, Yevstaviev was responsible for the scandal in which the slogan that aired on television during the election campaign of 1993 was changed

from "Your voucher, your choice" to "Your choice, Russia's Choice." "Russia's Choice" was the name of Chubais's political party. (See Janine R. Wedel, "Clique-Run Organizations and U.S. Economic Aid: An Institutional Analysis," *Demokratizatsiya: The Journal of Post-Soviet Democratization,* vol. 4, no. 4, Fall 1996, pp. 580-581.)

196. In a strange side story, Kokh arrived in New York in the spring of 1998 with an armful of notes that he gave to an "instant books" publisher, which assembled and printed a "book" about Russian privatization in a matter of weeks. Allegedly, this was an attempt by Kokh to escape prosecution in Moscow. (See Williamson, *Contagion: The Betrayal of Liberty: Russia and the United States in the 1990s,* chapter 13.) Later, in December 1998, Kokh was denied entry to the United States, having been implicated in dubious privatization deals and accused of corruption in Russia.

197. Fred Weir for the *Hindustan Times,* reported in *Johnson's Russia List,* no. 1367, November 15, 1997.

198. "Prosecutors Examine Chubais's Activities," *RFE/RL Newsline,* vol. 2, no. 39, part 1, February 26, 1998.

199. Russian television reported on May 28, 2000 that, during his recent trip to Washington, Chubais "was received at the highest levels—he met with Vice President [Albert] Gore, State Secretary [Madeleine] Albright, her deputy [Strobe] Talbott and Secretary of Treasury [Lawrence] Summers" (*Vremya,* ORT TV Channel, May 28, 2000, reported in *Johnson's Russia List* no. 4339, June 1, 2000).

200. *Kommersant Daily,* September 8, 1998; *Los Angeles Times,* September 9, 1998.

201. Michael R. Gordon and David E. Sanger, "Rescuing Russia: A Special Report; The Bailout of the Kremlin: How U.S. Pressed the IMF," *New York Times,* July 17, 1998, p.A1.

202. Adam Podgorecki, "Polish Society: A Sociological Analysis," *Praxis International,* vol. 7, no. 1, April 1987.

203. Summers, "The United States and Russia, Part II: Russia in Crisis," U.S. House of Representatives, Committee on International Relations, Washington, D.C.: U.S. House of Representatives, September 17, 1998, Hearing transcript, pp. 29-30.

204. See, for example, Barry Wood, "Russia's Economy," Voice of America, January 3, 2000 also in *Johnson's Russia List,* no. 4009, January 4, 2000; and "The State of the (Former Soviet) Union," Washington, D.C.: Carnegie Endowment for International Peace, January 6, 2000, also in *Johnson's Russia List,* no. 4031, January 13, 2000.

205. Putin worked under Pavel Borodin, the Kremlin's property manager, who has been linked to the Mabetex scandal. Swiss prosecutors have alleged that Mabetex Project Engineering, a Kremlin contractor, paid tens of thousands of dollars in credit card bills for members of the Yeltsin family. In one of his first acts, Putin signed a decree protecting Yeltsin from future prosecution and providing him with amenities such as a residence and a pension. See Paul J. Saunders, "The Real Vladimir Putin: A New Leader in the Old Mold," *Washington Times,* January 6, 2000, p. A15.

206. See, for example, Paul Starobin, "The Brain Trust Polishing Putin's Image," *Business Week,* January 31, 2000.

207. János Kornai, *Economics of Shortage,* Amsterdam, the Netherlands: North-Holland, 1980.

208. See, for example, Joseph L. Albini, R. E. Rogers, Victor Shabalin, Valery Kutushev, Vladimir Moiseev, and Julie Anderson ("Russian Organized Crime: Its History, Structure and Function," *Journal of Contemporary Criminal Justice,* vol. 11, no. 4, 1995, pp. 213-243). They explain that Russia's historical inheritance of tsarism

produced a system in which patrons and clients became the basic format of social interaction. Also see Merle Fainsod (*How Russia is Ruled*, Cambridge, MA: Harvard University Press, 1975), Jerry F. Hough (*The Soviet Prefects: The Local Party Organs in Industrial Decision-making*, Cambridge, MA: Harvard University Press, 1969), Jerry F. Hough and Merle Fainsod (*How the Soviet Union is Governed*, Cambridge, MA: Harvard University Press, 1979), Robert W. Orttung (*From Leningrad to St. Petersburg: Democratization in a Russian City*, New York, NY: St. Martin's Press, 1995), and Blair A. Ruble (*Leningrad: Shaping a Soviet City*, Berkeley, CA: University of California Press, 1990).

209. Personal letter from Lebed spokesman Vladimir Titov, August 28, 1996.

210. *Komsomolskaya Pravda*, May 1997.

211. Interview with Ronald Childress, former director of Rule of Law Consortium, ARD-Checchi joint venture in Russia, May 6, 1997.

212. "Popular Rule Group Wants Probe into U.S. Agencies' Presence," *Interfax in English*, April 30, 1997, cited in *Johnson's Russia List*, May 2, 1997.

213. Thomas A. Dine, "U.S. Aid for the Newly Independent States," *Problems of Post-Communism*, vol. 42, no. 3, May-June 1995, p. 29.

214. Interview with Laurier Mailloux, August 13, 1996.

215. Interview with William B. Taylor, August 9, 1996.

216. Interview with Thomas A. Dine, August 16, 1996.

217. Interview with Stanley R. Nevin, August 24, 1996.

218. Federal sources.

219. U.S. General Accounting Office, *Foreign Assistance: Harvard Institute for International Development's Work in Russia and Ukraine*, Washington, D.C.: GAO, November 1996, p. 6.

220. Conversations with Louis H. Zanardi of the GAO audit team.

221. S. Razgonov, *Moskovskie Novosty*, vol. 45, 1991; cited in I. Bremmer and R. Taras, *Nations and Politics in the Soviet Successor States*, Cambridge, United Kingdom: Cambridge University Press, 1993.

222. See Williamson, *Contagion: The Betrayal of Liberty*, chapter 3.

223. The Russian "population has suffered increasing hardship" since the ruble devaluation of August 1998. An estimated 38 percent was living in poverty at the close of the first quarter of 1999, as compared with 28 percent one year earlier. Real incomes in June 1999 were 77 percent of their June 1998 level. (*OECD Economic Outlook*, December 1999, p. 132.) Further, Russian citizens became poorer in 1999, even though wage arrears and absolute numbers below the poverty line trended down. "The average level of Russians' real cash income—incomes adjusted to account for inflation—decreased 15 percent," according to the Russian Statistics Agency. (Yevgenia Borisova, "Poverty Still Widespread Despite Modest Growth," *Moscow Times*, January 13, 2000, also in *Johnson's Russia List*, no. 4032, January 13, 2000.) An estimated 70 percent of Russians now live below or just above the poverty line.

224. *Frontline* "Return of the Czar" interview with E. Wayne Merry, PBS website www.pbs.org/wgbh/pages/frontline/shows\yeltsin\interviews\merry.html.

225. *Frontline* "Return of the Czar" interview with Thomas Graham, PBS website www.pbs.org/wgbh/pages/frontline/shows\yeltsin\interviews\graham.htm.

226. See Igor Kliamkin, "Elektorat Demokraticheskikh Sil," *Analiz Elektorata Politicheskikh Sil Rossii* (Analysis of the Electorate of Russia's Political Forces), Moscow, Russia: Carnegie Endowment for International Peace, 1995, pp. 16-17.

227. Information provided by Steve Grant, Office of Research, U.S. Department of State, July 10, 2000. A version of this is cited in Thomas E. Graham, Jr., "Putin's Russia:

Why Economic Reform Requires Political Support, Reflections on U.S. Policy Toward Russia," *East European Constitutional Review,* Winter/Spring 2000 (Reprinted in *Johnson's Russia List,* no. 4364, June 13, 2000). See also United States Information Agency, "Is Economic Reform in Russia Dead?," *Opinion Analysis,* Washington, DC.: USIA: Office of Research and Media Reaction, March 15, 1999, pp. 3-4. The ratio of Russians who had favorable attitudes toward U.S.-Russia rapprochement versus those who did not declined steeply from 1994 to 1999. In 1994 the ratio was 2.47, as compared with 1.67 in 1999. See Boris Dubin, "Vremia i Lyudi: O Massovom Vospriiatii Social'nykh Peremen," *Russian Public Opinion Monitor,* May-June 1999, pp. 22-23.

228. Opinion poll conducted in mid-November 1999 by the ROMIR group, a Russian polling organization, cited in James M. Klurfeld, "U.S. Errs by Treading on Russian Sensitivities," *Newsday,* December 2, 1999, reprinted in *Johnson's Russia List,* no. 3659, December 2, 1999.

229. Interview with Keith Henderson, July 24, 1996.

CHAPTER FIVE

1. Interview with Marek Kozak, June 18, 1998.

2. For a detailed description of the legal private sector, see Janine Wedel, *The Private Poland: An Anthropologist's Look at Everyday Life,* New York, NY: Facts on File, 1986, pp. 53-55.

3. *Studia i Materiały,* Ośrodek Prac Społeczno-Zawodowych Krajowa Komisja NSZZ "Solidarność," Warszawa, Poland, 1990.

4. Leila Webster, *Survey of Private Firms in Poland,* Washington, D.C.: World Bank, 1992.

5. For analysis of the role of the family, see Janine R. Wedel, *The Private Poland: An Anthropologist's Look at Everyday Life,* New York, NY: Facts on File, 1986, chapter 3, "The Ties that Bind"; and Jadwiga Korelewicz, "Social Differences—Feeling of Belonging—Belief in Oneself," study directed by Edmund Wnuk-Lipiński, Institute of Philosophy and Sociology, Polish Academy of Sciences, Warsaw, Poland, 1984.

6. Barbara Heyns, *The Dynamics of Market Transition,* final report submitted to the National Council on Soviet and East European Research, Washington, D.C., July 1995.

7. See, for example, Simon Johnson, Daniel Kaufmann, and Oleg Ustenko, "Complementarities, Formal Employment, and Survival Strategies," prepared for the National Academy of Sciences/National Research Council workshop on Economic Transformation—Households and Health, September 7-8, 1995.

8. See, for example, Victor Nee, "Markets and Inequality: Why Marx and Smith are Both Right," paper presented at the Conference on Inequality and Democracy, February 4-6, 1994, Rutgers University.

9. Public Law 101-179, *Support for East European Democracy (SEED) Act of 1989,* November 28, 1989, sec 201(a).

10. U.S. General Accounting Office, *Enterprise Funds: Evolving Models for Private Sector Development in Central and Eastern Europe,* Washington, D.C.: GAO, March 1994, p. 13.

11. Polish-American Enterprise Fund, *Annual Report 1991*, New York, NY: Polish-American Enterprise Fund, p. 18; Hungarian-American Enterprise Fund, *Annual Report 1991*, Washington, D.C.: Hungarian-American Enterprise Fund, p. 5.

12. U.S. General Accounting Office, *Enterprise Funds: Evolving Models for Private Sector Development in Central and Eastern Europe*, Washington, D.C.: GAO, March 1994, p. 13.

13. Development Alternatives, Inc., *Program Evaluation of the Central and Eastern Europe Enterprise Funds: Final Report*, Washington, D.C.: DAI, 1995, p. 3.

14. Ibid.

15. Polish-American Enterprise Fund, *Annual Report, 1991*, p. 2.

16. 1995 figures are from Development Alternatives, Inc., *Program Evaluation of the Central and Eastern Europe Enterprise Funds: Final Report*, Washington, D.C.: DAI, 1995, p. v.

    The $1 billion was distributed by the Funds to the following countries: Poland, Hungary, Slovakia, Romania, Bulgaria, Albania, Russia, Ukraine, Moldova, Belarus, Lithuania, Latvia, Estonia, Kazakhstan, Kyrgyz Republic, Uzbekistan, Turkmenistan, and Tajikistan (letter from USAID Enterprise Fund adviser [personal services contractor] Timothy Knowlton, May 17, 2000).

17. Materials supplied by *Polska Agencja Rozwoju Regionalnego* (the Polish Agency for Regional Development), Warsaw, Poland. For a history of the Struder program, see Marek Kozak and Andrzej Pyszkowski, eds., *Phare-STRUDER: A Pilot Regional Development Programme*, Warsaw, Poland: Polish Agency for Regional Development, 1999.

18. As of June 26, 1998, 1 ECU equaled $1.0925, according to the Federal Reserve Bank of New York.

19. Interviews with Marek Kozak, director of the Polish Agency for Regional Development, June 18, 1998, and May 29, 2000; and materials provided by Kozak, May 29, 2000.

20. Development Alternatives, Inc., *Program Evaluation of the Central and Eastern Europe Enterprise funds: Final Report*, Washington, D.C.: DAI, 1995, p. 10.

21. Development Alternatives, Inc., *Program Evaluation of the Central and Eastern Europe Enterprise funds: Final Report*, Washington, D.C.: DAI, 1995, pp. 3-4.

22. Ibid.

23. Sources include Piotr Kowalski, vice president of the Enterprise Credit Corporation, Polish American Enterprise Fund, interview of April 22, 1994.

24. Interview with Zdeněk Drábek, July 7, 1994.

25. Development Alternatives, Inc., *Program Evaluation of the Central and Eastern Europe Enterprise Funds: Final Report*, Washington, D.C.: DAI, 1995, p. 2.

26. Interview with Charles Huebner, April 25, 1994.

27. Public Law 101-179, *Support for East European Democracy (SEED) Act of 1989*, November 28, 1989, sec 201(a).

28. U.S. General Accounting Office, *Enterprise Funds: Evolving Models for Private Sector Development in Central and Eastern Europe*, Washington, D.C., GAO, March 1994, p. 30.

29. Development Alternatives, Inc., *Program Evaluation of the Central and Eastern Europe Enterprise Funds: Final Report*, Washington, D.C.: DAI, 1995, p. vi.

30. U.S. General Accounting Office, *Enterprise Funds: Evolving Models for Private Sector Development in Central and Eastern Europe*, Washington, D.C.: GAO, March 1994, pp. 55-57.

31. U.S. General Accounting Office, *Enterprise Funds: Evolving Models for Private Sector Development in Central and Eastern Europe,* Washington, D.C.: GAO, March 1994, pp. 60-62.

32. One program concentrating on small and medium-sized businesses was Caresbac, funded by USAID and other sources. In comparison with the Enterprise Funds, Caresbac appeared to operate with much less overhead and make more use of technical assistance resources available from Western voluntary organizations.

33. Interview with Henryka Bochniarz, April 18, 1998.

34. Interview with Zdeněk Drábek, July 7, 1994.

35. U.S. General Accounting Office, *Enterprise Funds: Evolving Models for Private Sector Development in Central and Eastern Europe,* Washington, D.C.: General Accounting Office, March 1994, pp. 20-21.

36. Interview with Zbigniew Brzezinski, March 10, 1994.

37. Development Alternatives, Inc., *Program Evaluation of the Central and Eastern Europe Enterprise Funds: Final Report,* Washington, D.C.: DAI, 1995, p. 7.

38. Interview with Henryka Bochniarz, April 18, 1998.

39. See, for example, Jane Perlez, "Polish Aid Fund Turns Profit, Posing a Problem," *The New York Times,* April 27, 1998, Page A9; and Michael M. Phillips, "Politics & Policy: Another Surplus to Fret About: Poland's," *The Wall Street Journal,* January 25, 1999, p. A20. For discussion within the Polish-American community, see "Polish American Enterprise Fund Liquidation Controversy," *Siec Polska,* May 19, 1999, and other articles in *Siec Polska.*

40. Polish-American Enterprise Fund, *Annual Report 1999,* p. 2.

41. *Newsletter of the Polish Embassy in Washington D.C.,* vol. VI, March-April 2000.

42. U.S. General Accounting Office, *Enterprise Funds: Evolving Models for Private Sector Development in Central and Eastern Europe,* Washington, D.C. GAO, March 1994, p. 28.

43. Letter from USAID Enterprise Fund adviser (personal services contractor) Timothy Knowlton, May 17, 2000, and fund annual reports.

44. Half of the Fund's board of directors were Americans (mostly political appointees) and half were Russians (Anatoly Chubais "had a great input" into the Russian list, says Towbin).

45. Interview with Robert Towbin, February 18, 1998.

46. Ibid.

47. Development Alternatives, Inc., *Program Evaluation of the Central and Eastern Europe Enterprise Funds: Final Report,* Washington, D.C.: DAI, 1995, p. 6.

48. James H. Holmes, "Prepared Statement of James H. Holmes, Coordinator for East European Assistance, U.S. Department of States, Before the House Committee on International Relations," *Federal News Service,* June 26, 1997.

49. Robert M. Rubin quoted in Leslie Eaton, "Public Money Foots the Bills for 'Privatized' Foreign Aid," *The New York Times,* February 7, 1996, p. A10.

50. Michal Illner, "The Regional Aspect of Post-Communist Transformation in the Czech Republic," *Czech Sociological Review,* vol. 2, no. 1, 1994, pp. 107-127.

51. See Jacek Szlachta, "Regional Regularities of Transformation Processes," *Regional Development in Poland* (Conference in Warsaw, September 30 to October 1, 1993), Warsaw, Poland: Friedrich Ebert Stiftung, 1994, pp. 12-23; and *Regional Development in Poland under Transformation,* Warsaw, Poland: Friedrich Ebert Foundation Warsaw Office, 1995, pp. 7-40.

52. Interview of April 22, 1994, with Jacek Szlachta, deputy director of Poland's Central Office of Planning, Regional Policy Department; and Szlachta, "Poland's Regional Development under Economic Transformation," prepared for the confer-

ence on "Regional Development in Poland," Sept. 30 to Oct. 1, 1993, Warsaw, Poland, and published by the Friedrich Ebert Stiftung in Poland, p. 16.

53. Interview of June 18, 1998, with Jacek Szlachta; *Rocznik Statystyczyny Województw* (Warsaw, Poland: Główny Urząd Statystyczny, 1997); and interview of May 29, 2000 with Jacek Szlachta, now professor at the Główna Szkoła Handlowa (Warsaw School of Economics).

54. Frances Pine and Sue Bridger, "Introduction," *Surviving Post-Socialism: Local Strategies and Regional Responses in Eastern Europe and the former Soviet Union,* Sue Bridger and Frances Pine, eds., London, United Kingdom: Routledge, 1998, p. 6.

55. Interviews of June 18, 1998 and May 29, 2000 with Jacek Szlachta.

56. The average value of the złoty during 1995 was 2.4244 (obtained from Narodowy Bank Polski).

57. Interviews with Witold Szwajkowski, chief operations officer, June 19, 1998, and Agata Szostek, international relations and credit director, May 29, 2000; and *Annual Report, Fundusz Mikro,* 1999. For further information, see website www.funduszmikro.com.pl.

58. Interview with Witold Szwajkowski, chief operations officer, June 19, 1998; *Annual Report, Fundusz Mikro,* 1997.

59. Christopher Bobinski, "Poland's Small Businesses Rise from the Flood," *Financial Times,* December 18, 1997, p. 3; and interviews with participants in other loan programs.

60. Materials provided by Polska Agencja Rozwoju Regionalnego, Warsaw, Poland; interviews with director Marek Kozak, June 18, 1998 and May 29, 2000, and with deputy director Jakub Sieracki, February 25, 1998.

61. See, for example, Development Alternatives, Inc., *Program Evaluation of the Central and Eastern Europe Enterprise Funds: Final Report,* Washington, D.C.: DAI, 1995.

62. Development Alternatives, Inc., *Program Evaluation of the Central and Eastern Europe Enterprise Funds: Final Report,* Washington, D.C.: DAI, 1995, p. ix.

63. Conversation with USAID Enterprise Fund adviser (personal services contractor) Timothy Knowlton, April 19, 2000.

64. U.S. General Accounting Office, *Enterprise Funds: Evolving Models for Private Sector Development in Central and Eastern Europe,* Washington, D.C.: General Accounting Office, March 1994, pp. 22-23.

65. Interviews with Zdeněk Drábek, former aid coordinator of Czechoslovakia, July 7, 1994; Leighton Klevana of the Slovak Enterprise fund, July 5, 1994; and Paul Gibian of the Czech and Slovak Enterprise funds, July 7, 1994.

66. Development Alternatives, Inc., *Program Evaluation of the Central and Eastern Europe Enterprise Funds: Final Report,* Washington, D.C.: DAI, 1995, pp. 4, 6, and 33.

67. See testimony of James H. Holmes, "Prepared Statement of James H. Holmes, Coordinator for East European Assistance, U.S. Department of States, Before the House Committee on International Relations," *Federal News Service,* June 26, 1997.

68. Interview with Barry Thomas, February 18, 1998.

69. Ibid.

70. Ibid.

71. Interview with Paul Gibian, July 7, 1994.

72. Development Alternatives, Inc., *Program Evaluation of the Central and Eastern Europe Enterprise Funds: Final Report,* Washington, D.C.: DAI, 1995, p. 39.

73. Conversations with USAID Enterprise Fund adviser (personal services contractor) Timothy Knowlton, April 19, 2000 and May 31, 2000.

CHAPTER SIX

1. Commission on Security and Cooperation in Europe, *Briefing On U.S. Assistance to Central and Eastern Europe and the NIS: An Assessment,* Washington, D.C.: Commission on Security and Cooperation in Europe, February 17, 1995, p. 46.

2. For details, see European Commission, *Regular Report from the Commission on Progress towards Accession by Each of the Candidate Countries,* October 13, 1999, www.europa.eu.int/comm/enlargement/report_10_99/intro/index.htm.

3. Arturo Escobar, *Encountering Development: The Making and Unmaking of the Third World,* Princeton, NJ: Princeton University Press, 1995, p. 4, and "The Invention of Development," *Current History,* vol. 98, no. 631, November 1999, pp. 382-386.

4. Peter Reddaway, "Questions about Russia's 'Dream Team,'" *Post-Soviet Prospects,* vol. 5, no. 5, Washington, D.C.: Center for Strategic and International Studies, September 1997.

5. The author would like to thank Erind Pajo for helpful discussion on this issue and for contributing the image of the bridge.

6. The concept of "transidentities" draws on Fredrik Barth's work exploring "repertoires" of identities and establishing that actors employ different identities depending on the situation. See Fredrik Barth, ed., *Ethnic Groups and Boundaries: The Social Organization of Culture Difference* (Boston, MA: Little, Brown, 1969).

7. See, for example, the comments of USAID official Thomas A. Dine in chapter 4.

8. As discussed in Chapter 4, "transactors" are players in a small, informal group who work together for mutual gain, while formally representing different parties. Although transactors may share the stated goals of the parties they represent, they have additional goals and ways of operating of their own. These may, advertently or inadvertently, subvert or subordinate the aims of those for whom they ostensibly act.

9. There is, of course, a sizable literature in social science, and especially in anthropology, on the "other." See, in particular, Edward Said, *Orientalism* (New York, NY: Pantheon Books, 1978); Benedict Anderson, *Imagined Communities: Reflections on the Origins and Spread of Nationalism* (London, United Kingdom: Verso, 1991); and Johannes Fabian, *Time and the Other: How Anthropology Makes its Object* (New York, NY: Columbia University Press, 1983).

10. Another international organization that has been seen as an integral part of joining "the West" is the North Atlantic Treaty Organization (NATO). After the Warsaw pact's collapse, NATO formed the North Atlantic Cooperation Council (NACC), which included NATO members as well as former Warsaw Pact countries. In 1994, NATO began the Partnership for Peace (PFP) program, under which non-NATO countries were permitted to begin participating in NATO military exercises and planning. More than 20 nations, including Russia and other former communist countries, joined PFP, which involved placing NATO advisers in the ministries of defense in the recipient countries. Despite involvement in PFP, not all countries were viewed as eventual members. Membership in NATO was a major part of the foreign policies of Poland, Hungary, and the Czech Republic, which were admitted on March 12, 1999.

APPENDIX 2

1. Cris Shore and Susan Wright, "Policy: A New Field of Anthropology," *Anthropology of Policy: Critical Perspectives on Governance and Power,* Cris Shore and Susan Wright, eds., London, United Kingdom: Routledge, 1997, p. 14.

2. Laura Nader, "Up the Anthropologist—Perspectives Gained from Studying Up," *Reinventing Anthropology,* Dell Hymes, ed., New York, NY: Vintage Books, 1974, pp. 284-311 (quote appears on pp. 292-293). See also Nader's "The Vertical Slice: Hierarchies and Children," *Hierarchy and Society: Anthropological Perspectives on Bureaucracy,* G. M. Britan and R. Cohen, eds., Philadelphia, PA: Institute for the Study of Human Issues, 1980. For a recent discussion of "studying up," see Susan Wright, "'Culture' in Anthropology and Organizational Studies," *Anthropology of Organizations,* Susan Wright, ed., London, United Kingdom: Routledge, 1994, pp. 14-17.

3. Eric R. Wolf, "American Anthropologists and American Society," *Reinventing Anthropology,* Dell Hymes, ed., New York, NY: Vintage Books, 1974, p. 261.

4. See, for example, Hugh Gusterson, *Nuclear Rites: A Weapons Laboratory at the End of the Cold War,* Berkeley and Los Angeles, CA: University of California Press, 1996, and "Nuclear Weapons and the Other in the Western Imagination," *Cultural Anthropology,* vol. 14, no. 1, February 1999, pp. 111-143; Gideon Kunda, *Engineering Culture,* Philadelphia, PA: Temple University Press, 1992; George Marcus, *Lives in Trust: The Fortunes of Dynastic Families in Late Twentieth-Century America,* Boulder, CO: Westview Press, 1992; Philip C. Parnell, "The Composite State: The Poor and the Nation in Manila," *Ethnography in Unstable Places,* Carol Greenhouse, Elizabeth Mertz, and Kay Warren, eds., Duke University Press, forthcoming 2001; and Cris Shore and Susan Wright, "Policy: A New Field of Anthropology," *Anthropology of Policy: Critical Perspectives on Governance and Power,* Cris Shore and Susan Wright, eds., London, United Kingdom: Routledge, 1997.

5. Akhil Gupta and James Ferguson, "Discipline and Practice: 'The Field' as Site, Method, and Location in Anthropology," *Anthropological Locations: Boundaries and Grounds of a Field Science,* Akhil Gupta and James Ferguson, eds., Berkeley, CA, University of California Press, 1997, p. 15.

6. Sherry B. Ortner, "Fieldwork in the Postcommunity," *Anthropology and Humanism,* vol. 22, no. 1, 1997, p.76. Increasingly, anthropologists have been conducting delocalized fieldwork among people connected with one another. For example, Ortner studied a high school graduating class that once had been part of an "actual on-the-ground community" that is now dispersed throughout the United States (ibid., pp. 61-80).

7. Jean Comaroff and John L. Comaroff, "Occult Economies and the Violence of Abstraction: Notes from the South African Postcolony," *American Ethnologist,* vol. 26, no. 2, 1999, p. 294.

8. Poland, the most populous nation in the region and the first to carry out a revolution and post-communist economic reforms received far more aid than any other single country in the initial aid push. Some 60 percent of U.S. grant aid and 36 percent of EU PHARE aid to the region was obligated to Poland during 1990-92 (appendix 1: tables 3.1 and 4.1).

9. J. Van Velsen, "The Extended-Case Method and Situational Analysis," *The Craft of Social Anthropology,* A. L. Epstein, ed., New York, NY: Tavistock Publications, 1967, p. 145.

10. As anthropologist George Marcus has put it, "In multi-sited ethnography, comparison emerges from putting questions to an emergent object of study whose contours, sites, and relationships are not known beforehand, but are themselves a contribution of making an account that has different, complexly connected real-world sites of investigation" (George Marcus, "Ethnography in/of the World System: The Emergence of Multi-Sited Ethnography," *Annual Review of Anthropology*, vol. 24, 1995, Annual Reviews Inc., p. 102).

11. In practice, this means representing myself accurately to informants (that I am an anthropologist, whom I work for, in what capacity, and the ends for which the information is gathered). It also means entering into agreements with my informants ("sources" to journalists) as to whether the information they are providing is "on background," "off the record," or "on the record" and not confusing those in publication.

12. For more on this topic, see Janine R. Wedel and David A. Kideckel, "Studying Up: Amending the First Principle of Anthropological Ethics," *Anthropology Newsletter*, vol. 35, no. 7, October 1994, p. 37.

13. Akhil Gupta and James Ferguson, "Discipline and Practice: 'The Field' as Site, Method, and Location in Anthropology," *Anthropological Locations: Boundaries and Grounds of a Field Science*, Akhil Gupta and James Ferguson, eds., Berkeley, CA, University of California Press, 1997, p. 37.

14. See Janine R. Wedel, "Tainted Transactions: An Exchange," *National Interest*, no. 60, Summer 2000, pp. 98-110.

SELECTED BIBLIOGRAPHY

REPORTS BY AID ORGANIZATIONS, DONOR OFFICIALS AND SPOKESPEOPLE, AND AID-FUNDED CONSULTANTS

Åslund, Anders. *How Russia Became a Market Economy*. Washington, D.C.: Brookings Institution, 1995.

Bernard, Richard P. "Regulation, Training, and Infrastructure Development: Current Resources and 1995-96 Projects." Briefing for the U.S. Agency for International Development, prepared by Richard P. Bernard, Executive Director, Resource Secretariat for the Russian Federation Commission on Securities and the Capital Market. 29 March 1995.

Boyko, Maxim, Andrei Shleifer, and Robert Vishny. *Privatizing Russia*. Cambridge, MA: MIT Press, 1995.

Commission of the European Communities. *The Phare Programme Annual Report 1996*. Brussels, Belgium: Commission of the European Communities, 1996.

Commission of the European Communities. *The Phare Programme Annual Report 1998*. Brussels, Belgium: Commission of the European Communities, March 2000.

Commission of the European Communities, TACIS Information Office. *TACIS Report on Activities 1992*. Brussels, Belgium: Commission of the European Communities, TACIS Information Office, 1993.

Commission on Security and Cooperation in Europe. *Briefing On U.S. Assistance to Central and Eastern Europe and the NIS: An Assessment*. Washington, D.C., 17 February 1995.

Court of Auditors. *Special Report Number 5/99 Concerning Phare Cross-Border Cooperation (1994 to 1998)*. Brussels, Belgium: Court of Auditors, February 2000.

Czech & Slovak American Enterprise Fund. *1993 Annual Report*. Washington, D.C.: Czech & Slovak American Enterprise Fund, 1993.

Dine, Thomas A. "U.S. Aid for the Newly Independent States." *Problems of Post-Communism*, vol. 42, no. 3, May-June 1995, pp.27-31.

Economies in Transition: Management Training and Market Economies Education in Central and Eastern Europe. Conference cosponsored by the White House and the United States Department of Treasury. Washington, D.C., 26 February 1991.

European Commission, Directorate General IA. *G-24 Scoreboard of Assistance Commitments to the Countries of Central and Eastern Europe, 1990-1994*. Brussels, Belgium: European Commission, Directorate General IA, March 1995.

European Commission, Phare Information Office. *How to Work with Phare?* Brussels, Belgium.

European Commission, Phare Information Office. *What is Phare?* Brussels, Belgium: May 1994.

European Commission, Tacis Information Office. *What is Tacis? Partnership and Cooperation with the New Independent States*. Brussels, Belgium: May 1994.

European Commission. *The Tacis Programme Annual Report 1996*. Brussels, Belgium: European Commission, July 1997.

European Commission. *The Tacis Programme Annual Report 1997*. Brussels, Belgium: European Commission, March 1998.

European Union. *Conclusions of the Presidency. Copenhagen, Denmark, 21-22 June 1993*. Brussels, Belgium: European Union, 1993.

Fundusz Mikro. *Annual Report for the Year Ending 30 September 1997*. Warsaw, Poland: Fundusz Mikro, 1997.

German Marshall Fund. *Environmental Partnership for Central Europe. Report 1995/96*. Washington, D.C.: German Marshall Fund, 1997.

Gershman, Carl. *The Future of Europe*. Prepared Statement of Carl Gershman, President of the National Endowment for Democracy, in hearings before the Committee on Foreign Relations and the Subcommittee on European Affairs of the United States Senate, One Hundred First Congress, Second Session, 13 December 1989; 17 January; 1 and 22 February; 1, 7, 21, 22, 28, and 29 March; 9 May; and 12 June 1990. Printed for the use of the Committee on Foreign Relations. Washington, D.C.: U.S. Government Printing Office, 1991.

Harvard Institute for International Development. *Impartial Oversight & Strategic Guidance for Privatization & Market Reforms in Russia*. (Cooperative Agreement Number: EPE-0005-A-00-5122-00. Russian Federation 1996 Workplan. Prepared for: U.S. Agency for International Development.) Cambridge, MA: HIID, 19 March 1996.

House of Representatives, Foreign Operation, Export Financing, and Related Programs Appropriations Bill. Washington, D.C., report 102-585, 18 June 1992, pp.34-36.

Howard, A. E. Dick. *Democracy's Dawn: A Directory of American Initiatives on Constitutionalism, Democracy, and the Rule of Law in Central and Eastern Europe*. Charlottesville, VA: University Press of Virginia for the United States Institute of Peace, 1991.

Hungarian-American Enterprise Fund. *Hungarian-American Enterprise Fund Annual Report, 1991*. Washington, D.C.: Hungarian-American Enterprise Fund, 1991.

Hutchings, Robert L. Statement of Ambassador Robert L. Hutchings, Special Adviser for East European Assistance, Department of State, before the Subcommittee on Foreign Operations, House Committee on Appropriations. Washington, D.C., 19 April 1993.

International Institute for Democracy. "Parliamentary Development Programmes: Evaluation and Beyond." Conference report. Berlin, Germany, 30-31 May 1997.

ISA Consult, European Institute, Sussex University, and GJW Europe. *Final Report: Evaluation of the Phare and Tacis Democracy Programme 1992-1997*. Brighton, Hamburg: ISA Consult, European Institute, Sussex University, and GWJ Europe, November 1997.

Jeffrey D. Sachs and Associates Inc., project documents. "Transformation of Centrally Planned Economies: The Lessons for Developing Countries." ("World Institute for Development Economic Research Project on the Transformation of Centrally Planned Economies: Report on Activities, First Half of 1991.")

Joint Hungarian-International Blue Ribbon Commission. *Financial Sector Reform and Enterprise Restructuring in Hungary*. Indianapolis, Indiana: Hudson Institute, December 1994.

Klaus, Václav. "Foreign Aid for a Post-Communist Country—Experience and Prospects." Speech before the Bretton Woods Committee, World Bank. Washington, D.C., 15 October 1993.

Kozak, Marek, and Andrzej Pyszkowski, eds. *Phare-STRUDER: A Pilot Regional Development Programme*. Warsaw, Poland: Polish Agency for Regional Development, 1999.

Medish. Mark C. *Confidential Report to The Special Adviser to the President and Coordinator of U.S. Assistance to the NIS (s/NIS/C), U.S. Department of State, and The Assistant Administrator for Europe and the NIS, U.S. Agency for*

International Development, on USAID Programs Supporting Commercial Law and other Legal Reform in the Russian Federation. Washington, D.C., September 1996.

Organisation for Economic Co-Operation and Development. *Aid and Other Resource Flows to the Central and Eastern European Countries and the New Independent States of the Former Soviet Union in 1992 and 1993.* Paris, France: OECD, 1995.

Polish-American Enterprise Fund. *1991 Annual Report.* New York, NY: Polish-American Enterprise Fund, 1991.

Polish-American Enterprise Fund. *1992 Annual Report.* New York, NY: Polish-American Enterprise Fund, 1992.

Polish-American Enterprise Fund. *1993 Annual Report.* New York, NY: Polish-American Enterprise Fund, 1993.

Polish-American Enterprise Fund. *1994 Annual Report.* New York, NY: Polish-American Enterprise Fund, 1994.

Polish-American Enterprise Fund. *1995 Annual Report.* New York, NY: Polish-American Enterprise Fund, 1995.

Polish-American Enterprise Fund. *1996 Annual Report.* New York, NY: Polish-American Enterprise Fund, 1996.

Polish-American Enterprise Fund. *1997 Annual Report.* New York, NY: Polish-American Enterprise Fund, 1997.

Polish American Enterprise Fund. *1999 Annual Report.* New York, NY: Polish American Enterprise Fund, 1999.

Public Law 101-179. Support for East European Democracy (SEED). Act of 1989, 28 November 1989.

Russian Privatization Center. *1994 Annual Report.* Moscow, Russia: Russian Privatization Center, 1994.

Russian Privatization Center. *1995 Annual Report.* Moscow, Russia: Russian Privatization Center, 1995.

Sachs, Jeffrey. "The Economic Transformation of Eastern Europe: The Case of Poland." *The American Economist* vol.36, no.2, Fall 1992, pp.3-11.

Soros, George. "Remarks by George Soros." U.S.-Russia Investment Symposium, Kennedy School of Government, Harvard University, 9 January 1998.

Summers, Lawrence H. *"Russia's Stake in Capital Market Development.* Kennedy School of Government." *Treasury News.* Washington, D.C.: Department of Treasury Office of Public Affairs, 9 January 1997.

Summers, Lawrence H. *"The Global Stake in Russian Economic Reform.* Speech before the U.S.-Russia Business Council." *Treasury News.* Washington, D.C.: Department of Treasury Office of Public Affairs, 1 April 1997.

Summers, Lawrence H. "Speech." *Russia Business Watch,* vol.5, no.2, Spring 1997.

Tacis Information Office. *Progress Report January 1993 through July 1993.* Brussels, Belgium: Commission of the European Communities.

Tacis Information Office. *Summary of Indicative Programs 1993-1995.* Brussels, Belgium: Commission of the European Communities.

UNDP, United Nations Office in Ukraine. *Development Cooperation: Ukraine.* Kiev, Ukraine: UNDP, United Nations Office in Ukraine, September 1994.

U.S. Department of State. *SEED Act Implementation Report: Fiscal Year 1991.* Washington, D.C.: Department of State, 31 January 1992.

U.S. Department of State. *SEED Act Implementation Report: Fiscal Year 1993.* Washington, D.C.: Department of State, January 1994.

U.S. Department of State. *SEED Act Implementation Report, Fiscal Year 1994.* Washington, D.C.: Department of State, January 1995.

U.S. Department of State. *SEED Act Implementation Report, Fiscal Year 1995.* Washington, D.C.: Department of State, February 1996.

U.S. Department of State. *Seed Act Implementation Report: Fiscal Year 1996.* Washington, D.C.: Department of State, February 1997.

U.S. Department of State. *SEED Act Implementation Report, Fiscal Year 1997.* Washington, D.C.: Department of State, February 1998.

U.S. Department of State. *Seed Act Implementation Report: Fiscal Year 1998.* Washington, D.C.: Department of State, March 1999.

U.S. Department of State. *Seed Act Implementation Report: Fiscal Year 1999.* Washington, D.C.: Department of State, March 2000.

U.S. Department of State. *United States Assistance and Economic Cooperation Strategy for the Newly Independent States. Approved January 14, 1994 by the Coordinator of U.S. Assistance to the New Independent States.*

U.S. Department of State. *United States Assistance and Economic Cooperation Strategy for Russia. Approved 19 May 1994 by the Coordinator of U.S. Assistance to the New Independent States.*

U.S. Department of State. *U.S. Assistance for Central and East Europe: Obligations FY 1990, 1991, SEED Act Implementation Report: Fiscal Year 1991.* Washington, D.C.: Department of State, 31 January 1992.

U.S. Department of State. *U.S. Assistance and Related Programs for the New Independent States of the Former Soviet Union: 1994 Annual Report.* Washington, D.C.: Department of State, January 1995.

U.S. Department of State, Office of the Coordinator of U.S. Assistance to the NIS. *U.S. Government Assistance to and Cooperative Activities with the New Independent States of the Former Soviet Union: FY 1995 Annual Report.* Washington, D.C.: Department of State, April 1996.

U.S. Department of State, Office of the Coordinator of U.S. Assistance to the NIS. *U.S. Government Assistance to and Cooperative Activities with the New Independent States of the Former Soviet Union: FY 1997 Annual Report.* Washington, D.C.: Department of State, January 1998.

U.S. Department of State, Office of the Coordinator of U.S. Assistance to the NIS. *U.S. Government Assistance to and Cooperative Activities with the New Independent States of theFormer Soviet Union: October 1995-March 1996.*

U.S. Department of State, Office of the Coordinator of U.S. Assistance to the NIS. *U.S. Government Assistance to and Cooperative Activities with the New Independent States of the Former Soviet Union: FY 1999 Annual Report.* Washington, D.C.: Department of State, January 2000.

USAID. *Action Plan for U.S. Assistance to Central and Eastern Europe.* Washington, D.C.: USAID, 1991.

USAID. *Obligation and Expenditure Report as of December 31, 1994. USAID Programs in the New Independent States of the Former Soviet Union.* Washington, D.C.: USAID, 9 February 1995.

USAID. *USAID Suspends Two Harvard Agreements in Russia.* A press release. Washington, D.C.: USAID Press Office, 20 May 1997.

The U.S. Russia Investment Fund. *1997 Annual Report.* New York, NY: TUSRIF, 1997.

Vasiliev, Sergei A. "The Political Economy of Russia's Reform." *Russian Economic Reform at Risk,* edited by Anders Åslund. New York, NY: St. Martin's Press, 1995.

ASSESSMENTS BY INDEPENDENT INSTITUTIONS AND ANALYSTS AND RECIPIENTS' CRITIQUES

Abalkin, Leonid. "Evaluation of USA Technical Aid in the Course of Democratic and Economic Transformations in Russia." Paper presented at The George Washington University, Washington, D.C., 26 February 1996.

Adams, Walter, and James W. Brock. *Adam Smith Goes to Moscow: A Dialogue on Radical Reform.* Princeton, New Jersey: Princeton University Press, 1993.

Ames, Mark, and Matt Taibbi. *The Exile.* New York, NY: Grove Press, 2000.

Bandow, Doug. "Uncle Sam as Investment Banker: The Failure of Washington's Overseas Enterprise Funds." *Policy Analysis of CATO Institute* no.260, 19 September 1996.

Barre, Raymond, William H. Luers, Anthony Solomon, and Krzysztof J. Ners. *Moving Beyond Assistance.* New York, NY: Institute for East West Studies, June 1992.

Biuro Informacynje. *Biuletyn Z Posiedzenia Komisji do Spraw Układu Europejskiego nr. 7.* Warsaw, Poland: Kancelarija Sejmu, Biuro Informacynje, nr. 311/II kad., 16 February 1994.

Bogdanowicz-Bindert, Christine A. *Interim Report: IDA Assessment.* A report commissioned by the European Union's PHARE program. December 1993.

Bratinka, Pavel. "Assistance Brings Greater Understanding." *G24 Newsletter.* Center for Foreign Assistance of the Ministry of the Economy, Prague, Czech Republic, December 1993.

Carothers, Thomas. *Assessing Democracy Assistance: The Case of Romania.* Washingon, D.C.: Carnegie Endowment for International Peace, 1996.

Carothers, Thomas. *Aiding Democracy Abroad: The Learning Curve.* Washington, D.C.: Carnegie Endowment for International Peace, 1999.

Checchi and Company Consulting, Inc. *Final Report: A Program Evaluation of A.I.D.'s Investment in Voluntary Assistance to Private Enterprise Development in Central and Eastern Europe.* Washington, D.C.: Checchi and Company Consulting, 1993.

Dąbrowski, Marek. *Western Aid Conditionality and the Post-Communist Transition.* Studies and Analyses 37. Warsaw, Poland: Center for Social and Economic Research, April 1995.

Development Economics Group/Louis Berger International, Inc., and Checci and Company Consulting, Inc. *Final Report: Privatization Phase II Program.* Evaluation submitted to AID. Washington, D.C., 30 July 1993.

Development Alternatives, Inc. *Program Evaluation of the Central and Eastern Europe Enterprise Funds: Final Report.* Washington, D.C.: Development Alternatives, 1995.

European Commission. *The Phare Programme: An Interim Evaluation.* Brussels, Belgium: June 1997.

Frontline "Return of the Czar." PBS website (www.pbs.org\wgbh\pages\frontline\shows\yeltsin\interviews\).

Harper, John, and Janine R. Wedel. "Western Aid to Central and Eastern Europe: What We are Doing Right, What We are Doing Wrong, and How We Can Do It Better." *Woodrow Wilson International Center for Scholars East European Studies Occasional Paper*, no. 41, September 1995.

Hughes, Kirsty, Philip Taylor, and Ian Christie. "Evaluation of Technical Assistance to Hungary." Policy Studies Institute. Published by the Department for Education and Employment as Research Series no. 70. (Excerpts republished in *The Skeleton at the Feast: Contributions to East European Anthropology*, edited by C.M.Hann. Canterbury, United Kingdom: University of Kent at Canterbury, Centre for Social Anthropology and Computing, 1995.)

Institute for East West Studies. *Annual Report 1992-93.* New York, NY: Institute for East West Studies, 1993.

Kádár, Béla. "Where Have all the Dollars Gone?" *Transition: The World Bank Newsletter About Reforming Economies*, vol.4, no.5, June 1993.

Kalabiński, Jacek. "The Marriott Brigade in Action." *Gazeta Wyborcza* (Warsaw, Poland), 21 June 1991.

Kalabiński, Jacek. "The Misfortune of the Marriott Brigade." *Gazeta Wyborcza* (Warsaw, Poland), 18 October 1991.

Kaplan, Sheila. "Conflicting Signals." *Legal Times* (Washington, D.C.), 25 February 1991.

Kotkin, Stephen. "Stealing the State." *The New Republic*, 13 April 1998.

Mendelson, Sarah E. and John K. Glenn. "Democracy Assistance and NGO Strategies in Post-Communist Societies." *Carnegie Endowment Working Papers*, Democracy and Rule of Law Project, no. 8. Washington, D.C.: Carnegie Endowment for International Peace, February 2000.

Ners, Krzysztof J. and Ingrid T. Buxell with Michael Palmer, Ewa Piwowar, and Daniel Linotte. *Assistance to Transition Survey 1995.* Warsaw, Poland: Institute for East West Studies, PECAT, 1995.

NIK. *List of Firms Recommended by the MWGZZ for Analysis and Asset Valuations of Privatizing Firms.* Warsaw, Poland: Ministerstwo Współpracy Gospodarczej z Zagranica or MWGZ, Economics Department, 1991.

NIK, Zespół Analiz Systemowych. *Informacja o Wynikach Kontroli Procesów Prywatyzacji Przedsiębórstw Panstwowych: Część I.* Warsaw, Poland: Najwyższa Izba Kontroli (NIK), Zespół Analiz Systemowych, June 1991.

Quigley, Kevin F.F. *For Democracy's Sake: Foundations and Democracy Assistance in Central Europe.* Washington, D.C.: Woodrow Wilson Center Press, 1997. Distributed by the Johns Hopkins University Press.

Reddaway, Peter. "Questions about Russia's 'Dream Team.'" *Post-Soviet Prospects,* vol.5, no.5. Washington, D.C.: Center for Strategic and International Studies, September 1997.

Robbins, Carla Anne, and Steve Liesman. "How an Aid Program Vital to New Economy of Russia Collapsed." *Wall Street Journal,* 13 August 1997.

Scheppele, Kim Lane. "The Soros Empire." *American and German Cultural Policies in Eastern Europe: Assessing Developments in the 1990s.* Washington, D.C.: American Institute for Contemporary German Studies, October 1999.

Siegel, Daniel, and Jenny Yancey. *The Rebirth of Civil Society: The Development of the Nonprofit Sector in East Central Europe and the Role of Western Assistance.* New York, NY: Rockefeller Brothers Fund, 1992.

Swiackiewicz, Tomasz. "Głowa w Mur." *Polityka* (Warsaw, Poland), no.36, 7 September 1991.

Taibbi, Matt. "Picked Clean: How a Small Clique of Americans Scavenged the Remains of Defrauded Russians." *Exile,* 15 January 1998. Reprinted in Johnson's Russia List (davidjohnson@erols.com, 16 January 1998, no. 2021).

U.S. General Accounting Office. *Eastern Europe: Status of U.S. Assistance.* Washington, D.C.: General Accounting Office, February 26, 1991, appendix 1.

U.S. General Accounting Office. *Enterprise Funds: Evolving Models for Private Sector Development in Central and Eastern Europe.* Washington, D.C.: General Accounting Office, March 1994.

U.S. General Accounting Office. *Environmental Issues in Central and Eastern Europe: U.S. Efforts to Help Resolve Institutional and Financial Problems.* Washington, D.C.: General Accounting Office, May 1994.

U.S. General Accounting Office. *Foreign Assistance: Assessment of Selected USAID Projects in Russia.* Washington, D.C.: General Accounting Office, August 1995.

U.S. General Accounting Office. *Foreign Assistance: Harvard Institute for International Development's Work in Russia and Ukraine.* Washington, D.C.: General Accounting Office, November 1996.

U.S. General Accounting Office. *Former Soviet Union: U.S. Bilateral Program Lacks Effective Coordination* Washington, D.C.: General Accounting Office, February 1995.

U.S. General Accounting Office. *Former Soviet Union: Assistance by the United States and Other Donors.* Washington, D.C.: General Accounting Office, December 1992.

U.S. General Accounting Office. *Poland: Economic Restructuring and Donor Assistance.* Washington, D.C.: General Accounting Office, August 1995.

U.S. General Accounting Office. *Poland and Hungary: Economic Transition and U.S. Assistance.* Washington, D.C.: General Accounting Office, 1 May 1 1992.

U.S. General Accounting Office. *Promoting Democracy: Progress Report on U.S. Democratic Development Assistance to Russia.* Washington, D.C.: General Accounting Office, February 1996.

U.S. General Accounting Office. Unpublished report. Washington, D.C.: General Accounting Office, August 1996.

Wedel, Janine R. "Beware Western Governments Bearing Gifts." *Wall Street Journal Europe*, 14 January 1992.

Wedel, Janine R. "Cliques and Clans and Aid to Russia." *Transitions, Changes in Post-Communist Societies*, vol.4, no.2, July 1997, pp.66-71.

Wedel, Janine R. "The Economist Heard 'Round the World, Part II." *World Monitor*, October 1990, pp.33-42.

Wedel, Janine R. "The Harvard Boys Do Russia." *Nation*, 1 June 1998, pp.11-16.

Wedel, Janine R. "Lessons of Western Technical Aid to Central and Eastern Europe." *Transition: The World Bank Newsletter About Reforming Economies*, vol.5, no.6, July-August 1994, pp.14-17.

Wedel, Janine R. "The Unintended Consequences of Western Aid to Post-Communist Europe." *Telos no.92*, vol.25, no.2, Summer 1992, pp.131-138.

Wedel, Janine R. "U.S. Aid to Central and Eastern Europe, 1990-1994: An Analysis of Aid Models and Responses." East-Central European Economies in Transition: Study Papers submitted to the Joint Economic Committee Congress of the United States, November 1994, pp. 299-335 (Republished as *East-Central European Economies in Transition*, edited by John P. Hardt and Richard F. Kaufman for the Joint Economic Committee Congress of the United States. New York, NY: M.E. Sharpe, 1995.)

Wedel, Janine R. "Clique-Run Organizations and U.S. Economic Aid: An Institutional Analysis." *Demokratizatsiya: The Journal of Post-Soviet Democratization*, vol. 4, no. 4, Fall 1996, pp. 571-602.

Wedel, Janine R. "Rigging the U.S.-Russian Relationship: Harvard, Chubais, and the Transidentity Game." *Demokratizatsiya: The Journal of Post-Soviet Democratization*, vol. 7, no. 4, Fall 1999, pp. 469-500.

Wedel, Janine R. "Tainted Transactions: Harvard, the Chubais Clan and Russia's Ruin." *The National Interest*, no. 59, Spring 2000, pp. 23-34.

Williamson, Anne. *Contagion: The Betrayal of Liberty—Russia and the United States in the 1990s*, forthcoming.

Williamson, Anne. "Russia's Fiscal Whistleblower: Chief Auditor Venyamin Sokolov says Western Loans Are Hijacked by the Corrupt Yeltsin Government." *MoJo Wire*, 16-22, June 1998.

"Współczesny Plan Marshalla?" *Nowa Europa* (Poland), 4 April 1994.

CENTRAL AND EASTERN EUROPE, ANTHROPOLOGY, DEVELOPMENT, SOCIAL SCIENCE, AND OTHER LITERATURE

Adams, Walter, and James W. Brock. *Adam Smith Goes to Moscow*. Princeton, NJ: Princeton University Press, 1993.

Albini, Joseph L., R.E. Rogers, Victor Shabalin, Valery Kutushev, Vladimir Moiseev, and Julie Anderson. "Russian Organized Crime: Its History, Structure and Function." *Journal of Contemporary Criminal Justice*, vol.11, no.4, 1995, pp.213-43.

Allardt, Eric, and W. Wesołowski, eds. *The General Outlines of Transformation*. Warsaw, Poland: IFIS PAN Publishing, 1994.

Amsden, Alice H., Jacek Kochanowicz, and Lance Taylor. *The Market Meets Its Match: Restructuring the Economies of Eastern Europe*. Cambridge, MA: Harvard University Press, 1994.

Amsden, Alice, Michael Intriligator, Robert McIntyre, and Lance Taylor. *Strategies for a Viable Transition: Lessons from the Political Economy of Renewal in Russia*. Institute for Policy Studies monograph. Washington, D.C., 1996.

Anderson, Benedict. *Imagined Communities: Reflections on the Origin and Spread of Nationalism.* Revised edition. London, United Kingdom: Verso, 1991.

Appadurai, Arjun. *Modernity at Large: Cultural Dimensions of Globalization.* Minneapolis, MN: University of Minnesota Press, 1996.

Arato, Andrew. "Civil Society Against the State: Poland 1980-81." *Telos,* no. 47, Spring 1981, pp.23-47.

Arato, Andrew. "Empire vs. Civil Society: Poland 1981-82." *Telos,* no. 50, Winter 1981-82, pp.19-48.

Barth, Fredrik, ed. *Ethnic Groups and Boundaries: The Social Organization of Cultural Difference.* Boston, MA: Little, Brown, 1969.

Bauer, Peter T. *Reality and Rhetoric: Studies in the Economics of Development.* Cambridge, MA: Harvard University Press, 1984.

Bennett, John W. "Anthropology and Development: The Ambiguous Engagement." *Production and Autonomy: Anthropological Studies and Critiques of Development,* edited by John W. Bennett and John R. Bowen. Lanham, MD: University Press of America, 1988.

Bernard, Michael H. *The Origins of Democratization in Poland.* New York, NY: Columbia University Press, 1993.

Bernstein, Jonas. "Loans for the Sharks?" *Moscow Times,* 19 December 1995.

Bivens, Matt, and Jonas Bernstein. "The Russia You Never Met." *Demokratizatsiya: The Journal of Post-Soviet Democratization,* vol. 6., no. 4, Fall 1998, pp. 613-647.

Boissevain, Jeremy. *Friends of Friends: Networks, Manipulators and Coalitions.* Oxford, United Kingdom: Basil Blackwell, 1974.

Bourdieu, Pierre. "What Makes a Social Class? On the Theoretical and Practical Existence of Groups." *Berkeley Journal of Sociology,* vol.32, no.1, 1987, pp.1-17.

Bourdieu, Pierre, and J.C. Passeron. *Reproduction in Education, Society and Culture.* London, United Kingdom: Sage, 1970.

Bozeman, Barry. *All Organizations Are Public: Bridging Public and Private Organizational Theories.* San Francisco, CA: Jossey-Bass, 1987.

Bremmer, I. and R. Taras. *Nations and Politics in the Soviet Successor States.* Cambridge, United Kingdom: Cambridge University Press, 1993.

Bruckner, Pascal. *The Tears of the White Man: Compassion as Contempt.* New York, NY: Free Press, 1983.

Bruno, Martha. "Playing the Co-Operation Game: Strategies Around International Aid in Post-Socialist Russia." *Surviving Post-Socialism: Local Strategies and Regional Responses in Eastern Europe and the Former Soviet Union,* edited by Sue Bridger and Frances Pine. London, United Kingdom: Routledge, 1998.

Bryant, Glenn. "State Duma Election Returns, 1995." *Demokratizatsiya: The Journal of Post-Soviet Democratization,* vol.4, no.3, Summer 1996, pp.420-421.

Bunce, Valerie. "Lessons of the First Postsocialist Decade." *East European Politics and Societies,* vol. 13, no. 2, 1999, pp. 236-243.

Bunce, Valerie. "The Political Economy of Postsocialism." *Slavic Review,* vol. 58, no. 4, Winter 1999, pp. 756-793.

Bunce, Valerie. *Subversive Institutions: The Design and the Destruction of Socialism and the State.* Cambridge, United Kingdom: Cambridge University Press, 1999.

Burawoy, Michael. *Industrial Revolution: The Russia Road to Capitalism.* Havens Lecture I, January 1995.

Burawoy, Michael. *The Politics of Production: Factory Regimes Under Capitalism and Socialism.* London, United Kingdom: Verso, 1985.

Burawoy, Michael, and János Lukács. *The Radiant Past: Ideology and Reality in Hungary's Road to Capitalism.* Chicago, IL: University of Chicago Press, 1992.

Burawoy, Michael, and Pavel Krotov. "The Soviet Transition from Socialism to Capitalism: Worker Control and Economic Bargaining in the Wood Industry." *American Sociological Review,* vol.57, February 1992, pp.16-38.

Carothers, Thomas. *Assessing Democracy Assistance: The Case of Romania.* Washington, D.C.: Carnegie Endowment for International Peace, 1996.

Cernea, Michael, ed. *Nongovernmental Organizations and Local Development: World Bank Discussion Papers.* Washington, D.C.: World Bank, 1988.

Cernea, Michael M., ed. *Putting People First: Sociological Variables in Rural Development.* Oxford, United Kingdom: Oxford University Press, 1985.

Cohen, Jean, and Andrew Arato. *Civil Society and Political Theory.* Cambridge, MA: MIT Press, 1992.

Comaroff, Jean, and John L. Comaroff, "Occult Economies and the Violence of Abstraction: Notes from the South African Postcolony." *American Ethnologist,* vol. 26, no.2, 1999, pp. 279-303.

Creed, Gerald, and Janine Wedel. "Second Thoughts from the Second World: Interpreting Aid in Post-Communist Eastern Europe." *Human Organization,* vol.56, no.3, Fall 1997, pp.253-264.

Dąbrowski, Janusz M., Michał Federowicz, and Anthony Levitas. "Polish State Enterprises and the Properties of Performance: Stabilization, Marketization, Privatization." *Politics and Society,* vol.19, no.4, 1991, pp.403-437.

Dąbrowski, Janusz M., Michał Federowicz, and Anthony Levitas. *State Enterprises in the Process of Economic Transformation 1992-1993: Research Findings.* Economic Transformation no.38. Warsaw, Poland: Gdańsk Institute for Market Economics, 1993.

Dąbrowski, Janusz M., Michał Federowicz, Tytus Kamiński, and Jan Szomburg. *Privatisation of Polish State-Owned Enterprises: Progress, Barriers, Initial Effects: The Third Report.* Economic Transformation no.33. Warsaw, Poland: Gdańsk Institute for Market Economics, February 1993.

Ekiert, Grzegorz, and Jan Kubik. "(Post)totalitarian Legacies, Civil Society, and Democracy in Post-Communist Poland, 1989-1993." Cornell University, Institute for European Studies *Working Paper,* no. 97.4.

Ellerman, David. "Voucher Privatization with Investment Funds: An Institutional Analysis." Policy Research Working Paper 1924. Washington, D.C.: The World Bank, Office of the Senior Vice President, Development Economics, May 1998.

Ermarth, Fritz W. "Seeing Russia Plain: The Russian Crisis and American Intelligence." *The National Interest,* Spring 1999.

Escobar, Arturo. "Anthropology and the Development Encounter: The Making and Marketing of Development Anthropology." *American Ethnologist,* vol.18, no.4, 1991, pp.658-682.

Escobar, Arturo. *Encountering Development: The Making and Unmaking of the Third World.* Princeton, NJ: Princeton University Press, 1995.

Escobar, Arturo. "Power and Visibility: Development and the Invention and Management of the Third World." *Cultural Anthropology,* vol.3, no.4, 1988.

Escobar, Arturo. "The Invention of Development," *Current History,* vol. 98, no. 631, November 1999, pp. 382-386.

Ethnographies of Transition: The Political, Social, and Cultural Dimensions of Emergent Market Economies in Russia and Eastern Europe. Package of papers for the conference with the same title, hosted by the Department of Sociology, University of California at Berkeley, 22-24 March 1996. Berkeley, CA: Department of Sociology of the University of California at Berkeley, February 1996.

Fabian, Johannes. *Time and the Other: How Anthropology Makes its Object.* New York, NY: Columbia University Press, 1983.

Ferguson, James. *The Anti-Politics Machine: "Development," Depoliticization, and Bureaucratic Power in Lesotho.* Cambridge, United Kingdom: Cambridge University Press, 1990.

Frydman, Roman, and Andrzej Rapaczynski. *Privatization in Eastern Europe: Is the State Withering Away?* Budapest, Hungary: Central European University Press, 1994.

Frydman, Roman, Andrzej Rapaczynski, John S. Earle, et al. *The Privatization Process in Central Europe.* Volume 1 of CEU Privatization Reports. Budapest, Hungary: Central European University Press, 1993.

Gal, Susan. "Bartok's Funeral: Representations of Europe in Hungarian Political Rhetoric." *American Ethnologist*, vol.18, no.3, August 1991, pp.440-458.

Gellner, Ernest. Keynote address at the conference on "The Anthropology of Politics in Eastern Europe," Zaborow, Poland, October 1990.

Gellner, Ernest. *Conditions of Liberty: Civil Society and its Rivals.* New York, NY: Allen Lane/Penguin Press, 1994.

Glinkina, Svetlana P. "Privatizatsiya and Kriminalizatsiya: How Organized Crime is Hijacking Privatization." *Demokratizatsiya: The Journal of Post-Soviet Democratization*, vol.2, no.3, Summer 1994, pp.385-391.

Glinkina, Svetlana P. *Kriminelle Komponenten der Russischen Wirtschaft: Typen und Dimensionen.* Köln, Germany: Berichte des Bundesinstituts für Ostwissenschaftliche und Internationale Studien, 1997.

Glinkina, Svetlana P. "The Ominous Landscape of Russian Corruption." *Transitions*, March 1998, pp. 16-23.

Goldman, Marshall I. "Privatization, Property Rights and Development Potential: Lessons from Poland and Russia." *Eastern Economic Journal*, vol. 25, issue 4, Fall 1999, pp. 389-398.

Grabher, Gernot, and David Stark, eds. *Restructuring Networks in Post-Socialism: Legacies, Linkages, and Localities.* Oxford, United Kingdom: Oxford University Press, 1997.

Graham, Thomas E. "Russia's New Non-Democrats." *Harper's Magazine*, vol.292, no.1751, April 1996, pp.26-28.

Graham, Thomas E., Jr. "Putin's Russia: Why Economic Reform Requires Political Support, Reflections on U.S. Policy Toward Russia." *East European Constitutional Review*, Winter/Spring 2000 (Reprinted in *Johnson's Russia List* no. 4364, June 13, 2000).

Grillo, R.D. and R.L. Stirrat, eds. *Discourses of Development: Anthropological Perspectives.* Oxford, United Kingdom: Berg, 1997.

Gronemeyer, Marianne. "Helping." *The Development Dictionary: A Guide to Knowledge as Power,* edited by Wolfgang Sachs. London, United Kingdom: Zed Books, 1992.

Gupta, Akhil and James Ferguson, eds. *Anthropological Locations: Boundaries and Grounds of a Field Science.* Los Angeles, CA: University of California Press, 1997.

Gupta, Akhil, and James Ferguson, eds. *Culture, Power, Place: Explorations in Critical Anthropology.* Durham, NC: Duke University Press, 1997.

Gurr, Lisa Anne. *The Unmaking of the Polish Working Class: Reform and Protest in the Ursus Mechanical Works, 1991-93.* Ph.D. dissertation, Northwestern University, 1998.

Gusterson, Hugh. *Nuclear Rites: A Weapons Laboratory at the End of the Cold War.* Berkeley and Los Angeles, CA: University of California Press, 1996.

Guttman, Daniel. *Contracting for Government.* Washington, D.C.: National Academy of Public Administration, January 1997.

Haggard, Stephen, and Andrew Moravcsik. "The Political Economy of Financial Assistance to Eastern Europe, 1989-1991." *After the Cold War: International Institutions and State Strategies in Europe, 1989-1991,* edited by Robert O. Keohane, Joseph S. Nye, and Stanley Hoffman. Cambridge, MA: Harvard University Press, 1993.

Hall, John, ed. *Civil Society: Theory, History, Comparison.* Cambridge, United Kingdom: Polity Press, 1995.

Hann, Chris. "Introduction: Political Society and Civil Anthropology." *Civil Society: Challenging Western Models,* edited by Chris Hann and Elizabeth Dunn. London, United Kingdom: Routledge, 1996.

Hann, Chris. *The Skeleton at the Feast: Contributions to East European Anthropology.* Canterbury, United Kingdom: University of Kent at Canterbury, Center for Social Anthropology and Computing, 1995.

Havel, Václav. "The Power of the Powerless." In *The Power of the Powerless: Citizens Against the State in Central-Eastern Europe*, edited by John Keane. Armonk, NY: M.E. Sharpe, 1985.

Hedlund, Stefan, *Russia's "Market" Economy: A Bad Case of Predatory Capitalism.* London, United Kingdom:UCL Press Limited 1999.

Herzfeld, Michael. *A Place in History: Social and Monumental Time in a Cretan Town.* Princeton, NJ: Princeton University Press, 1991.

Herzfeld, Michael. *The Social Production of Indifference: Exploring the Symbolic Roots of Western Bureaucracy.* New York, NY: Berg, 1992.

Heyns, Barbara. *The Dynamics of Market Transition: Final Report Submitted to the National Council on Soviet and East European Research.* Washington, D.C., July 1995.

Higgins, Benjamin. *A Path Less Travelled: A Development Economist's Quest.* Australian National University National Centre for Development Studies 2. Canberra, Australia: Australian National University, 1989.

Hobart, Mark. "Introduction: The Growth of Ignorance?" *An Anthropological Critique of Development*, edited by Mark Hobart. London, United Kingdom: Routledge, 1993.

Illner, Michal. "Post-Communist Transformation Revisited." *Czech Sociological Review*, vol.4, no.2, 1996, pp.157-169.

Illner, Michal. "The Regional Aspect of Post-Communist Transformation in the Czech Republic." *Czech Sociological Review*, vol.2, no.1, 1994, pp.107-127.

Jarosz, Maria, ed. *Polish Employee-Owned Companies in 1995.* Warsaw, Poland: Institute of Political Studies of the Polish Academy of Sciences, 1996.

Johnson, Simon, Daniel Kaufmann, and Oleg Ustenko. "Complementarities, Formal Employment, and Survival Strategies." Paper prepared for the National Academy of Sciences/National Research Council workshop on Economic Transformation-Households and Health, 7-9 September 1995.

Kamiński, Antoni Z. *An Institutional Theory of Communist Regimes: Design, Function, and Breakdown.* San Francisco, CA: ICS Press, 1992.

Kamiński, Antoni Z., and Joanna Kurczewska. *The Logic of Institutional Transformation: East Central Europe in Search of (a) New Political Order(s).* Unpublished Paper. Warsaw, Poland: Warsaw University, Institute of Sociology, October 1990.

Kamiński, Antoni Z., and Joanna Kurczewski. "Main Actors of Transformation: The Nomadic Elites." *The General Outlines of Transformation*, edited by Eric Allardt and W. Wesołowski. Warsaw, Poland: IFIS PAN Publishing, 1994.

Kamiński, Antoni Z. "Corruption Under the Post-Communist Transformation." *Polish Sociological Review*, vol. 2, no. II8, 1997, pp. 91-117.

Keane, John, ed. *Civil Society and the State: New European Perspectives.* London, United Kingdom: Verso, 1988.

Keane, John. *Democracy and Civil Society: On the Predicaments of European Socialism, the Prospects for Democracy, and the Problem of Controlling Social and Political Power.* London, United Kingdom: Verso, 1988.

Keane, John, ed. *The Power of the Powerless: Citizens Against the State in Central-Eastern Europe.* Armonk, NY: M.E. Sharpe, 1985.

Kelly, Robert J., Rufus Schatzberg, and Patrick J. Ryan. "Primitive Capitalist Accumulation: Russia as a Racket." *Journal of Contemporary Criminal Justice*, vol.11, no.4, 1995, pp 257-75.

Kideckel, David A. *Biting the Hand?: Cultural and Political Economy in Privatization Aid to Romania and Albania.* Unpublished Paper.

Kideckel, David A. *The Solitude of Collectivism: Romanian Villagers to the Revolution and Beyond.* Ithaca, NY: Cornell University Press, 1993.

Kideckel, David A. "Us and Them: Concepts of East and West in the East European Transition." *Cultural Dilemmas of Post-Communist Societies*, edited by Aldona Jawłowska and Marian Kempny.Warsaw, Poland: IFIS Publishers, 1994.

Kiss, Yudit. "Privatization Paradoxes in East Central Europe." *East European Politics and Society,* vol.8, no.1, Winter 1994, pp.141-152.

Kliamkin, Igor. "Elektorat Demokraticheskikh Sil." *Analiz Elektorata Politicheskikh Sil Rossii* (Analysis of the Electorate of Russia's Political Forces). Moscow, Russia: Carnegie Endowment for International Peace, 1995.

Kołodko, Grzegorz W. *From Shock to Therapy: The Political Economy of Postsocialist Transformations.* Oxford, United Kingdom: Oxford University Press, 2000.

Kołodko, Grzegorz W., and D. Mario Nuti. *The Polish Alternative: Old Myths, Hard Facts and New Strategies in the Successful Transformation of the Polish Economy.* Research for Action 33, World Institute for Development Economics Research, The United Nations University. Helsinki, Finland: UNU/WIDER, 1997.

Korelewicz, Jadwiga. "Social Differences—Feeling of Belonging—Belief in Oneself." Study directed by Edmund Wnuk-Lipinski, Institute of Philosophy and Sociology, Polish Academy of Sciences. Warsaw, Poland, 1984.

Kornai, János. *Economics of Shortage.* Amsterdam, Netherlands: North-Holland, 1980.

Kornai, János. "The Health of Nations: Reflections on the Analogy Between the Medical Science and Economics." *Kyklos,* vol.36, fasc.2, 1983, pp.191-212.

Kornai, János. *The Road to a Free Economy: Shifting from a Socialist System: The Example of Hungary.* New York, NY: Norton, 1990.

Kottak, Conrad. "When People Don't Come First." *Putting People First: Sociological Variables in Rural Development,* edited by Michael M. Cernea. New York, NY: Oxford University Press, 1985.

Kotz, David, with Fred Weir. *Revolution from Above: The Demise of the Soviet Union.* London, United Kingdom: Routledge, 1997.

Kowalski, Sergiusz. *Pierwszy Krok do Europy: O Komitetach Obywatelskich, Partiach Politycznych i Wyborach.* Warsaw, Poland: Ośrodek Prac Społeczno-Zawodowych przy KK NSZZ "Solidarność," 1990.

Kryshtanovskaya, Olga. "The Real Masters of Russia." *Argumenty i Fakty,* no.21, May 1997. Reprinted in Johnson's Russia List (davidjohnson@erols.com, May 1997).

Lampland, Martha. *The Object of Labor: Commodification in Socialist Hungary.* Chicago, IL: University of Chicago Press, 1995.

Lempert, David H. *Daily Life in a Crumbling Empire: The Absorption of Russia into the World Economy.* Volumes I and II, East European Monographs, Boulder. Distributed by Columbia University Press, New York. 1996.

Levitas, Anthony, and Piotr Strzałkowski. "What Does 'Uwłaszczenie Nomenklatury' (Propertisation of the Nomenklatura) Really Mean?" *Communist Economies,* vol.2, no.3, 1990, pp.413-416.

Lewenstein, Barbara, and Wojciech Pawlik. *A Miało Być Tak Pięknie: Polska Scena Publiczna Lat Dziewiędziesiątych.* Warsaw, Poland: Uniwersytet Warszawski, Instytut Stosowanych Nauk Społecznych, 1994.

Marcus, George, "Ethnography in/of the World System: The Emergence of Multi-Sited Ethnography." *Annual Review of Anthropology,* vol. 24, 1995, Annual Reviews Inc., pp. 95-117.

McIntyre, Michael. "Regional Stabilization Policy Under Transitional Period Conditions in Russia: Price Controls, Regional Trade Barriers and other Local-Level Measures." *Europe-Asia Studies,* vol.50, no.5, 1998, pp.859-871.

Millar, James R. "From Utopian Socialism to Utopian Capitalism: The Failure of Revolution and Reform in Post-Soviet Russia." *The George Washington University 175th Anniversary Papers.* Washington, D.C.: George Washington University, 1996.

Mouzelis, Nicos P. *Organisation and Bureaucracy: An Analysis of Modern Theories.* Hawthorne, NY: Aldine, 1968.

Murrell, Peter. "What is Shock Therapy? What Did it Do in Poland and Russia?" *Post-Soviet Affairs,* vol.9, no.2, 1993, pp.111-140.

Nader, Laura. "Up the Anthropologist: Perspectives Gained from Studying Up." *Reinventing Anthropology,* edited by Dell Hymes. New York, NY: Random House, 1972.

Nader, Laura. "The Vertical Slice: Hierarchies and Children." *Hierarchy and Society: Anthropological Perspectives on Bureaucracy,* edited by G. M. Britan and R. Cohen. Philadelphia, PA: Institute for the Study of Human Issues, 1980.

Nagengast, Carole. *Reluctant Socialists, Rural Enterpreneurs: Class, Culture, and the Polish State.* Boulder, CO: Westview Press, 1991.

Nee, Victor. "Markets and Inequality: Why Marx and Smith are Both Right." Paper presented at the "Conference on Inequality and Democracy," Rutgers University. NJ, 4-6 February 1994.

Nelson, Lynn D. and Irina Y. Kuzes. *Property to the People: The Struggle for Radical Economic Reform in Russia.* Armonk, NY: M.E. Sharpe, 1994.

Nelson, Lynn D. and Irina Y. Kuzes. *Radical Reform in Yeltsin's Russia: Political Economic and Social Dimensions.* Armonk, NY: M.E. Sharpe, 1995.

Nuti, Mario. "Mass Privatisation: Costs and Benefits of Instant Capitalism." *CIS-Middle Europe Centre, London Business School, Discussion Paper Series,* no.9, May 1994.

Offe, Claus. *Varieties of Transition: The East European and East German Experience.* Cambridge, MA: MIT Press, 1997.

Ortner, Sherry. "Fieldwork in the Postcommunity." *Anthropology and Humanism,* vol. 22, no. 1, 1997, pp. 61-80.

Ortung, Robert W. *From Leningrad to St. Petersburg: Democratization in a Russian City.* New York, NY: St. Martin's Press, 1995.

Parnell, Philip C. "The Composite State: The Poor and the Nation in Manila." *Ethnography in Unstable Places,* edited by Carol Greenhouse, Elizabeth Mertz, and Kay Warren. Unpublished manuscript.

Parnell, Philip C. *Escalating Disputes: Social Participation and Change in the Oaxacan Highlands.* Tuscon, AZ: University of Arizona Press, 1989.

Paul, Samuel, and Arturo Israel, eds. *Nongovernmental Organizations and the World Bank: Cooperation for Development.* Washington, D.C.: World Bank, 1991.

Pelczynski, Zbigniew A. "Solidarity and 'the Rebirth of Civil Society.'" *Civil Society and the State,* edited by John Keane. London, United Kingdom: Verso, 1988.

Pine, Frances, and Sue Bridger, eds. *Surviving Post-Socialism: Local Strategies and Regional Responses in Eastern Europe and the Former Soviet Union.* London, United Kingdom: Routledge, 1998.

Pistor, Katharina, and Joel Turkewitz. "Coping with Hydra-State Ownership after Privatization: A Comparative Study of Hungary, Russia, and the Czech Republic." Paper at a joint conference of the World Bank and the Central European University Privatization Project, "Corporate Governance in Central Europe and Russia," 15-16 December 1994. Washington, D.C.: World Bank, Policy Research Department, Transitions Economics Division, 1995.

Robertson, A.F. *People and the State: An Anthropology of Planned Development.* Cambridge, United Kingdom: Cambridge University Press, 1984.

Rocznik Statystyczny. Warsaw, Poland: Główny Urząd Statystyczny, 1985.

Rocznik Statystyczny Województw. Warsaw, Poland: Główny Urząd Statystyczny, 1997.

Roniger, Luis, and Ayşe Güneş-Ayata, eds. *Democracy, Clientelism, and Civil Society.* Boulder, CO: Lynne Rienner, 1994.

Rose, Richard. "Rethinking Civil Society: Postcommunism and the Problem of Trust." *Journal of Democracy,* vol. 5, no. 3, July 1994, pp. 18-30.

Rose, Richard. *Getting Things Done in an Anti-Modern Society: Social Capital Networks in Russia, Studies in Public Policy Number 304.* Glasgow, United Kingdom: Centre for the Study of Public Policy, University of Strathclyde, 1998.

Ruble, Blair A. *Leningrad: Shaping a Soviet City.* Berkeley, CA: University of California Press, 1990.

Rupnik, Jacques. "Dissent in Poland, 1968-78: The End of Revisionism and the Rebirth of Civil Society." *Opposition in Eastern Europe,* edited by Rudolf L. Tökés. Baltimore, MD: Johns Hopkins University Press, 1979.

Ryan, Dawn. "Cliques, Factions, and Leadership among the Toaripi of Papua." *Adaptation and Symbolism: Essays on Social Organization,* edited by Karen Ann Watson-Gegeo and S. Lee Seaton. Honolulu, HI: East-West Center, University Press of Hawaii, 1978.

Rykowski, Zbigniew. "Narodziny Demokratycznego Systemu Władzy. O Komitetach Obywatelskich w Latach 1989-92." *A Miało Byc Tak Pięknie: Polska Scena Publiczna Lat Dziewięćdziesiątych,* edited by Barbara Lewenstein and Wojciech Pawlik. Warsaw, Poland: Uniwersytet Warszawski, Institut Stosowanych Nauk Społecznych, 1994.

Sachs, Wolfgang, ed. *The Development Dictionary: A Guide to Knowledge and Power.* London, United Kingdom, Zed Books, 1992.

Said, Edward. *Orientalism.* New York: Pantheon Books, 1978.

Sampson, Steven. "The Informal Sector in Eastern Europe." *Telos,* vol. 66, Winter, 1986, pp.44-66.

Sampson, Steven. "Romanian Political Culture and NGOs." Paper presented at Sinaia NGO Conference, March 1994.

Sampson, Steven. "The Social Life of Projects: Importing Civil Society to Albania." *Civil Society: Challenging Western Models,* edited by Chris Hann and Elizabeth Dunn. London, United Kingdom: Routledge, 1996.

Seligman, Adam B. *The Idea of Civil Society.* Princeton, NJ: Princeton University Press, 1992.

Shelley, Louise I. "Post-Soviet Organized Crime: Implications for Economic, Social and Political Development." *Demokratizatsiya: The Journal of Post-Soviet Democratization,* vol.2, no.3, Summer 1994, pp.341-358.

Shelley, Louise I. "Post-Soviet Organized Crime: Implications for Economic, Social and Political Development." *Demokratizatsiya: The Journal of Post-Soviet Democratization,* vol. 2, no. 3, Summer 1994, pp. 341-358.

Shelley, Louise I. "Privatization and Crime: The Post-Soviet Experience." *Journal of Contemporary Criminal Justice,* vol.11, no.4, 1995, pp.244-56.

Shelley, Louise I. "Statement on Post-Soviet Organized Crime for House Committee on International Relations." 30 April 1996.

Shore, Cris, and Susan Wright, eds. *Anthropology of Policy: Critical Perspectives on Governance and Power.* London, United Kingdom: Routledge, 1997.

Silberman, James B., and Charles Weiss, Jr. *A History of the Technical Assistance Programs of the Marshall Plan and Successor Agencies, 1948-1961.* Washington, D.C.: World Bank Industrial Policy Group, November 1992.

Skilling, Gordon H. *Samizdat and an Independent Society in Central and Eastern Europe.* Basingstoke, United Kingdom: Macmillan, 1988.

Smith, Tony. "The Underdevelopment of Development Literature: The Case of Dependency Theory." *The State and Development,* edited by Atul Kohli. Princeton, NJ: Princeton University Press, 1986.

Squires Meaney, Connie. *Privatization and the Ministry of Privatization in Poland: Outsiders as Political Assets and Political Liabilities.* A Working Paper, University of California at Berkeley, Center for German and European Studies, April 1993.

Staniszkis, Jadwiga. "Political Capitalism in Poland." *Eastern European Politics and Societies,* vol.5, no.1, Winter 1991, pp.127-41.

Stark, David. "Path Dependance and Privatization Strategies in East and Central Europe." *East European Politics and Societies,* vol.6, no.1, Winter 1992, pp.17-54.

Stark, David. "Privatization in Hungary: From Plan to Market or From Plan to Clan?" *East European Politics and Societies,* vol.4, no.3, Fall 1990, pp.351-392.

Stark, David, and László Bruszt. *Postsocialist Pathways: Transforming Politics and Property in East Central Europe*. Cambridge, United Kingdom: Cambridge University Press, 1998.

Stavrakis, Peter J. "Bull in a China Shop: USAID's Post-Soviet Mission." *Demokratizatsiya: The Journal of Post-Soviet Democratization*, vol.4, no.2, Spring 1996, pp. 247-270.

Stiglitz, Joseph. "Whither Reform" speech by World Bank chief economist Joseph Stiglitz. (worldbank.org/knowledge/chiefecon/).

Szlachta, Jacek. *Regional Development in Poland under Transformation*. Warsaw. Poland: Friedrich Ebert Foundation Warsaw Office, 1995.

Tendler, Judith. *Inside Foreign Aid*. Baltimore, MD: Johns Hopkins University Press, 1975.

Tester, Keith. *Civil Society*. London, United Kingdom: Routledge, 1992.

Unger, Roberto Mangabeira. *Law in Modern Society: Toward a Criticism of Social Theory*. New York, NY: Free Press, 1976.

Uphoff, Norman. "Fitting Projects to People." *Putting People First: Sociological Variables in Rural Development*, edited by Michael M. Cernea. Oxford, United Kingdom: Oxford University Press, 1985.

Van Velsen, J. "The Extended Case Method and Situational Analysis." *The Craft of Social Anthropology*, edited by A. L. Epstein. New Brunswick, NJ: Transaction Books, 1978.

Verdery, Katherine. "Theorizing Socialism: A Prologue to the Transition." *American Ethnologist,* vol.18, no.3, August 1991, pp.419-439.

Verdery, Katherine. *What Was Socialism, and What Comes Next?* Princeton, NJ: Princeton University Press, 1996.

Waller, Michael J. "Organized Crime and the Russian State: Challenges to U.S.-Russian Cooperation." *Demokratizatsiya: The Journal of Post-Soviet Democratization*, vol.2, no.3, Summer 1994, pp.364-85.

Waller, Michael J., and Victor J. Yasmann. "Russia's Great Criminal Revolution: The Role of the Security Services," *Journal of Contemporary Criminal Justice*, vol.11, no.4, 1995, pp.276-97.

Ware, Alan. *Between Profit and State: Intermediate Organizations in Britain and the United States*. Cambridge, United Kingdom: Polity Press, 1989.

Watts, Michael J. "Development I: Power, knowledge, Discursive Practice." *Progress in Human Geography*, vol.17, no.2, 1993, pp.257-272.

Wedel, Janine. *The Private Poland: An Anthropologist's Look at Everyday Life*. New York, NY: Facts on File, 1986.

Wedel, Janine R. "The Demise of Solidarity and the Prospects for Democracy." *Eastern Europe Transformation and Revolution, 1945-1991: Documents and Essays*, edited by Lyman H. Legters. Lexington, MA: D.C. Heath, 1992.

Wedel, Janine R., ed. *The Unplanned Society: Poland During and After Communism*. New York, NY: Columbia University Press, 1992.

Wedel, Janine R. "Clique-Run Organizations and U.S. Economic Aid: An Institutional Analysis." *Demokratizatsiya: The Journal of Post-Soviet Democratization*, vol. 4, no.4, Fall 1996, pp.571-602.

Wedel, Janine R. *Clans, Cliques, and Captured States: How We Misunderstand 'Transition' in Central and Eastern Europe and the Former Soviet Union*, presented to the National Council for Eurasian and East European Research and the National Institute of Justice, 2000, and forthcoming as National Council *Working Paper.*

Wedel, Janine R. and David A. Kideckel, "Studying Up: Amending the First Principle of Anthropological Ethics," *Anthropology Newsletter,* vol. 35, no. 7, October 1994, p. 37.

Wittfogel, Karl A. *Oriental Despotism: A Comparative Study of Total Power*. New York, NY: Vintage Books, 1981.

Wolf, Eric. "American Anthropologists and American Society." *Reinventing Anthropology*, edited by Dell Hymes. New York, NY: Vintage Books, 1974, pp. 251-263.

Wood, Geof, ed. *Labelling in Development Policy: Essays in Honour of Bernard Schaffer.* London, United Kingdom: Sage, 1985.

Wright, Susan, ed. *Anthropology of Organizations.* London, United Kingdom: Routledge, 1994.

Wróblewski, Tadeusz. "The Opposition and Money." *The Unplanned Society: Poland During and After Communism,* edited by Janine R. Wedel. New York, NY: Columbia University Press, 1992.

Zavorotnyi, Sergei Zavorotnyi. "The Traces of 'Privatization' Go Overseas." *Komsomolskaya Pravda* (Moscow, Russia), 8 April 1997.

Zimmerman, Robert F. *Dollars, Diplomacy, and Dependency: Dilemmas of U.S. Economic Aid.* Boulder, CO: Lynne Rienner, 1993.

INDEX

Please note: Index includes only those names referenced in Interviews (appendix 3) and in the Bibliography, which are also referenced elsewhere in the text.

Abalkin, Leonid, 59, 144, 225, 259n46, 278n92

accountability, 10, 33, 126, 148, 154, 159, 171-174, 203-205

Adams, Walter, 248n24, 249n25, 255n4

Agency for International Development (AID). *See* United States Agency for International Development (USAID).

AID. *See* United States Agency for International Development (USAID).

aid
coordination of, 31-33, 35-38
delivery of, 8-11, 27-28, 102-103
East's expectations for, 4, 15-17, 22-25, 41, 45, 208
graduation from, 198, 208
language of, 2, 10, 21, 41-42, 84, 88-89, 91, 109-111, 208
reasons for, 21-22
successes of, 78-83, 117-122, 199-200
West's expectations for, 15-22, 41, 75, 208
See also donors; *names of specific individuals and agencies.*

aid relations,
dilemmas of, 6-7, 34-38, 39-41, 52-60, 197-202
phases of, 6-7, 10: Triumphalism, 7-8, 10, 23, 25, 43, 47, 59, 93, 118, 171, 195, 197, 199; Disillusionment, 7-8, 10, 43, 47, 58-59, 118,
171, 183, 195, 197, 199; Adjustment, 7-8, 10, 81-83, 118, 205-208
See also transactors and transactorship; transidentities and transidentity capabilities.

aid strategies

government-to-government links, 37-38
support of business, 175-194, 200
support of an exclusive political-economic group, 123-174, 200-205
support of "civil society" and NGOs, 37, 84-122, 193-194, 200
See also loans; technical assistance; aid, delivery of.

Albini, Joseph L., 286n208

Albright, Madeleine, 286n199

Allardt, Eric, 269n61

Allison, Graham, 277n80

Anderson, Benedict, 292n9

Anderson, Julie, 286n208

Andersson, Martin, 283n166

Andrew W. Mellon Foundation, 98

Antall, Jozsef, 20

anthropology
case studies, 9-11, 203, 221-222
of Central and Eastern Europe and/or former Soviet Union, 9, 245n7
of development, 8-11, 208, 220-224, 246n8, 246n9, 292n3
of globalization, 219-224, 245-246n4
of language, 10, 41-42, 208
of policy, 208, 219-220, 223-224, 293n1, 293n3, 293n4,
of political economy, 208, 224
reinvented, 219-220, 293n2, 293n3, 293n4
See also methods and methodology; social organization.

Appadurai, Arjun, 245n4

Arato, Andrew, 264n2, 268n49, 268n51

Arthur Andersen, 27, 149, 192. *See also* Big Six accounting firms *and* consultants and contractors.

Åslund, Anders, 146, 155-156, 165, 169-170, 240, 242, 281n154, 282n158, 282-283n159, 283n163, 283n164, 283n165, 283-284n166, 284n168, 284n169
asset valuations, 63-67
Atwood, Brian, 144
Austin, Jay, 120, 225, 271n103

Balcerowicz, Leszek, 67, 100, 255n6
Baldwin, Jeffry, 54, 226, 258n28
Bank of New York, 160, 165, 280n140, 285n179
Banque, Robert, 226, 263n108
Barre, Raymond, 249n27, 251n57
Barry, Robert, 45, 53, 226
Barth, Fredrik, 281n151, 292n6
Batory Foundation, 99, 121, 265n14
Bauer, P. T., 248n19
Bazilevich, Leonid, 134, 135, 226, 275n40, 275n41, 275n42, 275n50
Beltway Bandits, 27, 257n21
    See also consultants and contractors.
Belyaev, Sergei, 134
Bennett, John, 73, 261n88
Berlin Wall, 3, 5, 25, 86, 195, 207
Bernard, Michael H., 268n49, 268n50
Bernard, Richard P., 226, 272n1
Bernstam, Michael, 226, 283n161
Bernstein, Jonas, 161, 276n71, 285n182
Bielecki, Jan Krzysztof, 76, 104, 226, 262n97
Big Six accounting firms, 27-28, 51-55, 60-62, 65, 131, 257n17, 257n21. See also Arthur Andersen; Coopers & Lybrand; Deloitte & Touche; Ernst & Young; KPMG Peat Marwick; Price Waterhouse.
Bildt, Carl, 155, 283n164
Bivens, Matt, 276n71
Bobinski, Christopher, 291n59
Bochniarz, Henryka, 68-69, 185-186, 226, 290n33, 290n38
Bogdanowicz-Bindert, Christine A., 261n80, 262n94
Boissevain, Jeremy, 105-106, 268n57, 275n48
Bonner, Raymond, 285n179
Borodin, Pavel, 286n205
Borisova, Yevgenia, 287n223
Borodulin, Vladislav, 277n82
Borodziej, Wlodzimierz, 226, 263n110
Bourdieu, Pierre, 266n24
Boure, Eduard, 134, 146, 279n118
Bowen, John R., 261n88

Boycko, Maxim, 134, 136, 144-150, 156-157, 159, 163-164, 203-204, 226, 241, 272n6, 272n10, 277n84, 277n97, 278n100, 278n106, 285n178
Brademas, John, 246n1
Brasier, Mary, 250n49
Bratinka, Pavel, 61, 226, 259n49
Bremmer, I., 287n221
Bridger, Sue, 189, 266n22, 270n83, 270n85, 271n86, 291n54
Britan, G. M., 293n2
British Know How Fund, 27, 29, 32, 51-52, 79, 147
Brock, James W., 248n24, 249n25, 255n4
Bruckner, Pascal, 19, 248n18, 248n19
Bruno, Marta, 91, 113-114, 266n22, 270n83, 270n85
Brunswick and Brunswick-Warburg, 283n166
Bruszt, Laszlo, 262n98
Bryant, Glenn, 277n77
Brzezinski, Zbigniew, 184, 186, 227, 290n36
Bugaj, Ryszard, 48, 227, 256n9
Burawoy, Michael, 239n34, 256n11, Burkov, Sergei V., 144, 227, 278n93
Burson-Marsteller, 131
Bush, George, 18, 130, 182
business
    biznes, 175, 177-178, 180
    family, 177-180
    loans and grants to, 175-194
    local practices of, 61-62, 175-180, 191-193
    under communism, 177-179
Buxell, Ingrid T., 264n7, 270n76

Cadwell, Charles, 143-144, 227, 278n90, 278n91
Carana, 149-150
Caresbac, 290n32
Carothers, Thomas, 264n3, 265n17
Cassidy, Padraic, 280n140
Cenková, Jitka, 227, 254n93
Center for International Private Enterprise (CIPE), 16, 86
Central and Eastern Europe and Europeans
    environmental movement in, 115-118
    expectations for transition of. See aid, East's expectations for; West's expectations for.
    intelligentsia , 94-95, 98-99, 103-104, 106
    pride of, 38-43, 56-58

response to aid. *See* aid relations.
ritual of listening to foreigners, 3
social organization of, 103-122
views of West, 22-25, 41, 56-58
West's identification with, 18-19
See also business; privatization;
Visegrad countries; *and specific
countries, names, agencies, and
programs*
Central Europe
use of the term, xvii, 12-13, 16
Cernea, Michael, 246n8, 269n68
Charles Stewart Mott Foundation, 118
Chechnya, 120, 168
chemical reactions, 7-8, 208, 219
Chernomyrdin, Viktor, 154, 243, 282n159.
See also Gore-Chernomyrdin Commission.
Childress, Ronald, 167, 227, 287n211
Christie, Ian, 251n62
Chubais, Anatoly, 123, 125-129, 131-132,
134-136, 138-146, 150-168, 203-
205, 241-243, 273n17, 277n82,
277n85, 283-284n166, 285n178,
285n179, 286n198, 286n199,
290n44
Chubais Clan, 123-174, 200-201, 203-
205, 239-244, 274n37, 278n106,
282n155, 282n157, 285n195
Ciepiela, Cecilia, 227, 278n104, 279n126,
279n130
CIPE. *See* Center for International Private
Enterprise.
civil society, 16, 85, 85-89, 90, 95-110,
119, 200
clearing and settlement organizations
(CSOs), 143, 278n88, 278n89
Clifford, Deirdre, 227, 273n23, 276n61,
276n62, 276n63, 276n66, 278n103
Clinton, Bill, and Clinton administration,
127, 130
Cliques. *See* social organization.
Cohen, Jean 264n2
Cohen, R., 293n2
Cold War, 2-3, 7-8, 11, 17, 19, 25, 123,
195, 197-198, 201, 206
Coles, Walter, 142-146, 227, 276n61, 277-
278n86, 277n87, 278n95, 278n102,
278n109
Comaroff, Jean and John, 220, 293n7
communism, 3, 13, 21-23, 104, 177,
265n20, 287n213
collapse of, 1-2, 16, 18, 49, 89, 97-
98, 103, 106, 108
legacies of, 7, 38, 42, 167, 178, 197-
201, 206

practice of *ochkovtiratel'stvo*, 74-75
role of state under, 42, 53, 85, 89,
104-105, 101, 112, 177-180,
197, 201
Communist Bloc, 19, 27, 29, 175
company town, 49-51, 55, 71
Confederacy of Independent Poland
(KPN), 99-100
connections. *See* relationships.
consultants and contractors, 27-28, 46, 51-
52, 55-73, 79-82, 85, 91-92, 131-
132, 152, 156-157, 198-199, 202-
203, 208, 221
See also Big Six accounting firms,
econolobbyists *and* Marriott Brigade.
Cooperative Agreements, 153
Coopers & Lybrand, 27, 51-53. *See also*
Big Six accounting firms *and* consultants and contractors.
Credit Suisse First Boston (CSFB), 151,
162, 242
Creed, Gerald, 22, 24, 249n28, 249n36
CSOs. *See* clearing and settlement organizations.
Czech American Enterprise Fund, 188,
191-193
Czechoslovakia and Czech Republic, 4, 7,
11-12, 40, 96, 98, 102, 188, 191,
290n50. *See also specific names,
agencies and programs.*
Czerniawski, Jan, 227, 259n45

Dabrowski, Marek, 227, 284n168
Dart Management, Inc., 239, 280n140
Dean, Steve, 26, 227, 250n39, 250n42,
250n45, 250n46, 257n22, 258n24
Deloitte & Touche, 27, 53-54. *See also* Big
Six accounting firms *and* consultants
and contractors.
deniability, 158-159, 205
development, 11, 19-22, 208
critiques of, 10, 41-42, 78, 198,
263n103, 291n53, 246n8,
246n9, 254n100, 254-255n101,
255n102, 292n3. *See also*
anthropology, of
development.
geographical concentration of, 188-
191
See also aid, aid relations, aid strategies, donors, *and* Third World.
development anthropology. *See* anthropology, of development.
Dine, Thomas A., 136, 145, 148, 157, 195,
168-170, 227, 275n53, 275n54,

278n101,279n121, 283n165,
284n171, 284n172, 287n213,
287n216,
292n7
Dole, Elizabeth, 5
donors, 85-89, 101-102, 104, 108, 114-
115, 119, 125, 135, 137-138, 146,
149, 156, 159, 165, 173, 175, 177,
180, 182, 197-206, 219, 221, 223
See also British Know How Fund,
PHARE, TACIS, USAID, *and
other individual donors.*
Doyle, Larry, 69-70
Drábĕk, Zdenek, 40, 79, 183, 185, 228,
254n99, 263n105, 289n24, 290n34,
291n65
Drozdiak, William, 250n51
Dubin, Boris, 288n227
Duma, 129, 141, 143-145, 151, 158, 160,
167
Dunn, Elizabeth, 265n18, 266n23,
268n50, 269n66

Eagleburger, Lawrence, 250n49, 254n95
Eastern Europe. *See* Central and Eastern
Europe.
EBRD. *See* European Bank for Reconstruction and Development.
EC. *See* European Commission.
econolobbyists, 46-48, 199-200, 202. *See
also* Jeffrey Sachs.
Ekiert, Grzegorz, 108-109, 269n62,
269n67
Ellerman, David, 249n31, 262n99
Enterprise Funds, 18, 37, 82, 180-193,
289n12, 289n13, 289n14, 289n15,
289n16, 289n18, 288n10, 289n12,
289n16, 289n28, 289n29, 289n30,
290n31, 290n32, 290n35, 290n37,
290n39, 290n42, 290n43, 290n47,
291n61, 291n62, 291n63, 291n64,
291n65, 291n66, 291n72, 292n73.
See also specific funds.
environmental movement, 110, 115-118
Environmental Partnership, 121
Erlanger, Steven, 282-283n159
Ermarth, Fritz W., 276n71
Ernst &Young, 27. *See also* Big Six
accounting firms; consultants and
contractors.
Escobar, Arturo, 198, 246n9, 263n103,
292n3
ethnography across levels and processes,
8, 12, 219, 220, 223-224

European Bank for Reconstruction and
Development (EBRD), 27, 51, 147,
160, 186, 243
EU. *See* European Union.
European Commission (EC), 186, 247n14,
248n15, 292n2
European Recovery Plan, 247n6. *See also*
Marshall Plan.
European Union (EU), 17, 20, 27-
29, 33, 35-37, 41, 46, 51, 62, 69,
71-72, 79, 81, 82, 86-87, 102-
103, 115, 118, 147, 181, 190,
195, 198, 206-208, 217, 243,
256n13
extended case method, 222, 293n9

Fabian, Johannes, 292n9
Fainsod, Merle, 286n208
Fedorov, Boris, 147, 279n117, 285n183
Federal Securities Commission *or* Federal
Commission on Securities and the
Capital Market (Russia), 150, 151,
154, 157, 243-244, 272n1
Ferguson, James, 220, 224, 246n9,
263n103, 293n5, 294n13
fieldwork. *See* methods and methodology.
Finnish government, 281n154, 282n156
First Russian Specialized Depository, 154
First World, 17, 38, 56
flex organizations, 145-153, 156, 172
Foglizzo, Jean, 154, 283n160
Forum of Nongovernmental Initiatives
(FIP), 119-120
foundations, 5, 47, 87-89, 92-94, 111. *See
also individual foundations;* non-
governmental organizations.
Free Trade Union Institute of the AFL-
CIO (FTUI), 86, 96
Freedom Support Act, 26, 31, 216
FTUI. *See* Free Trade Union Institute.
Fyodorov, Boris, 285n184, 161

G-7 (Group of Seven), 17, 125, 279n111
G-24 (Group of Twenty-Four), 17-18, 26,
32, 209, 212, 247n10, 250n40,
251n57
Gaidar, Yegor, 126-128, 155, 240,
282n157, 282n159, 283n166
Gal, Susan, 246n2
Galuszka, Peter, 272n8
GAO. *See* General Accounting Office.
Gellner, Ernest, 264n2
General Accounting Office (GAO), 31, 35,
37, 50, 54, 56, 73, 109, 116-117,
131-132, 150-151, 158, 170, 185,
191, 224, 244, 249n27, 249n38,

252n75, 252n76, 253n88, 256n12,
257n15, 258n34, 257n16, 258n34,
258n35, 261n82, 261n83, 269n65,
271n91, 271n92, 271n94, 272n4,
274n26, 274n30, 274n31, 274n32,
278n89, 278n105, 279n110,
279n122, 279n134, 280n137,
280n138, 287n219, 287n220,
288n10, 289n13, 289n12, 289n28,
289n30, 290n31, 290n35, 290n42,
291n64
German Marshall Fund, 69, 118, 271n96,
271n97
Germany, 7, 27, 102, 247n10
Gershman, Carl, 96, 266n28, 266n29,
266n33, 266n35
Gibian, Paul, 193, 228, 291n65, 291n71
Ginsberg, Marianne, 118, 228, 271n96,
271n97
GKI. See State Property Committee.
GKOs, 163
Glenn, John K., 269n70, 270n72, 270n73,
271n87
Glinkina, Svetlana, 140, 252n52, 276-
277n73
globalization and global processes, 49,
220, 224, 245-246n4
Glowacki, Jacek, 228, 263n101
Gold, Michael N., 228, 258n31
Gorbachev, Mikhail, 126, 134
Gore, Albert, 243, 286n199. See also
Gore-Chernomyrdin Commission.
Gore-Chernomyrdin Commission, 158
Graham, Thomas E. Jr, 137, 172, 228,
276n58, 278n99, 287n225, 288n228,
287-288n227
Grant, Steve, 287-288n227
Green, Jerry, 162
Greene, Katrina, 250n45
Gronemeyer, Marianne, 41, 254n100
Gupta, Akhil, 220, 224, 293n5, 294n13
Gurr, Lisa Anne, 70, 77, 228, 260n66,
260n68, 260n72, 260n75, 263n102
Guttman, Daniel, 252n69, 257n21,
259n52
Győző, Antalfi, 260n64

Haggard, Stephen, 247n11, 250n40
Hall, Aleksander, 89-90
Hall, John, 264n2
Hann, C. M., 23, 104, 109, 114, 245n7,
249n29, 251n62, 266n23, 268n50,
269n66, 271n86
Harden, Blaine, 250n55, 255n104
Hardi, Peter, 116-117, 229
Hardt, John P., 252n78, 263n106

Harper, John, 250n43, 251n61, 251n66,
251n68, 252n71, 259n44
Hartelius, Dag, 283n163, 283n164
Harvard Institute for International Development (HIID), 38, 123-125, 129-
132, 139, 140- 147, 150-151, 153-
154, 156-159, 163, 165, 167-170,
203, 239-244, 279n110, 281n147,
284n168
Harvard Management Company (HMC),
158, 161-163, 169, 242-243
Harvard Project. See Harvard Institute for
International Development.
Harvard University, 48, 123, 127-128, 133,
145, 203-205, 249n3,
281n154,282n157, 285n186,
285n190, 287n219
JFK School of Government, 141,
277n80
See also Harvard Institute for Inter-
national Development.
Havel, Václav, 15, 20, 24, 85, 246n40,
249n34, 264n1, 268n49
Hay, Jonathan, 129, 131-133, 142, 148,
150-153, 156-159, 162-163, 167-
168, 203-204, 229, 239-241,
273n17, 273n18, 274n28, 274n29,
280n140, 280n142, 285n190
Hebert, Elizabeth, 151, 158, 240, 242,
280n142, 285n190
Hedlund, Stefan, 276n71
Helmer, John, 154, 280n141, 282n157
Helms, Jessie, 267n40
Henderson, Keith, 173, 229, 288n229
Henderson, Peter, 285n192
Herzfeld, Michael, 245n6
Heyns, Barbara, 178, 288n6
Higgins, Benjamin, 245n5
HIID. See Harvard Institute for Interna-
tional Development.
HMC. See Harvard Management Com-
pany.
Hobart, Mark, 42, 74, 78, 246n8, 255n102,
262n90, 263n104
Hodík, Jiří, 229, 259n51
Holmes, James H. 290n48, 291n67
Hoffman, Stanley, 247n11, 250n40
Horkusha, Mykola, 60, 229, 259n47
Hough, Jerry F., 281n148, 286n208
Hrbáčková, Jarmila, 45, 229, 254n93,
255n1
Hudson, Michael, 283n166
Huebner, Charles, 184, 229, 289n26
Hughes, Kirsty, 251n62
Humphreys, Michael B., 37, 229, 253n84,
253n85, 253n86

Hungarian-American Enterprise Fund, 184-186, 289n11
Hungary, 7, 11, 32, 34-36, 59, 75-76, 94, 97-98, 106. *See also* Monor *and specific names, agencies, and programs.*
Hutchings, Robert L., 31, 37, 251n60, 253n87
hyperinflation, 128

IBRD. *See* World Bank.
Ice, Janet, 209, 211
Icebreaker Fund, 162
ILBE. *See* Institute for Law-Based Economy.
ILBE Consulting, 152
Illner, Michal, 16, 188, 247n3, 290n50
IMF. *See* International Monetary Fund.
Indefinite Quantity Contracts (IQCs), 53-55, 257n23
Institute for Law-Based Economy (ILBE), 150-152, 241, 243, 280n140
institution building, 80-81, 117-120, 138, 171, 173-174
institutional nomads, 107, 269n61
International Bank for Reconstruction and Development (IBRD). *See* World Bank.
International Monetary Fund (IMF), 24, 26, 46-47, 62, 74, 76, 127-129, 154-155, 161, 163-164, 169, 171, 212, 240, 255n6, 282n157, 286n201
International Renaissance Foundation, 265n14
International Team for Company Assistance (ITCA), 68
IQC. *See* Indefinite Quantity Contracts.
Iran, 168, 201
Israel, Arturo, 269n68

Jacoby, Ruth, 229, 283n163
Jaruzelski, Wojciech, 98
Jawłowska, Aldona, 249n33
Jensen, Donald, 135, 275n52, 278n99
Johnson, David, 273n20
Johnson, Simon, 288n7
Jordan, Boris, 162-163, 242
Josefsson, Dan, 283n164
Kaczyński, Lech, 65, 230, 260n61
Kádár, Béla, 30, 230, 251n56
Kagalovsky, Konstantin, 280n140
Kagalovsky, Natasha Garfinkel, 280n140
Kalabiński, Jacek, 230, 255n3
Kamiński, Antoni, 64, 104, 112, 230, 260n59, 262n98, 267n47, 269n61, 270n78, 270n79, 270n82
Kaplan, Sheila, 63, 230, 260n56

Karns, Mark, 75, 230, 257n23, 262n93
Kaufman, Richard F., 252n78, 263n106
Kaufmann, Daniel, 288n7
Kawalec, Stefan, 5, 48, 55, 57, 230, 256n10, 258n33, 258n37
Kazár, Péter, 59, 230, 259n42
Keane, John, 249n34, 264n1, 264n2, 268n49
Kelly, Jack, 285n179
Kelly, Robert J., 277n75
Kempny, Marian, 249n33
Keohane, Robert O., 247n11, 250n40
Khasbulatov, Ruslan, 155, 283n161
Kideckel, David A., 24, 245n2, 245n7, 248n20, 249n33, 294n12
King, Alexander, 16
Kirkland, Lane, 184
Kiss, Yudit, 262n91
Kjaer, John, 230, 253n79
Klamkin, Murray S., 254n91
Klaus, Václav, 40, 254n98
Klevana, Leighton, 230, 291n65
Kliamkin, Igor, 287n226
Klimova, Rita, 23, 230, 249n30
Klurfeld, James M., 288n228
Knowlton, Timothy, 191, 194, 230, 289n16, 290n43, 291n63, 292n73
Koch, Thomas, 214, 267n43
Kohli, Atul, 245n5
Kokh, Alfred, 134, 163-164, 241, 275n46, 286n196
Kołodko, Grzegorz, 4, 57, 230, 241n2, 245n1, 259n39, 261n86, 262n98
Korelewicz, Jadwiga, 288n5
Kornai, János, 41, 249n25, 254n101, 286n207
Korzhakov, Alexander, 160
Kotkin, Stephen, 278n96
Kottak, Conrad, 246n8
Kotz, David M., 255n5, 272n13
Kováts, Kornél, 231, 254n89, 254n93
Kowalski, Piotr, 289n23
Kowalski, Sergiusz, 266n31
Kownacki, Piotr, 112, 231, 260n55, 270n81, 289n24
Kozak, Marek, 59, 82, 175, 231, 259n43, 288n1, 289n17, 289n19, 291n60
Kozminski, Jerzy, 187
KPMG Peat Marwick, 27, 53. *See also* Big Six accounting firms; consultants and contractors.
Kranish, Michael, 247n8
Krawczuk, Marek, 54, 231, 258n27, 258n29
Krizsa, Rozália, 66, 231, 260n64
Krotov, Pavel, 256n11

Kryshtanovskaya, Olga, 129, 133, 142, 273n20, 275n38, 277n83
Kubik, Jan, 108-109, 269n62, 269n67
Kuchma, Leonid, 168
Kudrin, Alexey, 134, 275n44
Kundrata, Miroslav, 118
Kurczewska, Joanna, 269n61
Kurczewski, Jacek, 269n63
Kuron, Jacek, 5
Kutushev, Valery, 287n209
Kuzes, Irina Y., 139, 275n55, 276n60, 276n68, 276n69, 276n71

Lake, Anthony, 283n162
Lampland, Martha, 245n7
Landau, Madeline, 269n60
Lasota, Irena, 99, 266n37
Lawina, Anatol, 67, 157, 231, 260n65
Lebed, Aleksandr, 136, 166, 276n56, 287n209
legacies of communism. See communism, legacies of.
Lempert, David H., 249n31, 275n39
Lepingwell, John W. R., 276n59
Levitas, Anthony, 259n54
Levitt, Arthur, Jr., 158
Lewandowski, Janusz, 52
Lewenstein, Barbara, 266n31
Lewicki, Zbigniew, 231, 254n93
Lieberman, Ira, 146-148, 231, 278n107, 278n108, 279n113, 279n116, 279n117, 279n124, 279n125
Liesman, Steve, 280n143, 280n144
Light, Jay, 162, 231, 285n189
Lindenberg, Grzegorz "Larry," 94-95
Lipton, David, 127, 131, 139, 154, 169-170, 231, 240, 242, 282n155, 282n157
Lis, Krzysztof, 52
loans, 175-194
Local Privatization Centers (LPCs), 148-150. See also Russian Privatization Center (RPC).
LOT Polish National Airlines, 50, 73
LPCs. See Local Privatization Centers.
Lubina, Lubo, 232, 254n93
Ludwiczak, Zdzisław, 232, 254n93, 254n96
Luers, William H., 249n27, 251n57
Lukacs, John, 247n5
Luzhkov, Yuri, 141, 277n81

Mabetex, 286n205
Mailloux, Laurier, 169, 232, 287n214
Manevich, Mikhail, 134, 275n45
Marcus, George, 294n10

Marriott Brigade, 45-46, 49, 55, 57-59, 203, 206-208, 255n2
Marshall Plan, 16-18, 30-31, 34, 38, 195, 247n6, 247n7, 248n17
Marshall Plan for Eastern Europe, 16-17, 29, 31, 38, 121
Marx, Karl, 49, 288n8
Matisová, Andrea, 232, 254n93
Mayhew, Alan, 32-33, 232, 251n63, 251n67, 257n21
Mazowiecki, Tadeusz, 65, 104, 109
McDonald, Kevin, 69-71, 232, 260n69, 260n74, 260n76
McMurtrie, Beth, 274n34
Meaney, Connie Squires, 259n54, 260n69, 262n96, 263n101
Medish, Mark C., 129, 232, 273n16, 279n114, 279n115, 280n135, 280n136, 282n159, 283n166, 283n165
Meijer, Isabella, 209
Menatep, 280n140, 282n155
Mendelson, Sarah E., 269n70, 270n72, 270n73, 271n87
Merry, E. Wayne, 140, 153, 171, 232, 276n72, 278n99, 281n150, 287n224
Mesler, Bill, 285n176, 285n184, 285n188
methods and methodology
  case studies, 9-11, 203, 221-222
  chemical reactions, 7-8, 208, 219
  ethnography across levels and pro-
    cesses, 8, 12, 219-220, 223-224
  extended case method, 222, 293n9
  studying through, 219, 223, 224, 293n1
  studying up, 219, 293n2
Meyer, Jack, 162-163, 285n188
Michnik, Adam, 85, 98-99, 107
Mientka, Walter, 39, 232, 254m92
Millar, James, 74, 140, 261n89, 262n91, 276n70
Minkin, Alexander, 164
Mirel, Pierre, 233, 253n79
Mitchem, Dennis, 149, 233, 279n127, 279n129, 279n131, 279n132
Moiseev, Vladimir, 287n209
Möller, Matthias, 233, 267n43
Monor, 65-66, 78
Montag-Girmes, Ralf-Dieter, 233, 278n106, 279n111
Moravcsik, Andrew, 247n11, 250n40
Morningstar, Richard L., 28, 144-145, 157, 170, 233, 250n44, 278n98, 283n165
Mossbacher, Robert, 250n49
Muenchow-Pohl, Bernd von, 267n43

multidisciplinary collaboration and studies, 224

Nader, Laura, 219, 293n2
Nádházi, Ágnes, 233, 254n89, 254n93
Nagengast, Carole, 245n7
Najwyższa Izba Kontroli (NIK), 62, 65, 67, 71-72, 112
National Bank of Ukraine, 169
National Democratic Institute for International Affairs (NDI), 85, 97, 100, 109
National Endowment for Democracy (NED), 86, 97-100
National Republican Institute for International Affairs (NRI), 85, 97, 100, 109
National Security Council (NSC), 131, 240, 242
National security waivers (for USAID grants), 130-131
NDI. See National Democratic Institute for International Affairs.
Necki, Zbigniew, 19
NED. See National Endowment for Democracy.
Nee, Victor, 288n8
Nelson, Lynn D., 139, 233, 275n55, 276n60, 276n68, 276n69, 276n71
Ners, Krzysztof J., 249n27, 250n51, 251n57, 264n7, 270n76
networks. See relationships.
Neuffer, Elizabeth, 248n17
Nevin, Stanley R., 28, 148, 169, 233, 250n47, 279n123, 287n217
Newly Independent States, 37, 131, 147, 157, 195, 240, 272n2, 273n23, 284n171, 287n213, 292n1
Ng, Renae, 233, 279n113
NGO and NGOs. See nongovernmental organizations.
NIK. See Najwyzsza Izba Kontroli.
NIS. See Newly Independent States.
nomenklatura, 61, 88, 177, 240n50
nongovernmental organizations (NGOs), 6, 26-27, 86-88,109-121, 200, 203, 269n68. See also foundations.
Norilsk Nickel, 161
North Atlantic Treaty Organization (NATO), 20, 41, 292n10
Novolipetsk Metal Factory, 162
Nowak, Stefan, 104-105, 268n52
NRI. See National Republican Institute for International Affairs.
NSC. See National Security Council.
Nuti, Mario, 233, 261n86

Nye, Joseph S., 247n11, 250n40

O'Brian, Timothy L., 285n179
ochkovtiratel'stvo, 74-75
ODA. See Overseas Development Administration or Official Development Assistance.
OECD. See Organization for Economic Cooperation and Development.
OECD Register, 33
Offe, Claus, 247n4, 254n90, 261n87
Official Development Assistance, 20
Open Society Institute (or Institutes), 86-87, 98, 156, 265n14, 265n15, 266n34. See also Stefan Batory Foundation.
Orekhov, Ruslan, 134, 157
Organization for Economic Cooperation and Development (OECD), 20, 33, 210, 214, 215
Orttung, Robert, 134, 275n42, 275n43, 286n208
Otto, Robert, 150, 233, 279n127, 279n133
Overseas Development Administration, 27

Pajo, Erind, 200, 201, 292n5
Palacka, Gabriel, 234, 259n50
Pallada Asset Management, 151-152, 158, 240
Pankrashchenko, Victor, 149
Pappalardo, Salvatore, 80-82, 234, 263n109, 263n115
Parnell, Philip C., 245n3, 293n4
Pascual, Carlos, 131, 170, 234, 240, 242, 274n25
Paskhaver, Alexander, 60, 234, 259n48
Passeron, J. C., 266n24
Patterson, David, 250n51
Paul, Samuel, 269n68
Pawlik, Wojciech, 266n31
Pelczynski, Zbigniew A., 246n40, 268n49, 268n51
Pennar, Karen, 272n8
Penoyar, William 234, 250n46
Perlez, Jane, 290n39
Peters, Gary, 234, 263n107
Petkova, Elena, 116, 234, 271n89, 271n93, 271n105
Pfaff, William, 246n1
PHARE (Poland and Hungary Aid in Restructuring the Economy), 17, 27, 32-34, 36-37, 51, 72, 86-87, 103, 181, 198, 212-213, 217, 247n9, 253n83, 253n84, 256n13
phases of aid relations. See aid relations, phases of.

Phillips, Michael M., 290n39
Pine, Frances, 189, 266n22, 270n83, 270n85, 271n86, 291n54
Pioneer First Voucher, 151
Piotrowski, Jan, 260n62
Pistor, Katharina, 234, 258n36
PMUs (program management units), 36
Podgorecki, Adam, 165, 286n202
Polakowski, Andrzej, 69-70, 234, 260n68, 260n70, 260n71, 260n73
Poland, 11, 23-24, 45-82, 85-91, 94-102, 104-106, 108-112, 119-121, 178, 181, 183-186, 188-190, 199, 266n26, 266n27, 290n51, 290-291n52, 293n8. *See also* Solidarity Movement, Ursus, *and specific names, agencies, and programs.*
Poland and Hungary Aid in Restructuring the Economy. *See* PHARE.
Polish Agency for Regional Development, 181-182
Polish-American Enterprise Fund, 82, 180-181, 186-187, 189, 289n11, 289n15, 289n23, 290n39, 290n40
Polish Humanitarian Action, 120
Polish Opposition, 95, 98
Polish Private Equity Fund, 184-185
Pomorski, Adam, 234, 271n106
Potanin, Vladimir, 161-162, 164, 242
Pressley, Donald, 133, 170, 234
Price Waterhouse, 27, 59, 69, 149, 279n127, 279n128. *See also* Big Six accounting firms *and* consultants and contractors.
privatization, 9, 26, 104 177, 194, 221, 222
 as yardstick for progress, 50
 by Big Six accounting firms, 51-52
 by decree, 142-144
 by *nomenklatura*, 61, 88, 177, 259n53
 definition of, 46
 ideology of, 49-51, 52-53, 73, 77
 in Russia, 123-125, 128-129, 138-143, 145, 159, 161-165, 286n196
 loans-for-share, 161-163
 of company towns, 45-51, 65-72
 voucher, 139-141, 143, 283n166, 285n195
privatization aid, 45-80, 167, 200-201. *See also* privatization, in Russia.
Putin, Vladimir, 134, 165, 241, 275n44, 286n205, 286n206, 288n227
Pyszkowski, Andrzej, 289n17

Quigley, Kevin F. F., 265n13, 265n14, 265n15, 266n37

Radio Free Europe, 24-25, 98
Radwanski, Witold, 234, 251n66
Rasbash, Andrew, 27, 234, 250n41, 253n79
Razgonov, S., 287n221
Razinkin, Vyacheslav, 155, 284n167
Reagan, Ronald, 15
Reddaway, Peter, 141, 201, 292n4, 277n78, 285n180
reform, 26, 47, 100, 125, 128-129, 131, 136-138, 140-145, 285n175, 288n227. *See also* privatization.
Reforma, 134
Reformers. *See* Chubais, Anatoly; Chubais Clan.
Regional Environmental Center, 115-118, 121, 200, 222
relationships, 6-7, 9-10, 46, 79, 195, 197-202, 207-208, 222
 dilemmas of aid relationships, 34-38
 See also aid relations, phases of; social organization.
Renaissance Capital, 162, 242-243
RICO, 280n140
Robbins, Carla Anne, 280n143, 280n144
Robertson, A. F., 246n8
Robinson, John, 247n8
Rockefeller Brothers Fund, 118
Rogers, R. E., 287n209
Rose, Richard, 268n54
Rozsypal, Pavel, 58, 235, 259n41
RPC. *See* Russian Privatization Center.
Rubin, Robert, 158
Rubin, Robert M., 290n49
Ruble, Blair A., 286n208
Ruch Obywatelski Akcja Demokratyczna (ROAD), 99
Rupnik, Jacques, 268n49, 268n51
Russia, 7, 12, 69, 100, 123-163, 194, 199, 201, 203-204, 206-207, 281n154, 282n157, 282n158, 282n159, 283n166, 284n169, 285n179, 285n180, 186n199, 286n201, 286n203, 286n204, 287n211, 287n223. *See also specific names, agencies, and programs.*
Russian-American Enterprise Fund, 187-188, 192
Russian Privatization Center (RPC), 163, 222, 229, 244, 275n46, 279n112
Ruszczynski, Marek, 266n32, 267n39, 267n40
Ryan, Dawn, 274n37, 275n48, 275n49

Ryan, Patrick J., 277n75
Rykowski, Zbigniew, 99, 235, 266n31, 266n36

Sachs, Jeffrey, 21, 47-49, 57, 69, 94, 126-129, 139, 146, 154-155, 168-170, 235, 239-240, 242, 249n26, 255n6, 256n7, 256n8, 272n5, 272n12, 273n17, 274n33, 276n64, 276n65, 280n139, 281n154, 282n155, 282n156, 282n157, 282n158, 282n159, 283n161, 283n162, 284n168
Sachs, Wolfgang, 246n8
Said, Edward, 292n9
Samecki, Paweł, 63, 235, 254n89, 260n57
Sampson, Steven, 87-88, 92, 110, 113-114, 245n7, 265n16, 265n18, 266n23, 269n69, 270n71, 270n84
Sanders, Paul J., 286n205
Saryusz-Wolski, Jacek, 30, 36, 57, 235, 259n40
Sasakawa Foundation, 281n154
Sawyer Miller, 285n196
Schatzberg, Rufus, 277n75
Schepple, Kim Lane, 265n14, 266n34
Schmidt, Klaus, 235, 253n79, 253n80
Seaton, S. Lee, 274n37, 275n48, 275n49
Second World, 11, 18, 21, 33-34, 38, 51, 56, 73, 76, 79, 110, 175, 195, 198
SEED. See Support for East European Democracy Act.
Seligman, Adam B., 264n2
Seymour-Smith, Charlotte, 235, 250n48
Shabalin, Victor, 287n209
Shelley, Louise, 140, 277n74, 277n75
Shishkin, Sergei, 151-152, 235-241
Shleifer, Andrei, 127, 129, 132-134, 139, 144-146, 151-152, 157-158, 162-163, 168, 235, 239-240, 272n6, 272n9, 272n10, 275n47, 277n84, 278n97, 278n100, 280n142, 282n155, 284n174, 284n173, 285n190
shock therapy, 21, 47, 128, 239, 248n24, 255n5
Shore, Cris, 219, 293n1, 293n4
Shpek, Roman, 168-169
Sidanko, 162
Siegel, Daniel, 270n75
Sieracki, Jakub, 291n60
Silberman, James B., 250n52
Sitnicki, Stanisław, 117
Skilling, Gordon H., 268n49, 268n51
Slovak-American Enterprise Fund, 191, 193

Slovakia, 12, 61, 191
Smith, Adam, 50, 168, 255n4, 267n48, 288n8
Smith, Edwin G. III, 263n108
Smith, Tony, 245n5
Smollett, Eleanor, 249n31
Sobchak, Anatoly, 134
social networks. See institutional nomads, relationships, and social organization.
social organization, 9, 88, 100, 103-109, 113-115, 129-130, 133-135, 177-180, 190, 203-205
  big men, 107-108
  cliques, 105-106, 133-135, 274n37
  See also institutional nomads and state, role of.
Sokolov, Veniamin, 147, 235, 279n119, 279n220, 281n152
Solidarity Movement, 25, 48, 68-69, 72, 88, 96, 98, 104
Solidarity-Opposition, 109, 269n64
Solomon, Anthony, 249n27, 251n57
Soros Foundation. See Open Society Institute (or Institutes); Stefan Batory Foundation.
Soros, George, 87, 98-99, 156, 161-163, 169-170, 240, 242, 255n6, 265n14, 285n186, 285n187, 285n192
Soviet Union, 18, 23, 121, 170, 177, 181n146, 291n54
środowisko, 105-106
St. Petersburg Clan. See Chubais Clan
Stalin, Joseph, 17
Stanford University, 157, 283n161
Staniszkis, Jadwiga, 259n54
Stark, David, 258n36, 262n98
Starobin, Paul, 286n206
Staszkiewicz, Wiesław, 81, 236, 263n110, 263n111, 263n112, 263n113, 263n114
state, role of, 42, 53, 85, 89, 104-105, 101, 112, 177-180, 197, 201
State Property Committee (GKI), 65-66, 75, 129, 138-140, 142, 145-146, 148, 163-164, 241, 243, 275n45, 275n46, 283n166
Stavrakis, Peter, 137, 276n57
Stefan Batory Foundation, 121, 265n14, 270n76, 271n106
Stefanowicz, Jan, 236, 267n47, 270n80
Stiglitz, Joseph, 276n71
Stritih, Jernej, 117
Struder program, 181-182, 189-190, 289n17
Strzałkowski, Piotr, 259n54

studying through, 219, 223, 224, 293n1
studying up, 219, 293n2
Suchocka, Hanna, 71
Summers, Lawrence, 127-129, 131, 154,
    158, 160, 163-165, 170, 239, 242,
    272n7, 273n19, 283n162, 284n174,
    285n175, 286n199, 286n203
Support for East European Democracy Act
    (SEED), 18, 31, 97, 111, 115, 180,
    184, 211, 247n12, 247n13, 247n14,
    256n13, 264n4, 264n5, 264n10,
    273n15, 288n9, 289n27
Svyazinvest, 163
Swedish government, 146, 155, 281n154,
    283n163, 283n166
Swiąckiewicz, Tomasz, 267n48
symbolic capital, 92
Szlachta, Jacek, 189, 236, 290n51,
    290n52, 291n53, 291n55
Szostek, Agata, 291n57
Szwajkowski, Witold, 236, 291n57,
    291n58

Taber, George M., 248n24
TACIS (Technical Assistance for the Com-
    monwealth of Independent States),
    37, 217, 256n13, 253n85, 253n86
Taibbi, Matt, 277-278n86, 280n142
Talbott, Strobe, 283n162, 286n199
Taras, R., 287n221
Taylor, Philip, 251n62
Taylor, William B., 144, 169, 236, 273n23,
    278n94, 284n171, 287n215
technical assistance, 30, 37, 45, 55, 59-61,
    76, 78-82, 198, 290n32
Technical Assistance for the Common-
    wealth of Independent States. See
    TACIS.
Tendler, Judith, 245n5
Tester, Keith, 264n2
Thatcher, Margaret, 51
Third World, 11, 18, 21, 33-34, 37-40, 57,
    172, 198
Thomas, Barry F., 192, 236, 291n68,
    291n69, 291n70
Thomas, David, 51-52, 236, 257n18,
    257n19, 257n20
Thomas, Scott, 236, 257n23
Titov, Vladimir, 236, 276n56, 287n209
Tökés, István, 116, 236, 271n88, 271n95
Tökés, Rudolf L., 268n49
Towbin, Robert, 187-188, 237, 290n44,
    290n45, 290n46
transactors and transactorship, 130, 145-
    165, 204-205, 281n154, 282n157,

282n159, 283n166, 284n168,
    284n169, 284n170, 292n8
transidentities and transidentity capabili-
    ties, 153-156, 159, 203-205,
    281n151, 292n6
transition, 4, 18, 22, 28, 85, 113, 118,
    281n146
    to democracy, 1, 2, 4, 13, 42, 74
    metaphors of, 2, 10, 21, 41-42, 208
    speed of, 21-22
Truman, Harry, 247n6
trust, 105-106, 113
Trzeciakowski, Witold, 29-30, 237,
    250n50, 250n53
Tula, 179
Turkewitz, Joel, 258n36

Ukraine, 7, 12, 20, 59, 168-171, 179, 204,
    206-208, 283n166, 284n168,
    284n169. See also specific names,
    agencies, and programs.
Ulyukaev, Alexei V., 282n159
United Export Import Bank (Unexim)
    161-162, 164, 242
United Nations Development Program
    (UNDP), 69
United States Agency for International
    Development (USAID), 1, 22, 26-
    28, 34-35, 46, 50-51, 53-56, 61, 65-
    66, 72-73, 75, 78-79, 86, 100, 117-
    118, 123, 125, 128, 130-133, 135-
    137, 139, 140-150, 158-166, 169-
    170, 173, 180-182, 186, 188, 190-
    194, 209, 211, 240, 243, 273n22,
    273n23, 274n35, 278n96, 278n103,
    279n126, 280n135, 280n136,
    280n139, 280n140, 284n168,
    285n195, 289n16, 290n32, 290n43,
    291n63, 292n73. See also donors.
United States Congressional Research
    Service, 81
United States Enterprise Funds. See Enter-
    prise Funds.
United States General Accounting Office.
    See General Accounting Office.
Uphoff, Norman, 246n8
Ursus, 67-71, 78, 221
USAID. See United States Agency for
    International Development
U.S. Congress, 86, 97, 181-182, 184, 189
U.S. Department of Justice and U.S. gov-
    ernment lawsuits, 130, 132, 151,
    158, 273n22, 274n35, 280n140,
    280n141, 282n155, 285n190,
U.S. Department of State, Office of the
    Aid Coordinator, 157, 242

U.S. Department of Treasury, 131, 171, 186, 239, 242, 282n159, 283n165 ,284n174, 285n175, 285n176
U.S. House of Representatives, Committee on International Relations, 158, 165, 285n187, 286n203, 290n48, 291n67
U.S. House of Representatives, Committee on Banking and Financial Services, 162, 285n187
U.S. Senate Foreign Relations Committee, 267n40
Ustenko, Oleg, 288n7

Vásárhelyi, Judit, 237, 271n90, 271n95
Vasiliev, Dmitry, 134, 146, 150-152, 154-158, 163, 203, 240-241, 243, 278n106
Velsen, J. Van, 206, 222, 293n9
Verdery, Katherine, 249n31, 255n103, 265n19
Vernikov, Andrei, 127-128, 237, 272n11
Visegrád countries, xvii, 11, 23, 39-40, 119, 207
Visegrád declaration, 20
Vishny, Robert, 237, 272n6, 272n10, 277n84, 278n97, 278n100
Voice of America, 24-25
volunteers and voluntary associations. See foundations and nongovernmental organizations.

Wahlbäck, Krister, 237, 283n164
Wałęsa, Lech, 15, 17, 20, 30, 43, 96, 107
Waller, J. Michael, 277n75
Ware, Alan, 270n77
Watson-Gegeo, Karen Ann, 274n37, 275n48, 275n49
Webster, Leila, 288n4
Wedel, Janine R., 245n7, 248n20, 248n21, 249n28, 249n30, 249n35, 249n36, 249n37, 250n43, 250n54, 251n61, 251n66, 251n68, 252n71, 252n75, 252n78, 255n5, 256n6, 256n7, 256n8, 258n37, 258n38, 259n40, 259n42, 259n43, 259n44, 259n51, 262n98, 263n106, 266n21, 266n25, 267n42, 268n49, 268n51, 268n53, 269n59, 269n63, 270n79, 276n56, 277-278n86, 277n88, 281n147, 281n149, 281n154, 282n158, 282n158, 283n166, 284n169, 285n177, 285n195, 288n2, 288n5, 294n11, 294n12, 294n14
Weir, Fred, 272n13, 255n5, 286n197

Weiss, Charles, Jr., 250n52
Wesolowski, W., 269n61
Wesseldijk, Enie, 237, 263n112
West as symbol, 17, 22
  as Demon, 23-24, 42-43, 167, 197, 207
  as Saint, 22-22, 25, 43, 197, 207
  as Savior, 22, 25
Williamson, Anne, 154, 161-163, 237, 272n13, 276n71,280n141, 281n153, 281n148, 282n159, 283n160, 283n166, 284n167, 288n230, 285n184, 285n185, 285n190, 285n197, 286n196, 287n222
Wisniewski, Piotr, 99
Wittfogel, Karl, 103, 267n46
Wnuk-Lipinski, Edmund, 288n5
Wolf, Eric R., 220, 293n3
Wood, Barry, 286n204
World Bank, 26-27, 32, 46, 51-52, 61, 74, 128-129, 147-148, 150, 152, 154, 157, 160, 178, 186, 239-240, 243, 280n140, 281n146 281n149
Wright, Susan, 219, 293n1, 293n2, 293n4
Wrinn, Joe, 274n34
Wróblewski, Tadeusz (pseudonym), 249n37, 266n25
Wrona, Tadeusz, 102, 237
Wülker, Margitta, 237, 267n43
Wygnanski, Jakub, 111, 119-121, 237, 270n74, 270n76, 271n99, 271n100, 271n101, 271n102, 271n104, 272n108, 272n109

Yakusha, Yuriy, 75, 238, 262n92
Yamey, B. S., 248n19
Yancey, Jenny, 270n75
Yasmann, Victor J., 277n75
Yavlinsky, Grigory, 282n159
Yeltsin, Boris, 126, 129, 136, 138, 141-142, 146, 157, 160, 163-164, 278n99,282n158, 285n179, 286n205
Yevstaviev, Arkady, 163, 285n195

Zagachin, Julia, 154, 240
Zanardi, Louis H., 131, 238, 274n24, 274n27, 280n137, 280n138, 287n220
Zavorotnyi, Sergei, 279n119
Zielinski, George, 238, 257n18, 257n19, 257n20
Zimmerman, Nancy, 151-152, 240, 242, 280n141, 285n190
Zyuganov, Gennady, 279n118

CPSIA information can be obtained
at www.ICGtesting.com
Printed in the USA
LVHW050716100322
713033LV00014B/1993

9 780312 238285